PHOTOGRAPHIC HANDBOOK OF THE

SEABIRDS

OF THE WORLD

PHOTOGRAPHIC HANDBOOK OF THE

SEABIRDS
OF THE WORLD

JIM ENTICOTT
& DAVID TIPLING

NEW
HOLLAND

First published in 1997 by
New Holland (Publishers) Ltd
London • Cape Town • Sydney • Singapore

24 Nutford Place
London W1H 6DQ
United Kingdom

80 McKenzie Street
Cape Town 8001
South Africa

3/2 Aquatic Drive
Frenchs Forest, NSW 2086
Australia

ISBN 1 85368 945 9 (hbk)

Commissioning Editor: Jo Hemmings
Assistant Editor: Sophie Bessemer
Copy-editor: David Christie
Designer: Alan Marshall, Wilderness Design
Topography: Richard Allen

Typeset by Alan Marshall, Wilderness Design
Reproduction by Modern Age Repro, Hong Kong
Printed and bound in Singapore by Tien Wah Press

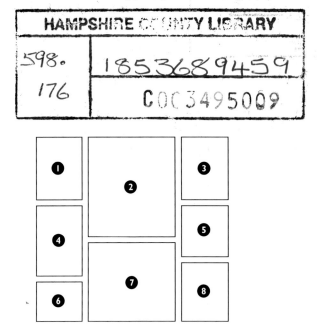

FRONT COVER PICTURES
1 White-tailed Tropicbirds
2 Great Cormorant
3 Franklin's Gull
4 Red-footed Booby
5 Guillemots
6 Wandering Albatross
7 Great Frigatebird
8 Southern Giant Petrel

Spine picture: Arctic Tern
Back cover picture: Magellanic Penguins

TOPOGRAPHY

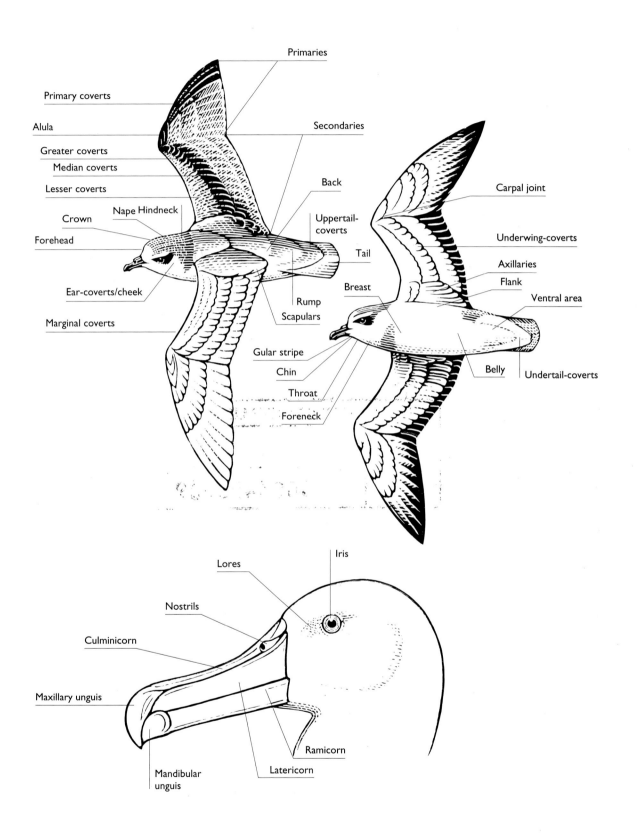

Primaries

Primary coverts

Alula

Greater coverts

Median coverts

Lesser coverts

Crown

Nape Hindneck

Forehead

Ear-coverts/cheek

Marginal coverts

Secondaries

Back

Uppertail-coverts

Tail

Rump

Scapulars

Gular stripe

Chin

Throat

Foreneck

Breast

Carpal joint

Underwing-coverts

Axillaries

Flank

Ventral area

Belly

Undertail-coverts

Lores

Iris

Nostrils

Culminicorn

Maxillary unguis

Mandibular
unguis

Lateicorn

Ramicorn

CONTENTS

CONTENTS

CONTENTS

ACKNOWLEDGEMENTS

AUTHOR'S ACKNOWLEDGEMENT

I could not have written this book without help and support from a lot of friends and colleagues. Briefly, I wish to thank Professors Roy Siegfried (Retired Director) and Geoff Brundrit (Acting Director) for allowing and indeed encouraging me to use the excellent Library at the Percy FitzPatrick Institute of African Ornithology (University of Cape Town). In addition, I thank Drs Phil Hockey and Peter Ryan, each for the extended loan of a very useful and expensive book, as well as passing an opinion on some of the more problematic photographs. The late Richard Brooke gave of his time and taxonomic knowledge to help me unravel Sibley & Monroe's new splits. I am also very grateful to Drs Alan Knox and Dr Bill Bourne for last-minute important comment and advice on the outstanding taxonomic conundrums. Michael Walters (Natural History Museum, Tring) also kindly passed an opinion.

Lesley Shackleton helped both my wife and me with logistical and moral support. E-mail figured largely in the preparation of this text, and I thank Dutch colleagues, particularly Martin van den Berg and Rolf de Buy. In the review, discussion and critical comment of earlier drafts of this text, I am grateful to Dr Tony (AJ) Williams, Dr Frank Zino, Caz Thomas and Clemens Portafee. I also 'stood on the shoulders of those who have assayed the height before us', and I am indebted to all those authors whose papers I have read, used and tried to incorporate. Jo Hemmings and particularly Sophie Bessemer of New Holland should also be thanked, as should Eve Gracie (formerly Struik Publishing, presently Black Eagle Publishing); as well as Pippa Parker (Struik Publishing) for professionalism above and beyond the call of duty. I also thank David Christie for his considerable knowledge as well as his editorial skills.

Lastly, without the patience and support of my son Daniel (who has not seen Wandering Albatross) and the unstinting practical and moral support of my wife Caz (who has), this book would not have been written.

PHOTOGRAPHIC EDITOR'S ACKNOWLEDGEMENT

To photograph a flying bird from the decks of a pitching ship, has been likened to photographing a bird on land whilst running on the spot! Such are the skills required to photograph birds at sea, that this book is not just a record of the world's seabirds, but is a testament to the skills of a dedicated band of photographers.

Never before has such a comprehensive set of photographs depicting seabirds been published. A few years ago such a project would have been impossible to complete; it is only in recent years that the increased ability to reach the remoter regions of the world has allowed many of the species featured to be photographed. The advancement in camera technology and film has also played a part in the quality of the images.

Despite this there are still a number of species, particularly from the southern oceans, that remain extremely difficult to observe, let alone photograph. Therefore it is inevitable that some images remain as record shots, these shots being the only images we have been made aware of. I have taken into consideration in my choice the aesthetic quality of the photograph as well as the usefulness as a means to an identification.

During my search for pictures, a number of people have given invaluable assistance. For their help my thanks are due to Alan Tate, Richard Porter, Simon Cook, Brian Chudleigh, Mike Carter, David Eades, Tony Palliser, Giff Beaton, Rich Stallcup, Julian Hough, Nigel Bean, Mark Brazil, Roger Tidman, Hadoram Shirihai, Adrian Plant, Phil Hansboro, Andy Swash, Bob Pitman, Mark Rauzon, Mark Cubitt, Gus Van Vliet, Kathy Meeth, Richard Bevan, Peter Pyle, Steve Gantlett (Birding World), Tony Marr, Steve Young, Pierre Devillers, David Cottridge, Alan Brady, Chris Haney, Killian Mullarney, and The New Zealand Department of Conservation. Thanks are due to Joan Thompson for relaying numerous e-mail messages. Jo Hemmings and Sophie Bessemer at New Holland Publishers deserve special thanks for their assistance throughout and for their patience and understanding when deadlines came and went during our search for the best pictures. Finally, Caz Thomas deserves a special mention for playing a major hand in sourcing photographs, relaying e-mail messages, faxes and calls from photographers.

Note: The publishers and authors would like to give special thanks to Killian Mullarney for so generously giving his time and for his invaluable help over some of the more difficult aspects of gull identification.

INTRODUCTION

Of some 9,700 bird species recognized to date, only about 300 (c 3%) can be considered seabirds (depending on one's definition of a seabird). Thus, while 9,400 landbirds inhabit some 30% of the globe (the land), the 300 seabirds inhabit the remaining 70% (the sea), coming to land generally only to breed. For most of the year they must derive their living from the marine environment.

Population and monitoring studies over the last 20 years have enhanced our knowledge of seabirds, and Birdlife International, in *Birds to Watch 2* (Collar et al. 1994), classifies 20% of seabirds as globally threatened, compared with 12% for all bird species: clearly, all is not well with the World's seabirds. While pelagic seabirds may be long-lived, they generally lay only one egg (which is not replaced if lost), breed once a year (in some cases once every two years), and consequently have a lower reproductive output than landbirds, which tend to be shorter-lived but lay larger clutches of eggs more frequently. Given that Man's track record of destruction (either directly, by taking eggs and killing birds, or indirectly, by the introduction of mammalian predators to islands) is not one to be proud of, seabirds must now contend with increasing degradation of the sea (heavy metals, oil pollution, plastic, etc) as well as increasing loss of life (gill nets and long-line fishing). Some seabird populations are now being reduced not only at their breeding sites but also more frequently on the open ocean. This does not bode well for large, long-lived seabirds, some of which do not breed until their tenth year.

While the long-term prospects for seabirds may look dark, there are a few rays of hope. South Africa's only overseas possession, Marion Island (Prince Edward Islands), is now apparently cat-free after an intensive ten-year eradication programme; time will tell if seabird populations on Marion increase. New Zealand, which probably has more breeding seabird species than anywhere else, is now able to eradicate rats on small to medium-sized islands; some formerly rare species are now recovering. Alec and Frank Zino from Madeira succeeded in bringing a halt to seabird slaughter on the Salvages, and are now committed to saving their rare and endemic *Pterodroma* petrels. Also David Wingate has almost single-handedly ensured the continued survival of the Bermuda Petrel.

Whether it is from the efforts of individuals, of conservation bodies or of governments, there should be some co-ordinated global marine conservation strategy for seabirds (as well as for all

marine life). The following one example should suffice. Monitoring studies indicate that Wandering Albatross populations are rapidly decreasing, to the extent that the bird is now classified as Vulnerable: numbers have fallen by some 50% in the last 20-30 years, mainly as a result of drowning on tuna long-lines. Having observed these ultimate flying machines at sea around the Southern Ocean and breeding on subantarctic islands, I find it a sobering thought that this awe-inspiring bird could become extinct in my or my son's lifetime. The fact that they fly does not in any way mean that they will not go the same way as the Great Auk.

This book is an attempt to illustrate the diagnostic characters of seabirds by a combination of photographs and written text. For reasons of space it has not been possible to illustrate every plumage phase and every subspecies, and in some cases – fortunately these are few – it has proved impossible to obtain any photographs.

Seabird identification often relies heavily on jizz and flight, as well as a colour combination of primarily browns, greys, white and black. All of these parameters become variable with different meteorological conditions: thus, a species' 'field variability' must be appreciated. There is no definitive at-sea 'seabird description', and I make no apology for the use of the words 'generally' and 'variable' in my descriptions.

Following Croxall et al. (1984), I have employed a strict definition of a seabird. While this includes all the Sphenisciformes and all the Procellariiformes, some non-marine Pelecaniformes and Lariiformes have been excluded (see Appendix I). Inevitably, a few decisions may appear a little arbitrary.

Since the publication of Harrison's *Seabirds: an Identification Guide* (1983) and *Seabirds of the World: a Photographic Guide* (1987), knowledge, taxonomy and technology have advanced considerably. There is a new taxonomy (Sibley and Monroe 1990), with taxa previously regarded as subspecies now being assigned specific status. In many cases, the visible differences become minimal in the field (eg Hawaiian and Galapagos Petrels), and this can hinder and even prevent specific

identification. Moreover, the 14 species of albatross recognized at present may soon be re-evaluated to constitute as many as 24 species. The new taxonomy has generated much heated discussion since its publication in 1990, and it was consequently decided to adopt an approach similar to that of Birdlife International (1994). For ease of use, the familiar sequence of families as used by Morony et al. (1975) has been maintained, but the order of birds within families follows that proposed by Sibley and Monroe. This appears to be the line of least resistance while the taxonomic debate continues at present. Different taxonomic interpretations from those of Sibley and Monroe are mentioned in the text, and in some cases the English names have conformed a little more to local usage, which in most cases is preferable.

With the increasing knowledge of the status, populations and distribution of seabirds, it is now possible to estimate a species' global population. While for many birds (especially burrow-nesters) these are, at best, estimates, I have tried to include such information where known, though in many cases figures just do not exist. Only by careful counting and monitoring over time will trends become apparent. All references to classified species are taken from *Birds to Watch 2* by Birdlife International (Collar et al. 1994): see Appendix II for the classification criteria.

Improved camera technology and the increased opportunities for the average birder to travel the globe have meant increased knowledge and more easily obtained photographs. Many of the photographs used here have not previously been published. There is now also a plethora of books on seabirds, as well as many new identification and distribution articles published in journals. I have drawn freely on these sources, the most important of which are listed in the bibliography.

A book of this kind does not get to be written and published without help from friends and colleagues. I hope that I have mentioned them all in the acknowledgements.

Sphenisciformes

17 species. Penguins are flightless marine seabirds, generally with dark upperparts and white underparts, which evolved in the Southern Hemisphere. They range in size from the Little Penguin (40 cm; 1 kg in weight) to the Emperor Penguin (110 cm; 40 kg), although some fossil penguins were much larger.

Penguins' closest relatives are the Procellariiformes, which may initially appear strange: non-flying seabirds closely related to the most accomplished fliers! However, they are at opposite ends of the continuum of marine exploitation, one diving and the other flying, both specialized and both successful.

Unlike auks, which have compromised between diving and yet retaining flight, penguins have opted totally for the underwater diving strategy. They have thus radiated into different sizes to feed on different foods, thereby dividing up the marine resource. This has meant that long-range foraging is out of the question, although the larger species are on a par with marine mammals such as seals – Emperor Penguins are able to dive to about 400 m and remain submerged for about 20 minutes. With the legs set well back on the body acting as a rudder, and the flippers acting as paddles, penguins literally 'fly' through the water. Penguins are social, colonial seabirds with some huge colonies on subantarctic islands. Young penguins form crèches and, generally, only one young is reared per year. The most extreme breeding strategies are employed by King and Emperor Penguins. Moulting penguins are also unique: they are unable to feed, and so they must be either on land or on ice.

Populations of some penguin species are increasing for various reasons. Five species (29%), however, are now classified as Vulnerable, with a further two classified as Near-threatened.

Procellariiformes

113 species. A large order of pelagic seabirds divided into four families, and ranging in size from the Least Storm-petrel (14 cm; 25 g) to the huge Royal Albatross (115 cm; 12 kg) – a weight-difference ratio of some 1:300, not exceeded by any other bird order. The order contains more individual birds than any other seabird order, ranging from Wilson's Storm-petrel (the World's most numerous seabird?) to some of the rarest, least-known and most enigmatic seabirds such as Magenta Petrel, Zino's Petrel and Fiji Petrel.

Procellariiformes are found in all oceans of the World. Their mobility has ensured almost unlimited radiation, although today most are found in the Southern Hemisphere, from where they originated. These are the truly pelagic seabirds in the strictest sense, with some undergoing vast annual migrations, while others spend many years at sea before returning to breed. Such wanderings inevitably mean that some birds occasionally become horribly lost and may turn up in bizarre locations (see Bourne's 1967 classic paper 'Long-distance vagrancy in the petrels').

Known as 'tubenoses' because their nostrils are external and tubular from the base of the upper mandible (nostrils separated in albatrosses but joined in the other three families), there is increasing evidence that these birds, which also have large olfactory bulbs in the brain, are able to smell their food from considerable distances. All have an extended glandular part of the stomach which helps produce the oil upon which their breeding strategy is based. They feed on fish, squid and plankton, with many feeding adaptations for long-distance foraging.

Procellariiformes are generally social and colonial breeders, using many breeding habitats (especially burrowing in the Procellariidae), but they do not use trees or bushes. They are extremely 'K-selected': the birds do not breed in some cases until they are seven to eleven years old, they lay one egg which is not replaced if lost, some species can breed only once every two years, but most birds are long-lived (up to 50 years for large albatrosses). Nevertheless, with increased man-induced mortality of pre-breeding and breeding birds at sea, mainly by long-line fishing, ever-growing numbers of species and populations are now declining (see above). It is difficult to quantify exact losses of seabirds annually to long-line fishing (as well as to drift nets and by trawling), but during 1990-94 over 30,000 Laysan Albatrosses and over 20,000 Black-footed Albatrosses were killed off Hawaii (ref. IUCN Draft Resolution June 1996) and, around New Zealand, up to 20,000 Shy Albatrosses and 10,000 Wandering Albatrosses are estimated to be killed every year by blue-fin tuna long-line fishing. These latter figures represent about 10% of the total population per year. Twelve of the 14 species of albatross have been recorded killed by long-line fishing, and six species are now rapidly declining. Furthermore, long-line fishing also kills penguins, petrels, shearwaters, gannets and skuas.

At present, 30 species (25%) of this order are classified as either Critical, Endangered, or Vulnerable, with a further 11 species Near-threatened.

Pelecaniformes

50 'seabird' species. A diverse and colourful order of mainly large seabirds consisting of pelicans, gannets and boobies, tropicbirds, cormorants and shags, and frigatebirds. These are the only birds to have all four toes connected by webs (totipalmate); and they have a gular or throat pouch, which is most developed in pelicans and frigatebirds. The upper mandible is hooked in pelicans, cormorants and frigatebirds and, apart from tropicbirds, all have very small nostrils which can lack an external opening. Cormorants and frigatebirds have a semi-permeable plumage; thus, cormorants have to dry their wings after swimming, whereas frigatebirds avoid getting wet.

Pelecaniformes are believed to be derived from Procellariiform stock, with their centre of origin in the Southern Hemisphere, though most are now found in tropical and warm-temperate latitudes. Although less marine than Procellariiformes, frigatebirds and tropicbirds are pelagic. Cormorants show most adaptive radiation, being of variable size, extending from the Arctic to the seas of the Antarctic, and containing a flightless representative.

Pelecaniformes have not explored the plankton feeding niche, and consequently there are no small species. Their food is mainly fish, with some tropical species additionally taking squid. Most species are social and colonial breeders, using all breeding habitats (but not burrowing), and trees and bushes are used extensively for nesting.

Breeding strategies are varied. Frigatebirds are the most 'K-selected', not breeding until seven to 11 years old, then breeding once every two years and having low breeding success, but adults live a long time. The remaining families are 'R-selected' to a variable degree: they have shorter adolescence (two to six years), lay several eggs in a season, but have relatively high annual rates of adult mortality. These latter species, with higher annual rates of reproduction and population turnover, are better placed than 'K-selected' species to absorb and recover from man-induced mortalities.

Eleven species (22%) are classified as Critical (one) or Vulnerable (ten), with a further five classified as Near-threatened.

Lariformes

About 107 'seabird' species. A large and diverse order of birds, comprising skuas, gulls, terns and noddies, skimmers, and auks.

The skuas are close relatives of the gulls. They are medium-sized to large piratical seabirds with hooked upper mandible, breeding in higher latitudes of both hemispheres and migrating towards and/or across the Equator in the non-breeding season. They are colonial breeders and are fiercely territorial; two eggs are laid on the ground. The *Catharacta* skuas are always dark with white flashes on the wings, whereas the *Stercorarius* skuas are polymorphic. *Stercorarius* species are circumpolar in the Northern Hemisphere, breeding in the arctic tundra and feeding on lemmings, young birds, insects, berries and carrion. Breeding success correlates with rodent abundance. None classified.

The gulls include 50 species of mainly grey, white and black seabirds varying in size from the Little Gull (25 cm; 90 g) to the Great Black-backed Gull (75 cm; 2 kg). Gulls are essentially birds of the Northern Hemisphere which have invaded the South, showing much speciation and adaptive radiation; they occupy many breeding habitats, both natural and man-made. Gulls breed colonially, laying several eggs usually on the ground, and young are fed in the nest on a variety of food – though only the kittiwakes have exploited the plankton feeding niche. Sewage works, landfill sites, reservoirs and fish factories have encouraged gulls inland in winter, to the point of their being a nuisance and even a danger to human and other bird populations. One species is classified as Endangered, four as Vulnerable, and two as Near-threatened.

Terns and noddies are smaller and more slender than gulls, with short legs, a forked tail and webbed feet, although they are not good swimmers. Size varies from the Least Tern (23 cm; 50 g) to the Caspian Tern (54 cm; 700 g) and coloration is generally similar to that of gulls, although some terns and the noddies are dark. As a group terns are more marine than gulls and, while some tropical species are sedentary, most are long-distance migrants. Terns are social and colonial breeders, using many breeding habitats, including trees and bushes (unlike most gulls), and one species (Inca Tern) burrows. Terns feed on fish, small squid and crustaceans, which they catch by plunging into the sea. Some tropical species lay only one egg, this being related to long-range foraging, while non-tropical species lay two to three eggs. Young terns form crèches, as do penguins and pelicans. Unlike gull populations, tern numbers are generally decreasing. Three species are classified (one Critical, two Vulnerable), and two are Near-threatened.

Auks are small black and white diving seabirds which originated in the north Pacific. They have a dense waterproof plumage, a short tail, and legs set well back on the body, and some have nuptial head plumes. Diving and flying have necessitated a compromise regarding wing size; long-distance foraging is sacrificed for an almost exclusive occupation of the diving niche. Subsequent adaptive radiation has led to feeding on different foods, as well as the evolution of a range of sizes from the Least Auklet (15 cm; 90 g) to the Guillemot (42 cm; 1 kg), the latter of which approaches the size limit to sustain flight. (The Great Auk weighed 5 kg and was flightless.) Six auks have gular pouches, thus increasing the amount of food carried to the young. One or two eggs are laid, and auks can breed when two to three years old. Breeding ecology varies considerably, as does post-hatching care of the young. Worldwide, auk numbers are now declining. One species is classified as Vulnerable and three are Near-threatened.

J.W. Enticott
Cape Town, June 1996

SYSTEMATIC LIST
OF SPECIES

PENGUINS

KING PENGUIN

Aptenodytes patagonicus L 94 cm (37 in)
The second largest penguin. Breeds on oceanic island groups in the cooler Subantarctic each side of the Antarctic Convergence.
IDENTIFICATION Immature Smaller than adult, with similar plumage pattern: white underparts but browner upperparts. Auricular patches paler than adult's, being lemon-yellow (or whitish in worn plumage); lower throat yellow, not orange; greyish tips to crown feathers; lower mandible stripe pinkish, becoming whiter with age. At sea, separated from immature Emperor Penguin by comma-shaped lemon-yellow or whitish auricular patches, whereas immature Emperor has darker head with lower and whiter auricular patch. Adult plumage attained at start of third year. **Adult** Smaller than Emperor Penguin, with different head pattern. Head and throat blackish-brown. Comma-shaped orange auricular patches on sides of neck extending further onto nape than Emperor's. Upperparts dark silvery bluish-grey (appearing blackish at a distance), separated from auricular patches by a thin black line which continues down sides of breast, thickening, and separating dark upperparts from white underparts. Tail black. Flipper silver-grey as upperparts, underside of flipper white with blackish band along leading edge and blackish tip (although variable). Underparts white with orange suffusion on lower throat, shading to yellowish on upper breast. Bill slightly decurved, blackish, with inner two-thirds of lower mandible pink or orange; iris brown; legs and feet dark grey to black.
DISTRIBUTION AND STATUS Southern Ocean, almost circumpolar (not south Pacific) between 45°S and 65°S. Breeds 46°S-55°S on Falklands, South Georgia, Prince Edwards, Crozets, Kerguelen, Heard and Macquarie Islands. Total population over 1 million pairs. Does not breed Antarctic Continent; status off southern South America unclear. Vagrants South America (including recent record as far north as Rio de Janeiro, Brazil), South Sandwich, Bouvet, Gough, South Africa, Australia, Tasmania, New Zealand and Antarctic Continent indicate wide pelagic dispersal when not breeding. Breeds colonially, twice in three years (unique breeding strategy). Numbers recovering after protection from persecution and with increased food supply.

EMPEROR PENGUIN

Aptenodytes forsteri L 112 cm (44 in)
The largest penguin. Breeds in winter (unique) in Antarctica and adjacent islands.
IDENTIFICATION Differs from King Penguin in larger size, darker head, different shape and colour of auricular patches, and smaller pale area on lower mandible. At sea, where identification of immature birds can be problematic, auricular patches extend to sea-surface level, unlike King Penguin. **Immature**
Smaller than adult. Plumage pattern as adult but paler, especially auricular patches, chin and throat, which are whiter; head browner; bill stripe on inner two-thirds of lower mandible pinkish-orange. Adult plumage attained after 18 months. **Adult** Head, throat and nape blackish. Auricular patches on sides of neck pale lemon-yellow or orange-yellow to (in worn plumage) whitish, extending onto upper breast, unlike King Penguin. Upperparts and tail bluish-black, not so dark as head (but colour shade dependent on distance and light intensity). Darker black stripe from sides of neck continues under flipper to flanks, separating dark upperparts from white underparts. Underparts glossy white, with lemon or orange suffusion on upper breast. Flipper bluish-black above (as upperparts), under surface white with narrow grey leading edge and small dark tip. Bill short and decurved, greyish-black, with inner two-thirds of lower mandible variable from lilac to orange; iris brown; legs and feet blackish-grey.
DISTRIBUTION AND STATUS Circumpolar. Breeds colonially at c 40 localities between 66°S and 78°S on the Antarctic Continent, Antarctic Peninsula and adjacent islands. Northern limit generally the open pack ice, but recorded at 40°S off Argentina. Total population 135,000-175,000 breeding pairs, representing perhaps 400,000-450,000 individuals. Vagrants Tierra del Fuego, South Orkneys, South Sandwich, South Georgia, Falklands, Kerguelen, Heard, New Zealand. Status appears stable.

GENTOO PENGUIN

Pygoscelis papua L 75 cm (30 in)
The largest *Pygoscelis* penguin and the least abundant. Generally found between 45°S and 65°S.
IDENTIFICATION Distinctively black and white. Combination of size, distinctive bill and head pattern prevents confusion with other penguins. Occasional albinos and partial albinos occur. **Immature** Smaller than adult, but similar plumage pattern. Bill smaller and duller; white bar over eye narrower and duller, usually reduced to white flecking near eye, although variable; white speckling on nape usually less extensive than adult's. Chin and throat usually grey, thus lacking adult's sharp demarcation between black and white. **Adult** The third largest penguin, with black upperparts and white underparts. Head, neck and throat slate-black, with conspicuous white triangular patches above and behind each eye, narrowing and usually meeting over crown; scattered white feathers on nape and shoulders impart speckled appearance to the blue-black upperparts; tail blackish with whitish base. Upper surface of flippers blue-black with narrow white leading edge and wider, more conspicuous white trailing edge. Under surface of flippers white with narrow darker leading edge and larger dark tip. Underparts white, sharply demarcated from black throat. Bill
pointed, orange-yellow to orange-red with black culmen and black tip; iris brown with white eyelids; feet orange-yellow with black soles.
DISTRIBUTION AND STATUS Circumpolar in subantarctic and antarctic waters between 45°S and 65°S. Breeds Antarctic Peninsula, South Shetlands, South Orkneys, Falklands, South Georgia, South Sandwich, Prince Edwards, Crozets, Kerguelen, Heard and Macquarie Islands. Total population c 280,000 pairs, 70% of which breed on the Falklands and South Georgia. Populations stable or slightly increasing, but not so much as either Adélie or Chinstrap Penguins. Northern populations are generally sedentary, while southern populations move north in winter. Vagrants have reached Argentina, Gough Island, South Africa, Tasmania, New Zealand and New Zealand subantarctic islands.

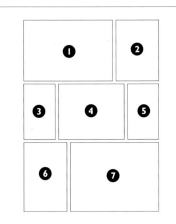

1 **King Penguin** (adults and juveniles at breeding colony, Bay of Isles, South Georgia, January)
2 **King Penguin** (breeding adults incubating egg, Volunteer Point, Falkland Islands)
3 **King Penguin** (juvenile, Bay of Isles, South Georgia, January)
4 **Emperor Penguin** (adults, Taylor Glacier, Antarctica)
5 **Emperor Penguin** (adults, Taylor Glacier, Antarctica)
6 **Gentoo Penguin** (pair of adults displaying, Falkland Islands)
7 **Gentoo Penguin** (adult at nest with chick, Falkland Islands, January)

PENGUINS

ADELIE PENGUIN

Pygoscelis adeliae L 71 cm (28 in)
Medium-sized *Pygoscelis* penguin, very widely distributed.
IDENTIFICATION Unlike Gentoo and Chinstrap Penguins, adult's head (including chin and throat) entirely black. Complete and partial albinos occasionally occur. **Immature** Similar plumage pattern to adult, but with chin and throat white or greyish. Eyelids dark, becoming white in the first year. Demarcation between dark head and white underparts occurs well below eye, whereas above eye in immature Chinstrap Penguin, which has a greyish chin, as well as a longer bill. Upperparts generally bluer than adult's. Chin and throat become black after moult at one year old. **Adult** Head, cheeks, chin, throat and upperparts, including flippers and tail, bluish-black, slightly variable with season, light intensity and distance. Conspicuous ring of white feathers around eye visible from a considerable distance. Upper surface of flipper bluish-black with narrow white trailing edge, under surface white with thin black leading edge and small blackish tip. Underparts white, sharply demarcated from blackish throat. Bill short and feathered for over half its length, thus appearing dark at base, remainder chestnut-red to dull orange with dark tip; iris red-brown; legs and feet flesh-pink with black soles.
DISTRIBUTION AND STATUS The most widely distributed antarctic penguin. Circumpolar: rarely north of 60°S. Breeds south of the Antarctic Convergence, with most breeding on the Antarctic Continent and Antarctic Peninsula, also on South Shetlands, South Sandwich, Bouvet and South Orkney Islands. Total population at least 2,610,000 pairs. Most move northwards after breeding, and vagrants have reached South America, Falklands, South Georgia, Prince Edwards, Heard and Macquarie Islands, Tasmania and New Zealand. Increase in numbers in recent decades resulting from a combination of recovery after persecution and increased food supply.

CHINSTRAP PENGUIN

Pygoscelis antarctica L 68 cm (27 in)
Medium-sized *Pygoscelis* penguin, possibly the most aggressive of all penguins.
IDENTIFICATION Has diagnostic thin black line from ear to ear, passing under the chin. Occasional albinos recorded. **Immature** Smaller and slimmer than adult, with similar plumage pattern except for chin, throat and cheeks being speckled with dark grey. Bill smaller than adult's but larger than Adélie Penguin's. Despite greyish cheeks, the demarcation of black and white is above the eye (unlike Adélie Penguin), with more white on the sides of the neck. The 'chinstrap' is acquired in the first year. **Adult** Forehead, crown, nape and long tail are blackish. Upperparts and flippers are bluish-black, the latter with narrow white trailing edge on upper surface. Under surface of flipper white with narrow blackish leading edge and small dark patch at tip. Cheeks white, with sharp demarcation from black crown passing above eye. Diagnostic thin black line from ear to ear separating white cheeks and chin from whitish throat ('chinstrap'). Rest of underparts white. Bill black; iris reddish-brown; legs and feet flesh-pink with black soles.
DISTRIBUTION AND STATUS Circumpolar south of the Antarctic Convergence. Fewer in Indian and Pacific Oceans, with 99% breeding in the Antarctic Peninsula and south Atlantic subantarctic and antarctic islands, where especially vast numbers (5 million pairs) in the South Sandwich group. Total population 6,500,000 pairs. Vagrants Gough, Prince Edwards, Crozets, Kerguelen, Macquarie Island, Australia and Tasmania. Increase in recent decades in numbers and range greater than for any other penguin, especially in the Antarctic Peninsula and adjacent islands, as a result of increased food availability and possibly climatic change.

ROCKHOPPER PENGUIN

Eudyptes chrysocome L 55 cm (22 in)
The smallest crested penguin.
IDENTIFICATION Diagnostic black occipital crest and drooping golden-yellow crests from above eye backwards, not reaching bill or joining across forehead. **Immature** As adult, but with less developed yellow superciliary stripe, smaller and browner bill, and chin and throat usually greyish (paler than adult). Eye reddish-brown, duller than adult. From Macaroni Penguin by smaller size, and different head and under-flipper patterns. **Adult** Head, cheeks and throat black. Yellow crest starts as narrow stripes above each eye, not extending to base of bill nor joining on forehead, continuing backwards to form long, wispy, silky-yellow feathers which can droop; intermixed are black feathers from occipital crest meeting on back of crown. (Yellow crest longer in *moseleyi*.) Upperparts and tail bluish-black, with bluish-grey sheen in fresh plumage. Upper surface of flipper bluish-black with narrow white trailing edge. Under surface of flipper white with narrow black leading edge, blackish tip and blackish base, but variable with subspecies. Bill reddish-brown with pinkish-flesh margin at base in *filholi*, whereas blackish in *chrysocome* and *moseleyi*; iris bright red; feet whitish to pinkish, soles black. *E. c. filholi* distinguished from immature Snares Island Penguin by smaller bill, less bare skin at bill base, narrower superciliary, and red (not dull red-brown) eye. *E. c. moseleyi* and *E. c. chrysocome* have black skin at bill base as Fiordland Crested Penguin, but smaller size, less robust bill, narrower superciliary, and presence of occipital crest. From Erect-crested Penguin by smaller size, shorter bill and narrower superciliary; from Macaroni and Royal Penguins by smaller size, shorter bill, and absence of orange-yellow crest plumes on forehead.
DISTRIBUTION AND STATUS Circumpolar in subantarctic and antarctic waters north of the northern limit of pack ice. Breeding range circumpolar from south of Antarctic Convergence to north of Subtropical Convergence on subantarctic and south-temperate islands in the Atlantic and Indian Oceans: *E. c. moseleyi* breeds Tristan da Cunha, Gough, Amsterdam and St Paul Islands; *E. c. chrysocome* breeds Falklands (2,500,000 pairs) and islands off southern South America; *E. c. filholi* breeds Prince Edwards, Crozets, Kerguelen, Heard, Macquarie, Campbell, Auckland and Antipodes Islands. Total population *c* 3,500,000 pairs. Dispersal north after breeding to 35°S off Argentina, reaching South Africa, Australia and New Zealand. One of the most numerous crested penguins; population appears stable.

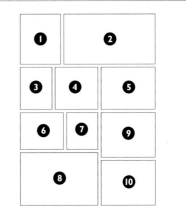

1 **Adélie Penguin** (adult, Antarctica, December)
2 **Adélie Penguin** (breeding colony, Hope Bay, Antarctica, December)
3 **Adélie Penguin** (adult, Hope Bay, Antarctica)
4 **Chinstrap Penguin** (adult, Half Moon Island, Antarctica)
5 **Chinstrap Penguin** (adult with chick, Bouvet Island)
6 **Rockhopper Penguin** (adult)
7 **Rockhopper Penguin** (adult, St Paul Island)
8 **Rockhopper Penguin** (adults in breeding colony with juvenile, New Island, Falkland Islands)
9 **Rockhopper Penguin, subspecies *E. c. moseleyi*** (adult, Gough Island)
10 **Rockhopper Penguin, subspecies *E. c. moseleyi*** (adult, Gough Island)

PENGUINS

FIORDLAND CRESTED PENGUIN

Eudyptes pachyrhynchus L 55 cm (22 in)
Eudyptes penguin breeding on South Island of New Zealand and adjacent islands. Classified as Vulnerable.

IDENTIFICATION Immature As adult, but with shorter crest and smaller, duller bill. Recently fledged birds have white chin and throat with grey cheeks similar to young Snares Island Penguin, but distinguished by lack of fleshy margin at base of bill. **Adult** Head blackish, with sulphur-yellow crest starting each side of base of bill (not meeting) and passing over eye, ending in a drooping crest which may contain some black feathers. Crest generally lies flat on head (unlike Snares Island and Erect-crested Penguins). Cheeks blackish, with whitish feather bases showing as three to six whitish cheek-stripes usually parallel with crest. Upperparts, throat, cheeks and tail bluish-black. Upper surface of flipper bluish-black with narrow white trailing edge. Underparts from throat white, clearly demarcated. Under surface of flipper white with narrow grey leading edge, blackish tip and dark brown base. Bill reddish-brown with some dark skin at base rather than fleshy margins; iris variable from greyish-brown to reddish; feet fleshy-pink, soles black. Male larger than female, with heavier bill and wider crest. Before moulting (December-March), upperparts become browner and crest fades to whitish; after moult, upperparts shiny dark blue.

DISTRIBUTION AND STATUS Breeds in dense vegetation and caves on west and south-east coasts of South Island, Solander and Stewart Island, New Zealand. Only *Eudyptes* penguin to lay in winter and rear chick in spring. Immatures reach South Australia, Tasmania and the Snares group in summer. Vagrants have reached North Island, Campbell and Auckland Islands; also recorded from Falkland Islands, which is more difficult to explain; movements at sea generally unknown. Total population estimated at 1,000-2,000 breeding pairs (perhaps as many as 5,000-10,000 pairs) remaining on predator-free islands; mainland colonies are threatened by stoats, rats, dogs and the native Weka Rail. Numbers apparently stable and little influenced by humans.

SNARES ISLAND PENGUIN

Eudyptes robustus L 63 cm (25 in)
Medium-sized *Eudyptes* penguin confined as a breeding bird to Snares Island (100 km south of Stewart Island). Classified as Vulnerable.

IDENTIFICATION Unlike Fiordland Crested Penguin, has fleshy margins at base of bill.
Immature As adult, but crest shorter and paler. Iris brown; bill smaller than adult, brownish with thin fleshy margins. Recently fledged birds have white chin and throat mottled with black; chin and throat soon become darker with age. **Adult** Head blackish. Narrow but conspicuous bright yellow crest starts as superciliary stripes from base of bill

(not meeting), continuing over eye to form long silky plumes drooping down sides of nape. Throat, cheeks, upperparts and tail bluish-black. Upper surface of flipper bluish-black with thin white trailing edge. Underparts from throat white, sharply demarcated. Under surface of flipper whitish with dark tip and base, with blackish stripe on leading edge. Bill large and heavy, reddish-brown, with flesh-coloured skin at base of lower mandible becoming triangular at gape; iris claret (but variable); legs and feet whitish-pink with black soles. Before moult (March), upperparts become browner and crest fades to pale yellow; after moult (May), upperparts have strong bluish tone. Most similar to Fiordland Crested and Erect-crested Penguins. From Fiordland Crested by larger bill, presence of bare pink skin at bill base, uniformly dark cheeks, and rear of crest bushier; from Erect-crested by larger bill and lack of velvet-black head and 'large-chinned' profile of that species, as well as lacking upward-sweeping brush-like crest.

DISTRIBUTION AND STATUS Breeds only on four islands in Snares group. Has reached mainland New Zealand, Stewart, Solander, Chatham, Antipodes and Campbell Islands. Vagrants to Australia, Tasmania and Macquarie Island, and Falklands. Total population estimated at 23,250 breeding pairs. Access to the islands controlled, thereby reducing threats to the population. No mammalian predation.

ERECT-CRESTED PENGUIN

Eudyptes sclateri L 67 cm (26 in)
Medium-sized *Eudyptes* penguin confined as a breeding bird to subantarctic islands south of New Zealand. Classified as Vulnerable.

IDENTIFICATION Immature As adult, but crest less pronounced, though still brush-like posteriorly. Under-surface pattern of flipper as adult. Recently fledged birds have white or greyish chin and throat. Bill dull brownish-orange, bare skin present but not conspicuous.
Adult Head, cheeks and throat velvet-black (not bluish-black as in other *Eudyptes* penguins). Golden-yellow crests start at base of bill (not meeting) near gape, broaden over eye, and end standing upright rather than drooping as in other *Eudyptes*. Upperparts and tail bluish-black. Upper surface of flipper bluish-black with narrow white trailing edge. Flippers and tail comparatively long. Underparts white, sharply demarcated from black of throat. Under surface of flipper whitish with broad black leading edge joining black tip and black base. Bill long and comparatively slim, reddish-brown to orange-brown, with exposed fleshy margins at base forming triangle at gape; iris brown; legs and feet pinkish-white with black soles. Before moulting (February), head becomes browner, superciliary fades, and upperparts develop bronze cast; after moulting (April), upperparts have a fresh strong bluish shade. Most similar to Snares Island Penguin, which has stouter, more orange bill, thinner drooping crest, and different underwing pattern.

DISTRIBUTION AND STATUS Breeds mainly on Bounty and Antipodes Islands, with smaller numbers on Auckland Island; formerly bred Campbell Island. Occasionally breeds New Zealand mainland. Winter distribution at sea unknown, but probably warmer waters off east coast of South Island. Recorded fairly regularly on mainland New Zealand, also Macquarie, Snares, Chathams; also recorded Australia, Tasmania, Kerguelen and Falklands. Estimated total population of *c* 200,000 pairs. Stable at present, with no known threats.

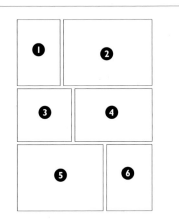

1 **Fiordland Crested Penguin** (adult, New Zealand)
2 **Fiordland Crested Penguin** (adults, New Zealand)
3 **Snares Island Penguin** (adults, Snares Island Group)
4 **Snares Island Penguin** (adults, Snares Island Group)
5 **Erect-crested Penguin** (adults, Antipodes Island)
6 **Erect-crested Penguin** (adult, Antipodes Island)

PENGUINS

MACARONI PENGUIN

Eudyptes chrysolophus L 70 cm (28 in)
Large *Eudyptes* penguin breeding on subantarctic islands of the Atlantic and Indian Oceans.
IDENTIFICATION Has massive bill, approaching that of Royal Penguin. **Immature** Plumage as adult, but with less extensive crest which is less orange and more yellow than adult's. Chin and throat dark grey in early stages. **Adult** Head, throat and nape blackish. Crest is conspicuous golden-orange rather than yellow, and starts on forehead, projects backwards over eye and droops downwards. Upperparts and tail bluish-black with whitish uppertail-coverts. Upper surface of flipper bluish-black with narrow white trailing edge. Underparts white; meeting of dark throat and white underparts forms more of a 'V' than in other *Eudyptes*. Under surface of flipper white with blackish leading edge, tip and base. Large bill reddish-brown, with pinkish fleshy margins forming a triangle at bill base; iris reddish-brown; legs and feet pale pinkish, soles black. Differs from other *Eudyptes* penguins (except Royal) in head plumes joining across forehead; differs from larger Royal Penguin in less robust bill, and absence of white or grey on sides of face, chin and throat.
DISTRIBUTION AND STATUS Most southerly-breeding *Eudyptes* penguin in subantarctic and antarctic waters (45°S-65°S) north of pack ice, breeding each side of Antarctic Convergence in south Atlantic and Indian Oceans; winter range generally 45°S-65°S. Total World population estimated at some 11,650,000+ pairs, with general trend of increase. Breeds southern South America, Antarctic Peninsula and adjacent islands, South Georgia (5 million+ pairs), Bouvet, Prince Edwards, Crozets, Kerguelen, Heard, McDonald Islands. Vagrants to South Africa, Australia, also Snares, Campbell and Macquarie Islands.

ROYAL PENGUIN

Eudyptes schlegeli L 76 cm (30 in)
The largest *Eudyptes* penguin. Confined as a breeding bird to Macquarie Island. Taxonomic status of white-faced birds outside Macquarie Island insufficiently understood.
IDENTIFICATION Massive bill, and white or greyish sides of face, chin and throat.
Immature As adult but smaller, with shorter head plumes and smaller, darker bill, and greyer on upper throat and above eye in early stages of immaturity. **Adult** Crown, nape and hindneck black. Long and conspicuous orange-yellow and black plumes start on forehead and project backwards along crown over eye, drooping behind eye. Upperparts and tail blackish with bluish sheen; some white on rump, but generally not visible in fresh plumage. Upper flipper blackish with narrow white trailing edge. Cheeks from crest to throat white (generally males) to pale grey (generally females), occasionally darker and

with much variability. Underparts white. Under flipper white with dark tip and base and with blackish leading edge. Bill huge, dark orange-brown, with bare skin at base forming pink triangle at gape; eye reddish-brown; legs and feet pinkish.
DISTRIBUTION AND STATUS Breeds in huge colonies at Macquarie and adjacent islets. Winters in subantarctic waters around Macquarie. Vagrants to South Australia, Victoria, Tasmania, New Zealand, Campbell, Snares Islands and Antarctica. Population *c* 1 million pairs. Previously heavily exploited for its oil, with many slaughtered over 50-year period up to 1918, but now recovered and stabilized.

YELLOW-EYED PENGUIN

Megadyptes antipodes L 66 cm (26 in)
Medium-sized, non-crested and secretive penguin, breeding South Island and adjacent islands of New Zealand. Classified as Vulnerable.
IDENTIFICATION Diagnostic pale yellow bands from eyes, meeting across hindcrown.
Immature Similar to adult, but pale yellow bands through eyes do not meet across hindcrown (extend to just behind eye, fully developed only after 18 months). Chin and throat mainly white, iris greyish-yellow; discoloration before moult more noticeable than in adult. **Adult** Crown, sides of face and chin pale yellow with black shaft streaks; blacker on crown; sides of face, head and throat with brownish tinge. Bands of pale yellow feathers start at gape, enclose the eyes and then enlarge and meet on hindcrown. Nape slate-grey. Back and tail uniform slate-blue. Upper surface of flipper darker than back: bluish-black with white trailing edge, very narrow white leading edge. Underparts white, sharply demarcated from yellowish throat. Under surface of flipper white. Bill long and slender, mainly reddish-brown; iris yellow; feet pinkish, soles black. Plumage duller before moult (February-March).
DISTRIBUTION AND STATUS Range 43°S-52°S around New Zealand. Resident, generally remaining near breeding sites all year, but some northward dispersal by juveniles and even some adults may take them 500-600 km from nesting area (has reached Cook Strait and North Island). Breeds solitarily under coastal vegetation or among roots on South Island (300-320 pairs), Stewart Island (300-400 pairs), Auckland Island (250-300 pairs), Campbell Island (560-700 pairs), also Codfish Island. Total breeding population 1,410-1,770 pairs, with total number of individual birds 4,028-5,057, though this species is difficult to census accurately because of its breeding habits. Probably the World's rarest penguin. Secretive species, and sensitive to human presence on landing beaches. Endangered on South Island from habitat clearance, fires, trampling of nests by cattle; eggs and chicks vulnerable to introduced predators, including

dogs, cats, pigs and stoats. Some losses to fishing nets. Fluctuating population, but trends unclear.

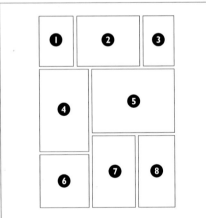

1 **Macaroni Penguin** (adult on nest platform, New Island, Falkland Islands)
2 **Macaroni Penguin** (breeding adult incubating egg, South Georgia)
3 **Royal Penguin** (adult, Macquarie Island)
4 **Royal Penguin** (breeding colony, Macquarie Island)
5 **Royal Penguin** (pair of adults, Macquarie Island)
6 **Yellow-eyed Penguin** (adult at nest, South Island, New Zealand)
7 **Yellow-eyed Penguin** (pair of adults, South Island, New Zealand)
8 **Yellow-eyed Penguin** (immature, Enderby Island, New Zealand)

PENGUINS

LITTLE PENGUIN

Eudyptula minor L 40 cm (16 in)
The smallest penguin, restricted to Australasian region. Nocturnal on land.
IDENTIFICATION Generally blue above and white below; no conspicuous head markings, and very short tail. **Immature** As adult, but smaller, with generally brighter blue on upperparts and smaller bill. **Adult** Head metallic blue-grey, paler on sides of face, merging into white chin and throat. Upperparts bluish, variable with wear and subspecies. Upper surface of flipper bluish-grey with white trailing edge, and white leading edge in 'White-flippered Penguin' *E. m. albosignata*. Tail short, bluish with black shafts; some show whitish on rump, uppertail-coverts, or whole tail. Underparts from chin whitish. Under flipper white with variable blackish patch at tip. Bill stout, and greyish-black; iris silvery-grey; legs and feet fleshy-white with black soles. Six subspecies recognized, on dorsal colour, bill dimensions and weight. Further study of New Zealand populations necessary to test subspecies validity. *E. m. albosignata*, 'White-flippered Penguin', differs from nominate in larger size, white margins to both leading and trailing edges of upper flipper, paler back; restricted to east coast of South Island, New Zealand.
DISTRIBUTION AND STATUS Breeds coastal mainland and islands of southern Australia, Tasmania and New Zealand, as well as Chatham Islands. Australian population probably under 1 million birds, but difficult to assess; regarded as stable, despite habitat destruction, predation and disturbance, latter including tourism (birds disoriented at night by motor launches using powerful searchlights). New Zealand population 25,000-50,000 pairs. Adults appear sedentary; immatures disperse more widely, but are not recorded outside the Australasian region. Vagrant Snares Island.

JACKASS or AFRICAN PENGUIN

Spheniscus demersus L 65 cm (26 in)
Uncrested black and white *Spheniscus* penguin breeding in South Africa and Namibia: Africa's only penguin. Classified as Near-threatened.
IDENTIFICATION Immature Head mainly greyish-black, thus lacking adult's distinctive head pattern. Blackish around eye, with whitish streaks above eye, on ear-coverts and on sides of neck. Upperparts, flippers and tail greyish-black. Underparts white, with dark grey chin, lower throat and upper breast. Adult pattern gradually emerges with age. Legs and feet pale flesh. **Adult** Back of head, ear-coverts and chin blackish; white bands from base of bill extend above eyes and around ear-coverts, meeting on upper breast and isolating black chin. Upperparts blackish-grey; tail blackish; upper surface of flipper blackish-grey with narrow white trailing edge. Underparts white, with one inverted horseshoe-shaped black breastband widening under flippers and extending to flanks

and thighs. A few birds may show a partial or complete second breastband between black chin and main horseshoe band, suggesting Magellanic Penguin. Under surface of flipper mainly white with dusky edges. Variable black spots on breast and belly. Bill black with blue-grey vertical bar at tip, and pinkish skin from base of upper mandible extending above and surrounding eye; iris dark brownish; legs and feet blackish with variable pink patches.
DISTRIBUTION AND STATUS Endemic to South Africa and Namibia, breeding in burrows on offshore islands and a few mainland sites. Population declined drastically since 19th century, and halved from *c* 295,000 birds in 1956 to *c* 170,000 birds in 1978. Main threats are seal competition, fisheries, and oil pollution; breeding colonies are also particularly sensitive to human disturbance. Non-breeders have reached Mozambique, Angola and even Gabon.

MAGELLANIC PENGUIN

Spheniscus magellanicus L 71 cm (28 in)
Largest and most numerous *Spheniscus* penguin, breeding on islands and coasts of southern South America.
IDENTIFICATION Strikingly black and white, with two black bands across breast.
Immature Lacks adult's distinctive pattern, having whitish-grey sides of face, chin and throat. Indistinct blackish-grey band, either partial or complete, across foreneck. Whitish supercilium and dark crown impart a slight capped appearance. Upperparts from crown to tail, including flippers, are greyer than adult's. Underparts white, lacking adult's distinct black breastbands. Immature Humboldt Penguin has darker brownish-grey sides of head, with more obvious pinkish fleshy margins at base of larger bill. **Adult** Head blackish, with broad white bands each side of crown, from base of upper mandible, above eyes and meeting on lower throat to enclose blackish chin. Upperparts, tail and upper surface of flipper blackish-grey, flipper with narrow white trailing edge; upperparts bluer in fresh plumage (after moult), whereas browner before moult. Underparts white with two blackish breastbands: the uppermost from sides of mantle across upper breast; the lowermost thinner, and extending from flanks below flipper and across upper breast as an inverted horseshoe band. Also isolated black feathers on white underparts on some birds. Under surface of flipper white with dusky edges. Stout black bill with transverse greyish bar near tip and fleshy pink margins at base, sometimes thinly joining pinkish eye-ring; iris brown; legs and feet blotched pinkish and black.
DISTRIBUTION AND STATUS Breeds Atlantic and Pacific coasts and islands of southern South America and the Falkland Islands. Total population several million, with estimates varying widely between 4,500,000 birds and 10 million birds; noticeable decline in numbers since end of 19th century, but range has at same time expanded northwards. Winter range

north to southern Brazil, occasionally Rio de Janeiro (23°S), and to *c* 30°S on Pacific coast. Vagrants South Georgia, possibly Tristan da Cunha; one record for Australia and another for New Zealand may have involved ship-assisted birds.

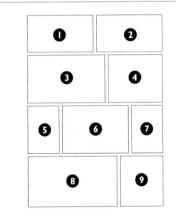

1 **Little Penguin** (Tanners Point, New Zealand)
2 **Little Penguin** (pair of adults at burrow, South Australia)
3 **Little Penguin** (adult at nest site, Waihi Beach, New Zealand)
4 **Jackass Penguin** (adult at nest, South Africa)
5 **Jackass Penguin** (immature, South Africa)
6 **Jackass Penguin** (pair of adults, South Africa)
7 **Magellanic Penguin** (adult, Falkland Islands)
8 **Magellanic Penguin** (adults coming ashore, Falkland Islands)
9 **Magellanic Penguin** (adult, Patagonia, January)

PENGUINS & ALBATROSSES

HUMBOLDT PENGUIN

Spheniscus humboldti L 65 cm (26 in)
Black and white *Spheniscus* penguin of the cool Humboldt Current off western South America. Classified as Near-threatened.
IDENTIFICATION Immature Lacks adult's distinctive head-and-breast pattern, having essentially dark brownish-grey upperparts and white underparts. Head brownish, with paler, greyer cheeks and brownish upper breast merging into white underparts. No whitish supercilium as in immature Magellanic Penguin; bill more stout than immature Magellanic's, with broader fleshy-pink margins at base.
Adult Head, chin and upper throat blackish, divided by narrow white stripes starting between each eye and upper mandible, passing over eyes and around ear-coverts, broadening and meeting on upper breast and continuing down body under the flipper to the flanks. Upperparts blackish-grey; tail blackish; upper surface of flipper blackish-grey with whitish trailing edge. Underparts white, with single black inverted horseshoe band extending from breast to flanks. Under surface of flipper mainly white. Occasionally, white underparts have isolated black feathers. Stout blackish bill with grey transverse bar near tip and extensive fleshy-pink margins at base and around eye; iris reddish-brown; legs and feet blackish. From Magellanic Penguin by narrower white head stripes, stouter bill with more extensive fleshy margins, and single black breastband; ranges overlap in north Chile but generally not in Peru.
DISTRIBUTION AND STATUS Breeds on coast of Peru (5°S) to *c* 33°S in Chile. Essentially sedentary, but non-breeders can reach north to Gulf of Guayaquil and south to *c* 37°S. Population (several thousand pairs) declining for a variety of reasons, now giving cause for concern; recently adversely affected by *El Niño*.

GALAPAGOS PENGUIN

Spheniscus mendiculus L 53 cm (21 in)
Smallest *Spheniscus* penguin, found only on Galapagos. Classified as Vulnerable.
IDENTIFICATION Immature Lacks adult's diagnostic head pattern and breastband, with dark grey head and upperparts and white underparts. Chin, cheeks and ear-coverts lighter grey, darkening on upper breast, forming indistinct demarcation against white underparts. **Adult** Head, including chin, blackish, with narrow white lines from eyes curving downwards around ear-coverts and meeting on lower chin. Upperparts blackish-grey, browner before moult and bluish-black after moult. Tail blackish. Upper surface of flipper blackish-grey; under surface white, with black at base. Underparts white with two indistinct brownish-grey bands across the upper breast; upper band is more distinct, and the narrower lower one extends under the flipper to the flanks and thigh. Bill is short, upper mandible black, base of lower mandible

yellowish; iris dark, pink eye-ring; legs and feet black. Smaller than Humboldt Penguin, with less distinct facial markings and breastbands, different bill coloration.
DISTRIBUTION AND STATUS Endemic to Galapagos, where a population of 6,000 to 15,000 birds bred on Isabela and Fernandina in 1977; this fell to 463 in 1984 following the *El Niño* of 1982/83, with numbers now apparently restored to a minimum of 3,000 pairs, although the 1995 census gave 844 birds (402 adults, 145 juveniles, and 297 indeterminates). Dogs prey on penguins on Isabela, and goats alter nesting habitat. Generally sedentary; small groups recorded from James, Santa Cruz and Floreana. One vagrant off Panama (probably ship-assisted). Birds must withstand air temperatures of 40°C and sea temperatures of 28°C by behavioural adaptations, which include moulting twice a year.

WANDERING ALBATROSS

Diomedea exulans L 115 cm (45 in), WS 250-350 cm (98-138 in)
Huge oceanic albatross of the Southern Ocean. One of the 'great albatrosses' – the largest seabirds. Classified as Vulnerable.
IDENTIFICATION Supreme user of dynamic soaring; wings more bowed in rough weather. Follows ships; occasionally attracted to trawlers. Variable plumage stages from brown juvenile to primarily white adult. **Juvenile** Head dark chocolate-brown with contrasting white face mask from base of bill, above eye to ear-coverts, and including chin and upper throat. Rest of plumage entirely dark chocolate-brown, apart from whitish underwing with black primary tips and narrow black trailing edge and brownish on axillaries (underwing essentially as adult). Bill pinkish; legs and feet pinkish. **Immature** Juveniles progressively whiten to adult plumage, going through numerous definable plumage phases. Head, mantle and rump develop whitish tips; belly and flanks become white, with brown breastband and undertail-coverts; blackish-brown upperwing develops whitish patch on inner wing; body becomes whitish with brown and grey vermiculations on saddle and flanks; tail starts to whiten, but retains dark tip and sides. Head, body and tail progressively develop more white, and white patch on upperwing joins white back to form whitish wedge on otherwise dark upperwings. White area of upperwing increases towards leading edge and outwards towards carpal; tail retains some dark tips. Bill pinkish; legs and feet pinkish. **Adult** Head white with pinkish ear stain. Body totally white. Upperwing white, with black primaries and narrower black on secondaries right up to body. Underwing white with blackish primary tips and narrow trailing edge. Tail white, though some dark outer feathers may be retained. Bill whitish-flesh to pinkish; iris brown, orbital ring pink or bluish; legs and feet pinkish or bluish-white. Very similar Royal Albatross does not undergo so many immature stages as

Wandering Albatross, fledging with head, body and tail mainly white. Wandering's upperwing whitens towards leading edge of wing, whereas Royal's whitens from leading edge backwards. Royal generally has whiter tail, body and head; also black cutting edges to mandibles visible at close range.
DISTRIBUTION AND STATUS Circumpolar in Southern Ocean. Breeds South Georgia, Tristan da Cunha group, Gough, Prince Edwards, Crozets, Kerguelen, occasionally Heard and Macquarie, also Antipodes, Auckland and Campbell Islands; total annual breeding population *c* 14,000 pairs (probably representing 100,000 birds). Breeds biennially. Age at first breeding generally eight to nine years, but now breeding earlier at South Georgia and Crozets, probably related to fishing mortality with perhaps 10% of the population killed each year (females more than males) mainly by drowning on long-lines where birds can gather in hundreds. Can live to 50 years. Pelagic when not breeding: range generally to Tropic of Capricorn, but regular to 10°S off western South America, western Southern Africa. Has wandered to California, Sicily, Portugal, Panama, St Helena, Fiji, Japan, Tonga.

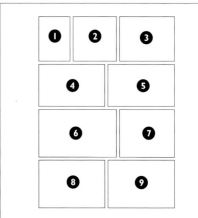

1 **Humboldt Penguin** (adult, Berlin Zoo, Germany)
2 **Humboldt Penguin** (adult, Berlin Zoo, Germany)
3 **Galapagos Penguin** (adults, Galapagos Islands)
4 **Galapagos Penguin** (adult, Galapagos Islands)
5 **Wandering Albatross** (adult on nest, South Georgia)
6 **Wandering Albatross** (adults at nest, South Georgia)
7 **Wandering Albatross** (immature, New Zealand, April)
8 **Wandering Albatross** (juvenile, New Zealand, April)
9 **Wandering Albatross** (immature, south Atlantic Ocean, November)

ALBATROSSES

AMSTERDAM ISLAND ALBATROSS

Diomedea amsterdamensis L 115 cm (45 in),
WS c 300 cm (118 in)
Recently (1983) described species, found only
at Amsterdam Island, Indian Ocean. Classified
as Critical.
IDENTIFICATION Similar to but smaller and
browner than Wandering Albatross. Resembles
immature Wandering Albatross, with dark
blackish-brown crown, hindneck, mantle, back,
rump, tail and wings. Whitish facial area similar
to juvenile Wandering Albatross. Lower
foreneck and upper breast dark blackish-
brown, this extending onto sides of breast and
flanks, enclosing whitish belly; undertail
blackish-brown. May occur in two forms,
differing in intensity of dark underparts – one
lighter, the other darker. Underwing similar to
Wandering Albatross, but with more extensive
brown at leading edge, and possibly a wider
dark trailing edge. Tibia dark. Eyelid white.
Dark cutting edge and tip to both mandibles:
probably only reliable 'plumage' characteristic
at present. One of the World's largest and
rarest seabirds.
DISTRIBUTION AND STATUS Amsterdam Island
(Indian Ocean). Breeds on central plateau at
500-600 m, with a population of c 70 birds
comprised of 15-19 pairs, of which only ten
breed annually. Formerly more numerous,
judging from the finding of large numbers of
bones. Cattle previously displaced the species,
so in 1987 cattle numbers reduced and fence
erected enclosing 400 ha. Mortality at sea
unknown, although at least two birds have been
drowned on long-lines (J.P. Croxall pers.
comm.) representing 3% of the total
population. Pelagic range unknown, may
disperse towards Australasia.

ROYAL ALBATROSS

Diomedea epomophora L 114 cm (45 in),
WS 305-350 cm (120-138 in)
Huge oceanic albatross of the Southern Ocean,
one of the 'great albatrosses'. Classified as
Near-threatened.
IDENTIFICATION Flight as Wandering Albatross.
Attracted to trawlers, but less of a ship-
follower than Wandering Albatross. May give
more humpbacked appearance than latter in
flight. Plumage similar to Wandering Albatross,
but with fewer stages to adult plumage. Two
subspecies, separable at sea; generally nominate
epomophora whiter than adult Wandering
Albatross, *sanfordi* darker. **D. e. epomophora
(Southern): Juvenile** Fledges with blackish
upperwing and dark tail tips. Much like juvenile
sanfordi, but without brownish on top of
crown, less blackish-brown vermiculation
across lower back, and blackish upperwing with
whitish at base of leading edge and the start of
whitish in centre of inner wing. Underwing as
Wandering Albatross. Tail white, tip
occasionally black but never on outer sides of
tail. **Immature** Upperwing shows
progressively larger white patch in centre of

inner wing, and then whitens from leading edge
backwards (unlike Wandering Albatross). Tail
becomes white. **Adult** Head, body, rump and
tail white. Upperwing mainly white, with black
primaries and narrower black secondary tips
right up to body. Generally, division of white
coverts and dark flight feathers more even than
in Wandering Albatross, as finer, more subtle
vermiculation across greater secondary
coverts. Underwing as Wandering Albatross.
Generally distinguished from old adult
Wandering Albatross by absence of brown on
crown, breast, lower back and tail and, at close
range, by dark cutting edges to mandibles. Bill
horn to pink with black cutting edges; iris dark
brown, orbital ring black; feet pinkish or bluish-
white. **D. e. sanfordi (Northern): Juvenile**
Much as adult *sanfordi*, but with blackish-brown
mottling on crown, blackish-brown
vermiculations on lower back, and blackish tip
to tail. Underwing has diagonal narrow black
leading edge from carpal to tip (unlike
epomophora and Wandering Albatross). **Adult**
Head, body, rump and tail white. Upperwing
blackish-brown, except for small white area
along base of leading edge. Underwing white
with black primary tips, narrow black trailing
edge and diagnostic narrow black leading edge
from carpal to wing tip.
DISTRIBUTION AND STATUS Circumpolar in
Southern Ocean. Breeds New Zealand only. *D.
e. sanfordi* on Chatham Islands (c 6,500 pairs)
and Taiaroa Head near Dunedin (15 pairs); *D. e.
epomophora* at Auckland (60 pairs) and
Campbell Islands (7,500 pairs). Breeds
biennially, first breeding at eight to nine years
old; pairs for life; can live to 50 years. Pelagic
when not breeding; range north to Tropic of
Capricorn but to 10°S off western South
America. Dogs and mustelids prey on mainland
New Zealand breeders.

WAVED ALBATROSS

Diomedea irrorata L 89 cm (35 in), WS 230-
240 cm (91-95 in)
The only tropical albatross, confined to the
Galapagos Islands and adjacent seas. Classified
as Near-threatened.
IDENTIFICATION Flight laboured, with flapping
beats, without dynamic soaring, as no regular
strong winds in species' range. Does not follow
ships; generally wary at sea. Associates with
Blue-footed Boobies when feeding.
Combination of large bill and short tail recalls
great albatrosses. Whitish head with yellow bill,
brownish upperparts and underparts; whitish
underwing with dark margins. **Juvenile**
Plumage essentially as adult, but with whiter
head and hindneck, bill darker yellow. **Adult**
Head white, with buffy lemon-yellow cast to
crown and nape extending onto hindneck as
barred or wavy vermiculated pattern. Body
chestnut-brown above, with greyish and whitish
vermiculated pattern from hindneck, becoming
stronger on rump and uppertail-coverts to
appear, from a distance, as a whitish horseshoe
rump patch which contrasts with uniform

brown tail. Chin, throat and upper breast
white, merging into brownish on lower breast
and belly with cross-patterned vermication,
especially on breast sides, flanks and belly.
Undertail brown. Upperwing chestnut-brown
without vermiculated pattern, but with whitish
shafts to primaries. Underwing whitish, with
fine greyish-brown vermiculated pattern on
axillaries and coverts; darker brownish margin
to entire underwing. Bill large and yellow; iris
dark brown; legs and feet pale bluish, projecting
beyond tail in flight.
DISTRIBUTION AND STATUS Breeds annually
Española (Hood Island), Galapagos, with c
15,000 pairs (1994); 10-50 pairs breed Isla La
Plata, off Ecuador. Dispersal east to coast of
Ecuador and Peru, generally 4°N to 12°S,
occasionally south to Mollendo; juveniles
probably remain here, returning to breed after
three years. La Plata population vulnerable to
predation by rats, cats and goats, as well as to
human disturbance. Recent work has shown
that birds feed over the continental shelf of
Peru in the breeding season, as well as
scavenging around the Galapagos Islands. The
proposed (1996) introduction of long-lining
around the islands for yellow-fin tuna, using
squid as bait, would almost certainly adversely
affect the population.

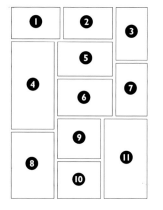

1 **Amsterdam Island Albatross** (adult,
Amsterdam Island, February)
2 **Amsterdam Island Albatross** (adult,
Amsterdam Island, February)
3 **Royal Albatross, subspecies D. e.
epomophora** (immature)
4 **Royal Albatross, subspecies D. e.
epomophora** (adult)
5 **Royal Albatross, subspecies D. e.
epomophora** (immature)
6 **Royal Albatross, subspecies D. e.
epomophora** (adult)
7 **Royal Albatross, subspecies D.e.
sandfordi** (adult, Chile)
8 **Waved Albatross** (adult, Galapagos Islands)
9 **Waved Albatross** (chick in nest, Galapagos
Islands)
10 **Waved Albatross** (adult on nest,
Galapagos Islands)
11 **Waved Albatross** (adult, Galapagos
Islands)

ALBATROSSES

SHORT-TAILED ALBATROSS

Diomedea albatrus L 89 cm (35 in), WS 215-230 cm (85-91 in)

Large, rare albatross of the north Pacific. Classified as Endangered.

IDENTIFICATION Not attracted to ships. Jizz recalls larger great albatrosses rather than smaller Pacific *Diomedea*. Various plumage stages from all-brown juvenile, progressively whitening through 'piebald' stages, to predominantly white adult with yellowish head, huge pink bill and distinctive upperwing pattern; adult the only white-bodied albatross of north Pacific. **Juvenile** Total plumage uniform blackish-brown, with whiter chin and thin whitish stripe from below eye to ear-coverts; primaries may show thin whitish shafts. Bill and legs pale pinkish-flesh. Plumage resembles that of smaller juvenile Black-footed Albatross, but differs in size, lack of white at base of bill, large pinkish bill and pinkish legs. **Immature** similar to juvenile, but forehead, bill base and chin whitish, shading to greyish on lores and ear-coverts, isolated from whitening underparts by dark blackish-brown throat. Off-white breast and belly shading to darker buffish-brown flanks, thighs, vent and undertail. Diagnostic white upperwing patch on inner greater coverts contrasts with otherwise dark upperwings and mantle. Pinkish bill and feet. *Next stage* Head whitish, but hindcrown, nape, hindneck and sides of neck sepia, this colour not joining across throat and thus forming dark cap. Upperparts sepia, with buff and white vermiculations to uppertail-coverts. Base of tail white, tip of tail blackish. Underparts off-white, with darker flanks, thighs and vent. Upperwing sepia, with second white patch on scapulars. Underwing brownish, but showing whitish tips to wing-coverts. Bill and legs as adult. *Next stage* Some breed in this phase. Head white; crown and sides of face yellowish-brown, becoming browner on nape with sharp division across hindneck. Upperparts whitish, with buffish-brown vermiculations on back and rump. Underparts white, with browner vermiculated flanks, thighs and vent. Upperwing sepia, with two larger, diagnostic white patches sometimes joining. Underwing progressively whitening on coverts. Tail black with white base. **Sub-adult** As adult, but with brownish nape and a few darker brown feathers on mantle and back. Undertail-coverts white. **Adult** Head white, shading to yellowish on crown, nape and, on some, across throat. Upper body white from nape to tail base, tip of tail black. Underparts white with some yellowish cast. White upperwing patches joined to each other and to white mantle – less well defined; primaries, primary coverts, secondaries and tertials black. Underwing white with blackish margin. Large pink bill with blue tip; iris blackish; legs and feet bluish-white.

DISTRIBUTION AND STATUS Formerly widespread in north Pacific Ocean, once breeding Bonin Islands, Ryukyu Islands, Taiwan and China, but brought close to extinction by Japanese plume-hunters. Breeds annually Torishima Island (600-650 birds 1994), Minami-Kojima (Senkaku Islands) (100 birds 1994) and Midway Atoll (one or two birds only; bred 1993). Pelagic range formerly to Bering Sea and western North America, but now rarely seen away from breeding islands. Mortality at sea from drift nets and long-line fisheries unknown, but some have been killed. Rats on Torishima may be a problem; however, this population is increasing at *c* 7% each year and doubles every ten years.

BLACK-FOOTED ALBATROSS

Diomedea nigripes L 81 cm (32 in), WS 193-213 cm (76-84 in)

Medium-sized, uniformly dark blackish-brown albatross of the north Pacific.

IDENTIFICATION Follows ships and is attracted to trawlers. Feet extend beyond tail in flight. Young birds resemble adults, but much plumage variation, and some adults may resemble rarer Short-tailed Albatross. **Juvenile** Whole plumage uniform sooty-brown, with narrow area of white at base of bill and whitish shafts on outer primaries. Bill and legs blackish. Differs from juvenile Short-tailed Albatross in smaller size, dark bill and legs, and white at base of bill. **Immature** Much as juvenile but with uppertail-coverts tipped white, sometimes forming whitish horseshoe over base of tail; undertail-coverts variably pale, from whitish to grey. **Adult** Head and neck blackish-brown, with narrow white area at base of bill extending from lower forehead to upper chin; some may show whitish eye-crescent below eye and extending backwards towards ear-coverts. Mantle and back blackish-brown, rump and uppertail-coverts usually white but variable, tail blackish-brown as upperparts. Underparts greyish-brown, slightly paler than upperparts, especially on breast and belly; some show whitish undertail-coverts and vent. Wings uniform blackish-brown, with outer primary shafts white. Bill blackish-brown (dark but variable); iris blackish-brown; legs and feet black. (Some Black-footed Albatrosses are noticeably paler than typical dark adults, with yellowish or pinkish bill and legs, paler brownish-white head, sandy-brown mantle with darker lower back contrasting with whiter rump and uppertail-coverts, and greyish-white underparts with darker brown breastband. These 'pale' birds have sandy-brown upperwings with darker primaries, but lack the white wing patches of Short-tailed Albatross; some may even show a whitish underwing and have whitish undertail-coverts.)

DISTRIBUTION AND STATUS North Pacific. Ranges at sea from *c* 30°N to *c* 55°N, from Taiwan and China north to Bering Sea and east to Baja California; the only albatross seen regularly off the Pacific coast of North America. Small but gradually increasing breeding populations on Torishima, Mukojima Islands (Bonin Islands), Kita-kojima (southern Ryukyus). Main stronghold now islands of Hawaiian archipelago (*c* 50,000 pairs), with large colonies breeding annually on Laysan, Lisianski, Pearl and Hermes Reef, Midway and French Frigate Shoals, with smaller numbers on other islands. Formerly bred on many other Pacific islands; population suffered from feather-hunters but now appears stable with some loss to periodic catastrophic weather and drift nets. Has occurred New Zealand (1884), the only Southern Hemisphere record. Can hybridize with Laysan Albatross.

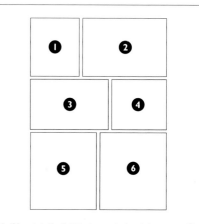

1 Short-tailed Albatross (sub-adult at sea off Torishima, Japan)
2 Short-tailed Albatross (breeding adult on nest, Midway Atoll, Hawaiian Chain)
3 Short-tailed Albatross (juvenile, Cordell Bank, off California, USA)
4 Black-footed Albatross (California, USA, May)
5 Black-footed Albatross (adult, Pacific coast, USA)
6 Black-footed Albatross (juvenile, Pacific coast, USA)

ALBATROSSES

LAYSAN ALBATROSS

Diomedea immutabilis L 80 cm (31 in), WS 195-203 cm (77-80 in)
Medium-sized, most common albatross of north Pacific.
IDENTIFICATION Will follow ships as mollymawks, but differs from latter in feet projecting slightly beyond tail. Superficially resembles Black-browed Albatross, but with different underwing pattern; white head and underparts enable easy separation from the other two north Pacific albatrosses. **Juvenile** Plumage as adult, but with darker bare parts.
Adult Head and neck white, with dark greyish-black eye patch from lores backwards through eye to ear-coverts and extending to malar region; lower lid of eye white. Mantle, back and scapulars blackish with slightly paler edges, extending to upper rump; lower rump and uppertail-coverts white, tail blackish-grey. Underparts white, under surface of tail blackish. Upperwing blackish-brown with some slightly paler edges, primaries blackish with white primary shafts. Underwing whitish in centre with narrow irregular black margins, broadest at wing tip (primaries) and just below carpal joint; coverts show variable blackish streaking, giving 'lined effect' to underwing pattern. Bill variable from yellowish to pinkish, with darker tip; iris dark; legs and feet whitish-flesh.
DISTRIBUTION AND STATUS North Pacific. Breeds north-west: Torishima (Mukojima Islands, Bonin Islands); central: stronghold mainly Laysan (105,000-132,000 pairs) and Midway Island (150,000-200,000 pairs), with smaller colonies on most other Hawaiian islands; and eastern: recently found breeding off western Mexico on Isla Guadalupe (1986) and Isla Clarion (1988), also probably San Benedicto and Rocas Alijos (small populations, but significant range extension eastwards). Total annual breeding population of some 362,000 pairs representing some 1,200,000-1,400,000 birds. Heavy persecution in the early part of 20th century, when huge numbers killed by Japanese feather-hunters and populations significantly reduced, and also suffered from egg-collecting and drift nets, but populations now slowly recovering and expanding. Pelagic range from c 30°N to c 55°N, from Japanese seas north to Bering Sea, and east to Pacific coast of North America, where regular but rare; southern limit not well known. Non-breeders wander widely over much of north Pacific, with large concentrations off Japan. Recorded twice in south-west Indian Ocean (1983, 1984), the only Southern Hemisphere records.

BLACK-BROWED ALBATROSS

Diomedea melanophris L 88 cm (35 in), WS 240 cm (95 in)
Medium-sized oceanic albatross of the Southern Ocean, the most familiar mollymawk.
IDENTIFICATION White head, black 'eyebrow', yellow-orange bill, dark upperparts and wings, and white underparts. The best-known mollymawk, with two identifiable subspecies.
Juvenile Head and neck mainly white, with blackish mark through eye; top of crown, nape and hindneck greyish, extending onto sides of lower neck as a partial or complete collar (variable: darkest birds can appear hooded). Mantle, back and scapulars blackish-grey, rump and uppertail-coverts white, tail grey. Underparts white; dark greyish tip to undertail. Upperwing blackish-brown, with whitish bases to outer primary shafts. Underwing blackish, with variable diffuse greyish-white central coverts (some also have greyish-white axillaries); becomes whiter with age. Bill dark olive-brown with black tip (occasionally appears all black); iris dark brown; legs and feet dark grey. **Immature** Much as juvenile, but bill becomes lighter yellowish-horn with dark tip (thus more contrast). Greyish of nape, hindneck and collar becomes paler and reduced in extent (if present at all). Underwing with more extensive whitish central stripe merging into blackish outer margins (some show blackish streaks across coverts): variable. Adult plumage acquired before adult bill colour.
Adult Head and neck white with black 'brow'. Mantle, back and scapulars blackish-grey. Upperwing blackish, with whitish bases to outer primary shafts. Rump and uppertail-coverts white, tail grey. Underparts white. Underwing with blackish margins and white centre more clearly demarcated than immature: dark leading edge approximately one third width of wing (widest of any mollymawk), black tip (primaries), narrower black trailing edge. Bill bright yellow-orange with redder tip; iris dark brown; legs and feet bluish-white. New Zealand subspecies *D. m. impavida* differs from nominate *melanophris* in more extensive black 'brow', especially in front of eye, honey-coloured iris, broader black leading edge to underwing. From similar immature and juvenile Grey-headed Albatross by bill colour, head pattern, collar and underwing pattern.
DISTRIBUTION AND STATUS Circumpolar from c 65°S to c 23°S (Tropic of Capricorn), but c 10°S off Peru and c 20°S off Namibia where cool upwellings. Breeds annually 46°S-56°S: Chile, Argentina, Falklands (c 70% world population), South Georgia, Crozets, Kerguelen, Heard, McDonald, Macquarie Islands, Antipodes. *D. m. impavida* at Campbell Island (may warrant specific status, as sympatry recorded with no hybridization). Total population over 500,000 pairs, but impact of fisheries and drowning by long-line fishing becoming a real threat; Kerguelen and Chile populations already decreased. Breeding success may be related to krill availability and prefers to feed and breed where there are large continental shelves (eg Falklands). Disperses to continental waters of Australia, New Zealand, South Africa and South America, with different populations to different areas. Recorded north in Pacific to Fiji, Tuamotu, Pitcairn, and annually in north Atlantic in small numbers; also Brazil, Kenya, Madagascar, Réunion and Rodrigues. This is the most frequently recorded albatross in the north Atlantic, having been seen as far north as Iceland and Spitsbergen (though fewer in north-west Atlantic): of particular note is a bird which regularly visited a gannetry in the Faeroes each summer from 1860 until 1894, when it was shot; and, more recently, a Black-browed Albatross has frequented the gannetry on Hermaness in the Shetlands, Scotland, every year since 1972 (except 1988 and 1989) and has even built a nest there.

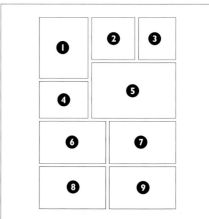

1 **Laysan Albatross** (pair, Hawaii)
2 **Laysan Albatross** (north Pacific Ocean)
3 **Laysan Albatross** (north Pacific Ocean)
4 **Laysan Albatross** (north Pacific Ocean)
5 **Black-browed Albatross** (adults feeding, south Atlantic Ocean)
6 **Black-browed Albatross** (pair of adults at nest, Falkland Islands)
7 **Black-browed Albatross** (adult off South Africa)
8 **Black-browed Albatross** (adult, south Atlantic Ocean)
9 **Black-browed Albatross** (sub-adult, south Atlantic Ocean)

ALBATROSSES

SHY ALBATROSS

Diomedea cauta L 90-99 cm (37 in), WS 220-256 cm (87-101 in)
Largest mollymawk, breeding mainly Australasia; three visually distinct subspecies which may prove to be separate species.
IDENTIFICATION Attracted to trawlers. From other mollymawks by size, paler mantle, whiter underwing with diagnostic dark pre-axillary notch. Three subspecies. *D. c. cauta,* **White-capped Albatross** (99 cm): **Juvenile/ immature** Head variable: some with full grey hood demarcated from white underparts, but with paler greyish-white cap; others have white head with pronounced grey collar from hindneck to foreneck, recalling juvenile Black-browed and Grey-headed Albatrosses. Rest of plumage much as adult. Bill darker than adult, medium grey with black tip. Further change of bill with head/neck variable and not well known, but adult plumage acquired fourth-fifth year before black tip to bill lost. **Adult** Forehead and crown white, forming white cap bordered by greyish-black 'eyebrow' and variable grey on cheeks and sides of head; hindneck, sides of neck and upper mantle white. Rest of mantle silvery-black, paler than blackish scapulars, lower back and upperwings. Rump and uppertail-coverts white, tail dark greyish. Underparts white, undertail greyish-black. Upperwing blackish-brown, darker than saddle, with outer primaries showing white shafts. Underwing white with narrow black border; dark pre-axillary notch at base of leading edge, usually separated from blackish border. Bill yellowish-grey with yellow tip; iris dark brown; legs and feet bluish-flesh. *D. c. salvini,* **Salvin's Albatross** (95 cm): **Juvenile** Much as nominate *cauta,* but generally with wholly grey hood (as dark as darkest *cauta*) which merges into mantle and also extends to (or just past) black pre-axillary notch on underwing; some have paler head with partial or complete grey collar from hindneck to foreneck. Under surface of primaries wholly black, forming larger blacker tip than in nominate *cauta*; lesser underwing-coverts may have greyish tips. Bill as nominate *cauta.* **Immature** Stages not well documented, but differs from nominate *cauta* in full grey hood which merges into greyish mantle, thus lacking white hindneck collar. Bill greyer than adult, with black tip to both mandibles. **Adult** Smaller than *cauta.* Head and neck uniform light grey (can appear brownish-grey), forming hood sharply demarcated from white underparts, with whitish cap on forehead and top of crown enhanced by greyish-black brow. Grey of hindneck merges into light grey mantle and back (paler than nominate *cauta*), which contrasts with darker blackish upperwings. Underwing as juvenile. Bill generally darker and browner than *cauta,* with black mandibular unguis, ivory-horn to yellowish culminicorn; side plates darker grey. From Buller's Albatross by underwing pattern and bill colour. *D. c. eremita,* **Chatham Island Albatross** (90 cm): **Juvenile** Much as adult but with hood dark grey, lacking

any paler cap on forehead and crown; grey of hindneck merges into dark grey of mantle and back, which is a similar shade to upperwing colour (unlike nominate *cauta* or *salvini*). Grey of hood can reach black pre-axillary notch as in *salvini,* but unlike nominate *cauta.* Some have greyish wash on upper breast. Solid black underwing tip (primaries) as *salvini,* unlike nominate *cauta.* Bill dark olive-brown with black tip. **Immature/ sub-adult** No available data (not described). **Adult** Smaller than nominate *cauta* and *salvini,* with proportionately shorter bill. Hood uniformly dark grey (darker than *cauta* or *salvini*), with perhaps paler grey (not white) hood. Underwing as *salvini,* with solid black primaries. Bill bright yellow with black subterminal spot (mandibular unguis).
DISTRIBUTION AND STATUS Circumpolar in northern subantarctic and southern subtropical waters. Total population *c* 155,000 pairs. *D. c. cauta* breeds Albatross Island, Pedra Branca, Mewstone (Australia *c* 7,500 pairs), Aucklands (New Zealand *c* 70,000 pairs); *D. c. salvini* Bounty (*c* 76,000 pairs) and Snares (New Zealand), small population at Crozets (may breed Prince Edward); *D. c. eremita* Chathams (New Zealand 4,000 pairs). More numerous over continental shelves than pelagic waters, generally to *c* 25°S, but to *c* 5°S off western South America. *D. c cauta* and *salvini* disperse to South America and South Africa (*salvini* less common), whereas *eremita* more sedentary. Vagrants Washington, Mauritius and Red Sea. Now large fatalities from long-line fishing: up to *c* 10,000 birds per year.

GREY-HEADED ALBATROSS

Diomedea chrysostoma L 81 cm (32 in), WS 180-220 cm (71-87 in)
Medium-sized cold-water albatross of the Southern Ocean. Classified as Near-threatened.
IDENTIFICATION Grey head, blackish bill with yellow ridges on upper and lower mandibles, and underwing pattern similar to Black-browed Albatross. **Juvenile** Head, neck, hindneck and throat dark grey (darker than adult), with paler ear-coverts and cheeks, small blackish 'eyebrow' and narrow white eye-crescent, less conspicuous than in adult. Hindneck merges into dark grey of mantle, becoming blackish-grey on scapulars and back; rump and uppertail-coverts white, tail dark grey. White underparts between throat and blackish undertail. Upperwing blackish-brown with paler primary shafts. Underwing blackish, with variable paler greyish central stripe: darkest underwing of any mollymawk. Bill blackish-grey. **Immature** Blackish bill, with tip faintly yellow. Crown and sides of face become whiter, but hindneck grey and extending as collar to throat and upper foreneck, thus not unlike sub-adult or juvenile Black-browed Albatross, although variable. Underwing becomes slightly paler, more resembling adult's pattern. **Sub-adult** Adult plumage acquired before full adult bill coloration. Head paler than adult, bill duller; underwing with greyish tips to coverts, thus

pattern not so well defined as full adult. **Adult** Head and neck light bluish-grey, forming distinct hood, with paler forehead and crown, short blackish 'eyebrow' and white crescent behind and below eye; hood sharply demarcated from white underparts. Mantle greyish-black. Back, scapulars and upperwings uniform blackish-brown, with whitish primary shafts. Rump and uppertail-coverts white, tail grey. Underwing white, with black wing tip (primaries), narrow black trailing edge, and broader black leading edge over approximately one third width (thus similar to Black-browed); demarcation quite sharp. Bill black, with bright yellow culmen and ramicorn (at close range tip orange-red); iris brown; legs and feet whitish-pink. Underwing pattern enables separation from Buller's, Yellow-nosed and Shy; from adult Black-browed by grey head, different bill colour. More care needed with non-adult Black-browed.
DISTRIBUTION AND STATUS Circumpolar in Southern Ocean. Breeds biennially subantarctic islands, 46°S-56°S: at South Georgia (*c* 48,000 pairs, one half of World population), Prince Edwards (*c* 7,000 pairs), Crozets (5,940 pairs), Kerguelen (7,900 pairs), Macquarie (*c* 100 pairs), Campbell (11,530 pairs), also at Diego Ramirez (*c* 20,000 birds 1981, subsequent decrease). Total population *c* 85,000 pairs, but increasing evidence of mortality from long-line fishing especially adult birds. Dispersal generally 65°S-35°S: immatures move north in winter. No reliable Northern Hemisphere records. Vagrants Tahiti.

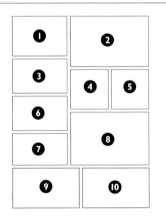

1 **Shy Albatross**, subspecies *D. c. cauta* (immature in flight, southeast Atlantic Ocean)
2 **Shy Albatross**, subspecies *D. c. cauta* (immature)
3 **Shy Albatross**, subspecies *D. c. cauta* (immature, south Atlantic Ocean)
4 **Shy Albatross**, subspecies *D. c. salvini* (immature in flight, off South Africa)
5 **Shy Albatross**, subspecies *D. c. salvini* (adult, Bounty Islands, November)
6 **Shy Albatross**, subspecies *D. c. eremita* (sub-adult, New South Wales, Australia, August)
7 **Grey-headed Albatross** (immature in flight, southern Indian Ocean)
8 **Grey-headed Albatross** (juvenile)
9 **Grey-headed Albatross** (adult)
10 **Grey-headed Albatross** (adult, south Atlantic Ocean, November)

ALBATROSSES

YELLOW-NOSED ALBATROSS

Diomedea chlororhynchos L 76 cm (30 in), WS 200-256 cm (79-101 in)
Smallest mollymawk of the Southern Ocean.
IDENTIFICATION Distinctive slender jizz, diagnostic underwing pattern, black bill with yellow culminicorn and orange tip. Two identifiable subspecies: Indian Ocean *D. c. bassi* have white head, Atlantic Ocean *D. c. chlororhynchos* have grey head. **Juvenile** *D. c. bassi*: Head and neck white, with short pale grey collar extending from mantle onto upper sides of neck (variable, but never complete collar); some have grey on nape. Dusky eye patch smaller than adult's, may be absent. Dark leading edge of underwing perhaps larger than in adult. Bill black for first year; culminicorn turns brown, then creamy, tip of bill becomes yellow; adult plumage acquired before adult bill colour. *D. c. chlororhynchos*: As juvenile *bassi* but with larger black triangular eye patch, though smaller than in adult. **Adult** *D. c. bassi*: Head and neck white with small blackish triangular patch before eye, light greyish wash on ear-coverts and cheeks. Mantle and back blackish-grey, lighter than blackish upperwings, but contrast reduced with age; whitish bases of outer primary shafts. Rump and uppertail-coverts white, tail grey. Underparts white, underside of tail blackish-grey. Underwing white, with black tip (primaries), narrow black trailing edge and broader black leading edge, all sharply demarcated from white centre. Bill black, bright yellow culminicorn becoming orange at tip; iris dark brown; legs and feet pinkish-blue. *D. c. chlororhynchos*: Much as *bassi*, but with head and neck pearl-grey (or bluish-grey), forming grey hood demarcated from white underparts; forehead and crown slightly paler (some also show paler chin and throat). Larger and blacker triangular patch before eye, and white crescent behind eye broader. Needs to be distinguished from adult Grey-headed and Buller's Albatrosses: underwing pattern of Yellow-nosed separates it from both, particularly Buller's (which in addition has different bill coloration).
DISTRIBUTION AND STATUS South Atlantic and southern Indian Oceans. Total population *c* 85,000 pairs. *D. c. chlororhynchos* breeds annually Tristan da Cunha group and Gough Island (27,000-40,000 pairs); *D. c. bassi* breeds annually at Prince Edwards (*c* 7,000 pairs), Crozets (4,430 pairs), Amsterdam (37,000 pairs), St Paul (seven pairs) and Kerguelen (50 pairs). Subtropical and warmer subantarctic waters of Atlantic Ocean, as well as Australasian seas: generally *c* 50°S-26°S, but further north in cool Benguela upwelling off west coast of South Africa. Atlantic birds not common in Indian Ocean but have reached New Zealand; Indian Ocean birds rare west of South Africa. Not recorded in Pacific east of Chathams. Accidental Cocos Keeling Island, Gulf of Mexico, Atlantic coast of North America, and recently Norway; also reported south of Britain. Status appears stable at

present; previously harvested on Tristan da Cunha group.

BULLER'S ALBATROSS

Diomedea bulleri L 78 cm (31 in), WS 205-213 cm (81-84 in)
Smallish to medium-sized, grey-headed mollymawk of the Pacific Ocean. Classified as Near-threatened.
IDENTIFICATION Will follow ships, and attends trawlers. Grey hood, white forehead, and diagnostic yellow and black bill; must be differentiated from other grey-headed species (Yellow-nosed, Grey-headed and Shy Albatrosses). **Juvenile** Much as adult, but with darker bill and darker head. White cap more extensive than adult's, reaching rear of crown, and blackish eye patch smaller. Grey on head and neck variable in extent and intensity: generally browner and less bluish-grey than adult (darkest are similar to adults, whilst palest with whiter head appear more collared than hooded). Grey of hindneck merges into grey of mantle, back and scapulars, which form a paler saddle contrasting with blackish upperwings; paler edges to scapulars and inner wing-coverts give scaly appearance to edges of saddle and inner upperwing. Underwing as adult. Bill brownish-horn with darker tip; gradually lightens with age. **Immature** Much as juvenile, but head becomes selectively greyer, less brown. Hood pale pearly-grey on chin, throat, cheeks, ear-coverts and nape, with whitish cap, whereas grey on hindneck, sides of neck and foreneck remains as darker rear half of hood. Tip of bill, culminicorn and ramicorn become paler and then yellowish; sides of bill darken to dull blackish. **Adult** Head and neck uniform grey, forming hood, with noticeable white cap on forehead and forecrown, hood sharply demarcated from white upper breast and underparts. White cap sharply defined at sides by greyish-black oval-shaped patch before and over eye; rear and bottom of eye with narrow white crescent. Hood merges into light grey mantle, which, with inner scapulars and back, forms a grey saddle contrasting with darker blackish upperwings. Rump and uppertail-coverts white, tail greyish-black. Underparts white from upper breast; undertail blackish. Upperwing brownish-black, with white bases to outer primary shafts. Underwing white in centre, with fairly broad blackish leading edge gradually broadening from carpal to body, thinner blackish trailing edge and blackish tip (primaries), sharply demarcated. Bill with maxillary unguis and culminicorn bright yellow, latericorn and upper half of ramicorn black, lower half of ramicorn and tip of mandibular unguis bright yellow; legs and feet bluish-flesh. From Grey-headed Albatross by white cap, different bill coloration, underwing pattern. From Atlantic Ocean Yellow-nosed Albatross by smaller eye patch, different bill coloration, paler mantle and wings, underwing pattern. From Shy Albatross of race *salvini* by smaller size and jizz, smaller bill, underwing pattern.

DISTRIBUTION AND STATUS South Pacific. *D. b. bulleri* breeds annually in autumn-winter period on Snares (*c* 8,500 pairs) and Solander (4,000-5,000 pairs). *D. b. platei* breeds annually on Chathams (*c* 18,000 pairs); recently found breeding Three Kings Islands north of New Zealand. Total population *c* 31,000 pairs, but suffering fatalities as a result of long-line fishing. Pelagic in subtropical and subantarctic south Pacific, with *D. b. bulleri* being comparatively sedentary with some dispersal across the southern Tasman Sea, whereas *D. b. platei* disperses eastwards across the South Pacific towards South America. Recorded in the South Atlantic off the Falklands (1987) and recently off Cape Town (1995). Adults tend to remain in New Zealand seas; especially numerous around Southland and Stewart Island.

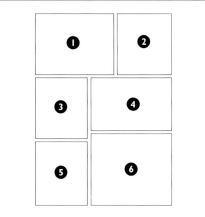

1 **Yellow-nosed Albatross** (adult, Gough Island)
2 **Yellow-nosed Albatross** (juvenile, south Atlantic Ocean, January)
3 **Yellow-nosed Albatross** (adult, off South Africa)
4 **Yellow-nosed Albatross** (adult, off South Africa)
5 **Buller's Albatross** (adult, New Zealand, November)
6 **Buller's Albatross** (adult, New Zealand, April)

ALBATROSSES

SOOTY ALBATROSS

Phoebetria fusca L 86 cm (34 in), WS 203 cm
(80 in)
Medium-sized sooty-brown albatross of the
south Atlantic and southern Indian Oceans.
Classified as Near-threatened.
IDENTIFICATION Apparently effortless flight
without active wing-flapping, especially in
strong winds; generally more manoeuvrable
than *Diomedea* species. Will follow ships.
Characteristic rakish jizz, slender body, long
narrow wings and long, pointed wedge-shaped
tail; very similar to Light-mantled Sooty
Albatross. **Juvenile** Sooty-brown plumage
much as adult. Bill, including sulcus (lower
mandible), usually black or greyish, although
variable. Pale brown or grey crescent above
and below eye. Nape variably paler, sometimes
forming indistinct paler collar which may
extend to upper mantle as paler fringes.
Mantle, back and rump sooty-brown; tail
slightly darker, not showing paler shafts.
Upperwing sooty-brown as upperparts,
primaries possibly slightly darker (with dark
shafts). **Immature** Much as juvenile, but with
variable paler nape: nape may show buffish or
whitish extending down sides of neck as a
paler collar, which may extend to upper
mantle as paler fringes, but not onto lower
mantle or back as on Light-mantled Sooty
Albatross. Tail and primaries have dark shafts.
Adult Generally uniformly sooty-brown. Sides
of face and ear-coverts slightly darker, with
whitish crescent above and below eye broken
only at lores. Back, mantle and abdomen
slightly lighter in shade than rest of plumage;
uppertail and primaries blackish with whitish
or yellowish shafts. Nape and sides of neck
wear paler. Bill blackish, with creamy or
orange stripe on sulcus; iris brown; legs and
feet greyish-flesh. Usually distinguished from
Light-mantled Sooty Albatross by darker
brown lower mantle, back and rump, although
some examples defy identification: Sooty has
heavier bill with creamy to orange sulcus
(bluish on Light-mantled Sooty), and generally
occupies warmer waters.
DISTRIBUTION AND STATUS South Atlantic and
southern Indian Oceans. Breeds biennially
(from July/August) on subantarctic islands
between 36°S and 49°S, total population *c*
15,000 pairs: Tristan da Cunha group (*c* 4,000-
5,000 pairs), Gough (5,000-10,000 pairs),
Prince Edwards (2,732 pairs), Crozets (2,260
pairs: recent rapid decline), Kerguelen (*c* 10
pairs), Amsterdam and St Paul (*c* 100 pairs).
Some populations, *eg* Nightingale Island
(Tristan da Cunha), subject to human
exploitation, chicks being taken for food; also
suffers from introduced predators at many
breeding localities. Generally the least colonial
albatross with occasional unexplained mass
desertion of nests. Usually solitary at sea and
rarely observed feeding; scavenging may be
important. Dispersal generally at 30°S-50°S in
subtropical and subantarctic waters, with most
near Subtropical Convergence, occasionally

further south (south of Antarctic
Convergence) in south-western Indian Ocean,
generally moving north in winter. Ranges west
in Atlantic to *c* 40°W and eastwards to
Australia and Tasmania (but not New
Zealand); more common than Light-mantled
Sooty Albatross in Australia. Accidental Cape
Horn, Mauritius, Réunion; apparently only one
record from south-east Pacific.

LIGHT-MANTLED SOOTY ALBATROSS

Phoebetria palpebrata L 84 cm (33 in), WS 185-
218 cm (73-86 in)
Medium-sized, sooty-brown, southern
circumpolar albatross. Formerly regarded as
conspecific with very similar Sooty Albatross,
but no hybridization in areas of sympatry
(displays and timing of breeding differ).
IDENTIFICATION Jizz, flight and general
coloration as Sooty Albatross, but generally a
bird of colder waters than Sooty Albatross,
and more of a ship-follower. Usually
distinguished by lighter-coloured upper body,
contrasting with darker head; different bill
colour at close range. **Juvenile** Generally
similar to adult, with uniform sooty-brown
plumage but with grey, not white, eye-
crescents (broken at lores); sulcus grey,
brownish or pale yellow (bluish in adult);
darker tail and primaries have dark (not
whitish) shafts. Paler upperparts show buffish
tips to lower mantle, back and rump, imparting
more scaly pattern than adult. **Immature**
Development of immature stages not well
documented (adults start to breed from seven
to 12 years of age). Generally as juvenile, but
increased buffish tips to lower mantle, back
and rump giving scaled or mottled appearance.
Underparts generally pale greyish-brown.
Adult Head to nape and upper foreneck dark
sooty-brown or blackish, with white eye-
crescents broken at lores. Hindneck, mantle,
back and rump variable ash-grey, palest on
mantle and back and edged brown on lower
back, rump and uppertail-coverts; uppertail
blackish with white shafts. Underparts from
foreneck pale brownish-grey. Upperwing dark
slate-brown, primaries darker, with whitish or
yellowish outer primary shafts. Bill black,
sulcus bluish; iris brown; feet and legs greyish-
flesh.
DISTRIBUTION AND STATUS Circumpolar in
Southern Ocean. Breeds biennially (starting
from September/October) on islands between
46°S and 55°S: South Georgia (8,000 pairs),
Prince Edwards (216 pairs), Crozets (2,280
pairs), Kerguelen (3,000-5,000 pairs), Heard
(200-500 pairs), Macquarie (500-700 pairs),
Campbell (1,000+ pairs), Auckland (5,000
pairs), Antipodes (*c* 1,000 pairs). At some
breeding islands formerly exploited for food.
World population estimated at perhaps *c*
150,000 birds, or some 25,000 breeding pairs.
At Crozets may breed once every three years;
on average one chick is fledged every five
years, thus has one of the lowest breeding

production rates for albatrosses. Populations
currently decreasing as a result of long-line
fishing which may kill 4,000 birds per year.
Pelagic from pack ice to *c* 35°S, but
occasionally to 20°S in Humboldt Current off
western South America; rare off South Africa,
but reaches Australia, Tasmania and New
Zealand. Summers in antarctic waters but does
not enter pack ice; in winter subantarctic and
even subtropical waters. Huge foraging range
for breeding birds. Accidental to southern
Brazil, Rodrigues, Marquesas, and recently
recorded off California – the only Northern
Hemisphere record.

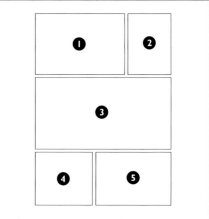

1 **Sooty Albatross** (adult, Gough Island,
November)
2 **Sooty Albatross** (adult, Gough Island,
November)
3 **Light-mantled Sooty Albatross** (breeding
pair, South Georgia, December)
4 **Light-mantled Sooty Albatross** (adult,
South Georgia)
5 **Light-mantled Sooty Albatross** (adult)

PETRELS

SOUTHERN GIANT PETREL

Macronectes giganteus L 87 cm (34 in), WS 195 cm (77 in)
Very large, scavenging, southern circumpolar fulmarine petrel.
IDENTIFICATION Size of a mollymawk, but proportionately shorter, narrower wings and bulkier body; often appears humpbacked. Laboured flight, four or five flaps and a glide; better in winds. Perhaps follows ships less than Northern Giant Petrel. Huge yellowish-green bill and distinctive jizz. Occurs in two plumage morphs: white morph unique and distinct, but dark morph closely resembles Northern Giant Petrel. **Juvenile** *Dark morph*: Entirely glossy sooty-black (white flecks on the head) with yellowish-green bill, but plumage soon fades to brownish-black and grey-brown, particularly on back and wings. Scattered white tips appear at base of bill, chin, throat and sides of face.
Immature Goes through progressively lighter immature stages, resembling adult but with greyish crown (not so capped as immature Northern Giant Petrel). Breast and underparts perhaps darker than immature Northern Giant Petrel, lacking the collar across throat; bill lacks reddish tip. Underparts as dark as upperparts, thus white-headed appearance. **Adult** *Dark morph*: Head, neck and upper breast off-white, with greyish-brown mottling on crown and nape. Upperparts mottled greyish-brown, with brownish-grey tail. Underparts mottled greyish-brown from upper breast, becoming darker on flanks and abdomen; slightly paler than upperparts. Upperwing greyish-brown. Underwing greyish-brown with pale leading edge to inner wing (dark on Northern Giant Petrel, although some show this), and pale silvery-grey bases to inner primaries and some secondaries giving scaly effect to underwing. Bill huge, nasal tube covering three-fifths of length, yellowish-horn to yellowish-green with pale green tip; iris brown; legs and feet blackish or blue-grey. *White morph*: up to c 10% of individuals in some populations. Juveniles and adults similar: wholly white except for asymmetrical black spots and patches scattered randomly through plumage; bare parts as dark morph. A much rarer totally white (leucistic) morph occurs. These are apparently the product of matings by spotted white morphs and are more likely to occur where the percentage of white morphs is high. Published records of these totally white birds are few but include the South Orkneys, south of Bouvet (Barry Rose, unpublished), Prince Edward, Crozets, Tasmania, and Macquarie. Plumage totally white with no black spots, bill horn coloured, iris dark, feet pink.
DISTRIBUTION AND STATUS Circumpolar in Southern Hemisphere from Antarctica to c 20°S in subtropical waters (c 15°S off western South America). Breeds (mainly from October) generally at 40°S-60°S on subantarctic and antarctic islands (eg South Orkney, South Shetland, South Georgia, Prince Edwards, Macquarie and Heard Islands), Antarctica and South America; also Gough, Diego Ramirez, Isla Noir, Chubut and Falklands. Total population c 36,000 pairs, some 40% of which in South Orkneys and South Shetlands, but numbers in both places declining. When breeding easily disturbed and relies on seals and penguins for food supply. Suffers mortalities from commercial fisheries, and gathers in thousands around long-liners; also some persecution in places (eg Falklands). Northward movement (north of 50°S) in winter, immatures moving further north than adults and further north than Northern Giant Petrel. In winter, numerous South America, South Africa, Australia and New Zealand. Vagrants Mauritius, New Guinea, Fiji, Tahiti; two records in Northern Hemisphere: Ushant (France) and Hawaii. Pelagic and inshore waters.

NORTHERN GIANT PETREL

Macronectes halli L 87 cm (34 in), WS 190 cm (75 in)
Very large, scavenging, southern circumpolar fulmarine petrel. Generally breeds north of Antarctic Convergence. Formerly treated as conspecific with Southern Giant Petrel.
IDENTIFICATION Jizz as Southern Giant Petrel, whose range partly overlaps (the two have hybridized); probably follows ships more than Southern Giant Petrel. Much as latter in plumage, but with horn-coloured bill with darker reddish tip. Only one plumage phase, but some geographical and individual variation. **Juvenile** Entirely glossy sooty-black with yellowish bill, which may lack reddish tip, but plumage soon fades to brownish-black and greyish-brown with whitish feather tips on base of bill, lores, sides of face and chin. Sequence thus similar to Southern Giant Petrel.
Immature Head and neck medium to dark grey, with clearer whitish forehead, lores, sides of face, chin and throat generally clearly demarcated across lower throat. Dark crown and nape contrasting with whitish face produces more capped appearance than Southern Giant Petrel. Upperparts mottled blackish, white and grey, tail blackish-grey. Underparts similarly mottled greyish-brown but paler than upperparts, although collar effect across upper throat. Upperwing greyish-brown. Underwing dusky-grey with pale silvery-grey bases to inner primaries and some secondaries. Leading and trailing edges of inner wing darker. **Adult** Crown and hindneck brownish-grey; less noticeable cap than immature, but head never completely white. Forehead, cheeks, chin and throat pale greyish to whitish, merging into brownish-grey of upperparts and underparts. Upperparts mottled greyish-brown: generally greyer than immature, with pale edges to mantle and wing-coverts. Underparts pale greyish-brown, lighter than upperparts, becoming almost whitish on old birds. Upperwing mottled greyish-brown as upperparts. Underwing dark with paler central coverts; bases of inner primaries and some secondaries silvery-grey; leading edge of inner underwing dark (some may be pale). Bill huge, nasal tube three-fifths of length, generally horn-coloured with darker tip, which may be brown or reddish; iris brown or grey (paler with age); legs and feet dark grey.
DISTRIBUTION AND STATUS Pelagic, marine and coastal from antarctic to subtropical waters, mostly subantarctic. Breeds (mainly from August) at 46°S-54°S at few localities: South Georgia, Prince Edwards, Crozets, Kerguelen, Macquarie, Campbell and Antipodes; total population c 7,000-12,000 pairs. Highly vulnerable to disturbance, avoids areas frequented by humans; some populations are increasing, however, evidently as result of improved food supply. Range circumpolar, 30°S-64°S, reaching South America, South Africa, Australia and New Zealand; regular visitor to Amsterdam and St Paul Islands.

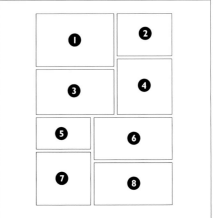

1 **Southern Giant Petrel** (totally white phase, presumed adult on water, Prince Edward Islands)
2 **Southern Giant Petrel** (adult, white morph, south Atlantic Ocean, January)
3 **Southern Giant Petrel** (immature, Falkland Islands, January)
4 **Southern Giant Petrel** (adult, Falkland Islands, January)
5 **Northern Giant Petrel** (adult on nest, Falkland Islands)
6 **Northern Giant Petrel** (adult, southern Indian Ocean)
7 **Northern Giant Petrel** (adult, southern Indian Ocean)
8 **Northern Giant Petrel** (juvenile, Victoria, Australia, May)

NORTHERN FULMAR

Fulmarus glacialis L 48 cm (19 in), WS 107 cm (42 in)

Medium-sized, stocky, polymorphic fulmarine petrel of the Northern Hemisphere.

IDENTIFICATION Colonial breeder and generally gregarious at sea, with huge numbers around trawlers; active ship-follower. Occasionally plunges, but obtains most food by surface-seizing; scavenges on carrion (eg dead seals and whales). Variable in colour, but with jizz and flight of a small albatross. Light morphs predominate in Atlantic: superficially resemble gulls and shearwaters, but told by colour, bill shape, thick neck, jizz and distinctive flight with stiff wings held straight out from body. Dark morphs predominate in Pacific: darker birds must be distinguished from Pink-footed and Flesh-footed Shearwaters. *Double light morph*: Head and neck white, with greyish around lores. Upperparts pale grey, mottled silvery, becoming browner with wear; tail pale grey, becoming whiter towards tip. Underparts white. Upperwing pale grey (as upperparts), becoming darker on carpal area and primaries; dark tips to primaries contrast with whitish bases and inner webs, which form conspicuous pale wing patch. Underwing white, with greyish carpal, primary tips and narrow trailing edge (secondaries). *Double dark morph*: More uniformly dark, with head, neck and underparts blue or smoky-grey. Carpal area and primaries correspondingly darker, but still with paler wing panel (though inconspicuous on some). Some wear darker to brownish. Bill stubby, yellow tips to both mandibles, base variable from olive-green to bluish-grey with darker nasal tubes; iris dark brown; legs and feet greenish to bluish-pink. Fisher recognized four morphs covering total plumage variability. The two extremes are outlined above. Between these are: *Light morph* (crown and hindneck light grey, breast white, belly white or light grey), and *Dark morph* (crown grey, not so dark as mantle and back, breast light grey).

DISTRIBUTION AND STATUS North Pacific and north Atlantic Oceans. Breeds in Atlantic in large numbers from Canadian Arctic and north-east USA south to Newfoundland, and from Arctic Ocean and Siberia to Britain and France; population expanding and increasing. In Pacific (also large numbers) from Kurile Islands east to Bering Sea and associated islands, eastern Siberia and Alaska; prospecting British Columbia. Typically nests on coastal cliff ledges, but also locally on cliffs and rock faces several kilometres inland, and in some places near human habitation (even sometimes on inhabited buildings along urban seafronts). Current World population put at several million pairs (one estimate gave 16 million pairs) following huge increase in numbers and range expansion in 19th and 20th centuries; this a result mainly of increase in food supply; growth still continuing in some areas, but at slower rate. In the past was heavily exploited for food, but only few killed now. Winters south to Japan and Baja California; dispersal south generally by young birds. In Atlantic, disperses south to *c* 34°N off north-east American coast and Bay of Biscay; stragglers south to New England and Madeira.

ANTARCTIC FULMAR

Fulmarus glacialoides L 48 cm (19 in), WS 117 cm (46 in)

Medium-sized, stocky, monomorphic fulmarine petrel of the Southern Ocean.

IDENTIFICATION Unmistakable in the Southern Ocean. Very gregarious, and very manoeuvrable in flight (but weakest walker on land of the fulmarine petrels). Feeds from surface of sea and will surface-dive/plunge; often feeds at night. Investigates ships and will feed on refuse, but not a persistent ship-follower; more regular at trawlers and whalers. Generally resembles a light-morph or double-light-morph Northern Fulmar but with darker, more contrasting upperwing pattern. Head white with greyish lores, shading to light grey on nape and hindneck. Mantle, back, rump and uppertail light grey. Underparts white, with light grey wash on breast sides and flanks. Upperwing variable, generally light greyish with blackish outer primaries, black decreasing inwards along secondaries as dark trailing edge; white bases of primaries form conspicuous pale wing patch. Occasional darker examples have primary coverts and alula dark grey to blackish, thus increasing blackish outer half of wing, with restricted whitish primary bases (primaries 4-8). Underwing whitish, with darker tips to flight feathers. Bill pink with blackish tip, nasal tube bluish, and often yellowish subterminal band between pink base and blackish tip; iris brown; legs and feet pinkish-blue.

DISTRIBUTION AND STATUS Circumpolar in Southern Ocean. Total population very large. Breeds on coasts of Antarctic Continent, Antarctic Peninsula and on islands well south of Antarctic Convergence: South Sandwich (1 million pairs), South Orkneys (maybe as many as 1 million pairs), also Elephant Island (71,000 pairs), Bouvet, Balleny Island, Peter the First Island. Status appears stable although adverse weather can affect breeding success; some predation from skuas and sheathbills, and commercial fisheries could represent a problem in the long term. May reach tropical waters in Humboldt Current off western South America; generally to 30°S in Atlantic and Indian Oceans, reaching South Africa, Australia and New Zealand (infrequently), with more in 'wreck' years. Most winter north of Antarctic Convergence.

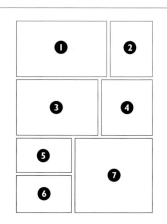

1 **Northern Fulmar** (adult incubating egg, Monach Islands, Scotland, July)
2 **Northern Fulmar** (adult, Isle of Skye, Scotland, July)
3 **Northern Fulmar** (adult, dark morph, north Pacific Ocean, June)
4 **Antarctic Fulmar** (south Atlantic Ocean, January)
5 **Antarctic Fulmar** (Victoria, Australia, September)
6 **Antarctic Fulmar** (Antarctica, January)
7 **Antarctic Fulmar** (Victoria, Australia, September)

ANTARCTIC PETREL

Thalassoica antarctica L 43 cm (17 in), WS 102 cm (40 in)

Distinctive and gregarious fulmarine petrel of the Southern Ocean, essentially a bird of the pack ice and surrounding iceberg zone.

IDENTIFICATION Medium-sized, with typical fulmarine petrel flight, but often flies high above sea surface, and flocks co-ordinated. Will follow ships and scavenge for food, especially in the ice. Feeds by surface-seizing, surface-plunging and pursuit-plunging; associates freely with Snow Petrels, Arctic Terns and various whale species; rests on icebergs and icefloes. Superficially somewhat resembles Cape Petrel, but shows clear-cut brown and white contrasting pattern on upperparts (unlike Cape Petrel's more chequered and spotted upperparts). **Juvenile** Plumage as adult in fresh plumage, but with a black bill. **Adult** Head, neck, chin and throat dark chocolate-brown, sharply demarcated from white underparts, but mottled brown and white on sides of neck and irregularly almost to upper flanks. Mantle, back and rump continuous dark chocolate-brown; lower rump, uppertail-coverts and tail white, tail with narrow brown terminal band. Underparts white from upper breast to tail, tail with narrow brown tip. Upperwing with leading edge (inner coverts and outer three to five primaries) dark chocolate-brown, as upperparts; inner primaries, greater coverts and secondaries contrastingly white, with narrow brown trailing edge to secondaries. Underwing white, with brown leading edge from armpit to just below carpal joint; narrower and irregular brownish tips to primaries and trailing edge of wing. Bill olive-brown; iris brown; legs and feet greyish-flesh. By summer chocolate-brown fades variably to lighter brownish, especially on hindneck, which may become whitish and thus form a pale hindcollar isolating brown head from mantle; throat may also become whitish.

DISTRIBUTION AND STATUS Circumpolar in Southern Ocean. Breeds at 35 colonies on Antarctica, up to 250 km inland (does not breed Balleny Islands, Scott Island or Adelaide Island). Sea study counts estimate 4-7 million pairs (10-20 million birds), thus unknown colonies exist (SCAR 1996). Population appears stable; breeding success may be related to krill availability. Range in summer north to 62°S-63°S, in winter pelagic dispersal north to near Antarctic Convergence at 48°S-55°S in all three oceans; regular visitor Signy, Bouvet, occasionally Prince Edwards, Crozets, Kerguelen and Heard Islands. Vagrants to South Georgia, Falklands, South Africa, Australia, New Zealand; occasionally more in 'wreck' years (eg 1978).

CAPE or PINTADO PETREL

Daption capense L 39 cm (15 in), WS 86 cm (34 in)

Distinctive and gregarious medium-sized fulmarine petrel, reaching further north than others, even across the Equator.

IDENTIFICATION Typical fulmarine flight, but more flapping and less gliding than Antarctic Petrel; flies higher in strong winds. Feeds from surface, also dives from surface and in flight. Quarrelsome over food, which is probably located by smell; can feed at night. Avid ship-follower. Plumage distinctive, with chequered sooty-black and white upperparts and wings and mainly white underparts. Head, neck, chin and throat sooty-black to black, darker and usually more clearly demarcated from white underparts than Antarctic Petrel, although some show whitish or mottled chin and throat. Upper mantle black; lower mantle, back, rump and uppertail-coverts white with boldly chequered black chevrons, generally appearing whiter from mantle to uppertail-coverts. Tail mostly white with broad blackish terminal band. Underparts from throat (usually) white, undertail-coverts with blackish tips; black terminal band to undertail. Upperwing mainly blackish, with conspicuous white primary patch from white bases to innermost five to six primaries, their coverts and inner webs of outer primaries; second white patch on innermost greater, median and some adjacent lesser coverts which may or may not join whitish lower back. Underwing white with equal blackish margins on leading and trailing edges, and blackish primary tips. Bill black; iris brown; legs and feet black. Subspecies *australe* from New Zealand offshore islands smaller, with less white and more black on upper surface of wings and possibly more black on upper mantle. Many birds, however, appear intermediate.

DISTRIBUTION AND STATUS Circumpolar in antarctic and subantarctic seas, avoiding pack ice. Breeds on coasts of Antarctic mainland, Antarctic Peninsula and many antarctic and subantarctic islands north to Crozets. New Zealand population (5,000-10,000 pairs) on subantarctic islands. Elsewhere mostly on South Sandwich, South Orkneys, Elephant Island, South Georgia and South Shetlands. Population appears stable, probably several million birds. Outside breeding season pelagic to c 25°S in all three oceans, although further north in Benguela Current off western South Africa and especially in Humboldt Current off western South America, where it reaches Galapagos and the Equator. Vagrant to St Helena, Kenya, Mauritius, Réunion, Marquesas; possible Northern Hemisphere records off California and Mexico, but most other such claims unsubstantiated.

SNOW PETREL

Pagodroma nivea L 32 cm (13 in), WS 78 cm (31 in)

Small, lightly built, unmistakable white petrel generally confined to the Southern Ocean pack ice and surrounding adjacent waters.

IDENTIFICATION Appears long-winged in erratic and buoyant flight, with rapid shallow wingbeats and much changing of direction, generally without long period of gliding. Tail appears square when folded but distinctly wedge-shaped when fanned. Follows ships in pack ice. Feeds by aerial dipping and contact-dipping, surface-diving, surface-seizing and pursuit-diving; will hover before descending to water. Partially nocturnal, and food probably located by smell. Flocks roost on icebergs and icefloes, often with Cape Petrels and Antarctic Petrels, and freely associates with whales. Plumage entirely white with faint ivory wash, contrasting with dark brown iris, blackish bill and bluish-black legs and feet. At very close range may show very pale vermiculations on upperparts, tail and wing-coverts; primaries may show very slight grey wash. Against the ice, at extreme distance or in poor light, some birds can look comparatively pale greyish; these may be immatures. Two subspecies, smaller nominate *nivea* and larger *confusa*; much hybridization and most colonies are mixed.

DISTRIBUTION AND STATUS Circumpolar in Southern Ocean. Breeds south of Antarctic Convergence on Antarctic Continent (up to 400 km inland), Antarctic Peninsula and numerous antarctic islands. Total population several million birds. Generally less numerous east coast of Antarctic Peninsula and west Antarctica because of persistent pack ice; large numbers breed west Antarctic Peninsula, South Georgia, South Orkneys and South Sandwich. In austral winter ranges to c 50°S in south-west Atlantic (north of South Georgia and Bouvet breeding sites), whereas generally to c 55°S in Indian and Pacific Oceans. Vagrants Heard Island, Kerguelen, Falklands. Not recorded South America, South Africa or Australia.

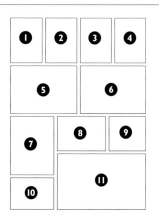

1 **Antarctic Petrel** (worn adult, Antarctica)
2 **Antarctic Petrel** (worn adult, Southern Ocean)
3 **Antarctic Petrel** (Antarctica)
4 **Cape Petrel** (Antarctica, January)
5 **Cape Petrel** (at nest site)
6 **Cape Petrel** (Deception Island, Antarctica, December)
7 **Cape Petrel** (subantarctic)
8 **Snow Petrel** (pair at nest site, Queen Maud Land, Antarctica)
9 **Snow Petrel** (Antarctica)
10 **Snow Petrel** (Antarctica)
11 **Snow Petrel** (Antarctica)

KERGUELEN PETREL

Lugensa brevirostris L 36 cm (14 in), WS 81 cm (32 in)

Medium-sized, dark, southern circumpolar petrel with distinctive jizz and flight. Plumage appearance highly variable with light conditions.

IDENTIFICATION Appears noticeably large-headed, with steep forehead and thick neck, gradually tapering to slightly wedge-shaped tail. Unlike most *Pterodroma* petrels, can be seen drifting into wind almost motionless at up to 50 m above sea. In lighter winds flight more typical of *Pterodroma*, but has curious fast wing-flicking action usually accompanied by rapid changes of direction. Usually solitary at sea, and generally does not follow ships. Head, upperparts and upperwings fairly uniform dark slate-grey, usually appearing blackish at a distance; back and mantle slightly paler than wings and tail. Underparts slate-grey, generally a shade paler than upperparts. Underwing slate-grey, similar to underparts, but with paler whitish inner leading edge formed by pale edges to marginal coverts, widest at wingpit and tapering gradually to carpal joint. Primaries and greater primary coverts silvery-grey, forming pale wing tip often extending to outer secondaries. Patch around eye often appears darker than rest of head, but in some lights (especially strong sunlight) whole head and neck appears darker than rest of body, imparting strong hooded appearance. At a distance, in diffuse light, general appearance can be uniformly blackish, whereas in strong light underbody and underwing appear slaty greyish-brown with silvery-white on underwing tip and leading edge of inner wing. Plumage wears to greyish-brown, often with paler chin and throat. Outer undertail-coverts may also appear silvery. Bill black; iris brown; legs and feet brown to grey. Distinguished from Great-winged Petrel by smaller size, thicker appearance (especially head and neck), generally greyer rather than blackish-brown coloration (but dependent on distance and light conditions), and characteristic flight.

DISTRIBUTION AND STATUS Circumpolar in all three oceans in subantarctic and antarctic seas. Very common throughout range, locally abundant; total World population probably numbers several hundred thousand individuals. Breeds Tristan da Cunha group and Gough Island, Prince Edwards (tens of thousands of pairs), Crozets (tens of thousands of pairs), and Kerguelen (up to c 50,000 pairs). Populations appear stable, but black rats exist on Possession (Crozets), also cats on some islands, eg Kerguelen; preyed on by skuas at Prince Edwards, and to lesser extent also at Gough and Tristan da Cunha. Ranges from pack ice to c 30°S, with fewer in Pacific Ocean. Recorded to 24°S off Brazil in south Atlantic; irregular vagrant off South Africa; occasionally 'wrecked' Australia, New Zealand, otherwise uncommon visitor. Has reached Somalia and Red Sea.

MASCARENE PETREL

Pterodroma aterrima Length 36 cm (14 in), WS ? Small to medium-sized, uniformly dark, Indian Ocean *Pterodroma*, very rare and little known. Only recently rediscovered, at Réunion, but breeding grounds remain unknown. Status at sea complicated by difficulties of identification. Classified as Critical.

IDENTIFICATION Flight apparently undescribed: probably swift, with typical high *Pterodroma* arcs. Plumage wholly blackish-brown with lighter greyish-black underwing. Smaller than Great-winged Petrel and larger than both Bulwer's and Jouanin's Petrels, with large bill, shorter, squarer tail, longer wings. More uniformly dark, and lacking any definable paler coverts (usually visible on Bulwer's and Jouanin's). Larger size and stocky body probably impart heavier and more powerful jizz. Bill black; iris brown; legs and feet pink and black. From dark shearwaters (Wedge-tailed and Flesh-footed) by large stubby *Pterodroma* bill, gadfly jizz and different flight. From dark-morph Herald Petrel by absence of white on underwing from primaries across wing-coverts, and absence of white between carpal and body on inner underwing.

DISTRIBUTION AND STATUS Indian Ocean. Formerly found on Rodrigues, where subfossil remains have been discovered; now presumed extinct there. Four specimens were collected on Réunion in the 19th century (others also collected but now lost). Two birds were found dead in 1970 and 1973. Since 1964 there have been observations of birds south of Réunion, generally between October and March; despite searches, however, no nests have been found. The species may breed in winter. No reliable at-sea records away from the immediate area of Réunion. Threats are unknown, but probably include predation by mammals (cats, dogs and rats) as well as illegal hunting by local inhabitants, which has recently had a drastic effect on the population of Barau's Petrel. Breeding biology completely unknown; existing population probably very small.

BECK'S PETREL

Pterodroma becki L c 29 cm (11 in), WS ? Rare and hardly known *Pterodroma* of the western Pacific Ocean, similar to and considered by some to be a smaller subspecies of Tahiti Petrel. Classified as Critical.

IDENTIFICATION Field appearance and flight totally unknown. Plumage apparently identical to that of larger Tahiti Petrel: see latter species. Separated as a species mainly on size. Beck's Petrel, at c 29 cm, is only slightly larger than the *Cookilaria* petrels, and considered to be 15% smaller than Tahiti Petrel. The bill is more slender than latter's.

DISTRIBUTION AND STATUS Western Pacific. Known from two specimens collected at sea about 1928: one east of New Ireland and north of Buka, Papua New Guinea; the other north-east of Rendova Island, Solomon Islands. What may have been this species has been reported off Wuvulu Island (north-east New Guinea), off the Admiralty Islands, the Bismarck archipelago and the Solomon Islands. Bougainville Island (Papua New Guinea) has been suggested as a likely breeding place. Threats are unknown at present, but probably include introduced mammalian predators.

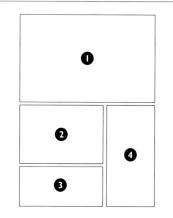

1 **Kerguelen Petrel** (worn adult on ship's deck, off Tristan da Cunha)
2 **Kerguelen Petrel** (Gough Island)
3 **Kerguelen Petrel** (southern Indian Ocean)
4 **Kerguelen Petrel** (southern Indian Ocean)

PETRELS

TAHITI PETREL

Pterodroma rostrata L 39 cm (15 in), WS 84 cm (33 in)

Medium-sized tropical Pacific *Pterodroma* very similar in plumage to Phoenix Petrel, but differing in jizz and flight.

IDENTIFICATION Distinctive jizz: long, narrow wings held perpendicular to body with primaries curling upwards at wing tip, longish body gradually tapering to tail, and long neck but small head making bill appear large (Phoenix Petrel generally flies with wings held forward, bending at carpal joint, but not curling upwards at tip). Flight generally low over water with loose wingbeats, wings generally bowed when gliding. In stronger winds flight more albatross-like than typical *Pterodroma*, lacking latter's sudden direction changes. Usually seen singly; does not follow ships. Plumage dark with contrasting white underparts. Head and neck uniform dark sooty-brown. Upperparts uniform dark sooty-brown, slightly paler on uppertail-coverts (but variable); tail dark brown. Lower breast, belly and vent white, sharply demarcated from dark of head and across upper breast, but dark continues down sides of breast to flanks; undertail white, narrowly bordered dark brown. Upperwing uniform dark sooty-brown. Underwing dark brown, appearing uniform at a distance, but when close shows a variable narrow whitish stripe down centre of underwing from pale median coverts. Bill black (larger than that of Phoenix Petrel); iris dark brown; legs and feet flesh and black. Distinguished from similar, slightly smaller Phoenix Petrel by jizz and flight; in addition, Phoenix Petrel has darker upperparts without paler uppertail-coverts, has white leading edge to inner underwing (underwing otherwise generally darker, without central stripe), and has whitish chin and throat. The two overlap in range in eastern Pacific.

DISTRIBUTION AND STATUS Tropical Pacific Ocean. Breeds Society and Marquesa Islands and New Caledonia; population total unknown. Widespread in eastern tropical and subtropical Pacific Ocean between Mexico and Peru, extending to near Taiwan, Kiribati as far as 7°N, central Pacific to 6°N. Range overlaps with that of similar Phoenix Petrel in eastern Pacific. Has occurred eastern Indian Ocean (Banda Sea, New Guinea, Bismarck archipelago, Coral Sea). Recorded off New South Wales, Australia.

FIJI PETREL

Pterodroma macgillivrayi L 30 cm (12 in), WS ?
Very rare, uniformly dark petrel known only from Gau Island (Fiji). Classified as Critical.

IDENTIFICATION Flight details unrecorded. Resembles a large Bulwer's Petrel, but with heavier bill, larger head and neck, shorter tail, and plain dark upperwing. Plumage wholly dark chocolate-brown, much as Bulwer's Petrel but more uniform. Face and head slightly darker, imparting slight hooded effect. Lacks pale upperwing bars across coverts of Bulwer's Petrel, but centre of underwing appears slightly paler and greyish. Bill black, comparatively shorter than that of Bulwer's Petrel, but stouter and more robust; iris brown; feet with tarsus pale blue, webs black with pale blue patch on centre of inner web. Feet appear large for size of bird. Differs from Bulwer's Petrel in more thickset jizz with heavier bill, shorter tail, comparatively more rounded wings and proportionately larger head.

DISTRIBUTION AND STATUS South-west Pacific seas around Fiji. One specimen (probably a juvenile) collected on Gau Island in 1855. A search started in May 1983, and the species was rediscovered in April 1984 when one adult was caught by spotlighting. In 1985 a fledgling was found, but this died later. Subsequently the number of observations has risen to eight (mostly juveniles), although no nests have been found. Villagers do not hunt petrels on Gau, but rats and cats are present on the island and may pose a threat; there are no pigs or mongooses on Gau.

CHATHAM ISLAND PETREL

Pterodroma axillaris L 30 cm (12 in), WS 67 cm (26 in)

Small to medium-sized Pacific *Pterodroma*, very rare. Classified as Critical.

IDENTIFICATION Very rare and not well known; flight probably similar to that of Black-winged Petrel. Plumage greyish above, with dark 'M' mark, white below, with diagnostic underwing pattern. Crown, nape and hindneck uniform light grey, extending onto foreneck and sides of breast as partial grey collar; forehead, lores, chin, throat and narrow supercilium white; blackish patch through and under eye contrasts with both grey head and white face. Mantle, back, scapulars, uppertail-coverts and uppertail uniform light grey, tail with darker tip; rump blackish. Underparts white; undertail-coverts white, with dark tip to undertail. Upperwing light grey, with blackish-brown primaries and inner coverts forming 'M' from wing tip to wing tip, joining across blackish rump. (With wear, upperwing darkens and the 'M' mark is reduced, thus more contrast with mantle.) Underwing white centrally with broad blackish margins: black trailing edge continues around wing tip (primaries) onto leading edge; continuous and more extensive blackish leading edge from primary coverts and over carpal joint, then extending diagonally inwards and continuing to similarly broad blackish axillaries and joining with innermost dark secondaries (a unique pattern within the *Pterodroma* genus); inner leading edge of underwing white, extending narrowly towards carpal joint and towards axillaries. Bill black; iris dark brown; legs and feet flesh-pink and black. Generally very similar to Black-winged Petrel, but distinguished by unique and extensive black underwing pattern extending to axillaries.

DISTRIBUTION AND STATUS South Pacific Ocean. Breeds only at Rangitira Island (formerly Southeast Island) in the Chatham Islands, east of New Zealand. Population estimated at 200-400 individuals, possibly as many as 800. Previously occurred also on Chatham Island and Mangere Island. May disperse to north Pacific in non-breeding season (absent from Chathams June-November); only one record away from Chatham Islands, at 120 km to south-east. Recorded once from mainland New Zealand. Removal of sheep and cattle has hopefully enabled existing vegetation to recover; however, population is not expanding and has suffered recent complete breeding failure. Threats include man, cats, pigs, rats and dogs as well as competition for nesting burrows with diving petrels, prions and Black-winged Petrels (a recent colonist).

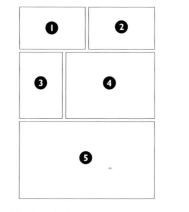

1 **Tahiti Petrel** (October)
2 **Tahiti Petrel** (November)
3 **Tahiti Petrel** (November)
4 **Chatham Island Petrel** (Rangitira Island, New Zealand)
5 **Chatham Island Petrel** (Rangitira Island, New Zealand)

PETRELS

BLACK-WINGED PETREL

Pterodroma nigripennis L 30 cm (12 in), WS 67 cm (26 in)
Medium-sized Pacific *Pterodroma*.
IDENTIFICATION Flight rapid and strong; will soar and hang motionless. Usually not a ship-follower. Plumage greyish-brown above with 'M' across wings, mostly white below; underwing white with blackish borders and diagonal dark bar. Crown, nape and hindneck light grey, extending onto foreneck and sides of breast as partial grey collar; forehead and lores white, narrowing to form pale supercilium; short black patch through and below eye, contrasting with grey head and white chin and cheeks. Mantle, scapulars and upper back light grey; rump blackish-brown; uppertail-coverts and tail light grey, tail tip darker. Underparts white, but grey of partial collar can extend to leading edge of underwing and onto flanks; white undertail-coverts; undertail shows narrow dark border. Upperwing light grey, with blackish-brown primaries and inner wing-coverts forming 'M' from wing tip to wing tip, joining across blackish-brown rump. (With wear, upperwing darkens and 'M' reduces; dark wings contrast with grey mantle and upper back.) Underwing mainly white, with blackish trailing edge enlarging to extensive dark wing tip (primaries) and narrowing onto leading edge; thicker black leading edge from base of outermost primary, extending over carpal joint and then diagonally across coverts to centre of wing; inner leading edge white. Bill black; iris dark brown; legs and feet flesh-pink (can be bluish) and black. Grey cap and mantle shared with Cook's, Pycroft's and Chatham Island Petrels. Cook's and Pycroft's have narrower dark leading edge to underwing, diagonal bar starts at carpal (not inward of carpal as on Black-winged), and have narrower dark trailing edge, less black at wing tip, and partial collar less pronounced. From Chatham Island by underwing pattern (lacking black axillaries). Gould's, Stejneger's and Bonin all have darker head and different underwing pattern.
DISTRIBUTION AND STATUS Pelagic in subtropical and tropical south-west and central Pacific. Breeds Norfolk Island, Lord Howe Island, Kermadecs (Macauley over 1,100,000 birds), Chathams, Three Kings, New Caledonia, and Austral group (Rapa); has expanded breeding range westwards. Total population a few hundred thousand breeding pairs. In non-breeding season (July-November) disperses north to central north Pacific (south-east of Japan, up to 31°N north of Hawaii), extending east to Baja California and Central America south to Galapagos and Peru; occurs regularly off eastern Australia and Tasman Sea, Fiji and Tonga. Heavily preyed on by cats.

WHITE-NECKED PETREL

Pterodroma cervicalis L 43 cm (17 in), WS 97 cm (38 in)
Large south-west Pacific *Pterodroma*, formerly sometimes treated as conspecific with Juan Fernandez Petrel. Classified as Vulnerable.
IDENTIFICATION Flight appears effortless and graceful with few wingbeats, slower than that of *Cookilaria* petrels; typical *Pterodroma* flight in stronger winds. Usually solitary; not attracted to ships. Dark-capped with diagnostic white hindneck collar; grey above with obvious 'M' across wings, white below with blackish underwing borders. Crown, nape and sides of head to below eye black, forming small but conspicuous black cap; forehead, lores, cheeks, chin and throat white, extending around hindneck to form diagnostic white hindcollar. Mantle, upper back and scapulars medium grey, with paler edges giving scaled appearance close up; grey of mantle extends down sides of neck to form short partial collar; lower back and rump blackish, uppertail-coverts medium grey. Tail medium grey with whiter sides. Underparts white; white undertail has narrow dark tip. Upperwing medium brownish-grey, with blackish-brown primaries and wing-coverts forming 'M' from wing tip to wing tip across lower back and rump. (As with similar species, such as Juan Fernandez, the upperparts become browner with wear, showing less scaling and less conspicuous 'M', and the tail may also darken.) Underwing white, narrow black trailing edge broadens at wing tip and extends narrowly along outer primary; narrow black bar from carpal extends diagonally inwards across coverts towards centre of wing. Bill black; iris brown; legs and feet pinkish and black. White hindneck separates this species from similar-sized Juan Fernandez; smaller Barau's has grey, not white, hindneck.
DISTRIBUTION AND STATUS South-west Pacific in breeding season. Breeds Macauley (Kermadecs) and Philip Island (off Norfolk Island, Australia). Former colony on Raoul (Kermadecs) probably wiped out by feral cats. Estimated total population of at least 50,000 pairs; goats have been removed from Macauley Island. Occurs occasionally Tasman Sea and east coast of Australia; common c 1,600 km from Kermadecs, north to Fiji and Tonga waters. Moves north May-November after breeding to central and north Pacific waters between Equator and Hawaii, occasionally further east to c 110°E. Vagrant New Zealand, and one record off Crozets (Indian Ocean).

MOTTLED PETREL

Pterodroma inexpectata L 34 cm (13 in), WS 74 cm (29 in)
Medium-sized *Pterodroma* of the Pacific and south-east Indian Oceans.
IDENTIFICATION Typical *Pterodroma* flight and generally solitary; not usually at trawlers or following ships. Plumage grey and white with dark 'M' across upperwings, diagnostic grey belly patch, and distinct white underwing with striking black diagonal bar. Crown and nape slate-grey, merging into paler medium grey mantle; forehead white with darker scaling, narrow white supercilium; lores, chin and throat white, contrasting with blackish eye patch. Scapulars medium grey, lower back and rump blackish-brown; tail medium grey with blackish tip, outer tail feathers white. (In fresh plumage, upperparts have narrow white fringes giving scaled appearance.) On underparts, slate-grey of hindneck can extend onto sides of neck as partial collar and also along sides of breast to join diagnostic grey belly; upper breast white; vent and undertail-coverts white, sharply separated from grey belly. Upperwing medium grey, with darker blackish primaries and greater coverts forming 'M' across upperwings. Underwing white with thin dark trailing edge; also larger, more noticeable broad black leading edge along outer primary coverts, extending inwards from carpal joint diagonally across secondary coverts to centre of inner wing. Bill black; iris dark brown; legs and feet flesh and black. Juvenile similar to adult, but paler: white fringes extend to nape and hindcrown, with broader white tips on upperparts. Collared Petrel is smaller, with cap contrasting with grey mantle, and has darker upperwings without 'M' mark, and narrower black on underwing.
DISTRIBUTION AND STATUS South-east Indian Ocean and Pacific Ocean: antarctic and subantarctic waters. Breeds on South Island, Stewart and Snares Islands (New Zealand), previously on Bounty, Antipodes, Auckland and Chatham Islands. Total population 10,000-50,000 pairs. Strictly pelagic throughout range; in non-breeding season disperses north through the Tropics to winter in far north Pacific. In the Pacific concentrates over cool currents along central subarctic front; numerous in Bering Sea. Recorded Atlantic seaboard of USA, Chile, Galapagos, eastern tropical Pacific, Drake Passage to Prydz Bay; uncommon to south Alaska, accidental to south-east Australia.

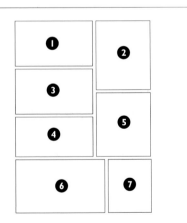

1 **Black-winged Petrel** (Lord Howe Island, Australia, March)
2 **Black-winged Petrel** (Philip Is., off Norfolk Island, Australia, February)
3 **Black-winged Petrel** (digging a burrow at night, Norfolk Island, Australia)
4 **White-necked Petrel**
5 **White-necked Petrel** (at nest site, Philip Is., off Norfolk Island, Australia, February)
6 **Mottled Petrel** (April)
7 **Mottled Petrel**

PETRELS

BONIN PETREL

Pterodroma hypoleuca L 30 cm (12 in), WS 67 cm (26 in)

Medium-sized north-western Pacific *Pterodroma*.
IDENTIFICATION Typical *Pterodroma* flight; does not follow ships. Plumage greyish above, blackish on crown to nape, with dark 'M' mark across wings, and white below with diagnostic dark underwing patches. Crown, nape and hindneck blackish-grey, extending below eye and onto foreneck and sides of breast as partial collar; forehead white, scaled with blackish, extending partially over eye as narrow supercilium; lores, chin and throat white. Mantle and back medium bluish-grey, with whitish fringes giving scaled appearance; lower back and rump blackish-brown, tail dark grey. Underparts white; undertail has dark blackish border. Upperwing greyish-brown, with blackish primaries and greater coverts forming 'M' from wing tip to wing tip, joining across lower back. Underwing white; bold blackish trailing edge broadens at wing tip (primaries) and extends narrowly onto leading edge there joining blackish patch on primary coverts, narrowing at carpal joint, and then extending diagonally inwards as a second blackish bar across secondary coverts. No other *Pterodroma* shows this diagnostic underwing pattern. Bill black; iris dark brown; legs and feet pinkish-flesh, distally black. Hawaiian Petrel is larger, with longer-winged jizz, browner upperparts lacking 'M' mark, and different underwing pattern. Cook's and Stejneger's Petrels are smaller, with different head and underwing patterns.
DISTRIBUTION AND STATUS Subtropical western and central north Pacific. Breeds Volcano and Bonin Islands south of Japan and on north-west Hawaiian chain, where Midway colony is being devastated by rats. Total population estimate several hundred thousand breeding pairs. Disperses widely over central and northern Pacific to *c* 30°N and to Taiwan, Japan and Sakhalin.

GOULD'S PETREL

Pterodroma leucoptera L 30 cm (12 in), WS 71 cm (28 in)

Small south Pacific *Pterodroma*. Apparently not classified by BirdLife International, despite low population levels.
IDENTIFICATION Flight normally slower than that of Cook's Petrel, but occasionally interspersed with more erratic and bounding flight. Does not follow ships; usually solitary at sea. Plumage grey above, with contrasting blackish head, white face and dark 'M' across upperwings, and white below, with dark underwing borders extending diagonally across secondary coverts. Crown, nape and hindneck sooty-black, extending below eye to join blackish suborbital patch reaching to sides of neck and sides of upper breast to form extensive dark cap (the darkest of any small *Pterodroma* and clearly marked); forehead white, scaled with dark feathers; lores, base of bill, chin

and throat white, contrasting with cap. Mantle and back dark bluish-grey to dark grey, rump and uppertail-coverts darker grey. Short and rounded tail greyish-brown with darker tip; outer tail feather has inner web grey to brownish-grey. Underparts white. Upperwing dark brownish-grey, with blackish-brown primaries and greater coverts forming indistinct 'M' from wing tip to wing tip, joining across lower back; inner webs of primaries have whitish wedge at base; secondaries grey. Underwing white, with blackish border which forms extensive blackish carpal area that extends diagonally inwards across secondary coverts. Underwing bar more marked than on Stejneger's, Cook's or Pycroft's (which also have paler head), but less than on Black-winged, Chatham Island or Bonin. Bill black; iris dark brown; legs and feet off-white, distally black. Recently described (1978) subspecies *P. l. caledonica* (New Caledonia Petrel) is similar to Gould's but slightly larger, with a bigger bill; back paler grey, thus more contrast with rest of upperparts; paler chest sides; less prominent underwing bar from carpal towards wing-coverts; and white or mainly white inner web on outer tail feathers.
DISTRIBUTION AND STATUS Tropical and subtropical Pacific. Breeds (October-April) only at Cabbage Tree Island (Australia). Population 250-300 pairs, but stable. No rats or cats exist on breeding island, but some birds caught by the sticky seeds of the bird-lime tree (*Pisconia umbellifera*); also, some predation by raptors and ravens, and rabbits have removed the vegetation. Rarely seen away from Cabbage Tree Island, thought to feed in Tasman Sea during breeding season. Absent from breeding island May-October, and may disperse to north Tasman Sea and eastwards towards central Pacific. *P. l. caledonica*, breeding in central mountains of New Caledonia, disperses west and mainly east in subtropical and tropical south Pacific from Australia (Tasman and Coral Seas) to eastern Pacific, reaching Galapagos Islands; non-breeders may remain in eastern Pacific.

COOK'S PETREL

Pterodroma cookii L 26 cm (10 in), WS 66 cm (26 in)

Small south Pacific *Pterodroma*. Classified as Vulnerable.
IDENTIFICATION Rapid *Pterodroma* flight with fast wingbeats, flying in high arcs. Ignores ships. Pale grey above, with darker 'M' across upperwings, and white below, with narrow black underwing borders extending diagonally a short way across secondary coverts. Crown, nape and hindneck grey, with whitish margins extending to sides of neck and upper breast sides as short incomplete collar; forehead white, with darker scaling on forecrown, also narrow white supercilium; lores, chin and throat white; dark grey-black patch in front of and below eye which merges into grey of head behind eye. Mantle, back and uppertail-coverts grey, rump blackish. Tail slightly darker grey than mantle,

with blackish-brown tip; outer tail feathers paler than centre. Underparts entirely white. Upperwing grey, with blackish primaries and greater coverts forming 'M' from wing tip to wing tip, joining across blackish rump. (Wings become browner with wear.) Underwing mainly white, with narrow blackish trailing edge broadening slightly at tip (primaries) and extending onto leading edge; small blackish carpal patch extends diagonally across wing-coverts – short and tapering to a point. Comparatively long and slender bill black; iris brown; legs and feet bluish (yellowish webs) and black. Immatures slightly paler than adults, with more prominent white edges to upperparts. From Black-winged, Chatham Island, Gould's and Stejneger's Petrels by paler crown and nape merging into similarly coloured mantle, also by whiter underwing with shorter black diagonal bar. Criteria for separation from Pycroft's and De Filippi's still evolving – see those species.
DISTRIBUTION AND STATUS South Pacific Ocean. Breeds Codfish Island, Little Barrier and Great Barrier Islands (off New Zealand). Total population recovering, and now estimated at 10,000-50,000 pairs after Weka Rails removed from Codfish and feral cats from Little Barrier. Rats are still on Codfish, Little Barrier and Great Barrier, and cats on Great Barrier. Formerly food for Maoris. Range subtropical Pacific in breeding season, extending west into Tasman Sea and offshore Australia and east of New Zealand; rarely, subantarctic Pacific. Winters in eastern Pacific between Baja California and Chile, with many off Peru, where range overlaps with that of De Filippi's Petrel; also north to at least 34°N north of Hawaii, and Aleutian Islands to 46°N.

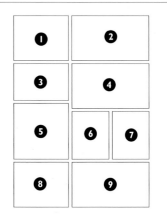

1 **Bonin Petrel** (at nest site, Hawaiian Islands, March)
2 **Bonin Petrel** (at nest site, Hawaiian Islands, March)
3 **Bonin Petrel** (Hawaiian Islands)
4 **Gould's Petrel** (at nest site, Cabbage Tree Island, Australia, November)
5 **Gould's Petrel**
6 **Gould's Petrel** (Victoria, Australia, December)
7 **Gould's Petrel** (Tasman Sea, February)
8 **Cook's Petrel** (off Little Barrier Island, New Zealand, November)
9 **Cook's Petrel** (at nest site, New Zealand)

PYCROFT'S PETREL

Pterodroma pycrofti L 26 cm (10 in), WS 66 cm (26 in)

Small south Pacific *Pterodroma*, very rare and poorly known. Classified as Vulnerable.

IDENTIFICATION Behaviour at sea unknown, but assumed to be similar to that of Cook's Petrel. Grey above, with darker 'M' mark across upperwings, and white below with narrow black underwing borders extending diagonally across secondary coverts. Crown, nape and hindneck dusky grey, extending to sides of neck and upper breast to form dusky partial collar; forehead white with grey scaling, indistinct white supercilium; darker grey suborbital patch from just in front of eye to ear-coverts. Mantle and back medium grey, paler than head; rump brownish-black, uppertail-coverts medium grey. Tail grey, with darker tip and paler outer tail feathers. Underparts white. Upperwing brownish-black, with darker primaries and wing-coverts forming 'M' from wing tip to wing tip, joining across brownish-black rump. (Upperwing wears darker, reducing 'M' mark and reducing contrast on upperparts.) Underwing mainly white, with dark trailing edge broadening at tip (primaries) and extending narrowly onto leading edge, and dark at carpal joint on leading edge extending diagonally inwards across coverts. Bill black; iris dark brown; legs and feet bluish-grey. Extremely similar to Cook's Petrel and doubtfully distinguishable at sea: Pycroft's Petrel is slightly smaller, with shorter wings, shorter bill, slightly longer tail, and has darker crown and nape giving darker cap, browner upperparts with less distinct 'M', and darker eye mark.

DISTRIBUTION AND STATUS South-west Pacific. Breeds on 11 islands off North Island, New Zealand. Total population estimates vary from under 2,000 birds, with a breeding population of not more than 300 pairs, to *c* 10,000 birds with a breeding population of 2,000-2,500 pairs. Predated by cats, rats, and tuataras (*Sphenodon punctatus*). Distribution at sea unknown, but absent from colonies April to October, with no confirmed records off Australia and no reliable New Zealand sight records, but numerous beachcasts. Recorded on Kermadecs in 1898; one north Pacific record indicating possible dispersal northwards after breeding, and recently recorded central and eastern Pacific, implying wide dispersal.

COLLARED PETREL

Pterodroma brevipes L 30 cm (12 in), WS 71 cm (28 in)

Small, polymorphic, south Pacific *Pterodroma*, sometimes considered a subspecies of Gould's Petrel.

IDENTIFICATION Not a ship-follower. Grey above, with blackish head and dark 'M' mark across upperwings, white face and underwing, and extremely variable below, from white through intermediates to dark. Crown, nape and hindneck sooty-black, extending below eye to join blackish suborbital patch reaching to sides of neck and upper breast (on some, forming full collar); forehead white, scaled with dark feathers; lores, base of bill, chin and throat white, isolated from whitish underparts by complete breastband on some examples. Mantle and back medium grey, lighter than on Gould's Petrel; rump and uppertail-coverts darker grey. Tail greyish-brown, lacking whitish outer tail feathers; tail appears long compared with other *Cookilaria* petrels. Upperwing dark brownish-grey, with blackish-brown primaries and greater coverts forming indistinct 'M' from wing tip to wing tip, joining across lower back; primaries lack white wedges on inner margins; secondaries grey. Underwing white with blackish border, latter more extensive on carpal joint and extending diagonally inwards across secondary coverts (pattern more pronounced than on Cook's Petrel, but less so than on Black-winged Petrel). Underparts variable, and polymorphism may vary geographically among different populations: *palest* as Gould's Petrel, white with no breastband (distinguished from Gould's by more extensive dark on leading edge of underwing, which also shows distinct demarcation between white coverts and dark primary bases, whereas Gould's Petrel has basal area of inner primaries white); *intermediates* have partial or complete collar across upper breast which is variably greyish and separates white throat from whiter lower breast and belly; *dark* has wholly grey underparts except for white chin and throat and blackish upper breast (dark birds have broader dark underwing pattern, and 'M' across upperwings may be less conspicuous). Bill black; iris dark brown; legs and feet light grey to intense blue, distally black.

DISTRIBUTION AND STATUS South Pacific Ocean. Breeds in Fiji group on Gau, Kadavu (where heavily exploited) and possibly Ovalu; may have been extirpated by mongooses on Vitilevu and Vanualevu. Also breeds Vanuatu, Rarotonga (Cook Islands), and possibly on Ta'u in American Samoa (but not Western Samoa). A larger form may exist in the Solomon Islands. Some dispersal along the South Equatorial Current and Equatorial Counter Current between 10°N and 10°S eastwards almost to the Galapagos Islands. Recorded Phoenix Islands. Some populations may be more sedentary.

DE FILIPPI'S PETREL

Pterodroma defilippiana L 26 cm (10 in), WS 66 cm (26 in)

Small eastern Pacific *Pterodroma* breeding off Chile and dispersing northwards probably only to Galapagos. Classified as Vulnerable.

IDENTIFICATION Plumage essentially similar to Cook's Petrel, but with longer, thicker bill, shorter wings, longer, more wedge-shaped tail and more languid, horizontal flight. Crown, nape and hindneck grey, extending to sides of neck and upper breast sides as short, incomplete collar; forehead white, with darker scaling on forecrown and narrow white supercilium; lores, chin and throat white, extending upwards across cheeks and behind auriculars to form a short half-collar (often lacking or insignificant on Cook's Petrel); dark greyish-black patch around and below eye and merging into grey of head (similar to Cook's Petrel). Mantle, back and uppertail-coverts grey (with wear, head and mantle appear darker, as Cook's Petrel); rump blackish. Tail longer and broader than Cook's, uniformly grey centrally without the dark tip shown by Cook's or Pycroft's Petrels; outer tail feathers paler than centre, generally less white than Cook's Petrel. Underparts white. Upperwing grey, with blackish primaries and greater coverts forming 'M' from wing tip to wing tip, joining across blackish rump. Underwing mainly white, with narrow blackish trailing edge broadening slightly at tip (primaries) and extending onto leading edge; small blackish carpal patch extends diagonally across wing-coverts (longer than on Cook's Petrel). Bill black; iris brown; legs and feet purple-bluish with black webs. Identification criteria for separation of Cook's, De Filippi's and Pycroft's Petrels still evolving, and published data somewhat contradictory at present; flight of De Filippi's Petrel apparently more sluggish than that of Cook's Petrel, with less high arcing.

DISTRIBUTION AND STATUS Eastern Pacific. Breeds (June-January) above ground on ledges or in caves (*contra Birds to Watch 2*: not in burrows), and visits colonies in daylight. Breeds Des Venturadas, on San Ambrosio (10,000 birds in 1970) and San Felix (150-200 pairs in 1970, population reduced by cats); and Juan Fernandez, on Robinson Crusoe (Mas a Tierra), where now very few, if any (population reduced considerably by cats and coatis), and Santa Clara ('hundreds and thousands in 1986' but 100-200 in 1991, reduced by rats). Absent from breeding grounds March-June and disperses north off Peru almost to Galapagos.

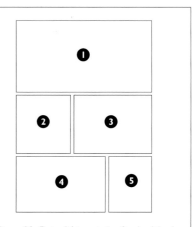

1 **Pycroft's Petrel** (at nest site, Stanley Island, New Zealand)
2 **Pycroft's Petrel** (Stanley Island, New Zealand)
3 **Pycroft's Petrel** (Stanley Island, New Zealand)
4 **Collared Petrel** (Gau, Fiji)
5 **De Filippi's Petrel**

PETRELS

STEJNEGER'S PETREL

Pterodroma longirostris L 26 cm (10 in), WS 66 cm (26 in)
Small Pacific *Pterodroma* breeding only on Juan Fernandez Islands.
IDENTIFICATION Smallest and fastest *Cookilaria* petrel, with flight probably less erratic than that of Cook's Petrel; does not follow ships. Grey above, with whitish face contrasting with darker crown and nape, and dark 'M' across wings, and whitish below, with blackish underwing margins and diagonal bar from carpal across secondary coverts. Crown and nape blackish-grey, extending to enclose blackish eye patch contrasting with whitish forehead, lores, forecrown, cheeks and chin. Hindneck dark grey, extending to sides of neck and upper breast sides as partial collar. Mantle and back mid grey; rump blackish, lower rump and uppertail-coverts grey; long tail brownish-black. Underparts, including undertail-coverts, white. Upperwing blackish-brown, with blackish primaries and greater coverts forming indistinct 'M' from wing tip to wing tip, joining across blackish rump. Underwing white, with narrow blackish trailing edge and tip (primaries) narrowly extending onto leading edge; slightly thicker black at carpal joint extending diagonally inwards onto coverts as an inconspicuous bar. Bill black; iris brown; legs and feet pale bluish. Immatures much as adults, but mantle and back lighter grey and thus contrasting more with dark head. Distinguished from Gould's, Collared, Black-winged, Chatham Island and Bonin Petrels by whiter underwing, and generally whiter forecrown. Cook's and Pycroft's Petrels have similar underwing pattern, but Cook's has longer bill, paler crown and nape not contrasting with mantle, and more prominent 'M', while Pycroft's has whitish stripe above eye and less extensive dark eye patch.
DISTRIBUTION AND STATUS South-east Pacific. Breeds only Juan Fernandez Islands, with a total population of *c* 131,000 pairs. Breeds with Juan Fernandez Petrel but feral cats prefer smaller Stejneger's Petrel, giving cause for concern. Presumed distribution limited to south-eastern Pacific in breeding season (south to 49°S), but not well known. Non-breeding range north Pacific Ocean from Japan to western USA, with most in subtropical north-west Pacific. Accidental to New Zealand, but no Australian records.

PHOENIX PETREL

Pterodroma alba L 35 cm (14 in), WS 83 cm (33 in)
Medium-sized, dark, tropical Pacific *Pterodroma*.
IDENTIFICATION Highly pelagic; avoids land except when breeding. Has typical *Pterodroma* flight. Generally solitary at sea, and does not follow ships. Dark sooty-brown above and on head and upper breast, sharply demarcated from white underparts, with contrasting dark underwing. Very similar to Tahiti Petrel. Head,

neck and upper breast sooty-brown; variable white chin and throat, with scattered brownish tips to lower throat. Brown of head continues narrowly along breast sides to flanks and thighs; lower breast, belly, vent and undertail-coverts white. Blackish under surface of tail. Upperparts uniform sooty-brown, appearing blackish at sea and darker than Tahiti Petrel. Tail blackish-brown. Upperwing sooty-brown; primary shafts blackish. Underwing sooty-brown, with variable white on leading edge of inner wing extending almost to carpal joint; slightly paler primaries and secondaries may show as silvery wing flash along trailing third of underwing. Bill black; iris dark brown; legs and feet flesh and black. See Tahiti Petrel for differences from that species. Intermediate Kermadec and Herald Petrels do not have the contrasting black and white plumage of Phoenix, which has a darker underwing than either and lacks the white primary shafts of Kermadec Petrel.
DISTRIBUTION AND STATUS Tropical and subtropical central Pacific Ocean. Breeds Phoenix, Marquesas, Tuamotu, Tonga, Line (including Christmas Island), Pitcairn Islands, also possibly Raoul Island (Kermadecs); no fixed breeding season. Total population probably tens of thousands of breeding pairs – data lacking for most islands. Range extends north to north of Hawaii (25°N), while also south-west to Kermadecs. Tentative sight records from Fiji; no Australian records. Susceptible to *El Niño* on Christmas Island. Regular equatorial Pacific.

HERALD PETREL

Pterodroma arminjoniana L 37 cm (15 in), WS 95 cm (37 in)
Medium-sized polymorphic *Pterodroma* found discontinuously in all three tropical oceans.
IDENTIFICATION Flight buoyant; usually ignores ships. Plumage morphs similar to those of Kermadec Petrel, but all lack white primary shafts on upperwing and generally show more extensive white on underwing. *Pale morph*: Head and neck mainly ash-brown, merging into whitish with scaling on forehead and lores; clearer white on chin and throat. Dark of head and neck extends to sides of upper breast, forming variable collar which may isolate white chin and throat from white underparts, and extends narrowly along sides of breast to flanks; undertail-coverts blackish with white tips. Mantle and back dark ash-brown, with paler edges visible at close range; tail blackish-brown. Upperwing darker than mantle, greyish-brown, with faint 'M' across wings and back; primary shafts dark. Underwing dark grey, with whitish patch on primaries; brownish tips to primary coverts separate secondary whitish patch on inner underwing formed by white bases to primary coverts, greater coverts and secondaries; whitish on leading edge of inner underwing extending almost to carpal. Bill black; iris dark brown; legs and feet pinkish and black. *Dark morph*: Blacker than Kermadec

Petrel, darker than Murphy's and Providence Petrels. Essentially no 'M' mark on upperwing. Head and body slate-brown. Otherwise as pale morph, though some have reduced white primary patch on underwing. Legs and feet black. *Intermediate morph*: Generally as pale morph, but with darker head, upper breast and undertail-coverts; lower breast and belly variably mottled brownish-grey and white. Complicated by partial albinism. More delicate build and buoyant flight help to distinguish this species from Kermadec Petrel.
DISTRIBUTION AND STATUS Tropical and subtropical Atlantic, Indian and Pacific Oceans. Atlantic: breeds Trinidade and Martin Vaz Islands; pelagic range not well known, thought to be mainly sedentary but occasionally recorded north Atlantic; post-juvenile dispersal probably very wide. Indian: breeds Round Island, Mauritius and possibly Cocos-Keeling Islands; population in severe decline; pelagic range not well known. Pacific: breeds Raine Island, Chesterfield Reefs, Ducie, Henderson, Oeno, Tuamotus, Marquesas, Tonga, Easter Island, Pitcairn, Gambier, possibly also Cook Islands and New Caledonia; pelagic range north to *c* 40°N in central Pacific, few north Pacific sightings, dispersal generally south of Equator in Pacific; rare off east coast of Australia, and no records New Zealand.

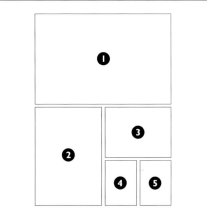

1 **Stejneger's Petrel** (in fern forest, Juan Fernandez Islands)
2 **Phoenix Petrel** (Christmas Island, Pacific Ocean)
3 **Phoenix Petrel** (Christmas Island, Pacific Ocean)
4 **Herald Petrel** (pale morph)
5 **Herald Petrel** (dark morph, off Pacific Coast, USA)

PETRELS

HAWAIIAN PETREL

Pterodroma sandwichensis L 43 cm (17 in), WS 91 cm (36 in)

Large, long-winged Pacific *Pterodroma*. Classified as Vulnerable.

IDENTIFICATION Typical *Pterodroma* flight, flapping less in high winds. Brownish-grey above, with dark cap and variable white on rump, and white below, with dark-margined underwing showing dark diagonal and variable dark axillaries. Almost identical to Galapagos Petrel. Upper crown and nape dark blackish-brown, extending below eye level and to sides of foreneck and upper breast as short partial collar; forehead, lores, chin and throat white, sharply demarcated from blackish cap. Upperparts dark brownish-grey (velvet-brown), slightly paler than cap; some individuals show variable white on sides of rump, normally two oval patches. Tail blackish-brown. Underparts white. Upperwings brownish-grey (velvet-brown) with darker primaries and secondaries, but no 'M' mark. Underwing white, with blackish trailing edge widening at tip (primaries) and extending narrowly onto leading edge; blackish carpal extending diagonally inwards across coverts; white axillaries may show small blackish patch. Bill black; iris brown; legs and feet bluish-flesh, webs black. Differs from White-necked Petrel in dark neck sides, darker upperparts lacking distinctive 'M', and different underwing pattern.

DISTRIBUTION AND STATUS Pacific Ocean. Breeds Hawaiian islands and ranges throughout central Pacific, with vagrants Japan, Philippines, Moluccas. Formerly common, with large colonies on all the main islands. Population now reduced to c 900 pairs, in the Haleakala NP on Mani (may also breed Kauai, Molokai and Lanai). Suffers predation from introduced cats and mongooses, and fledglings killed by hitting street lights.

GALAPAGOS PETREL

Pterodroma phaeopygia L 43 cm (17 in), WS 91 cm (36 in)

Large, long-winged Pacific *Pterodroma*, almost identical to Hawaiian Petrel. Classified as Critical.

IDENTIFICATION Almost wholly identical to Hawaiian Petrel: for description, see that species. Lighter in weight than Hawaiian Petrel, with shorter wing and tarsus and with longer and thinner bill; wing area smaller and wing loading lower than in Hawaiian Petrel. Differences subjective, however, and evidence is accumulating that Galapagos birds differ in size parameters depending on which island they breed on. At-sea ranges may overlap, though Galapagos Petrel tends to be more sedentary, ranging in warm waters from northern Peru to Mexico.

DISTRIBUTION AND STATUS Pacific Ocean. Known to breed only on Galapagos Islands. Populations declining by around 30% per annum on Santa Cruz (c 9,000 pairs) and Floreana (c 1,000 pairs); no data for Santiago or San Cristobal, where breeding also occurs. Preyed on by dogs, cats, pigs and rats, and nesting habitat destroyed by goats, donkeys, cattle and horses. Latest (1994) assessment suggests 10,000-50,000 pairs in four colonies.

KERMADEC PETREL

Pterodroma neglecta L 38 cm (15 in), WS 92 cm (36 in)

Medium-sized tropical and subtropical Pacific *Pterodroma* which is polymorphic.

IDENTIFICATION In light winds has leisurely flight on broad and long wings: deep beats and long unhurried glide, with banking in broad arcs. Solitary at sea and ignores ships. Occurs in three morphs; much plumage variation, complicating identification, but all morphs show whitish primary patch on underwing, and a whitish skua-like flash (whitish primary shafts) on upperwing. *Pale morph*: Head mainly white, with forehead, crown and nape variably mottled grey and brown; some can show darker eye patch. Mantle and back pale ashy-brown with whitish margins; tail short, squarish and blackish-brown. Underparts white, with variable brown partial collar on sides of upper breast. Upperwing blackish-brown; primaries blackish, with white shafts forming pale wing flash on upperwing (no 'M' mark). Underwing dark greyish-brown, with conspicuous white patch at base of primaries and smaller whitish area inside this (from whitish greater primary coverts), the darker primary-covert tips thus bisecting pale area; some show small whitish area on leading edge of underwing between carpal and body. Bill black; iris brown; legs and feet pinkish and black. *Dark morph*: Plumage entirely blackish-brown except for whitish scalloping on forehead, base of bill and chin. *Intermediate morph*: Continuous gradation between light and dark morphs: wings above and below as pale morph, but underparts variable, from whitish with greyish breastband, to brownish-grey and white, to dark greyish-brown. Morphs generally resemble those of smaller polymorphic Herald Petrel, but latter has darker head, paler underwing with white extending to secondaries and secondary coverts, and lacks white flash on upperwing. Providence Petrel is larger, greyer on mantle, back and upperwing than dark-morph Kermadec Petrel and showing head/mantle contrast, and has dark primary shafts.

DISTRIBUTION AND STATUS Pelagic in subtropical and tropical south Pacific, dispersing to central north Pacific. Breeds on islands in south Pacific at 25°S-35°S, from Lord Howe to Juan Fernandez Islands, including Kermadecs, Austral, Pitcairn (formerly Easter Island), Tuamotu, also San Ambrosio and San Felix Islands off Chile. Population on Raoul (Kermadec Islands) now 5,000-10,000 pairs, on the verge of extinction caused by cats, rats and humans. Total population unknown at present.

Eggs are collected at Pitcairn. Non-breeding birds disperse transequatorially to c 39°N in the central Pacific and to offshore Californian, Mexican, Peruvian and Chilean waters; also recorded west to Japan. Vagrant New Zealand and east coast of Australia.

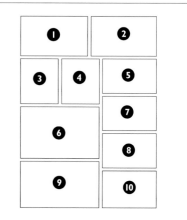

1 **Hawaiian Petrel** (May)
2 **Hawaiian Petrel** (feeding on squid, March)
3 **Hawaiian Petrel** (November)
4 **Hawaiian Petrel** (August)
5 **Galapagos Petrel**
6 **Kermadec Petrel** (dark morph with chick, South Meyer Is., Kermadec Islands)
7 **Kermadec Petrel** (light morph, North Meyer Is., Kermadec Islands)
8 **Kermadec Petrel** (dark morph, Norfolk Island, Australia, January)
9 **Kermadec Petrel** (intermediate morph, North Meyer Is., Kermadec Islands)
10 **Kermadec Petrel** (dark morph, Norfolk Island, Australia, January)

PETRELS

JUAN FERNANDEZ PETREL

Pterodroma externa L 43 cm (17 in), WS 97 cm (38 in)

Large south-eastern Pacific *Pterodroma*, closely resembling White-necked Petrel from the Kermadec Islands in south-western Pacific.

IDENTIFICATION Strictly pelagic. Flight graceful and effortless, slower than that of *Cookilaria* petrels. Generally solitary, and not attracted to ships. Plumage grey above, with dark cap, obvious 'M' mark across wings, variable white rump, and white below. Dark brownish-grey cap on crown and nape extending to below eye level, where appears darker, cap sharply demarcated from medium grey hindneck; forehead, lores, sides of face, chin and throat white. Grey of hindneck extends onto sides of neck as a short, partial collar. Mantle, back and scapulars medium grey or brownish-grey, with paler edges giving scaled appearance noticeable at close range; lower back and rump blackish; uppertail-coverts slate-grey with white bases (when exposed, may show as variable white horseshoe over base of tail). Tail slate-grey, appears long. Underparts, including undertail-coverts, white; undertail shows narrow dark border. Upperwing medium brownish-grey, with blackish-brown primaries and greater coverts forming 'M' mark from wing tip to wing tip across lower back and rump. (With wear, upperparts become browner, showing less scaling and less conspicuous 'M', and hindneck may become paler.) Underwing white, with narrow black trailing edge becoming broader at wing tip (primaries) and then narrowing and extending along outer primary; discrete blackish patch at carpal, which may extend diagonally inwards across coverts towards centre of wing. Bill black; iris brown; legs and feet pinkish and black. Distinguished from similar White-necked Petrel by lack of blackish cap contrasting sharply with white nape, and less extensive dark leading edge to underwing; otherwise similar in size, shape, flight and plumage. From Barau's and Stejneger's Petrels by size and underwing pattern. Hawaiian Petrel has darker, more extensive cap and more extensive dark on underwing. Buller's Shearwater has different jizz and flight, dark forehead and whiter underwing.

DISTRIBUTION AND STATUS Pacific Ocean. Breeds Isla Alejandro Selkirk (Juan Fernandez Islands) (c 1 million pairs). Despite breeding in a national park (established 1935) suffers from introduced predators, mainly cats, rats and coatis (*Nasua nasua*). South to 50°S in breeding season; subtropical and tropical south-east Pacific. Disperses to north Pacific between Equator and 20°N, and 90°W (off Galapagos) to c 170°W. Vagrant to New Zealand and Australia.

BARAU'S PETREL

Pterodroma baraui L 38 cm (15 in), WS 96 cm (38 in)

Medium-sized Indian Ocean *Pterodroma*.

Classified as Critical.

IDENTIFICATION Only *Pterodroma* in the Indian Ocean with 'Cookilaria-like' underwing pattern. Typical *Pterodroma* flight, slower than that of *Cookilaria* petrels; wings flexed more in strong winds, making more broad arcs. Not so strong a flier as Soft-plumaged Petrel or Great-winged Petrel. Very occasionally follows ships; generally solitary at sea. Plumage grey above, with dark cap and dark 'M' across wings, and white below, with well-defined dark diagonal bar across underwing-coverts. Crown and nape blackish-grey, forming dark cap extending to below eye, where blacker; forehead, lores and cheeks white. Hindneck medium grey, extending onto sides of neck as narrow half-collar. Mantle, upper back and scapulars medium brownish-grey, with whitish edges giving scaled appearance; lower back and rump blackish; uppertail-coverts and tail medium grey. Underparts, including undertail-coverts, white; undertail has narrow dark border. Upperwings mostly medium grey, with blackish-brown primaries and coverts forming 'M' from wing tip to wing tip across lower back and rump. (With wear, upperparts become darker, with less scaling, and 'M' less prominent.) Underwing mainly white, with narrow and sharp dark trailing edge (secondaries), broader but less defined dark tip (primaries) extending narrowly onto leading edge; larger blackish patch across carpal joint extends diagonally inwards across coverts towards centre of wing. Bill black; iris dark brown; legs and feet flesh-pink and black.

DISTRIBUTION AND STATUS Pelagic in tropical and subtropical Indian Ocean. Breeds Réunion and Rodrigues at high altitudes (2,700 m) on cliffs and peaks of volcanic cirque. Estimated population 3,000 pairs (1991), but numbers believed to be halved through shooting by locals. Dispersal north then east to west Australia in tropical and subtropical Indian Ocean, also south of Java and Sumatra; not recorded in north-western Indian Ocean or New Zealand. One record south-east Australia, and also near Christmas Island. Winters north and east of Réunion. When breeding, forages south to Subtropical Convergence.

MURPHY'S PETREL

Pterodroma ultima L 40 cm (16 in), WS 97 cm (38 in)

Medium-sized to large, plump, central south Pacific *Pterodroma*.

IDENTIFICATION Buoyant flight even in low winds, generally vertical banking followed by long glides; in higher winds flight more dramatic, resembling a fast Sooty Shearwater. Does not follow ships. Fairly uniform greyish-brown plumage, with indistinct 'M' mark across upperwings, whitish throat and base of bill, and pale bases to undersides of primaries. Head and nape dark brownish-grey, sometimes appearing as dark hood; throat mottled white, extending to whitish base of bill (both variable, but throat always whiter than forehead). Nape merges

into slightly paler mantle and back, which are a medium bluish-grey with some gloss in fresh plumage (glossiness recalls a dull Kerguelen Petrel, appearing more grey than brown), becoming browner with wear; rump and tail brownish-grey to dark grey. Tail shorter and less wedge-shaped than Providence Petrel. Underparts uniform medium dark grey, merging into whitish throat. Upperwing greyish-brown, with indistinct darker 'M' mark across upperwing surface; upperwing-coverts and secondaries paler grey, as mantle. Underwing generally dark, with silvery-grey primaries contrasting with darker primary tips (underwing flash not so well defined as on either Providence or Kermadec Petrels); greater under primary coverts medium-grey. Bill black; iris dark brown; legs and feet flesh-coloured, distally black. Wings narrower and shorter than on either Providence or Kermadec Petrels; dark Kermadec and Herald Petrels are smaller, browner, and lack greyish-white around the face; Providence Petrel is similar in size, but lacks the 'M' mark across upperwings and has a whiter underwing.

DISTRIBUTION AND STATUS Pacific Ocean. Breeds at 22°S-28°S on six islands among Austral, Tuamotu, Pitcairn, Rapa, Oeno. Dispersal not well known but northwards, and recorded Hawaii, French Frigate Shoals and Oahu. Has occurred Cook Islands. Also recorded north Pacific to 54°N and 300-400 miles (480-640 km) off Californian coast; probably regular eastern Pacific. Beached bird northern California.

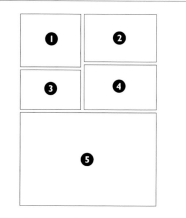

1 **Juan Fernandez Petrel** (Juan Fernandez Islands, Chile)
2 **Juan Fernandez Petrel** (Juan Fernandez Islands, Chile)
3 **Barau's Petrel**
4 **Murphy's Petrel**
5 **Murphy's Petrel** (at nest, Henderson Island, south Pacific Ocean)

PROVIDENCE or SOLANDER'S PETREL

Pterodroma solandri L 40 cm (16 in), WS 94 cm (37 in)
Medium-sized to large Pacific *Pterodroma*. Classified as Vulnerable.

IDENTIFICATION Steadier flight than Murphy's or Herald Petrel: in light winds, slow easy flaps and long glides. Fairly uniform greyish-brown, with distinct wedge-shaped tail. Must be distinguished from several other all-dark *Pterodroma*. Head and neck greyish-brown, with darker patch in front of eye; forehead, cheeks and chin much paler and white, recalling race *gouldi* of Great-winged Petrel, but scaled on forehead and chin (never with only throat white as Murphy's Petrel). Hooded effect from above and below. Mantle mottled slaty greyish-brown (much as Murphy's Petrel), back darker brownish-grey, uppertail-coverts dark brown; tail greyish-brown and wedge-shaped. Underparts with throat and upper breast greyish-brown (thus head darker than underparts, imparting hooded appearance); rest of underparts paler greyish-brown, and may show whitish tips on belly in worn plumage. Upperwing similar to Murphy's Petrel, but has even less pronounced 'M' mark: wings broad and long, dark slate-brown (darker than mantle), with primaries blacker with no white shafts. Underwing dark grey, with conspicuous whitish bases to primaries and greater primary coverts forming whitish underwing flash bisected by dark primary-covert tips (differs from Murphy's Petrel's 'silver flash', and quite well demarcated). Stout bill black, larger than on Murphy's, Kermadec and Herald Petrels; iris brown; legs and feet greyish-black. From race *gouldi* of Great-winged Petrel, which has similar face pattern, by overall lighter colour and lighter underwing. Murphy's Petrel is darker, with a dark underwing and indistinct 'M' on upperparts. Dark Kermadec and Herald Petrels have no grey on face, but both have pale primaries on underwing.

DISTRIBUTION AND STATUS Pacific Ocean. Breeds in winter on Lord Howe (c 27,000 breeding pairs representing some 96,000 birds, not 96,000 pairs as stated in del Hoyo), where some predation from mammals. Exterminated from Norfolk Island 200 years ago, by convicts, pigs and goats, but recently found breeding on nearby Philip Island. Subtropical and tropical south-western Pacific, with some dispersal to west and north Pacific and Bering Sea to edge of continental shelf, but rarely near shore (regular east of Japan; fewer Gulf of Alaska, offshore south California). Regular off east coast Australia, a feeding area for breeding birds. Accidental to New Zealand, with a few sightings in eastern Pacific.

GREAT-WINGED PETREL

Pterodroma macroptera L 41 cm (16 in), WS 97 cm (38 in)
Medium to large, almost circumpolar southern *Pterodroma*.

IDENTIFICATION Jizz and flight typical of genus. Flight strong and impetuous in strong winds, with typical *Pterodroma* pendulum progression; less bounding in calmer conditions. Feeds mainly at night. Rarely follows ships, but gathers at trawlers; otherwise generally solitary at sea. Plumage uniformly dark, with variably paler face depending on subspecies. *P. m. macroptera*: Head and neck blackish-brown, with slightly paler and greyer face extending from forehead and lores around base of bill to chin (merges into darker head); variable, some appearing dark-faced. Upperparts, including tail, uniform blackish-brown. Upperwing a similar uniform blackish-brown; in fresh plumage, may show silvery greater secondary coverts. Underwing blackish-brown, with primaries and secondaries paler greyish-black, but intensity variable with light conditions; leading edge of underwing generally darker than flight feathers. Underparts uniform blackish-brown. Bill blackish; iris dark brown; legs and feet black. *P. m. gouldi*: As nominate *macroptera*, but pale grey face more extensive and more conspicuous, extending further onto forehead and chin, and contrasting with dark stubby bill and darker head colour. Providence Petrel, which is similar in size, shape and flight, has greyer upperparts and more white on underwing. Dark Kermadec Petrel has whitish underwing, white on upperwing and slower flight. Dark Herald Petrel has more white on underwing, which also has white leading edge. Kerguelen Petrel is smaller, with different jizz and flight, and different underwing pattern, plus a hooded appearance to head. White-chinned Petrel is larger and browner.

DISTRIBUTION AND STATUS Subtropical, subantarctic and, more rarely, antarctic waters. *P. m. macroptera* breeds Tristan da Cunha group and Gough Island, Prince Edwards, Crozets, Kerguelen and Australia. *P. m. gouldi* breeds North Island, New Zealand. Ranges eastern south Atlantic, Indian Ocean, and Pacific Ocean east of New Zealand to 130°W, rarer south-west Atlantic, west coast South America; generally 30°S- 50°S. Regular off South Africa, Australia and New Zealand. Possible increase in Australian region over last 20 years as muttonbird-collecting has declined.

MAGENTA PETREL

Pterodroma magentae L c 38 cm (15 in), WS 102 cm (40 in)
Medium-sized, very rare Pacific *Pterodroma*, little known and rarely seen. Classified as Critical.

IDENTIFICATION Rarely seen at sea, even at Chatham Islands; not seen in day, and avoids land apart from when breeding. Typical *Pterodroma* flight. Solitary at sea; avoids ships. Plumage sooty-grey above, with dark head and dark underwing contrasting with white underparts. Much as Phoenix Petrel, or Atlantic Petrel with white undertail-coverts. Head, neck and upper breast sooty greyish-brown, appearing as dark hood sharply demarcated from white lower breast; paler whitish on face, with scaling on forehead from base of bill almost extending to eye, and whitish chin to level of gape; between these white facial areas is a small darker area in front of eye on lores. Upperparts uniform sooty greyish-brown as head, mantle with slightly paler fringes. Uppertail dark brown; tail slightly wedge-shaped. Dark of hood extends narrowly along breast sides to flanks; lower breast, belly and undertail-coverts white; undertail has thin dark border. Upperwing with flight feathers blackish-brown, dark brown wing-coverts fringed slightly paler; no visible 'M' mark across upperwings, although flight feathers have whitish inner webs. Underwing uniformly blackish, with suggestion of whitish on primaries, but no white on leading edge (armpit to carpal). Bill black; iris brown; legs pinkish, feet pink and black. From Soft-plumaged Petrel by larger size, bulkier jizz and larger bill; upperparts uniformly darker than on Soft-plumaged Petrel, with no 'M', different head and breast patterns, and underwing which lacks pale leading edge from wingpit to near carpal.

DISTRIBUTION AND STATUS Pacific Ocean. Breeds only on Chatham Islands, foraging east or south of Chathams; recent probable sight records west of Chile and near Mas Afuera and Mas a Tierra. Total population estimates vary from 45-70 birds to 100-150 birds with probably fewer than 10 pairs breeding (no chicks 1994). Nests in dense forest, which was cleared for pastoral development; remaining forest damaged by wind and introduced herbivores. Introduced predators (cats, rats, Wekas) common. Rediscovered 1978, formerly food for Maoris.

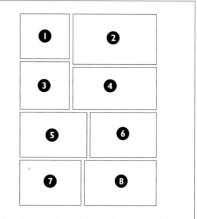

1 **Providence Petrel** (off Sydney, Australia)
2 **Providence Petrel** (off Sydney, Australia)
3 **Great-winged Petrel subspecies P. m. gouldi** (Australia, December)
4 **Great-winged Petrel subspecies P. m. gouldi** (at breeding site)
5 **Great-winged Petrel subspecies P. m. macroptera** (southern Indian Ocean)
6 **Magenta Petrel** (Chatham Islands)
7 **Magenta Petrel** (Chatham Islands)
8 **Magenta Petrel** (Chatham Islands)

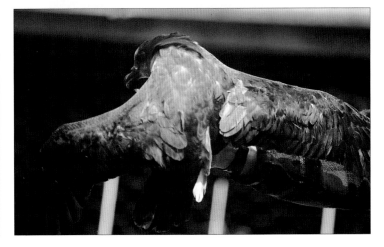

61

PETRELS

WHITE-HEADED PETREL

Pterodroma lessonii L 43 cm (17 in), WS 109 cm (43 in)

Large and striking, greyish, southern circumpolar *Pterodroma*, generally a bird of colder waters.

IDENTIFICATION Very strong, typical *Pterodroma* flight; briefly investigates ships. One of the most beautiful birds of the Southern Ocean, dark greyish above with contrasting white head, and white below with dark underwings. Forehead and forecrown white, merging into very light vermiculated grey hindcrown, nape and hindneck; grey extends variably onto sides of neck in pale grey half-collar which may almost join across upper throat; chin and throat white; distinctive black streak through eye, broadest in front of eye. At sea, head usually appears white with contrasting blackish eye-stripe – greyish collar generally visible on very close (or dark) birds. Mantle, scapulars and upper back medium pearly-grey; lower back and rump darker, brownish-grey; uppertail-coverts greyish, as mantle. Tail with central third greyish (as uppertail-coverts), sides whiter, with very thin white terminal band generally seen only on very close birds. Underparts white; undertail white to very pale grey. Upperwings darker than mantle, dark greyish-brown, with variable and indistinct blackish 'M' across upperwing joining across lower back and rump. Underwing dark greyish-black, darkest on wing-coverts; primaries and secondaries with silvery cast; whitish leading edge from wing join almost to carpal. Bill black; iris dark brown; legs and feet flesh-pink. From Soft-plumaged Petrel by larger size and larger, whiter head. Grey Petrel is larger, with grey head and undertail.

DISTRIBUTION AND STATUS Circumpolar in Southern Ocean, from Antarctic Continent to *c* 30°S. Rare South Africa; more numerous south Australia, New Zealand, South America. Most move north in winter. Not a common bird in south Atlantic. Breeds Crozets, Kerguelen (abundant), Auckland and Antipodes, Macquarie Island; may possibly breed on Prince Edwards and Campbell Island. Total population probably 100,000 breeding pairs; suffers some predation.

FEA'S PETREL

Pterodroma feae L 35 cm (14 in), WS 95 cm (37 in)

Medium-sized north Atlantic *Pterodroma*. Classified as Vulnerable.

IDENTIFICATION Flight generally low over surface, glides interspersed with six to eight rapid wingbeats; in higher winds direction becomes more semicircular, with higher banking and gliding, and wing shape becomes more angled back. Generally rests in small groups on the sea in calm weather, flying more often when windy, and can form feeding frenzies of 100-200 birds when food, usually tuna, becomes abundant. Greyish above, with darker head and 'M' mark across upperwings, and white below (no breastband), with contrasting dark

underwings. Forehead white, forecrown scaled darker, generally not extending above eye as paler supercilium; brownish-grey crown and upper nape merging into darker eye mask and lighter, greyer lower nape. Lower nape and hindneck unmarked pale grey, extending slightly to breast sides and enhancing darker and browner crown and eye mask. Mantle and back a shade darker than nape and hindneck, with light brownish feather edges; lower back and upper rump darker brownish-grey. Tail colour variable: generally greyish-white outer feathers with darker brownish-grey centre (some appear darker at sea), but constantly lighter than Soft-plumaged Petrel. Underparts white from forecrown to undertail-coverts; no breastband, although some show darker flecking at sides of foreneck and also on lower breast sides. Upperwing variable greyish-brown, with darker blackish-brown primaries and secondary coverts forming variable 'M' from wing tip to wing tip across lower back; some birds show darker secondary tips which isolate a paler wedge of grey on the secondaries between their tips and wing-coverts; greyish of mantle extends onto scapulars and inner wing-coverts. Underwing variable, generally dusky grey (can appear blackish at sea) with variable whitish central stripe; whitish inner leading edge from body, decreasing towards carpal joint. Bill black; iris brown; legs and feet pink and black.

DISTRIBUTION AND STATUS Subtropical north-east Atlantic. Breeds on four islands in the Cape Verdes (Fogo, Santo Antao, São Nicolau and São Tiago), with *c* 1,000 pairs; hunted for food and medicinal uses, and by mammals. Around 200 pairs breed on Bugio in the Desertas Special Protection Area. Sight records off eastern seaboard of USA and Britain and Ireland may indicate wide north Atlantic dispersal. Birds recently trapped in the Azores may prove to be a link between the other *Pterodroma* species on both sides of the north Atlantic.

ZINO'S PETREL

Pterodroma madeira L 32-33 cm (13 in), WS 83 cm (33 in)

Small to medium-sized north Atlantic *Pterodroma*, probably the Atlantic Ocean's rarest seabird. Classified as Critical.

IDENTIFICATION Identical in plumage to Fea's Petrel (see that species), but with structural and other differences. Zino and Zino (1986) state 'we have been unable to find any constant distinguishing feature in the plumage of either bird'. Structural differences between the two species are fully described in the above paper (see Selected Bibliography). Briefly, there is no overlap in weight, wing length or bill parameters. Thus, Zino's Petrel is a smaller and lighter bird with shorter wings and a shorter, lighter bill than Fea's Petrel. How, and in fact whether, these differences are detectable in birds at sea is perhaps a matter of individual interpretation. Zino and Zino state: 'However, despite the considerable difference in size between the Bugio and Madeira bird, we have

found it impossible to distinguish one from the other at sea'. Intense further study reiterates this conclusion (F. Zino pers. comm. 1996), and a 1995 British attempt at identification and separation of the three '*mollis* species' is contradictory and unreliable. From personal experience, the author suggests that specific identification may be possible if Zino's and Fea's Petrels are seen together (but even around Madeira this is unlikely); identifying isolated individuals with absolute certainty is, however, probably impossible on present knowledge.

DISTRIBUTION AND STATUS Subtropical north-east Atlantic Ocean. A very small population was known to breed on Madeira during 1903-09 (Schmitz). Single young (with down) were found in Funchal in 1940 and 1951. Not rediscovered breeding in Madeira until 1969, when eight birds and six eggs were found. A 1981 claim of 20 or so nests at a different locality has never been conclusively corroborated. In 1985 and 1986, rats were found at the original breeding site and no birds bred; poison was put down in 1987 but, while petrels returned, they did not breed successfully until 1989. In 1991 a new threat appeared: ten Zino's Petrels were found dead on the breeding ledges, killed by cats. Birds bred in 1992, fledging four young despite cats still being trapped. Eight young fledged in 1993, five in 1994, and four in 1995 (F. Zino *in litt.*). The 1996 population is estimated at 10+ pairs attempting to breed (max. 20 pairs), but again cats have been trapped at the site (F. Zino pers. comm. 1996). Distribution at sea and dispersal completely unknown, although some individuals have been ringed. Bones of Zino's Petrel have been found on Porto Santo. The continued survival of this species is now increasingly falling on the shoulders of one person.

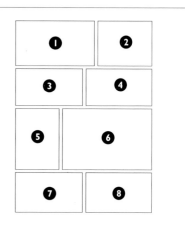

1 **White-headed Petrel** (off Tasmania, Australia)
2 **White-headed Petrel** (off Tasmania)
3 **[Presumed] Fea's Petrel** (off Madeira, August)
4 **[Presumed] Fea's Petrel** (off Madeira, August)
5 **[Presumed] Fea's Petrel** (off Bugio, August)
6 **Fea's Petrel** (burrow site, Bugio, off Madeira, July)
7 **Zino's Petrel** (Madeira, June)
8 **Zino's Petrel** (Madeira, July)

SOFT-PLUMAGED PETREL

Pterodroma mollis L 34 cm (13 in), WS 89 cm (35 in)
Medium-sized, almost circumpolar southern *Pterodroma*.

IDENTIFICATION Typical *Pterodroma* flight; occasionally follows ships. Mostly dark above and on underwings, and white below with dark breastband. Crown, nape and hindneck greyish-brown or slate-brown, extending over sides of neck and upper breast to form usually a continuous breastband; forehead white, usually scaled with darker feathers, and extending above eye as a narrow whitish supercilium; black patch before, around and below, and usually behind, eye. Lores, chin and throat white, isolated from remaining white underparts by breastband; undertail-coverts white. Greyish-brown of head merges into slate-grey of mantle and upper back (these with paler fringes in fresh plumage, becoming a browner grey when worn); tail slaty brownish-grey. Upperwing dark greyish-brown (darker than saddle), darker blackish-brown primaries and secondary coverts forming variable 'M' mark from wing tip to wing tip; intensity of pattern is light-dependent. Underwing variable, generally dusky grey (appearing blackish at a distance) with narrow whitish leading edge on inner wing from body almost to carpal joint; variable whitish central stripe on flight feathers with darker coverts, some tips of which may be white. Enigmatic variable dark morph rarely seen at sea or on breeding grounds, but occurs in south Atlantic and Indian Oceans: generally recalls Kerguelen Petrel, being wholly dark sooty-grey, perhaps with indistinct darker breastband, and less white on underwings; differences in jizz and flight should aid identification. Bill black; iris brown; legs and feet flesh-pink and black. Atlantic Ocean birds (nominate *mollis*) have a narrower breastband, greyer mantle, and whiter outer tail feathers than Indian Ocean birds (*dubia*), which also have more extensive facial marks. Antipodes birds probably same as nominate *mollis*.

DISTRIBUTION AND STATUS South Atlantic, Indian and west Pacific Oceans. Breeds Tristan da Cunha group and Gough Island (nominate *mollis*); Prince Edwards (thousands), Crozets (tens of thousands) and Kerguelen (all *dubia*), probably also Amsterdam and Macquarie Islands; and Antipodes Islands.

ATLANTIC PETREL

Pterodroma incerta L 43 cm (17 in), WS 104 cm (41 in)
Large, stocky, long-winged Atlantic *Pterodroma*, the only one endemic to south Atlantic. Not well studied. Classified as Vulnerable.

IDENTIFICATION A large *Pterodroma* with strong and fast flight, especially in rough weather, with a tendency to flap once or twice at peaks of glides (unlike most *Pterodroma*). Investigates ships at sea, but not a persistent ship-follower. Plumage uniformly dark brown above and on upper breast, with contrasting white lower breast and belly and brown ventral region. Head and upper breast rich dark brown, tending to appear slightly greyer on nape and chin and often with slightly darker suborbital patch, but this dependent on light conditions. Upperparts from hindneck to tail uniform rich dark brown, perhaps appearing a shade darker on rump. (Many birds in worn plumage show paler and greyer nape and hindneck, almost forming whitish collar in extreme examples; similarly, some show paler and greyer forehead, chin and throat almost joining white underparts and enhancing dark suborbital patch; upperparts and upperwing-coverts may also show paler edges.) Underparts white, cleanly demarcated from brown upper breast at level of leading edge of wing; vent, undertail-coverts and undertail brown, enhancing comparatively long-tailed appearance. Upperwing rich dark brown, uniform with mantle; primaries slightly darker, but no 'M' mark across wings and back. Underwing brown, primaries slightly paler and greyer, but no definable pale central stripe. Bill black; iris brown; legs and feet pink, distally blackish.

DISTRIBUTION AND STATUS South Atlantic Ocean, occasionally into Indian Ocean. Breeds in winter only at Tristan da Cunha group (a few hundred pairs) and Gough Island (thousands of pairs). Generally 50°S-20°S in south Atlantic, with a few recorded off Cape Horn, one record off Brazil, and regularly to 20°S off south-western Africa. Most breeding birds appear to disperse west towards South America. Rare in Indian Ocean, generally single birds (numerous reports in the literature are more probably of Soft-plumaged Petrel); vagrant Red Sea at Eilat (Israel).

BERMUDA PETREL

Pterodroma cahow L 38 cm (15 in), WS 89 cm (35 in)
Medium-sized, long-winged *Pterodroma*, restricted to Bermuda and surrounding seas. Classified as Endangered.

IDENTIFICATION Flight typical of *Pterodroma*; does not follow ships. Dark above, with darker cap, and white below with variable breastband. Crown, nape and hindneck blackish-brown, joining dark suborbital patch on ear-coverts to form dark cap; forehead white with some dark scaling, extending narrowly over eye as weak supercilium; lores, cheeks, chin and throat white. Upperparts dark greyish-brown, shading to blackish on rump; pale uppertail-coverts may form narrow whitish band. Tail blackish, comparatively longer than on Soft-plumaged Petrel. Underparts white, with dusky sides to upper breast which may form complete breastband; tip of undertail dark. Upperwing blackish-grey, coverts with paler edges, but no visible 'M' mark. Underwing white, with narrow blackish trailing edge widening at wing tip (primaries) and extending narrowly onto leading edge; some may show short diagonal bar from carpal joint inwards towards centre of wing across wing-coverts. Bill black; iris blackish-brown; legs and feet whitish-pink, distally black. Resembles Black-capped Petrel, but slightly smaller, and upperparts lack white hindcollar and white rump.

DISTRIBUTION AND STATUS Bermuda and presumably surrounding seas. Thought extinct for 300 years, then rediscovered in 1935, followed by 18 pairs found breeding on Nonsuch Island in 1951. Intensive management since 1961 has resulted in a slow but steady increase to 32 pairs in 1982, 44 breeding pairs in 1993 and 45 breeding pairs in 1994. Pelagic range unknown, but absent from colonies from May to October.

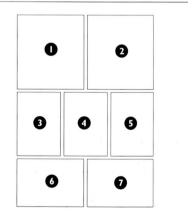

1 **Soft-plumaged Petrel** (south Atlantic Ocean)
2 **Soft-plumaged Petrel** (south Atlantic Ocean)
3 **Atlantic Petrel** (south Atlantic Ocean, July)
4 **Atlantic Petrel** (underparts, worn plumage, south Atlantic Ocean)
5 **Atlantic Petrel** (upperparts, worn plumage, off Uruguay)
6 **Bermuda Petrel** (juvenile, Nonsuch Island)
7 **Bermuda Petrel** (juvenile, Nonsuch Island)

BLACK-CAPPED PETREL

Pterodroma hasitata L 40 cm (16 in), WS 95 cm (37 in)

Large, long-winged Caribbean *Pterodroma*. Classified as Endangered.

IDENTIFICATION Typical *Pterodroma* flight; does not follow ships. Springs clear of water when flushed from sea surface. Plumage dark above, with small blackish cap, variable white hindneck and white rump, and white below, with blackish underwing border and bar along secondary coverts. Upper crown and nape blackish-brown, joining blackish suborbital patch on ear-coverts to form small but distinct black cap; forehead, lores, chin and throat white. Hindneck white. Upperparts dark brown, shading to blackish on lower back; rump and uppertail-coverts white, forming (usually) broad 'U' across rump. Tail blackish-brown. Underparts white, with narrow dark partial collar at sides of upper breast; tip of undertail blackish. Upperwing blackish-brown, primaries and secondaries slightly darker, but no visible 'M' mark. Underwing white, with blackish trailing edge widening at wing tip (primaries) and extending onto leading edge, widening at carpal joint and extending diagonally inwards towards centre of wing across secondary coverts. Bill black; iris blackish-brown; legs and feet pinkish-white, distally black. From Bermuda Petrel by larger size, heavier bill, white hindcollar and white rump, browner cap and darker brown upperparts, but note that some atypical birds have reduced or no white hindcollar and/or white rump; the darkest examples thus resemble Bermuda Petrel, and may be indistinguishable at sea. The all-dark Jamaican Petrel (*P. h. caribbaea*), considered to be a melanistic race of Black-capped, was plentiful 200 years ago but is now considered extinct, although it may conceivably survive in the Blue and John Crow Mountains of north-eastern Jamaica.

DISTRIBUTION AND STATUS Caribbean, where formerly widespread, but now known to breed only on Haiti, Dominican Republic, Cuba, and probably Dominica in Windward Islands. Total population a few thousand pairs (undiscovered colonies probably still exist). Predation by introduced mammals and human exploitation for food remain threats. Dispersal south to Dutch Antilles (and possibly Brazil) and north to Atlantic seaboard of USA along Gulf Stream; regular but uncommon off USA – occasionally prone to displacement by hurricanes. One recently recorded at sea in north-east Atlantic; one found inland in Norfolk, England (1850).

BLUE PETREL

Halobaena caerulea L 29 cm (11 in), WS 62 cm (24 in)

Small, prion-like, circumpolar petrel of Southern Ocean.

IDENTIFICATION Flight prion-like in light winds, though with more frequent gliding on bowed wings; in stronger winds, becomes more

Pterodroma-like. Gregarious, often with prions; occasionally follows ships. Plumage bluish-grey above, black-capped and white-faced, with dark 'M', and diagnostic white tip to grey tail. Lores, forehead and forecrown to eye or just above eye white, joining with white chin and throat and extending upwards behind ear-coverts; crown, nape, suborbital patch and ear-coverts dark blackish-grey, forming neat black cap. Hindneck bluish-grey, extending to sides of neck and sides of upper breast to form incomplete dark collar. Mantle, back, rump and uppertail-coverts bluish-grey, slightly darker on lower back; inner scapulars tipped white. Tail noticeably square; bluish-grey with narrow white on outer feathers, narrow blackish-grey subterminal band and wider, more conspicuous white tip (very visible at sea). Underparts white, greyish undertail lacking blackish tip or central blackish wedge of various prion species. Upperwing mainly bluish-grey; outer four primaries, primary coverts and greater coverts darker, forming narrow blackish-brown 'M' from wing tip to wing tip, joining across lower back (with wear, 'M' mark becomes browner and thus less distinct); trailing half of upperwing behind 'M' paler grey than rest of upperwing and mantle. Underwing generally white with narrow and indistinct slightly darker greyish border, often irregular. Bill black; iris blackish-brown; legs and feet bluish-grey with paler webs. Distinguished from prions by white forehead, dark cap and half-collar, more contrasting upperparts, white tip to tail.

DISTRIBUTION AND STATUS Circumpolar in Southern Ocean from pack ice north to *c* 30°S, but to *c* 20°S off Peru. Regular but uncommon South America, South Africa, Australia and New Zealand. Breeds subantarctic islands: Diego Ramirez, Chile (*c* 2 million birds), various islands around Cape Horn, South Georgia (70,000 pairs), Prince Edwards (tens of thousands), Crozets (tens of thousands), Kerguelen (*c* 200,000 pairs) and Macquarie Island (500-600 pairs); total population several million birds. Subject to predation by introduced mammals, and susceptible to 'wrecks' in bad weather.

BROAD-BILLED PRION

Pachyptila vittata L 28 cm (11 in), WS 61 cm (24 in)

Largest prion, found around Subtropical Convergence in New Zealand and south Atlantic Ocean.

IDENTIFICATION Flight generally slower and with more gliding than that of other prions. Very gregarious; generally not a frequent ship-follower. Blue-grey above, with 'M' mark and dark tip to tail, dark-headed appearance and large blackish bill. Forehead, crown and nape bluish-grey, slightly darker than hindneck; short and narrow white supercilium above and behind eye; blackish-grey suborbital patch from in front of eye to ear-coverts; chin and throat white. Hindneck bluish-grey, extending to sides of neck and sides of upper breast to form conspicuous

partial collar, which may become complete. Mantle, back, rump and uppertail-coverts bluish-grey, darker on lower back; scapulars with narrow white tips. Tail bluish-grey, with narrow black terminal band not extending to outer feathers. Underparts white. Undertail white with blackish central streak. Upperwing mainly bluish-grey, with blackish outer primaries, primary coverts and inner wing-coverts forming 'M' from wing tip to wing tip, joining across lower back; inner primaries and secondaries behind 'M' noticeably paler grey than rest of upperparts. Underwing white with indistinct narrow greyish trailing edge. Huge, broad and deep 'duck-like' bill, appearing black at sea; iris dark brown; legs and feet bluish with cream-flesh webs. Large size, large black bill, large head with steep forehead, dark-headed appearance, partial collar and narrow dark tail band help separate it from other prions.

DISTRIBUTION AND STATUS Mainly near Subtropical Convergence; may reach subantarctic and tropical waters outside breeding season. Breeds New Zealand islands (Stewart, Foveaux Straits, Snares, Chatham Islands) and Tristan da Cunha group. Total population several hundred thousand birds (abundant at Gough Island). Some predation by introduced mammals and skuas. In New Zealand, some birds remain all year and others disperse to Tasman Sea, but rarely Australia; rare south of Subtropical Convergence in New Zealand. In south Atlantic, some remain all year, while others disperse to 10°S in Atlantic off South Africa and into western Indian Ocean. Vagrants to Falkland Islands, Madagascar and Réunion.

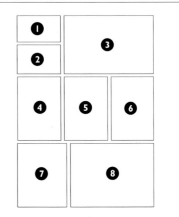

1 **Black-capped Petrel** (off North Carolina, USA, August)
2 **Black-capped Petrel** (Atlantic Ocean, off Georgia, USA)
3 **Blue Petrel**
4 **Blue Petrel** (at sea off Falkland Islands, December)
5 **Blue Petrel** (southern Indian Ocean)
6 **Broad-billed Prion** (at sea off south Australia, October)
7 **Broad-billed Prion** (at nest site, Southeast Island, New Zealand, September)
8 **Broad-billed Prion** (at nest site, Mangere Island, Chatham Islands, December)

SALVIN'S PRION

Pachyptila salvini L 28 cm (11 in), WS 57 cm (22 in)

Medium-sized prion of the Indian Ocean.

IDENTIFICATION Flight similar to that of Antarctic Prion, and plumage almost identical. Generally indistinguishable from Antarctic at sea, but with less grey on sides of breast; shorter wingspan than either Broad-billed or Antarctic Prion. Forehead, crown and nape bluish-grey, slightly darker than hindneck; short and narrow white supercilium; grey to dark grey suborbital patch from in front of eye to ear-coverts; chin and throat white. Hindneck bluish-grey, extending to sides of neck and sides of upper breast as partial collar (less apparent than on either Broad-billed or Antarctic Prion). Mantle, back, rump and uppertail-coverts light bluish-grey, darker on lower back. Tail light grey, with narrow black terminal band not extending to outer feathers. Underparts white, undertail with blackish central streak. Upperwing mainly bluish-grey, with blackish outer primaries, primary coverts and inner wing-coverts forming 'M' mark from wing tip to wing tip, joining across lower back; inner primaries and secondaries behind 'M' noticeably paler grey than rest of upperparts. Underwing white with indistinct narrow greyish trailing edge. Bill bluish with some black, less robust than that of Broad-billed Prion but longer and broader than Antarctic Prion's; iris dark brown; legs and feet bluish with creamy-flesh webs.

DISTRIBUTION AND STATUS South Indian Ocean, from Africa to Australia, Tasman Sea and New Zealand. *P. s. salvini* breeds Prince Edwards (hundreds of thousands), Crozets (six to eight million pairs); *P. s. macgillivrayi* (previously considered a subspecies of Broad-billed Prion) at St Paul and Amsterdam (a few pairs, now reduced by rats and cats). At Crozets, Est Island is predator free and although Cochons has cats they cannot enter breeding burrows. Subantarctic waters, outside breeding season extending to subtropics off Africa, Australia and New Zealand. Pelagic distribution not well known owing to difficulties of identification at sea. Not recorded South America, Atlantic Ocean or south Pacific Ocean (excluding New Zealand).

ANTARCTIC PRION

Pachyptila desolata L 27 cm (11 in), WS 61 cm (24 in)

Medium-sized prion of the Southern Ocean.

IDENTIFICATION Flight erratic, glides interspersed with rapid wingbeats, wings generally bowed. Highly gregarious, often feeding in thousands; generally not a frequent ship-follower. Very similar to Broad-billed and Salvin's Prions, but with marginally more extensive partial collar; bill smaller than Broad-billed Prion's, appearing bluish at sea. Forehead, crown and nape bluish-grey, slightly darker than hindneck; short and narrow white supercilium

(varies geographically); blackish-grey suborbital patch from in front of eye to ear-coverts; chin and throat white. Hindneck bluish-grey, extending to sides of neck and sides of upper breast to form conspicuous partial collar. Mantle, back, rump and uppertail-coverts bluish-grey, darker on lower back; scapulars have narrow white tips. Tail bluish-grey, with narrow black terminal band not extending to outer feathers. Underparts white, undertail with blackish central streak. Upperwing mainly bluish-grey, with blackish outer primaries, primary coverts and inner wing-coverts forming 'M' mark from wing tip to wing tip, joining across lower back; inner primaries and secondaries behind 'M' noticeably paler grey than rest of upperparts. Underwing white with indistinct narrow greyish trailing edge. Bill mainly pale blue, less robust than Broad-billed Prion's; iris dark brown; legs and feet bluish with creamy-flesh webs. From Broad-billed Prion by smaller size and smaller, paler head, smaller bluish (not black) bill, and possibly longer supercilium enhancing paler-faced appearance. Probably not reliably distinguishable from Salvin's Prion at sea.

DISTRIBUTION AND STATUS Most southerly prion. Almost circumpolar, but fewer in southern central Pacific. Breeds antarctic and subantarctic islands: South Georgia (22 million pairs, breeding in rat-free areas), South Sandwich (over 10,000 pairs), South Orkneys (over 100,000 pairs), Elephant Island (440 pairs), Crozets (hundreds of pairs), Kerguelen (2-3 million pairs), Heard Island (10,000 pairs), Macquarie (49,000 pairs) and Auckland Islands (100,000-1 million pairs). Threatened by krill-harvesting, introduced mammalian predators, and some ingestion of plastic. Ranges from pack ice to 40°S, but further north in subtropics off South Africa, Australia and South America in non-breeding season. Reaches 12°S off Peru and 24°S off Brazil.

SLENDER-BILLED or NARROW-BILLED PRION

Pachyptila belcheri L 26 cm (10 in), WS 56 cm (22 in)

Small Southern Ocean prion.

IDENTIFICATION Flight generally fast and erratic, with rapid wingbeats between short glides, usually low over surface. Not a frequent ship-follower, and less gregarious than other prions. Pale bluish-grey above, with indistinct 'M' mark and narrow black tail tip, thin bluish bill; small, comparatively pale head. Forehead, crown and hindneck uniform pale bluish-grey; lores and supercilium whiter, broader and longer than on any other prion, enhancing pale-headed appearance and contrasting with dark bluish-grey suborbital stripe from in front of eye to ear-coverts; chin and throat white. Bluish-grey of hindneck extends onto sides of neck and upper breast sides as a partial collar, but can be absent. Mantle, back, rump and uppertail-coverts pale bluish-grey, darker on lower back; scapulars narrowly tipped white.

Tail pale bluish-grey, with narrow black tip not extending to whitish or pale grey tail sides. Underparts white, with blackish central streak on undertail. Upperwing mainly pale bluish-grey, with outer primaries, primary coverts and inner wing-coverts forming blackish but comparatively pale 'M' mark from wing tip to wing tip, joining across lower back; inner primaries and secondaries behind 'M' paler grey than rest of upperparts. Underwing white with indistinct narrow greyish trailing edge. Bill pale blue and blackish, very slender at base; iris dark brown; legs and feet bluish with creamy-flesh webs. From all other prions by combination of pale face, broad supercilium, pale upperparts with indistinct 'M', narrow tail band, and undertail pattern.

DISTRIBUTION AND STATUS Distribution not well known, probably circumpolar in subantarctic and antarctic waters south to pack ice, ranging north to c 30°S (or further) in non-breeding season. Breeds on islands between Subtropical and Subantarctic Convergences in Indian, Atlantic and Pacific Oceans: Isla Noir (southern Chile) and possibly other islands off Tierra del Fuego, Falklands (c 1 million pairs), Crozets (tens of pairs), Kerguelen (c 1 million pairs), and possibly Macquarie and South Georgia. Threatened by introduced mammals. Regular off Chile, Peru (to c 15°S), Argentina, Australia; more numerous North Island of New Zealand than South Island. Falkland Islands population disperses west; Indian Ocean population east. Rare off South Africa, but vagrant to Java.

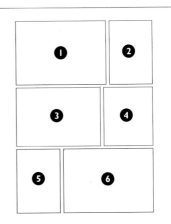

1 **Salvin's Prion** (flock, Crozet Islands, Indian Ocean)
2 **Antarctic Prion** (off Macquarie Island, January)
3 **Antarctic Prion** (Signy Island)
4 **Slender-billed Prion** (South Georgia, December)
5 **Slender-billed Prion** (South Georgia, December)
6 **Slender-billed Prion** (at nest site, Falkland Islands)

FAIRY PRION

Pachyptila turtur L 25 cm (10 in), WS 58 cm (23 in)
Smallest prion, probably circumpolar in Southern Ocean.

IDENTIFICATION Generally flies very close to surface, with rapid changes of direction. Gregarious, but not a ship-follower. Plumage bluish-grey above, with 'M' mark and prominent broad black tail band, pale head lacking dark contrasts. Forehead, crown and hindneck pale blue-grey; lores and supercilium to ear-coverts white, merging into crown; ill-defined dusky grey suborbital patch merging into grey of lower ear-coverts; chin and throat white. Blue-grey of hindneck extends onto sides of neck and sides of upper breast as short partial collar. Mantle, back, rump and uppertail-coverts pale bluish-grey, darker on lower back; narrow white tips to scapulars. Tail pale bluish-grey with broad blackish terminal band, outer feathers paler grey. Underparts white, undertail with blackish tip. Upperwing mainly pale bluish-grey, with darker outer primaries, primary coverts and inner wing-coverts forming blackish 'M' mark from wing tip to wing tip, joining across lower back; inner primaries and secondaries behind 'M' paler grey than rest of upperparts. Underwing white with indistinct greyish trailing edge. Bill short and stubby, pale blue and black; iris dark brown; legs and feet bluish with creamy-flesh webs. From Fulmar Prion by lighter upperparts, less distinct 'M' mark, narrower black tail band.

DISTRIBUTION AND STATUS Pelagic distribution not well known; probably circumpolar, moving to subtropical seas in non-breeding season, especially Indian Ocean, south-east Australia and New Zealand. New Zealand birds present all year. Breeds Falklands (*c* 3,000 pairs), South Georgia (several hundred pairs), Prince Edwards (thousands of pairs), Crozets (tens of thousands of pairs), St Paul ('a dozen burrows'), Kerguelen (1,000-10,000 pairs), Australia (not quantified, but many sites in Victoria and Tasmania), New Zealand and offshore islands (*c* 1 million pairs), and also present on Macquarie and Heard Islands. Some colonies suffer predation by introduced mammals. Rare vagrant to South Africa (eight beached and two sightings), Namibia and South America.

FULMAR PRION

Pachyptila crassirostris L 28 cm (11 in), WS 58 cm (23 in)
A rare, little-known and localized prion of subantarctic waters.

IDENTIFICATION Habits as those of Fairy Prion, but with characteristic 'loop-the-loop' flight manoeuvres high in the air. Plumage bluish-grey above, pale-headed, with 'M' mark and broad black tail band. Forehead mottled white and grey, merging into light grey crown and hindneck; narrow white supercilium extending behind eye; indistinct narrow greyish-black suborbital patch merging into greyish ear-coverts; lores, chin and throat white. Hindneck light grey, this extending marginally to sides of neck and sides of upper breast. Mantle, back, rump and uppertail-coverts pale bluish-grey, darker on lower back. Tail pale bluish-grey with broad blackish terminal band, latter the widest of any prion. Underparts white, occasionally with pale greyish wash; undertail white with blackish tip. Upperwing mainly pale bluish-grey, with darker outer primaries, primary coverts and inner wing-coverts forming blackish 'M' mark from wing tip to wing tip, joining across lower back; inner primaries and secondaries behind 'M' slightly paler than rest of upperparts. Underwing mainly white, with greyish wash towards trailing edge. Bill more robust than Fairy Prion's, pale grey and greyish-black; iris dark brown; legs and feet bluish with lighter webs. Doubtfully distinguished from Fairy Prion at sea by paler face and upperparts, more distinct 'M' mark, broader blackish tail band and bigger bill; probably best identified by distinctive looping flight.

DISTRIBUTION AND STATUS Distribution at sea little known, owing to difficulty of identification. Breeds New Zealand subantarctic islands and thought to remain near breeding areas all year; has been recorded 1,660 km ESE of Chatham Islands, most easterly record to date. No acceptable Australian records, and the least common prion in New Zealand. Not recorded south Atlantic or South America. Breeds Heard (1,000-10,000 pairs), Auckland (1,000-5,000 pairs), Snares (1,000-5,000 pairs), Chathams (1,000-5,000 pairs), Bounty Island (76,000 pairs). Total New Zealand population *c* 90,000 pairs. Unusual in visiting nesting sites in daytime, only prion to do so.

BULWER'S PETREL

Bulweria bulwerii L 26 cm (10 in), WS 67 cm (26 in)
Small, all-dark, tropical petrel with characteristic long-winged and long-tailed jizz.

IDENTIFICATION Characteristic jizz, with long wings generally held well forward and appearing set well to fore on body, accentuated by small head and bill; long tail is folded to a narrow point in normal flight, the wedge shape only occasionally noticed. In calm conditions flight is purposeful and direct, with a few wingbeats followed by a short glide; in stronger winds wings become more angled, with more buoyant and erratic flight, sometimes developing into rapid changes of direction and zigzagging more characteristic of some *Pterodroma*; rarely more than 2-3 m above sea surface. Buoyant flight, with wings almost acting as hydrofoils, correlates with having the lowest wing loading of any tubenose. Not particularly gregarious at sea; will rest on the sea; generally not a ship-follower. Whole plumage sooty-brown, becoming paler and greyer on lores, chin and upper throat (not normally visible on birds at sea). Upperwing sooty-brown, with paler diagonal bar across inner wing-coverts usually visible at up to *c* 250 m; wing bar is greyish-brown when fresh but fades to pale buffish-white, and broadens towards the carpal joint. Bill black; iris dark brown; legs and feet pinkish with darker webs. Dark-morph Wedge-tailed Shearwater is larger and broader-winged, with shearwater flap-and-glide flight. Other dark shearwaters are larger than Bulwer's Petrel, with different jizz and flight. Jouanin's Petrel is larger and heavier, with larger head, bigger bill, broader wings and shorter, broader tail, but can show similar pale wing bar, and also (*contra* Harrison) similar low flight.

DISTRIBUTION AND STATUS Tropical and subtropical Atlantic, Indian and Pacific Oceans. Breeds in Atlantic on Azores, Madeira, Desertas, Salvages, Canary Islands, Cape Verde Islands (total Atlantic population tens of thousands of breeding pairs); and in Pacific off eastern China, formerly Taiwan, Ryukyus, Izus, Bonin, most islands in Hawaiian group (perhaps 400,000 birds), Phoenix and Marquesas (total Pacific population several hundred thousand pairs). Some populations suffer from human and mammalian predation (eg Midway and Desertas). Post-breeding dispersal not well known, but probably within subtropical and tropical seas; some Pacific birds may enter Indian Ocean. Vagrants South Africa, Ireland, Britain, Australia; not recorded New Zealand.

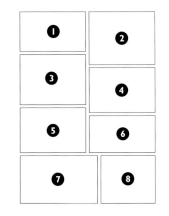

1 **Fairy Prion** (off Port Macdonnell, South Australia, June)
2 **Fairy Prion**
3 **Fairy Prion** (Victoria, Australia, November)
4 **Fairy Prion** (pair at nest cavity, Mangere Island, Chatham Islands, November)
5 **Fulmar Prion** (pair Bounty Islands)
6 **Fulmar Prion** (Bounty Islands)
7 **Bulwer's Petrel** (Grand Salvage Island)
8 **Bulwer's Petrel**

JOUANIN'S PETREL

Bulweria fallax L 31 cm (12 in), WS 79 cm (31 in)

Small to medium-sized, all-dark petrel of Indian Ocean.

IDENTIFICATION Flight is variable with wind speed, being generally *Pterodroma*-like, but even in strong winds does not fly more than 8 m above the sea surface (*contra* Harrison). Not a ship-follower. In all respects recalls a big Bulwer's Petrel; must also be distinguished from Wedge-tailed Shearwater. Whole plumage sooty blackish-brown, some with paler and greyer chin and forehead (more noticeable than on Bulwer's Petrel). In fresh plumage upperwing appears uniform, but with wear develops a variable paler area across wing-coverts; this may appear as a paler bar, much as on Bulwer's Petrel, or a line of distinct pale spots. Bill black; iris brown; legs and feet pink with darker tips. From Bulwer's Petrel by larger size and heavier appearance, larger head, bigger bill, shorter and comparatively broader tail. Distant birds distinguished from Wedge-tailed Shearwater by jizz and structure, flight, and also dark bill usually held downwards, whereas Wedge-tailed Shearwater has longer, more slender, pale bill usually held more horizontal.

DISTRIBUTION AND STATUS Indian Ocean. Not a well-known species (described in 1955). May breed regularly in the interior desert of Oman, where the only nest to date has been found, or on offshore islands (eg Kuria Muria); breeding could be timed to coincide with the peak of the south-west monsoon. Recorded at sea in southern Red Sea, Gulf of Aden, Arabian Sea, southwards to Kenya and the Mozambique Channel. Recently shown to disperse eastwards in tropical waters south of India and Sri Lanka east as far as Sumatra. Vagrants: three off Italy (1953) possibly ship-assisted, but one in Hawaii much more difficult to explain.

WHITE-CHINNED PETREL

Procellaria aequinoctialis L 55 cm (22 in), WS 140 cm (55 in)

A surprisingly large and heavily built, dark blackish-brown petrel with circumpolar distribution in the Southern Ocean.

IDENTIFICATION The largest *Procellaria*, seen regularly from the coast off South Africa. Flight purposeful and strong, with slow wingbeats interspersed with long periods of gliding, often soaring in strong winds well above surface (reminiscent of albatrosses). Swims well, and will dive for food with wings outstretched; congregates around trawlers, competing for food, and habitually follows ships for long periods. Plumage uniformly dark but for variable white chin and upper throat, with a large pale bill. Head and neck blackish-brown, with variable white on chin and occasionally upper throat (totally absent on some). Although the white head markings on *P. a. conspicillata* are somewhat variable in extent, occasional birds of nominate *P. a. aequinoctialis* show more variable symmetrical or asymmetrical white markings on the head and occasionally on the wings. Some of these may appear similar to typical *P. a. conspicillata* and such birds should be identified carefully. Upperparts blackish-brown, with lighter brownish tips to mantle and back visible at close range; tail slightly darker blackish-brown (tips of feet can project slightly beyond tail). Underparts blackish-brown, more uniform and a shade lighter than upperparts. Upperwing blackish-brown as upperparts, with lighter brownish tips to scapulars and inner wing-coverts visible at close range; primaries generally appear slightly blacker at sea than rest of upperwing, but can show whitish shafts. Underwing-coverts blackish-brown as underparts, primaries and secondaries paler and greyer and appearing silvery (the intensity of which is light-dependent). Bill large and powerful, variable from greenish-horn to pale ivory in colour, generally appearing whitish at sea; iris blackish-brown; legs and feet blackish. For differences from Westland Petrel, see that species. *P. a. conspicillata* has more extensive white on head, generally encircling eye.

DISTRIBUTION AND STATUS Circumpolar in Southern Ocean, generally at 60°S-30°S. Breeds South Georgia (2 million pairs), Falklands, Tristan da Cunha group (100 pairs); *P. a. conspicillata* on Inaccessible, 1,000 pairs; *P. a. aequinoctalis*, Prince Edwards (tens of thousands), Crozets (tens of thousands), Kerguelen (hundreds of thousands), Antipodes, Auckland and Campbell Islands (10,000-50,000 pairs), also possibly Gough Island and Macquarie Island. Total population several million birds. Now known to be suffering large fatalities from long-line fishing, where birds can gather in thousands and drown by day and by night. Mainly subantarctic zone in breeding season, with fewer to edge of pack ice. In non-breeding season northward dispersal to subtropical upwellings, especially South America (to 6°N in Humboldt Current), South Africa (to c 12°N in Benguela Current), southern Australia and around New Zealand.

PARKINSON'S or BLACK PETREL

Procellaria parkinsoni L 46 cm (18 in), WS 115 cm (45 in)

Medium-sized, stocky, uniformly dark New Zealand petrel with dark-tipped pale bill. Classified as Vulnerable.

IDENTIFICATION The smallest *Procellaria*. Flight similar to that of Westland and White-chinned Petrels, perhaps easier and less laboured; in stronger winds becomes more albatross-like, with higher banking and soaring. Swims well; will dive for food. Generally solitary at sea in non-breeding season, more gregarious when breeding; will follow ships, and attends trawlers. Not seen from land. Jizz and plumage similar to Westland Petrel, but slighter, with more slender wings. Head and neck blackish-brown, can appear darker than rest of plumage.

Upperparts and uppertail blackish-brown. Underparts blackish-brown, slightly paler than upperparts. Upperwing blackish-brown as upperparts; when fresh, may have silvery appearance. Underwing-coverts blackish-brown, with paler greyish primaries and secondaries giving silvery appearance to trailing edge (as on Westland and White-chinned Petrels). With wear, whole plumage becomes browner. Bill short and compact, yellowish-horn (appearing whitish at a distance) with blackish tip; iris dark brown; legs and feet black. From Westland Petrel by smaller size, thinner neck, shorter and thinner wings, less laboured flight, smaller bill.

DISTRIBUTION AND STATUS Pacific Ocean. Breeds New Zealand: Great and Little Barrier Islands (Hauraki Gulf, North Island) at high altitude in forest; formerly bred on mainland New Zealand. Population 3,000-4,000 birds. Little interference from introduced rats and cats on Great Barrier, and although cats were eliminated from Little Barrier in 1980, some birds there may still be taken by Maoris for food. Now suffering fatalities at sea from long-line fishing. In breeding season (austral summer, unlike Westland Petrel) frequents subtropical waters around North Island and generally eastwards, but ranges into Tasman Sea and probably regular off east coast of Australia. After breeding, dispersal into eastern tropical Pacific Ocean (March to November) off Mexico, Central America and Ecuador. Seen at sea near Galapagos Islands.

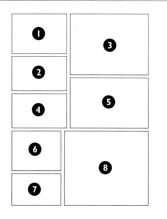

1 **Jouanin's Petrel** (off Socotra Island, Arabian Sea, Indian Ocean)
2 **Jouanin's Petrel** (Arabian Sea, Indian Ocean, July)
3 **White-chinned Petrel** (at breeding site, Falkland Islands)
4 **White-chinned Petrel subspecies *P. a. conspicillata*** (Inaccessible Island)
5 **White-chinned Petrel** (off Tierra del Fuego, November)
6 **White-chinned Petrel** (off South Africa)
7 **Parkinson's Petrel** (off Sydney, Australia, October)
8 **Parkinson's Petrel** (Great Barrier Island, New Zealand, March)

PETRELS & SHEARWATERS

WESTLAND PETREL

Procellaria westlandica L 51 cm (20 in), WS 137 cm (54 in)

A large and heavily built, all-dark New Zealand petrel with dark-tipped creamy-white bill. Classified as Vulnerable.

IDENTIFICATION Flight as that of White-chinned Petrel. Swims well, and will dive for food. Generally solitary at sea in non-breeding season, but flocks gather and compete for food around trawlers in the breeding season. Will follow ships (*contra* Harrison). Plumage dark all over. Head and neck blackish-brown, can appear darker than rest of plumage, imparting hooded effect. Upperparts blackish-brown, with slightly paler tips visible at close range; tail blackish-brown. Underparts blackish-brown, much as upperparts. Upperwing blackish-brown as upperparts, with lighter brownish tips to scapulars and inner wing-coverts, primaries generally slightly darker; some primary coverts may show whitish shaft streaks. Underwing-coverts blackish-brown as underparts, with primaries and secondaries paler and greyer, appearing silvery (the intensity of which is light-dependent): pattern very similar to that of White-chinned. Bill large, creamy-coloured with black tip; iris dark brown; legs and feet blackish. From White-chinned by dark bill tip; White-chinned lacking the white chin is probably indistinguishable from Westland Petrel unless the bill is well seen, since size, structure and flight very similar. From smaller Parkinson's Petrel by bulkier jizz, broader wings giving more laboured flight, thicker neck and larger, heavier bill.

DISTRIBUTION AND STATUS Pacific Ocean. Breeds colonially (in winter) in dense forest in Punakaiki region, west coast of South Island, New Zealand. Increasing population now estimated at 20,000 birds; may have quadrupled in the last 30 years, linked to increased trawler offal within 200 km of breeding colonies. Rafts gather offshore at dusk, before flying to colonies. Some predation by introduced mammals, and fed on by man until 1974. During breeding season (March-December) generally around New Zealand continental-shelf waters north of Subtropical Convergence; can reach south to subantarctic waters. Rare visitor to south-east Australia, mainly in summer. After breeding, disperses east to central and eastern Pacific along 40°S; rare around New Zealand between December and February.

GREY PETREL

Procellaria cinerea L 50 cm (20 in), WS 120 cm (47 in)

Large, southern circumpolar *Procellaria* with ash-grey upperparts and wings.

IDENTIFICATION Flight in light winds gliding, with brief rapid wingbeats, becoming more albatross-like in higher winds, often high above sea surface at peaks of glides. Pursuit-plunges for food using wings underwater. Usually solitary at sea; will follow ships and cetaceans.

Plumage grey above, dark-capped and with yellowish bill, and white below, with dark underwings and undertail. Crown and nape slate-grey, from ear-coverts below eye to bill as a cap, which can appear darker than rest of upperparts; lower hindneck greyish-white, demarcating cap; chin, throat and foreneck white. Upperparts ash-grey with paler fringes, wearing to brownish-grey. Tail blackish-brown, darker than upperparts, thus upperparts generally 'darker at both ends'. Underparts white, with undertail blackish. Upperwing ash-grey, wearing to brownish-grey, at sea looking slightly darker than mantle and back; primaries and tail become blackish, contrasting more with brownish-grey of inner wing-coverts and uppertail-coverts. Underwing dark grey, darker than upperparts; primaries and secondaries slightly paler, often showing as silvery trailing edge, but can also show very faint whitish central stripe on inner wing. Bill slender and more shearwater-like than on other *Procellaria*, greenish-yellow to horn-coloured, with yellow tip, black culmen; iris dark brown; legs and feet flesh-grey.

DISTRIBUTION AND STATUS Pelagic range circumpolar, generally from c 60°S to 30°S; uncommon north of Subtropical Convergence. Breeds in winter on cool temperate and subantarctic islands: Gough Island (thousands), Tristan da Cunha group (50-100 pairs), Prince Edwards (thousands), Crozets (thousands; eliminated by cats on Cochons), Kerguelen (5,000-10,000 pairs), Amsterdam Island; Campbell Island and Antipodes (10,000-50,000 pairs), and formerly Macquarie Island. Northern range unclear, but recorded at 18°S in Atlantic Ocean (with one near Ascension at 8°S), 20°S in Indian Ocean, and possibly to 6°S off Peru. Rare visitor South Africa, southern Australia; more numerous New Zealand, where common. Eastwards, occasional in Tasman Sea. Formerly preyed on by cats (Marion Island) and now by rats (Crozets and Campbell) and by skuas. Also large fatalities from long-line fishing.

CORY'S SHEARWATER

Calonectris diomedea L 46 cm (18 in), WS 113 cm (44 in)

Large, heavy-bodied Atlantic shearwater.

IDENTIFICATION Flight easy and powerful in light winds, several wingbeats then a long rambling glide on bowed and sometimes angled wings; with more wind more albatross-like, soaring higher than most other shearwaters; a deceptively strong flier. Will follow ships; attends trawlers. Plumage grey-brown above, white below, with dark-tipped pale (yellow) bill; generally rather featureless, lacking any distinctive contrasts. Forehead and crown dark grey, extending from ear-coverts below eye to bill, with some whitish mottling, but generally capped appearance gradually merging into lighter brownish-grey hindneck, sides of neck and sides of breast. Mantle, back, scapulars and uppertail-coverts greyish-brown with paler edges, slightly darker across lower back;

whitish tips to uppertail-coverts may form variable white horseshoe mark over tail base. Tail dark brown. Chin and throat usually white, sometimes mottled greyish; rest of underparts white, with dark undertail. Upperwing with primaries and secondaries blackish-brown; coverts greyish-brown with narrow paler edges, often forming variable indistinct brownish 'M' mark from wing tip to wing tip across lower back. Underwing mainly white, with dark greyish border and tip narrowest on leading edge. Bill variable yellowish with dark tip; iris dark brown; legs and feet dusky pinkish-flesh. Race *borealis* (Azores) larger, and darker on mantle and head, while *edwardsii* (Cape Verdes) much smaller, with shorter dark bill, longer tail, shorter wings, and darker above.

DISTRIBUTION AND STATUS Breeds north Atlantic; transequatorial migrant to south Atlantic and Indian Oceans. Nominate *C. d. diomedea* breeds Mediterranean (c 26,000 pairs); *borealis* breeds Azores, where the most abundant seabird (c 500,000 pairs), Salvages (15,000 pairs), Canary Islands (thousands: most abundant Procellariiform, breeds on all islands); *edwardsii* breeds Cape Verdes (large colonies). Total population several million birds. Some colonies heavily exploited. In Southern Hemisphere between November and May: south-west Atlantic off Brazil, Uruguay and Argentina, mainly off South African coast. In Indian Ocean east to Amsterdam and St Paul Islands and south to Prince Edwards: summer population estimated at 250,000 birds. Not recorded Australia; one record New Zealand.

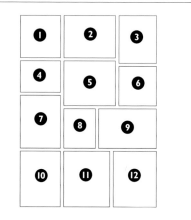

1 **Westland Petrel** (off Kaikoura, New Zealand, April)
2 **Westland Petrel** (at breeding site)
3 **Westland Petrel**
4 **Grey Petrel** (Prince Edward Islands, May)
5 **Grey Petrel** (Prince Edward Islands, May)
6 **Grey Petrel** (Prince Edward Islands, May)
7 **Cory's Shearwater, subspecies C. d. borealis** (Grand Salvage Island)
8 **Cory's Shearwater** (off South Africa)
9 **Cory's Shearwater** (at breeding site)
10 **Cory's Shearwater** (off North Carolina, USA, May)
11 **Cory's Shearwater, subspecies C.d. edwardsii** (off Dakar)
12 **Cory's Shearwater** (off Eilat, Israel)

STREAKED SHEARWATER

Calonectris leucomelas L 48 cm (19 in), WS 122 cm (48 in)

A large, mainly Pacific shearwater.

IDENTIFICATION Flight much as Cory's Shearwater's, easy and purposeful, albatross-like. Generally gregarious at sea. Distinctive jizz: slender bill, small head, long neck, long broad wings with carpal joints held well forward, and wings bowed down and angled back from carpal. Plumage brownish above, with whitish face, and white below, with broad dark trailing edge and tip to underwing. Forehead, lores and forecrown white, increasingly streaked brown towards dark brown of rear crown, nape and hindneck; ear-coverts and cheeks white, streaked dark brown; white eye-ring (unique for a shearwater). Chin, throat and foreneck white (sometimes streaked). Mantle, back, scapulars, rump and uppertail-coverts dark brown, with narrow paler brownish-whitish fringes appearing scaled when close; uppertail-coverts may have variable whitish 'V' over base of uniformly dark brown tail. Underparts white, with variable dark brown partial collar from hindneck onto sides of neck and upper breast; undertail white with narrow blackish tip. Upperwing has inner wing-coverts dark brown with narrow paler brownish-white fringes (as mantle), contrasting with darker blackish-brown secondaries and primaries but forming indistinct 'M' mark from wing tip to wing tip. Underwing mainly white on coverts, with blackish flight feathers forming contrasting broad dark trailing edge and tip (primaries) narrowly extending to carpal joint on forewing; some coverts with variable narrow brownish streaks extending towards inner wing. Bill long and slender, horn-coloured with greyish tip; iris dark brown; legs and feet flesh-pink.

DISTRIBUTION AND STATUS North-west Pacific. Breeds (March-November) in large numbers on Japanese islands (especially Izus), the most abundant breeding seabird in Japan (1 million+ pairs); also in large numbers off eastern China and Korea, with c 150 breeding pairs south-east Russia. Total population several million birds. Threats include human exploitation, fishing nets, and introduced predators (mainly cats and rats). Dispersal south to tropical western Pacific to winter between Japan and Australia; recorded south Australian waters down both east and west coasts, but not New Zealand. Limited penetration of Indian Ocean west to Sri Lanka and Maldives, and has occurred off South Africa and also in eastern Pacific off California. More surprisingly, several records at top of Red Sea (Eilat and Aqaba).

WEDGE-TAILED SHEARWATER

Puffinus pacificus L 43 cm (17 in), WS 101 cm (40 in)

Large, slender-bodied, polymorphic shearwater of the Indian and Pacific Oceans.

IDENTIFICATION Unhurried flight, with slow measured wingbeats. Associates with cetaceans and large feeding flocks of terns and noddies; attends trawlers, but generally not a ship-follower. Characteristic jizz: small-headed and long-tailed, with broad wings held forward at carpals, bowed and angled back from carpal to tip. Occurs in dark and light morphs. *Dark morph*: Fairly uniform blackish-brown, with blacker primaries and uppertail. Upperparts blackish-brown. Underparts blackish-brown, paler greyish-brown on chin, throat and face. Scapulars narrowly tipped greyish-brown, appearing scaled to base of inner wing; inner wing-coverts paler and browner than rest of upperwing, forming pale panel contrasting with black secondaries; darker lesser wing-coverts form inconspicuous 'M' across upperwings with darker primaries. Underwing dark greyish-brown with slightly paler flight feathers. Bill long and slender, greyish with darker tip; iris brown; legs and feet flesh-white (can show up against dark undertail). *Light morph*: Dark brown of crown and nape extends from ear-coverts below eye to bill, often looking slightly hooded; chin, throat and foreneck white. Upperparts similar to dark morph, but paler greyish-brown. Underparts white, undertail-coverts brown; undertail blackish, enhancing dark 'rear end'. Upperwing much as dark morph. Underwing mainly white, with dark trailing edge and tip. Bare parts as dark morph. Dark morph distinguished from marginally larger Flesh-footed by slightly longer appearance, more angled wings, longer wedge-shaped (not rounded) tail, absence of distinct white on under primaries, darker and thinner bill. Pale morph from larger Pink-footed by slighter jizz, more angled wings, longer tail, thinner greyish-based (not pink-based) bill, paler head and whiter underwing.

DISTRIBUTION AND STATUS Breeds on many islands throughout tropical and subtropical Pacific and Indian Oceans; total population over 1 million breeding pairs. Tropical birds thought to be mainly sedentary whereas north and south subtropical populations more dispersive towards the tropics, but exact movements not well known. Ranges east in Pacific to Mexico and west in Indian Ocean to southern Africa, and north to Aden; absent from south Atlantic. Common Australia; fewer New Zealand.

BULLER'S SHEARWATER

Puffinus bulleri L 46 cm (18 in), WS 97 cm (38 in)

Large, slender-bodied Pacific shearwater.

IDENTIFICATION Flight in low winds slow, measured wingbeats on bowed wings then long glides close to water; in stronger winds glides higher, with very little flapping. Feeds mainly by surface-seizing; will join feeding flocks. Usually ignores ships, but will attend trawlers. Size, flight and jizz as Wedge-tailed. Plumage grey-brown above, with dark cap and tail and broad dark 'M', and white below. Forehead, crown and nape blackish-brown, forming dark cap

from ear-coverts through eye to upper mandible, demarcated from white chin, throat and cheeks. Light grey of hindneck extends behind dark cap to grey patches on sides of upper neck and sides of breast. Mantle, back and scapulars uniform light grey, rump dark brownish-grey, uppertail-coverts light grey; uppertail black. Underparts clean white, with undertail greyish-black. Upperwing with primaries blackish-brown, frosted grey inner primaries continue with light grey secondaries; broad blackish bar diagonally on inner wing forms (with blackish primaries) broad 'M' from wing tip to wing tip, joining across rump; inner wing in front of diagonal bar light grey, as mantle; greater and median secondary coverts silvery-grey. Underwing white, with greyish tips to flight feathers forming narrow grey trailing edge and tip (primaries) extending more narrowly onto leading edge to carpal. Bill long and slender, dark grey with black tip; iris dark brown; legs and feet fleshy-pink.

DISTRIBUTION AND STATUS Subtropical New Zealand waters in breeding season, north to 33°S, and extending west into Tasman Sea regularly to south-east coast of Australia; Breeds on islands off North Island, New Zealand: estimated total population c 2.5 million birds; Poor Knight's Island population increasing (c 200,000 breeding pairs) after removal of pigs. Post-breeding dispersal to north Pacific, where widespread off Japan and Russia, north to Alaska, offshore British Columbia to central Californian coast; irregular south to Peru and Chile, occasionally Galapagos. Recorded north-west Atlantic off New Jersey.

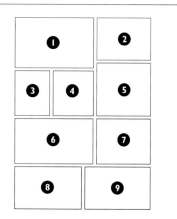

1 **Streaked Shearwater** (off southern Izu Islands, Japan, March)
2 **Streaked Shearwater** (off southern Izu Islands, Japan, March)
3 **Streaked Shearwater** (off southern Izu Islands, Japan, March)
4 **Wedge-tailed Shearwater** (Australia)
5 **Wedge-tailed Shearwater** (at nest site, Australia)
6 **Buller's Shearwater** (New Zealand, May)
7 **Buller's Shearwater** (Chile, February)
8 **Buller's Shearwater** (New Zealand, April)
9 **Buller's Shearwater** (at nest site, Poor Knight's Island, New Zealand)

SHEARWATERS

FLESH-FOOTED SHEARWATER

Puffinus carneipes L 43 cm (17 in), WS 103 cm (41 in)

Large, broad-winged and bulky blackish-brown shearwater of the Indian and Pacific Oceans.
IDENTIFICATION Flight steady and unhurried in calm conditions, with long glides interspersed with slowish deep wingbeats; in stronger winds fewer wingbeats and longer banking glides, as other *Puffinus* species. Can dive well; joins flocks of gulls and terns. Attracted to fishing trawlers. All-dark plumage, with diagnostic dark-tipped pale horn bill and pink legs and feet. Head and neck blackish, slightly darker than upperparts, becoming dark brownish-grey on chin, throat and lores. Upperparts blackish-brown with brownish fringes, becoming paler with wear, imparting scaled appearance. Tail blackish-brown, slightly wedge-shaped, feet not extending beyond tail. Underparts dark brownish, with undertail blackish-brown. Upperwing blackish-brown as upperparts, with darker black primaries; wing-coverts and scapulars have brown fringes as upperparts. Underwing dark brownish on coverts, with paler greyish primaries and secondaries appearing silvery in good light. Bill more robust than that of other *Puffinus* shearwaters, variable pale horn with blackish tip; iris dark brown; legs and feet variable flesh-pink, darker at tips (can show up against dark undertail). Larger than Sooty and Short-tailed Shearwaters, with darker underwing, diagnostic bill, pale feet and slower flight. From Wedge-tailed Shearwater by heavier build with comparatively shorter, rounded tail, wings held straighter, with pale primaries on underwing, and bill differences.
DISTRIBUTION AND STATUS Pacific and Indian Oceans. In Pacific breeds Lord Howe (20,000-40,000 pairs) and North Island and central New Zealand (50,000-100,000 pairs); in Indian Ocean breeds St Paul (600 pairs) and southern coast of western Australia (common). Total population several hundred thousand birds. In the Pacific moves north after breeding, to winter north of Subtropical Convergence; some move east to west coast of North America. Indian Ocean population moves west after breeding, across ocean, past Maldives and Laccadives, to Arabian Sea and Gulf of Oman; some move southwards to South Africa.

PINK-FOOTED SHEARWATER

Puffinus creatopus L 48 cm (19 in), WS 109 cm (43 in)

Large, thickset and broad-winged polymorphic Pacific shearwater. Classified as Vulnerable.
IDENTIFICATION Flight steady and unhurried, much as that of Flesh-footed Shearwater. Dark grey-brown above, variable below, with strong dark-tipped pink bill. Occurs in three morphs.
Pale morph: Head and hindneck dark grey-brown, darker than upperparts, often imparting capped or hooded appearance, and merging into greyish speckling on cheeks, sides of neck and sides of upper breast. Upperparts dark greyish-brown, with narrow whitish fringes on mantle, back and scapulars giving scaled appearance. Tail blackish-brown. Underparts mainly white from chin to tail, with speckling or barring on sides of neck, sides of upper breast and flanks, extending to thighs; undertail-coverts mottled brown and white; undertail dark blackish-brown. Upperwing has inner coverts greyish-brown with whitish fringes, as mantle and scapulars, and primaries and secondaries darker; sometimes shows indistinct 'M' mark across upperwings. Underwing with primaries and secondaries blackish-brown, forming broad dark trailing edge and tip; coverts mainly white with variable small dark streaks, and darkish-streaked triangle at axillaries. Large bill pinkish to yellowish with dark tip; iris dark brown; legs and feet pink.
Dark morph: Upperparts as pale morph. More strongly hooded appearance, with darker cheeks and sides of neck. Chin and throat speckled greyish-brown, underparts generally greyer. Underwing pattern much darker, with whitish central stripe. *Intermediate morph:* Commonest morph. Underparts vary between above two extremes. For differences from Wedge-tailed Shearwater, see latter.
DISTRIBUTION AND STATUS Eastern Pacific Ocean. Breeds on Juan Fernandez group (Chile), at Mas a Tierra (a few thousand pairs) and Santa Clara (3,000 pairs; no threats), and also Mocha Island. Population large, but decreasing through predation by cats and coatimundis and soil erosion caused by goats and rabbits. Some birds caught in fishing gear, mainly in winter. Disperses north to seas off western North America (April-November), generally north of 10°N, from Mexico to British Columbia, occasionally Gulf of Alaska and south Bering Sea. Vagrants Hawaii, Line Islands, Australia and New Zealand.

GREAT SHEARWATER

Puffinus gravis L 47 cm (19 in), WS 109 cm (43 in)

Large, long-winged, mainly Atlantic and Indian Ocean shearwater.
IDENTIFICATION Flight usually with fairly rapid wingbeats followed by low long glides, wings held straighter than Cory's Shearwater; higher flight with increased winds, more albatross-like. Gregarious at sea; regularly follows ships and attends trawlers. Will dive for food. Plumage dark brown above, with blackish cap and tail and contrasting whitish hindneck and uppertail-coverts, and largely white below. Forehead, crown, nape and ear-coverts dark brown, forming blackish cap extending just below eye level and sharply demarcated from white of chin, throat and foreneck, which extends onto hindneck as a white collar separating cap from mantle. Mantle, back, rump, basal uppertail-coverts and scapulars dark greyish-brown to blackish, with paler greyish-brown to whitish fringes imparting scaled appearance; distal uppertail-coverts white, forming horseshoe mark above tail. Uppertail blackish. Underparts white, with greyish-brown short partial collar at sides of upper breast, variable blackish-brown belly patch (often difficult to see at sea), greyish-brown rear flanks, and blackish-brown undertail-coverts and undertail. Upperwing with primaries, primary coverts and secondaries blackish-brown, and inner wing-coverts dark greyish-brown with narrow whitish fringes as mantle. Underwing mainly white; blackish-brown flight feathers form dark trailing edge and tip, narrowly extending onto leading edge; variable diagonal blackish-brown bar extending from trailing edge across lesser coverts towards carpal joint, often with smaller parallel bar in front, from centre of underwing. Bill long and slender, dark blackish-brown; iris dark brown; legs and feet flesh-pink.
DISTRIBUTION AND STATUS Almost exclusively Atlantic and Indian Oceans. Breeds (September-May) only at Falklands (very few: hundreds) and at Tristan da Cunha group (conservative estimate of 5+ million pairs) and Gough Island (estimated 600,000 to 3 million pairs). Annual harvest of Nightingale Island population by Tristan islanders. Ranges over south Atlantic and south-west Indian Ocean in breeding season (c 38°S-52°S), east in Indian Ocean to at least 65°E. Dispersal to north Atlantic (May-November) generally in anticlockwise direction, reaching north to c 66°N, with concentrations on both sides of north Atlantic Ocean. Vagrants to north Pacific off California; one off Australia (1989). No definite accepted records for New Zealand.

1 **Flesh-footed Shearwater** (Mayor Island, New Zealand, February)
2 **Flesh-footed Shearwater** (Victoria, Australia, December)
3 **Flesh-footed Shearwater** (New Zealand, April)
4 **Pink-footed Shearwater** (Pacific coast, USA, July)
5 **Pink-footed Shearwater** (Pacific coast, USA, July)
6 **Pink-footed Shearwater** (California, USA, September)
7 **Great Shearwater** (off South Africa, September)
8 **Great Shearwater** (south Atlantic Ocean, December)
9 **Great Shearwater** (off Southern Ireland, August)

SHEARWATERS

SOOTY SHEARWATER

Puffinus griseus L 44 cm (17 in), WS 105 cm (41 in)
Medium-sized to large, sooty-brown shearwater of all three oceans.

IDENTIFICATION Flight deceptively swift and agile on long but comparatively narrow wings: several stiff and rapid wingbeats followed by long glides; in higher winds wings more swept back, with less flapping and higher glides, often with quickish direction changes, usually following swells rather than *Pterodroma*-like. Gregarious; can form huge feeding flocks, often with other species. Readily plunges for food, using wings underwater; swims well. Generally ignores ships, but regular at trawlers. Plumage mainly dark, with variable pale underwing. Head and neck blackish-brown, slightly greyer on chin and throat. Mantle, back, rump, uppertail-coverts and tail blackish-brown (intensity of upperparts colour variable with light conditions). Underparts dark brownish-grey, generally slightly lighter than upperparts. Upperwing blackish-brown, primaries and secondaries slightly darker; at close range, inner wing-coverts may show slightly paler tips and trailing edge of secondaries may appear slightly paler (not extending to primaries). Underwing generally blackish-brown, with variable paler central stripe formed by whitish tips to coverts, usually more extensive below carpal joint; underwing may appear silvery in strong light. Bill long and slender, greyish-black; iris dark brown; legs and feet pinkish-black, often extending slightly beyond tail. Difficult to separate from Short-tailed Shearwater, but latter is generally smaller, with shorter bill and steeper forehead, and head may show more hooded appearance; Short-tailed's underwing-coverts generally greyer and more even along underwing, but much variation in both species.

DISTRIBUTION AND STATUS Mainly Pacific Ocean, breeding primarily on New Zealand islands where some colonies are vast eg Snares Island 2,750,000 pairs, also Aukland, Campbell, Chatham, Antipodes, Stewart Islands. Also smaller numbers at Macquarie, New South Wales and Tasmania (Australia). Fewer numbers breed southern South America and the Falkland Islands. Total population several million birds. The only shearwater that can legally be sold in New Zealand: annual harvest c 250,000 young. Range in breeding season south to iceberg belt. Transequatorial dispersal in all three oceans with most (April-September) north to north Pacific, reaching Bering Sea, fewer in north Atlantic and northern Indian Ocean; has reached Eilat (Israel).

SHORT-TAILED SHEARWATER

Puffinus tenuirostris L 42 cm (17 in), WS 98 cm (39 in)
Medium-sized, mainly Pacific shearwater, very similar to Sooty Shearwater and likewise a transequatorial migrant.

IDENTIFICATION Flight with several rapid and stiff wingbeats followed by gliding; in increased wind, higher glides with less flapping. Gregarious; can form huge flocks, often with other species. Generally not a ship-follower. Plumage sooty-brown, much as that of Sooty Shearwater. Head and neck blackish-brown, merging into dark brownish-grey at about eye level (head may appear slightly hooded at times). Mantle, back, rump, uppertail-coverts and tail blackish-brown. Underparts dark brownish-grey, generally slightly lighter than upperparts, often with small whitish chin. Upperwing sooty-brown; primaries and secondaries slightly darker, with greyish gloss. Underwing generally blackish-brown, with variable paler central area (which may be greyish or, more rarely, whitish) formed by paler tips to coverts, with leading edge of inner wing and axillaries generally darkest part; underwing may appear silvery in strong light. Bill short and stubby, blackish-grey; iris dark brown; legs and feet blackish. For separation from Sooty Shearwater, see that species.

DISTRIBUTION AND STATUS Mainly Pacific Ocean. Breeds (September-May) west Australia (a few pairs), South Australia (c 3,000 pairs), Victoria (1.45 million burrows), New South Wales (25,700 pairs), Tasmania (5.6 million breeding pairs). Total population estimated at 23 million breeding birds. Long history of human exploitation on Tasmania; now only nestlings harvested (c 300,000 young taken per annum). Ranges south to Antarctica at 65°S (February), otherwise mainly over continental-shelf waters in breeding season. After breeding migrates mainly to north Pacific, a few to north-east Indian Ocean. Recently reported sight record off south-east coast of South Africa. Main Pacific passage via Fiji, rapidly across Tropics between Hawaii and Marshall Islands, to main wintering area off Aleutian Islands (also Gulf of Alaska and Bering Sea). Leaves Alaska late September, offshore Washington to California (November-February), then south through central Pacific to breed. Uncommon migrant New Zealand.

CHRISTMAS SHEARWATER

Puffinus nativitatis L 36 cm (14 in), WS 76 cm (30 in)
Medium-sized, slender-bodied, uniformly dark shearwater of the tropical Pacific Ocean.

IDENTIFICATION Flight buoyant, generally more flapping on stiff wings, with less gliding than Sooty, Short-tailed or Wedge-tailed Shearwater, usually very low over sea surface. Often seen close to breeding islands; associates with multi-species flocks. Has comparatively short and rounded wings, long slender bill and slightly wedge-shaped tail. Plumage essentially uniform sooty-brown, appearing all dark at sea. Head and neck dark brown, slightly paler on chin and throat. Upperparts dark brown; tail blackish-brown, quite long and slightly wedge-shaped. Underparts dark brown, similar to upperparts. Upperwing as mantle; outer primaries and some coverts may be reflective in some lights. Underwing fairly uniform dark brown, with no white visible on coverts. Bill long and quite slender, blackish; iris brown; legs and feet dark brown, and do not extend beyond tail. From Sooty and Short-tailed Shearwaters by smaller size, dark brown underwing, shorter and less pointed wings. From similar all-dark (but variable) Heinroth's Shearwater by larger size, dark underwing, absence of white belly, dark feet. From dark-morph Wedge-tailed Shearwater by smaller size, darker plumage, shorter tail, different jizz and flight.

DISTRIBUTION AND STATUS Tropical and subtropical Pacific. Breeds on most Hawaiian islands, with most on Laysan (1,500-2,000 pairs) and Lisianski (400-600 pairs), these populations having declined from exploitation and predation; also Pitcairn, Gambier, Tuamotu, Australs, with more on Line (1,000-10,000 pairs) and Phoenix (10,000-100,000 pairs), Easter Island and Sala y Gomez Island (c 1,000 birds). Probably remains near tropical colonies throughout year, but subtropical colonies vacated in non-breeding season. Pelagic range not well known, but recorded in east Pacific off south-west Mexico, Central America and off Peru, possibly from Easter Island. One record New Zealand.

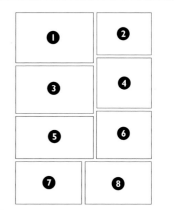

1 **Sooty Shearwater** (at nest site, Kidney Island, Falkland Islands)
2 **Sooty Shearwater** (California, USA, September)
3 **Short-tailed Shearwater** (pair at nest site)
4 **Sooty Shearwater** (off South Africa, September)
5 **Short-tailed Shearwater** (Magadan, Russia)
6 **Christmas Shearwater**
7 **Christmas Shearwater** (at nest site)
8 **Christmas Shearwater** (breeding pair, Laysan Island, Hawaii)

SHEARWATERS

MANX SHEARWATER

Puffinus puffinus L 34 cm (13 in), WS 82 cm (32 in)

Medium-sized north Atlantic shearwater, common and locally abundant.

IDENTIFICATION Flight in low winds consists of rapid, stiff-winged beats followed by shearing glides, generally low over sea with slight rising and falling; in stronger winds less flapping, higher shearing up to 10 m above sea surface. Gregarious; readily swims and dives. Not a persistent ship-follower, but attends trawlers. Blackish cap (to below eye) and blackish upperparts sharply demarcated from white underparts, giving the sharpest contrast of any similar black and white *Puffinus*. Forehead, crown and nape blackish, forming dark cap extending to ear-coverts, below eye, and to base of upper mandible, and sharply demarcated from white of chin, throat and lower cheeks, which curl up behind dark ear-coverts. Hindneck blackish, this extending to sides of neck and upper sides of breast, less demarcated than cap. Upperparts to tail blackish, wearing to blackish-brown. Underparts white, with variable dark flank spots, black thigh patch, and thin dark rim to undertail; white can appear to extend narrowly onto sides of rump in late summer. Upperwing blackish, becoming browner with wear. Underwing white with sharply defined blackish margins and tip (primaries); blackish trailing edge (flight feathers) broader than leading edge; some birds may show narrow dark diagonal bar from carpal across lesser coverts. Bill long and slender, blackish with grey base; iris dark brown; legs and feet pale flesh and black.

DISTRIBUTION AND STATUS Atlantic Ocean. Breeds north-east America (Newfoundland, Labrador, Gulf of St Lawrence to Gulf of Maine, 11-150 pairs; Massachusetts, 1-10 pairs, increasing), Iceland (1,000-10,000 pairs), France (c 10 pairs), Wales (125,000-135,000 pairs), England (1,000-1,500 pairs), Faeroes (10,000-15,000 pairs), Ireland (20,000-50,000 pairs), Scotland (80,000-100,000 pairs), Channel Islands (c 10 pairs), Azores, Madeira and possibly Canary Islands. Some colonies suffer from predation and human exploitation. Rare in breeding range November-January. Dispersal southwards July, return March. Concentrations south Atlantic (10°S-40°S) off Brazil and Argentina, fewer South Africa. Vagrant Australia and New Zealand. Recently recorded north-east Pacific off Washington, also sight records California.

YELKOUAN SHEARWATER (including BALEARIC SHEARWATER)

Puffinus yelkouan L 34-37 cm (14 in), WS 87 cm (34 in)

Recently separated from Manx Shearwater, and occurs as two subspecies in the Mediterranean Sea.

IDENTIFICATION Normal flight a fluttering flap-and-glide, low over sea surface, becoming higher in stronger winds. Both subspecies larger than Manx Shearwater, with variably browner upperparts merging into variably dark underparts, especially flanks, undertail-coverts and axillaries. **P. y. yelkouan, Yelkouan Shearwater**: Slightly larger than Manx Shearwater, with browner upperparts and darker underparts. Head dark greyish-brown, extending to eye, or just below, including ear-coverts, usually quite sharply demarcated from whitish on chin and sides of face, although some may show whitish mottling on forehead and around eye. Hindneck, mantle and back dark greyish-brown in fresh plumage, generally darker than on Balearic Shearwater and may appear dark grey without any brown; mantle fades paler through wear, but never becomes as pale as palest Balearic Shearwater. Tail browner than mantle; feet project slightly. Underparts whitish from chin and sides of face to lower belly, but with variable greyish-brown wash on undertail-coverts, extending onto flanks on some birds; pale birds similar to pale Balearic Shearwater. Upperwing dark greyish-brown, primaries slightly darker. Underwing with greyish-brown flight feathers forming dark trailing edge extending variably onto axillaries; underwing-coverts whitish with variable brownish wash, with very narrow dark leading edge to wing. (Underwing generally between clearly demarcated Manx Shearwater and duskier Balearic, although latter more variable.) Demarcation of upperparts and underparts not so sharp as on Manx Shearwater. **P. y. mauretanicus, Balearic Shearwater**: Larger and heavier than both Manx and Yelkouan Shearwaters. Head variable, mainly dusky brown, merging into dusky white chin and throat; on intermediate and dark birds the forehead, forecrown and ear-coverts are darkest, and may extend to lores and hindcrown; may show paler eye-ring and variable whitish sides to neck. Fading in summer may give paler nape and hindneck, suggesting paler collar. Upperparts dusky dark brown, slightly paler than Yelkouan Shearwater; tail darker brown, feet extending slightly. Underparts variable, from very pale (resembling Cory's and Yelkouan Shearwaters) to very dark (almost recalling Sooty Shearwater), but most are intermediates with a dark brownish-grey breastband separating whitish chin and throat from whitish belly (these have similarly dark flanks, vent and undertail-coverts): pale birds most resemble Yelkouan Shearwater with no breastband (thus white or off-white from chin to lower belly), but with greyish-brown vent and undertail-coverts; darkest birds recall Sooty Shearwater, but usually have paler chin and whitish on central belly (as well as structural differences). Upperwing dusky brown, with darker primaries and darker inner leading edge; when worn and faded, may show paler mid-wing panel, paler spots on wing-coverts, and suggestion of a paler rump. Underwing variable, usually dusky white with brownish trailing edge (flight feathers), tip (primaries) and axillaries; generally darker than Yelkouan Shearwater (though some may be as pale), and very dark birds may even suggest Sooty Shearwater with contrast between the dark axillaries and white to off-white coverts (these dark birds may be immatures).

DISTRIBUTION AND STATUS Mediterranean Sea. *P. y. yelkouan* breeds France and eastern Algeria eastwards to Aegean Sea and Turkey (has bred Black Sea, off Bulgaria; may breed Tunisia), with most off Italy, former Yugoslavia, Greece; total population several thousand pairs. Dispersal north-east through Bosporus towards Black Sea, also westwards towards Gibraltar in some years: not yet proved to leave Mediterranean via Gibraltar Straits. *P. y. mauretanicus* breeds Balearic islands (and possibly north-east Spain), where still relatively abundant (c 1,000-5,000 pairs) and widely distributed, but now outnumbered by Cory's Shearwater at breeding sites; threatened by rats, harvested for food and used as bait by fishermen; disperses westwards into Atlantic Ocean, moving generally north to Scotland and Scandinavia (regular Channel Islands and south-west England), and has been recorded south to Madeira and Atlantic coast of Morocco; may have reached South Africa.

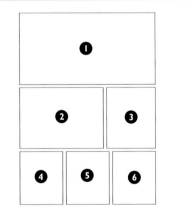

1 **Manx Shearwater** (adult at breeding colony, Skokholm Island, Wales, May)
2 **Manx Shearwater** (juvenile, Bardsey Island, Wales)
3 **Manx Shearwater** (adult, north Atlantic)
4 **Manx Shearwater** (adult off St Kilda, Scotland, July)
5 **Yelkouan Shearwater** (Islas Ciés, Spain, May)
6 **Yelkouan (Balearic) Shearwater** subspecies *P. y. mauretanicus* (Kent, England, September)

SHEARWATERS

TOWNSEND'S SHEARWATER

Puffinus auricularis L 33 cm (13 in), WS 76 cm (30 in)

Medium-sized eastern Pacific shearwater. Treated as conspecific with Newell's Shearwater by Sibley and Monroe, but as a separate species by BirdLife International, who classify it as Vulnerable.

IDENTIFICATION Flight generally low and fast, with rapid wingbeats and very little gliding. Blackish-brown above and white below, with contrasting blackish undertail-coverts; birds on the sea surface show latter feature, unlike similar Newell's and Manx Shearwaters. Forehead, crown and nape blackish-brown, forming dark cap and extending to ear-coverts below eye and to base of upper mandible, variably sharply demarcated from white of chin, throat and lower cheeks which curls up behind dark ear-coverts. Hindneck blackish-brown, extending to sides of neck and upper breast sides, becoming mottled blackish and less demarcated than head. Upperparts blackish-brown (a shade browner than either Newell's or Manx Shearwater). Tail blackish. Underparts white, with blackish thigh patch, white on flanks extending narrowly onto sides of rump; undertail-coverts variable, generally all dark with variable small area of white at base, usually evenly and squarely demarcated (appear all dark at sea, unlike Newell's or Manx Shearwater). Upperwing blackish-brown. Underwing mainly white, with broad dark trailing edge (flight feathers) and tip (primaries) extending more narrowly to carpal joint; short, indistinct dark diagonal bar from central wingpit towards carpal joint (possibly more noticeable than on Newell's or Manx). Bill blackish; iris blackish; legs and feet blackish with pinkish webs. Black-vented Shearwater is slightly larger and browner, without strong upperpart/underpart demarcation, lacks white extension onto rump sides, and has darker underparts much more like Yelkouan Shearwater's. See also Newell's Shearwater.

DISTRIBUTION AND STATUS Eastern Pacific. Breeds only on three islands of Las Islas Revilla Gigedo group, 650 km west of Mexico. The population on Clarion has almost been exterminated by feral pigs; that on Socorro has been estimated at 1,000 pairs, with heavy predation by feral cats; the San Benedicto population was essentially wiped out by a volcanic eruption in 1952, although there is now some recolonization. The most endangered seabird of the region. Pelagic dispersal not well known, possibly south-east to just north of the Galapagos Islands.

NEWELL'S SHEARWATER

Puffinus newelli L 33 cm (13 in), WS 76 cm (30 in)

Medium-sized, black and white Hawaiian shearwater. Classified as Vulnerable.

IDENTIFICATION Flight typical of small shearwaters, with less flapping and more shearing in higher winds. Much as Manx Shearwater, but comparatively longer-tailed, with white of flanks extending further onto rump sides, and undertail-covert pattern between those of Manx and Townsend's Shearwaters. Forehead, crown and nape blackish, forming dark cap and extending to ear-coverts, below eye and to base of upper mandible, sharply demarcated from white of chin, throat and lower cheeks which curls up behind dark ear-coverts. Hindneck blackish, extending to sides of neck and upper breast sides. Upperparts blackish. Tail blackish, and comparatively longer than on either Townsend's or Manx Shearwater. Underparts white with blackish thigh patch, white on flanks extending onto sides of rump (further than on Manx Shearwater, but much as on Townsend's); undertail-coverts between all dark of Townsend's and all white of Manx, never all white (generally, inner coverts whitish, extending and tapering to a 'V' shape or point about halfway to undertail tip, and outer coverts dark). Upperwing blackish. Underwing white with sharply defined blackish margins and tip (primaries), blackish trailing edge (flight feathers) broader than leading edge; short, indistinct dark diagonal bar from wingpit towards carpal joint. Bill blackish; iris blackish; legs and feet blackish with pinkish webs. From Townsend's Shearwater by slightly longer wings, with marginally blacker (less brown) upperparts, with sharper and better-defined demarcation (especially around ear-coverts and sides of breast), possibly greater extension of white onto rump sides, and whiter inner undertail-coverts usually tapering to a point or 'V'-shaped (unlike the darker, more extensive and square-ended pattern of Townsend's).

DISTRIBUTION AND STATUS North Pacific: Hawaii and surrounding seas. Now breeds only on Kauai (rediscovered 1967), with c 8,000 adults nesting in burrows on mountainous grassy slopes (total population c 10,000, perhaps more). Kauai is free of mongooses, but fledglings are attracted to street lights; there is now a programme to collect and release these young (c 1,500 per year), as well as to control lighting. Formerly bred on Maui and Molokai, where exterminated by cats, rats, pigs, mongooses, dogs and Barn Owls. Undiscovered colonies may exist elsewhere in Hawaii. Pelagic dispersal not well known, but moves eastwards towards California.

BLACK-VENTED SHEARWATER

Puffinus opisthomelas L 34 cm (13 in), WS 82 cm (32 in)

Medium-sized eastern Pacific shearwater. Classified as Vulnerable.

IDENTIFICATION Flight generally low and fast, rapid wingbeats interspersed with short glides. Occasionally follows ships. Brownish above, gradually merging into variably whitish underparts, with dark undertail-coverts, underwing borders and axillaries. Dark brown of head extends below eye level, merging into paler chin and throat; pale colour of chin and throat may extend onto rear of ear-coverts. Hindneck brownish, this extending onto sides of neck and upper breast, sometimes forming complete breastband. Upperparts dark brown. Tail brown, and comparatively long. Underparts variable, generally whitish with dusky flanks, but darker birds may show continuous brownish breastband enhancing dark head and neck, and more rarely underparts may be uniform pale greyish; all show brownish undertail-coverts. (Pattern and extent of variation not unlike Balearic Shearwater.) Upperwing brownish. Underwing dull whitish centrally, merging into broad dark trailing edge (flight feathers) and tip (primaries) with narrower dark leading edge; axillaries extensively smudged brown, continuous with dark flanks or showing as dark flanks extending diagonally across coverts towards carpal joint. Bill blackish; iris blackish; legs and feet blackish with paler webs. From Townsend's Shearwater by slightly larger size, browner upperparts merging into more dusky underparts and underwing, and no extension of white onto sides of rump.

DISTRIBUTION AND STATUS Eastern Pacific Ocean from California to Galapagos. Breeds in winter (November-August) off Baja California, on Isla Guadalupe (c 2,500 pairs), Islas San Benito (250-500 pairs), Islas Natividad (5,000-10,000 pairs); reports from other islands, including in Gulf of California, unsubstantiated. Preyed on by cats on Islas Natividad; also possible mortalities from gill-net fisheries. Populations heavily reduced, mainly by predation. Post-breeding dispersal northwards along Californian coast to Monterey Bay (October-November), extending further north to Mendicino County when water is warm (some may even reach Vancouver Island); some also move south to just north of Galapagos.

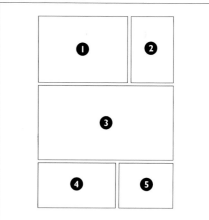

1 **Townsend's Shearwater**
2 **Newell's Shearwater** (Kauai, Hawaii)
3 **Newell's Shearwater** (at breeding site)
4 **Black-vented Shearwater** (California, USA, September)
5 **Black-vented Shearwater** (California, USA, September)

SHEARWATERS

FLUTTERING SHEARWATER

Puffinus gavia L 33 cm (13 in), WS 76 cm (30 in)
Small to medium-sized New Zealand
shearwater.
IDENTIFICATION Flight typically low and direct,
with rapid wingbeats and short glides on stiff
wings; higher in strong winds. Gregarious,
forming mixed feeding flocks in inshore waters;
swims and dives well. Ignores ships and
trawlers. Smaller than Manx but larger than
Little Shearwater; almost identical to Hutton's
in size, shape and appearance, with much
overlap. Forehead, crown and hindneck
blackish-brown, forming dark cap extending
over ear-coverts, below eye, to base of bill and
generally sharply demarcated from chin, throat
and lower cheeks. Dark of hindneck extends to
form variable partial collar at sides of neck and
sides of upper breast. Upperparts generally
dark brown or blackish-brown, though variable
with light conditions, becoming rusty-brown
when worn (November-January). Tail blackish-
brown, feet tips extending slightly. Underparts
mainly white with dark thigh patch, margins of
undertail dark; white on lower flanks extends
upwards narrowly to sides of rump. Upperwing
dark brown or blackish-brown. Underwing
mainly white, with broad dark trailing edge
(flight feathers) and tip (primaries) extending
narrowly along leading edge; variable dark
axillaries, which may extend as diagonal bar
from trailing edge of wing towards carpal joint.
Bill long and slender, greyish-black; iris dark
brown; legs and feet flesh-white. Very similar to
Hutton's, which is slightly larger, with bigger
head and larger body. Generally, Hutton's has
darker and blacker upperparts more constantly
throughout the year, with a darker head and
thus more hooded appearance (lacking
Fluttering's demarcation), and generally darker
underwing.
DISTRIBUTION AND STATUS New Zealand and
Australia. Breeds (August-February) North
Island, and central New Zealand (c 100,000 to
1 million pairs). Slight decline in north of range
as competition with larger and more aggressive
Buller's, also mammalian predation and taken
for human food in the past. Generally in warm
subtropical continental-shelf waters, a more
northerly distribution than Hutton's. Dispersal
of immatures and non-breeding birds to waters
off South Island, New Zealand, and across the
Tasman Sea to south and east Australia where
some remain over the summer. Vagrants New
Caledonia and Vanuatu.

HUTTON'S SHEARWATER

Puffinus huttoni L 38 cm (15 in), WS 90 cm
(35 in)
Medium-sized New Zealand shearwater, very
similar to Fluttering. Classified as Endangered.
IDENTIFICATION Typical flight in light winds low
and direct, with rapid wingbeats and short
glides on stiff wings; higher in stronger winds,
with fewer beats. Gregarious; forms mixed
feeding flocks; swims and dives well. Ignores

ships. White below, with dusky-looking
underwing. Forehead, crown and hindneck
blackish-brown, forming dark cap extending
below eye level and merging into whitish of
chin and throat. Dark of hindneck extends to
sides of neck and sides of upper breast,
imparting hooded appearance, becoming
slightly mottled on foreneck and generally
merging into whiter underparts. Upperparts
and uppertail uniform blackish-brown.
Underparts white from lower breast to
undertail-coverts, except for small dark thigh
patch and thin dark margin to undertail; white
of lower flanks extends upwards narrowly to
sides of rump. Upperwing blackish-brown,
primaries slightly darker than coverts.
Underwing mainly whitish, with broad dark
trailing edge (flight feathers) and tip (primaries)
extending narrowly along leading edge, and
variable greyish-brown triangle on inner wing
between trailing edge and body, extending
diagonally towards carpal joint; generally darker
than on Fluttering, but variable. Bill dark grey,
generally longer than Fluttering's; iris dark
brown; legs and feet dark grey and pinkish.
Prefers more open water than Fluttering, which
see for other differences.
DISTRIBUTION AND STATUS Australasian seas.
Breeds (August-April) 12-18 km inland from
coast (at 1,200-1,800 m) on Seaward Kaikoura
Range, north-east South Island (New Zealand),
where discovered in 1965. Two known
colonies, and total population fewer than
200,000 pairs. Evidence of decline, with
introduced stoats taking adults and chicks; red
deer, chamois and goats trample burrows and
graze vegetation, but deer and chamois
numbers have been reduced since 1970 and
tussock grass has subsequently regenerated.
Adults remain in New Zealand waters, but
dispersal of mostly immature birds across
Tasman Sea to Australia in non-breeding
season, when recorded around most of
Australian continental shelf; status off northern
Australia unclear.

MASCARENE SHEARWATER

Puffinus atrodorsalis L ?, WS ?
Recently described (1995) small, black and
white *Puffinus* shearwater from the western
Indian Ocean. Subsequent to the initial 1995
publication it has been shown that DNA
analysis does not support the specific status of
atrodorsalis at present. However, considerably
more evidence is required before any firm
taxonomic category can be applied to it, as well
as a complete review of the *P. lherminieri-
assimilis* complex (Morgan JH et al. 'Further
notes on the taxonomy of *P. atrodorsalis*',
BBOC in press). Thus for the present it
remains 'species inquirendae'; however, photos
and field data are presented here.
IDENTIFICATION In calm conditions, flies with
wingbeats (slower than Little) interspersed
with low shearing; above force 4 flight becomes
more undulating, but still weaker than that of
Manx. Intermediate in size between Manx and

Little. Very black (above) and white (below)
appearance, as Manx, with white undertail-
coverts, and comparatively long wings, tail and
bill. Blackish crown extends to just below eye,
encloses blackish loral patch and imparts
hooded appearance, sharply demarcated from
white underparts, but with greyish-white
mottling on lower ear-coverts. Hindneck,
mantle, back, rump and uppertail uniformly
black. Foreneck, throat, breast, flanks and
undertail-coverts white, latter separated from
rest of white underparts by narrow blackish-
brown band extending from rump onto thigh;
slight blackish-brown mottling on sides of neck
and breast. Upperwings blackish, with indistinct
whitish tips to greater coverts. Underwing-
coverts pure white, with narrow blackish-
brown leading edge to wing; flight feathers
dusky grey to blackish, axillaries white. Bill long
and slender, bluish-grey; inner tarsus, inner
toes and webs bluish-grey, rest of legs and feet
black. 15% smaller than Manx, 5% larger than
Audubon's or Little, but with comparatively
longer wings, tail and bill (proportions nearer
Audubon's than Little). Lacks the brownish hue
to upperparts and undertail-coverts of
Audubon's.
DISTRIBUTION AND STATUS Western Indian
Ocean. Breeding grounds unknown at present,
but believed to be in the Comoro Islands
and/or Réunion. Birds observed at sea north
and south of Comoros, west and south of
Aldabra, Mozambique Channel and east of
Maputo (4°S-29°S and 32°E-57°E). Vagrants
Durban (South Africa) and Eilat (Israel).

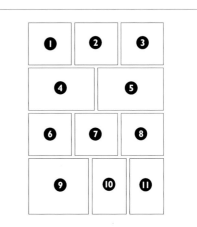

1 **Fluttering Shearwater** (Victoria, Australia,
March)
2 **Fluttering Shearwater** (off Sydney,
Australia)
3 **Fluttering Shearwater** (Pelorus Sounds,
New Zealand, March)
4 **Fluttering Shearwater** (at nest site)
5 **Hutton's Shearwater** (at nest site)
6 **Hutton's Shearwater** (June)
7 **Hutton's Shearwater** (New South Wales,
Australia, May)
8 **Mascarene Shearwater** (Eilat, Israel, June)
9 **Mascarene Shearwater** (Eilat, Israel, June)
10 **Mascarene Shearwater** (type specimen)
11 **Mascarene Shearwater** (type specimen)

SHEARWATERS

AUDUBON'S SHEARWATER

Puffinus lherminieri L 30 cm (12 in), WS 69 cm (27 in)

Small but rather stocky shearwater of all three oceans. Complicated taxonomy in need of thorough revision; Sibley and Monroe have separated Persian, Bannerman's and Heinroth's Shearwaters as good species.

IDENTIFICATION Normal flight a series of stiff wingbeats followed by short glides low over surface, in stronger winds becoming higher, with more gliding and less flapping. Gregarious or solitary at sea, but can form large feeding flocks, sometimes with other species. Dives and swims well; often rests on sea. Not attracted to ships. Wings short and broad, tail comparatively long. Variably blackish-brown above and white below, with usually dark undertail-coverts. Forehead, crown and hindneck blackish-brown, extending from bill base, just below eye, to rear of ear-coverts and generally sharply demarcated from white chin, throat and lower cheeks; whitish cheeks may curve up slightly behind ear-coverts. Dark of hindneck extends slightly onto sides of neck and sides of upper breast. Upperparts blackish-brown, becoming lighter and brownish-grey with wear. Tail blackish-brown, feet not projecting. Underparts white with small blackish thigh patch; no extension of white flanks onto sides of rump; undertail-coverts usually brownish, undertail brownish, giving dark rear end. Upperwing brownish, primaries slightly darker and without paler inner webs. Underwing mainly white, with broad dark trailing edge (flight feathers) and tip (primaries) extending into very narrow dark leading edge, but pattern variable. Bill blackish with paler base; iris brown; legs and feet flesh-pink with blackish tips. Dark undertail-coverts and undertail giving dark rear end helps separation from most similar *Puffinus* species. For differences from Little Shearwater, see that species. Manx Shearwater is larger, with proportionately longer wings and shorter tail, blackish-blue upperparts, and white undertail-coverts. **Note:** Many subspecies described, with much geographical variation; *subalaris* (Galapagos) and *bailloni* (Mascarene Islands) have white undertail-coverts. Sibley and Monroe split both Persian and Bannerman's Shearwaters from Audubon's as separate species. I have cautiously included them under Audubon's Shearwater until a thorough revision of the Little/Audubon's complex is completed. *P. l. bannermani*, Bannerman's Shearwater: Locally in north-west Pacific (Bonin and Volcano Islands). Has paler greyish head and hindcollar, contrasting strongly with slaty-black back; underwing-coverts, sides of neck and sides of upper breast mottled with blackish and grey; may show paler feather edges on upperwing-coverts, mantle and rump. *P. l. persicus*, Persian Shearwater: North-west Indian Ocean (Arabian Sea, Gulf of Aden, Somalia, southern Red Sea, Straits of Hormuz and north-west India; has been found breeding

Kuria Muria group, off Oman). Slightly larger, with longer bill and darker underwing, also variable mottling on flanks and axillaries; much as Balearic or Black-vented Shearwater.

DISTRIBUTION AND STATUS Breeds in tropical and subtropical waters of all three oceans. Atlantic: breeds Bahamas and West Indies (*P. l. lherminieri*); Caribbean islands south to Venezuela (*P. l. loyemilleri*). Indian: breeds Comoros (*P. l. temptator*); Aldabra (*P. l. colstoni*: dark under-tail coverts); Amirantes, Seychelles, Maldives, Chagos (*P. l. nicolae*); Mascarene Islands (*P. l. bailloni*): some colonies huge. Pacific: breeds Bonin and Volcano Islands (*P. l. bannermani*); New Hebrides (*P. l. gunax*); Fiji, Phoenix, Line Islands, Marquesas, Gambier, Galapagos (*P. l. dichrous*); possibly Tuamotu, Society Islands, Samoa and Tokelau. Total population probably several tens of thousands of breeding pairs. Pelagic movements not well known; generally believed to remain near breeding sites.

LITTLE SHEARWATER

Puffinus assimilis L 27 cm (11 in), WS 62 cm (24 in)

Small shearwater, widely distributed in all three oceans.

IDENTIFICATION Normal flight in calm conditions a 'flutter and glide' low over sea surface, with less shearing than other *Puffinus* species; shears more in stronger winds, but keeps low. Dives and swims well. Will investigate ships, but not a follower. The smallest shearwater, very compact, with comparatively short, broad and rounded wings. Generally black above and white below, with usually white-faced appearance; underwing very white, undertail-coverts usually white. Forehead, crown, nape and hindneck bluish-black or slate-black; lores, chin, throat and cheeks white with demarcation usually above eye, imparting comparatively white-faced appearance (race *elegans* has demarcation below eye, thus darker, fuller cap); some may show dark mottling around eye, shortish white supercilium and whitish ear-coverts, but all variable. Dark of hindneck extends only slightly onto sides of neck. Upperparts bluish-black or slate-black with greyish shade when fresh, becoming browner when worn (though variable). Tail blackish. Underparts white, with no extension of white flanks onto sides of rump; undertail-coverts white (dark on race *boydi*), undertail blackish-grey. Upperwing bluish-black or slate-black, primaries with concealed white inner webs; flight feathers develop brownish tone with wear. Underwing white, with narrow dark trailing edge (flight feathers) and tip (primaries) extending very narrowly onto leading edge. Bill greyish-black, appearing black at sea; iris dark brown; legs and feet bluish-grey (diagnostic). Audubon's Shearwater is larger, with more thickset jizz and longer bill, wing and tail, darker face, browner upperparts, (usually) darker undertail-coverts, broader trailing edge to underwing,

flesh-pink legs; flight more gliding and less flapping than Little Shearwater's.

DISTRIBUTION AND STATUS Subtropical and subantarctic waters of all three oceans: few precise data for some populations. Pelagic movements not well known; generally believed to remain near breeding sites, although *elegans* probably more migratory than other subspecies – birds from the Antipodes have reached Chile. **Atlantic:** *P. a. baroli* breeds Azores, Desertas, Salvages and Canary Islands; *boydi* on Cape Verdes (has dark undertail-coverts and perhaps should be included with Audubon's Shearwater); *elegans* on Tristan da Cunha group and Gough Island. **Indian:** *P. a. tunneyi* breeds Amsterdam and St Paul Islands and islands off Western Australia. **Pacific:** *P. a. assimilis* breeds Norfolk and Lord Howe Islands; *kermadecensis* on Kermadec Islands; *haurakiensis* on islands off east coast of North Island, New Zealand; *elegans* on Chatham Islands, Antipodes Islands; *myrtae* on Rapa, Austral Islands (may breed elsewhere on Pacific islands). Some colonies exploited by humans and preyed on by introduced mammals.

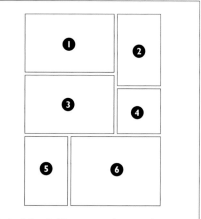

1 **Audubon's Shearwater** (on nest, Aride Island, Seychelles)
2 **Audubon's Shearwater**
3 **Audubon's Shearwater**
4 **Audubon's Shearwater** (Costa Rica, April)
5 **Little Shearwater subspecies** *P. a. elegans* (south Atlantic Ocean)
6 **Little Shearwater**

SHEARWATERS & DIVING-PETRELS

HEINROTH'S SHEARWATER

Puffinus heinrothi L 27 cm (11 in), WS ?
Small, rare and virtually unknown shearwater of
the tropical western Pacific, probably breeding
at Bougainville, in Solomon Islands. Classified as
Endangered.

IDENTIFICATION Generally dark-plumaged, but
variable below. Head, neck and upper breast
sooty-brown, shading to whitish on chin and
upper throat. Upperparts and uppertail uniform
sooty-brown. Underparts variable: darkest
birds are sooty-brown, a shade lighter than
upperparts, dark extending to undertail; lighter
birds have a variable whitish central belly patch
(may be difficult to see at sea) which merges
into otherwise sooty-brown underparts.
Upperwing sooty-brown as upperparts.
Underwing whitish centrally, with dark trailing
edge (flight feathers) and tip (primaries)
narrowly extending onto leading edge; dark of
axillaries extends as dark triangle from inner
trailing edge towards carpal joint. Bill very long
and slender, blackish; iris variable from brown
to bluish; legs and feet light brown or flesh-
coloured, distally black. From Sooty and Short-
tailed Shearwaters by smaller size, whiter
underwing and (if present) whitish belly. Has
previously been considered conspecific with
Audubon's Shearwater, but separated as a
species by Sibley and Monroe.
DISTRIBUTION AND STATUS Tropical western
Pacific (Melanesia). Hardly known, rarely seen
at sea, and never found breeding. Previously
recorded from seas near Rabaul, New Britain.
In 1979, one fledged individual was found at
Arawa, Bougainville, the first record for 50
years. Another (adult) in 1980 at Panguna
indicated probable breeding in the Crown
Prince Range, Bougainville. Recent reports of
birds at sea around Bougainville and in the
Bismarck Sea include one flock of 250 between
Buka and Kieta. Additional observations near
Kolombangara, Solomon Islands, suggest that
the birds could also breed there in mountain
forests. Threats are unknown at present, but
Kolombangara has pigs and dogs and the birds
may suffer from increasing loss of breeding
habitat.

PERUVIAN DIVING-PETREL

Pelecanoides garnotii L 22 cm (8.5 in), WS ?
Small diving-petrel, restricted to the Humboldt
Current off western South America. Rapidly
diminishing population this century, and now
classified as Endangered.
IDENTIFICATION Characteristic jizz; blackish
above and white below. Head mostly blackish,
darker than on Common or South Georgian
Diving-petrel; lores and forehead a browner
black than crown, nape and hindneck,
extending to ear-coverts and sides of neck; chin
and throat white. Upperparts from mantle to
tail glossy blackish; tips of scapulars variably
whitish, forming pale, often irregular, diagonal
stripe. Underparts mainly white, with sides of
upper breast mottled greyish (may form

indistinct breastband); flanks and axillaries
deepish grey, undertail whitish. Upperwing
glossy blackish, outer primaries a browner
black; secondaries blackish, tipped white.
Underwing-coverts mainly whitish-grey, flight
feathers darker grey; leading edge may be
narrowly whitish. Bill black; iris dark brown;
legs and feet blue, webs black. General
appearance at sea more black and white than
Common Diving-petrel. For differences from
Magellan Diving-petrel, see that species:
separable at sea.
DISTRIBUTION AND STATUS Restricted to
Humboldt Current off western South America,
from Peru to Chiloé in Chile. Breeds in austral
winter and early spring, to coincide with
upwelling, on offshore islands from Isla Lobos
de Tierra (6°S) in Peru to Chiloé (43°S).
Mainland colonies have been reported, but
without detail. Formerly abundant numbers
have rapidly declined, a result of guano
extraction destroying nesting sites, exploitation
by man for food, predation by mammals (eg
foxes on Chanaral Island), and competition
with commercial fisheries. Peru population
estimated at 1,500 birds (mainly on San Gallan
Island and La Vieja Island) while the main Chile
population is found on Pan de Azucar Island
and Choros Island (possibly 500 pairs).

MAGELLAN DIVING-PETREL

Pelecanoides magellani L 19 cm (7.5 in), WS ?
The smallest diving-petrel, confined to
southern South America.
IDENTIFICATION Can be aged and identified at
sea, although there is a range overlap with both
Common and Peruvian Diving-petrels. **Juvenile**
As adult, but with smaller bill; scapulars, lower
back and rump lack variable whitish tips. **Adult**
Forehead and lores blackish-brown; crown,
nape and hindneck blackish, shading to blackish-
grey on cheeks, suborbital region and ear-
coverts, sharply demarcated from white chin
and throat; whitish crescent curls from below
ear-coverts upwards and backwards towards
upper hindneck, imparting a capped and
collared appearance and perhaps extending
narrowly above ear-coverts towards eye.
Upperparts glossy black, with narrow whitish
tips to lower back and upper rump; scapulars
greyish, with variable white tips usually forming
whitish stripe along top of closed wing. Tail
blackish. Underparts white, with greyish
mottling on upper breast sides, flanks and
axillaries; undertail greyish with narrow
blackish tip. Upperwing has primaries blackish-
brown with paler inner webs, secondaries
blackish with narrow white tips; coverts
blackish with white tips and fringes. Underwing
mainly white, with dusky grey primaries
forming dark tip and trailing edge, extending
more narrowly onto secondaries. Note that
whitish tips to wing-coverts, secondaries, back
and rump in fresh plumage (August) become
reduced or absent in worn plumage (March).
Bill black; iris dark brown; legs and feet blue
with black webs.

DISTRIBUTION AND STATUS Eastern Pacific;
southern South America. Found in fjords and
inlets of southern Chile, Patagonia and Tierra
del Fuego. Occurs north to Chiloé Island
(Chile) and Puerto Deseado (Patagonia) during
winter. Common; no evidence of population
changes.

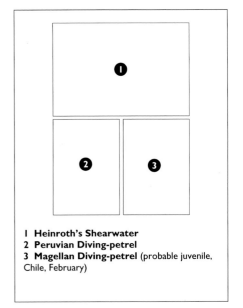

1 **Heinroth's Shearwater**
2 **Peruvian Diving-petrel**
3 **Magellan Diving-petrel** (probable juvenile,
Chile, February)

DIVING-PETRELS & STORM-PETRELS

SOUTH GEORGIAN DIVING-PETREL

Pelecanoides georgicus L 20 cm (8 in), WS 32 cm (13 in)
Small subantarctic diving-petrel. At sea, separation from Common Diving-petrel considered virtually impossible.
IDENTIFICATION Flight low, fast and direct with rapid whirring wingbeats, often plunging into waves. Usually in small groups near breeding islands. Excellent swimmer and diver, using wings underwater (like small penguin); feeds mainly on euphausiids (Common Diving-petrel feeds on copepods). Not a ship-follower, but attracted to ships' lights at night. Stocky jizz, with short neck and tail, small wings; blackish above and whitish below. Forehead, lores and suborbital area dark brownish; crown, nape and hindneck blackish, shading to bluish-grey on sides of neck and ear-coverts and occasionally extending upwards behind ear-coverts; chin and throat generally white, lower throat sometimes showing greyish mottling. Upperparts glossy black; scapulars greyish-white with grey tips, which may form a diagonal stripe; tail glossy black. Underparts white, with variable greyish mottling on sides of breast and flanks; undertail light grey. Upperwing has primaries blackish-brown with whitish inner webs, secondaries blackish-brown with narrow white tips, coverts blackish-brown with broad glossy black fringes. Underwing with coverts white, axillaries greyish, primaries and secondaries grey. Bill black; iris black-brown; legs and feet blue, webs blackish. Doubtfully distinguished at sea from Common by smaller size, less dark plumage, pale tips to scapulars, white tips to secondaries, blacker upperwing with paler inner webs of primaries (brown on Common), and white underwing-coverts (grey on Common).
DISTRIBUTION AND STATUS Subantarctic islands. Breeds South Georgia (2 million pairs), Prince Edwards (thousands), Crozets (millions), Kerguelen (1-2 million pairs), McDonald (c 10,000 pairs), Heard Island (10,000-100,000 pairs), Codfish Island, New Zealand (30-35 pairs). Pelagic dispersal not well known. Some populations (South Georgia) are sedentary, other sites (Crozets) deserted in non-breeding season. One record Australia. Status stable, but predation by skuas, rats and cats.

COMMON DIVING-PETREL

Pelecanoides urinatrix L 23 cm (9 in), WS 35 cm (14 in)
Small, southern circumpolar diving-petrel, very similar to South Georgian Diving-petrel. Most widespread and most dispersive of the genus.
IDENTIFICATION Forehead and lores glossy black, fading to dark brown; crown, nape and hindneck glossy black, shading to bluish-grey on sides of neck and ear-coverts and sometimes extending upwards behind ear-coverts; chin white. Throat white with variable grey mottling, which may form complete indistinct collar on darkest birds (generally darker than South

Georgian Diving-petrel). Upperparts glossy black when fresh, mantle and back acquiring dark brown tips when worn; some scapulars have whitish tips when fresh (less noticeable than on South Georgian). Tail glossy black, becoming blackish-brown when worn. Underparts white, with variable grey collar extending onto breast sides; flanks and undertail-coverts have greyish wash. Upperwing with primaries and secondaries blackish-brown, fading to dark brown, primaries with brownish inner webs; secondaries sometimes have narrow white tips when fresh; coverts blackish-brown. Underwing-coverts variably grey, with flight feathers greyish-black, coverts perhaps darker than on South Georgian. Bill black; iris dark brown; legs and feet blue, webs blackish. See South Georgian for possible differences at sea. In the hand, inner webs of outer primaries brown, and differs in bill shape and size, otherwise plumage and habits as South Georgian.
DISTRIBUTION AND STATUS Circumpolar between 35°S and 55°S. Distribution at sea complicated by problems of identification. Breeds on Diego Ramirez and islands off southern Chile (large population), Falklands (10,000 pairs), South Georgia (3.8 million pairs), Tristan da Cunha group (hundreds to thousands of pairs), Gough Island ('breeds'), Prince Edwards (extinct Marion Island owing to cats), Crozets (millions of pairs), Kerguelen (abundant), formerly Amsterdam and St Paul Islands, and breeds Heard, McDonald and Macquarie Islands; also Campbell, Auckland, Antipodes, Snares Islands, Stewart Island, Codfish, Solander Islands, Chathams and many offshore islands off North Island, New Zealand (New Zealand population 100,000 to 1 million pairs); Tasmania and also Victoria. Most populations stable, but some declining from cats, rats and also livestock grazing and trampling. Movements at sea not well known, but occasionally seen in mid-ocean.

WILSON'S STORM-PETREL

Oceanites oceanicus L 17 cm (7 in), WS 40 cm (16 in)
Small, blackish-brown storm-petrel found commonly in all three oceans.
IDENTIFICATION Normal flight purposeful, without Leach's Storm-petrel's bounding and less gliding, reminiscent of hirundines. Feeding flight slower; patters on surface. Gregarious, and a ship-follower. Short rounded wings, short square tail and yellow-webbed feet; plumage uniformly dark, with pale diagonal bar on upperwing and conspicuous white 'U' on rump. Head uniformly blackish-brown. Upperparts blackish-brown, with sharply defined white 'U'-shaped patch on rump joining white sides to lower flanks. Tail blackish, short and square-ended (feet may project slightly). Underparts blackish-brown, with white sides to lower flanks joining white on rump. Upperwing: primary coverts, primaries and secondaries blackish, darker than upperparts; greater

coverts greyish to greyish-brown, forming pale diagonal bar from carpal joint to trailing edge of inner wing, this becoming more prominent in worn plumage (May-October), often with whitish tips; remaining coverts blackish-brown. Underwing-coverts blackish-brown, with flight feathers blackish-grey; may show faint pale area along coverts. Bill very small, black; iris dark brown; legs and feet blackish with yellow webs. Between British and Leach's Storm-petrel in size; wing shape short, with little bend at carpal joint and rounded tips. From Leach's and Madeiran Storm-petrels by size, jizz, tail shape, more extensive white rump, and flight. From British (which has similar jizz) by size, paler upperwing bar, lack of pale underwing bar, and flight.
DISTRIBUTION AND STATUS Breeds Antarctic Continent, Antarctic Peninsula, and many subantarctic islands; circumpolar in summer. Reputed to be one of the World's most numerous seabirds with a total population of several million pairs, some colonies being vast (eg South Shetland Islands c 1 million pairs). Post-breeding dispersal (about May-November) north of Equator in all three oceans: has reached 77°N in Atlantic, Persian Gulf in Indian Ocean, and Japan and Washington in Pacific Ocean where less numerous. Some predation by rats and cats (Crozets and Kerguelen), otherwise stable. Large scale krill exploitation may affect population, and breeding success affected by snow blocking burrows.

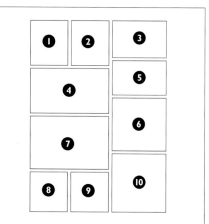

1 **South Georgian Diving-petrel** (at sea, off South Georgia)
2 **South Georgian Diving-petrel** (South Georgia, December)
3 **South Georgian Diving-petrel** (Codfish Island, New Zealand)
4 **Common Diving-petrel** (Southeast Island, New Zealand, September)
5 **Common Diving-petrel** (Snares Island, January)
6 **Common Diving-petrel** (Snares Island, January)
7 **Wilson's Storm-petrel** (at breeding site)
8 **Wilson's Storm-petrel** (south Atlantic Ocean, December)
9 **Wilson's Storm-petrel** (off South Africa)
10 **Wilson's Storm-petrel** (south Atlantic Ocean, December)

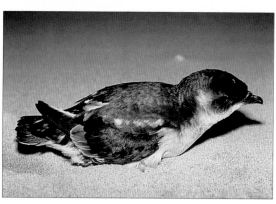

STORM-PETRELS

ELLIOT'S or WHITE-VENTED STORM-PETREL

Oceanites gracilis L 15 cm (6 in), WS ?
Very small eastern Pacific storm-petrel, little known but not particularly rare, though only one nest has been found.

IDENTIFICATION Normal flight buoyant and low over water, with rapid, fairly shallow wingbeats; patters on surface with wings raised in shallow 'V' and legs dangling. Gregarious; follows ships. Plumage mainly dark, with white rump, white belly and indistinct pale area on underwing. Head uniformly blackish-brown. Upperparts mainly blackish-brown, with well-demarcated white on rump extending to sides of lower flanks. Tail blackish, short and square-ended (in flight, feet usually extend beyond tail, more so than on Wilson's Storm-petrel). Underparts usually blackish-brown on upper breast, flanks and undertail-coverts, enclosing white belly of variable size, white of belly separated from white on sides of rump by narrow brownish thighs; undertail blackish. Primary coverts, primaries and secondaries blackish, darker than upperparts; greater coverts paler, brownish-grey, forming pale diagonal bar from carpal joint to trailing edge of inner wing; rest of coverts dark brownish. Underwing dark brown, with whitish-grey central area on coverts. Bill small, black; iris brownish; legs and feet black with yellow webs. Much like a diminutive Wilson's Storm-petrel in jizz, with variable white belly, and paler underwing; feet project comparatively more.

DISTRIBUTION AND STATUS Eastern Pacific, from Galapagos to central Chile in Humboldt Current; pelagic dispersal unknown but may range northwards to Colombia and Panama. Numerous at Galapagos: 'many thousands', but breeding sites remain undiscovered. Not yet proved to breed in Peru, where status and numbers unknown. Only nest found was on Chingungo Island (29°S) off Chile. Breeds in austral winter and spring, to coincide with upwelling. Threats and status/population remain unknown.

GREY-BACKED STORM-PETREL

Garrodia nereis L 17 cm (7 in), WS 39 cm (15 in)
Smallest Southern Ocean storm-petrel.
IDENTIFICATION Normal flight fast and direct, with continuous fluttering wingbeats and no gliding. Feeding flight slower and more variable; patters on surface with outstretched wings. Can be gregarious; will follow ships, and attracted to trawlers and long-liners. Plumage blackish-grey above, with darker head, pale grey rump and dark-tipped grey tail, and white below, with dark-margined underwing. Head, neck and upper breast blackish-grey, sharply demarcated from white underparts and forming blackish hood. Hood merges into ash-grey mantle and back; rump and uppertail-coverts paler, clearer ash-grey. Uppertail ash-grey with narrow blackish tip (feet extend beyond tail in normal flight). Underparts white from upper breast downwards; undertail blackish. Upperwing: primary coverts, primaries and secondaries blackish; greater coverts pale greyish-white, forming pale diagonal bar from carpal to trailing edge of inner wing; remaining coverts blackish-grey. Underwing mainly white centrally, with broad dark margin that is thicker and blacker on leading edge (marginal coverts) and shades around tip of wing to thinner greyish-black trailing edge (primaries and secondaries). In fresh plumage mantle, scapulars, rump and most wing-coverts narrowly fringed white, imparting scaled appearance, becoming reduced when worn, when mantle thus appears duller ash-grey. Bill black; iris dark brown; legs and feet blackish.

DISTRIBUTION AND STATUS Mainly subantarctic zone of all three oceans, generally northwards to *c* 35°S (Subtropical Convergence), while south of Antarctic Convergence at South Georgia. Range contraction around breeding islands in summer; possibly circumpolar in non-breeding season. Few records in eastern Pacific. Wide range, but known colonies are not huge and not well known. In Atlantic, breeds at Falklands, South Georgia, Gough Island; in Indian Ocean, at Prince Edwards, Crozets, Kerguelen (3,000-5,000 pairs); in Pacific, probably at Macquarie, Chathams (10,000-12,000 birds), Antipodes, Auckland, probably Campbell Island. Total population of 10,000-50,000 pairs appears stable, but not well known. May suffer from introduced mammalian predators (eg on Possession, in Crozets).

WHITE-FACED STORM-PETREL

Pelagodroma marina L 20 cm (8 in), WS 42 cm (17 in)
Medium-sized to large, distinctive storm-petrel found in all three oceans.
IDENTIFICATION Normal flight erratic, prion-like, with banking and short glides on bowed wings, rapid jerky wingbeats recalling Common Sandpiper. Feeding flight more variable: uses feet to 'push off' from sea surface, will face into wind with wings outstretched, using feet (aerial dipping and contact-dipping). Not normally a ship-follower. Brownish-grey above, with dark flight feathers and tail, grey rump, and patterned face, and white below. Crown and nape dark sooty-grey, imparting capped appearance, becoming browner-grey on hindneck and sides of neck (Cape Verde subspecies *P. m. eadesi* has whiter forehead and variable whitish hindneck); forehead, lores, supercilium, chin and throat white; dark grey suborbital stripe from before eye to rear of ear-coverts, not joining brownish-grey on sides of neck. Mantle, back and scapulars brownish-grey; rump and uppertail-coverts contrasting pale grey; tail slightly forked, blackish-brown and contrasting with pale grey rump (feet extend beyond tail in normal flight). Underparts white, with narrow extension of brownish-grey from hindneck and sides of neck onto sides of upper breast (some New Zealand birds of *P. m.*

maoriana may show a complete breastband); undertail blackish-brown. Inner wing-coverts brownish-grey as mantle; greater coverts have whitish tips and fringes forming variable diagonal bar on inner wing from carpal joint towards trailing edge; primary coverts, primaries and secondaries blackish-brown. Underwing mainly white, with very narrow dark leading edge and broader blackish tip (primaries) and trailing edge (flight feathers). In fresh plumage mantle, back, scapulars and inner wing-coverts mid grey, with wear generally becoming browner with more conspicuous paler greater coverts. Bill blackish; iris dark brown; legs (extremely long for size of bird) and feet blackish with yellowish webs. Unlikely to be confused, but note that Grey Phalarope at sea resembles White-faced Storm-petrel in plumage and size.

DISTRIBUTION AND STATUS Temperate and subtropical regions of all three oceans. Breeds Salvages, Cape Verdes, Tristan da Cunha group and Gough Island; Western and South Australia, Victoria, Tasmania, New South Wales, New Zealand, Stewart Island, Auckland and Chathams (New Zealand population over 1 million breeding pairs); may breed on St Helena, Amsterdam and Kermadecs. General dispersal from temperate breeding sites to subtropics and tropics. Vagrant Germany; recently recorded South Africa. Vulnerable to gull predation and to humans collapsing burrows as well as human exploitation.

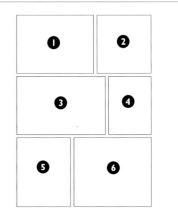

1 **Elliot's Storm-petrel** (Isabela, Galapagos Islands, November)
2 **Grey-backed Storm-petrel** (Victoria, Australia, February)
3 **Grey-backed Storm-petrel** (at breeding site, Kidney Island, Falkland Islands)
4 **Grey-backed Storm-petrel** (off Tasmania, October)
5 **White-faced Storm-petrel** (Victoria, Australia, February)
6 **White-faced Storm-petrel** (adult at breeding site, Southeast Island, New Zealand, September)

STORM-PETRELS

BLACK-BELLIED STORM-PETREL

Fregetta tropica L 20 cm (8 in), WS 46 cm (18 in)
Medium-sized, southern circumpolar storm-petrel.

IDENTIFICATION Normal flight erratic, low and zigzagging; does not patter, but uses feet against sea surface. May investigate ships but not a follower; readily attracted to chum. Associates with cetaceans, and probably locates food by smell. Blackish above, with white rump, and generally white below, with variable blackish central stripe from blackish head and upper breast to blackish undertail-coverts. Head and hindneck blackish-brown, this extending to upper breast; chin whitish. Mantle and back blackish-brown; rump and uppertail-coverts white, sharply demarcated and extending narrowly onto white flanks; tail blackish (feet extend slightly beyond tail in normal flight). Throat and upper breast blackish-brown, this colour normally extending as thin black central belly stripe to black undertail-coverts and undertail, with white flanks, thighs and sides of belly (black and white of underparts usually fairly sharply demarcated); some birds may lack blackish central stripe on belly and abdomen. Upperwing-coverts dark brown, greater coverts with whitish fringes and tips appearing as pale diagonal bar on inner wing from carpal joint to trailing edge; primary coverts, primaries and secondaries blackish. Underwing with whitish triangular central coverts enclosed by dark leading edge, broader dark tip (primaries) and broad trailing edge (flight feathers) narrowing at inner secondaries. Bill black; iris dark brown; legs and feet blackish.

DISTRIBUTION AND STATUS Circumpolar in antarctic and subantarctic waters. Breeds South Shetlands, Elephant Island (28,500 pairs), South Orkneys, South Georgia (c 50,000 pairs), Tristan da Cunha group and Gough Island, Prince Edwards, Crozets, Kerguelen; Antipodes and Auckland (c 50,000-100,000 pairs); possibly breeds Bouvet, South Sandwich, Heard Island. Total population c 150,000 pairs. Widespread breeding distribution, but nowhere abundant, dispersing north to subtropical and tropical waters of all three oceans; gathers in hundreds around long-liners. Reaches Northern Hemisphere in Atlantic and Indian Oceans. More southerly distribution than White-bellied Storm-petrel.

WHITE-BELLIED STORM-PETREL

Fregetta grallaria L 20 cm (8 in), WS 46 cm (18 in)
Medium-sized, southern circumpolar storm-petrel.

IDENTIFICATION Normal flight much as that of Black-bellied Storm-petrel; 'skips' with feet on sea surface, feeds by dipping and pattering. Generally not a ship-follower, but may investigate ship's wake briefly. Plumage blackish above, with white rump, and variably white below from upper breast to undertail-coverts (darkest examples from Lord Howe may be completely dark below). Head and hindneck blackish-brown, extending to upper breast and sharply demarcated from white underparts; chin dark. Mantle, back, scapulars and upper rump blackish-brown, with paler white fringes imparting scaled appearance; uppertail-coverts white, clearly demarcated and extending to join white of flanks. Tail blackish, darker than mantle (unlike Black-bellied Storm-petrel, feet generally not extending beyond tail in normal flight). Underparts white from upper breast to vent; undertail-coverts generally dark (some may show white traces), undertail blackish. (Note that birds from Lord Howe show continuous gradation from white underparts to all-dark underparts, including underwing.) Upperwing-coverts dark brownish with indistinct paler fringes; greater coverts paler greyish-brown with whitish fringes, showing as indistinct pale diagonal bar from carpal joint to trailing edge; primary coverts, primaries and secondaries blackish (as uppertail). Underwing with whitish central triangular-shaped wing-coverts bordered by blackish-brown leading edge of wing, broader blackish-brown tip (primaries) and broad dark trailing edge (flight feathers) narrowing towards innermost secondaries. Bill black; iris dark brown; legs and feet black.

DISTRIBUTION AND STATUS Subtropical Atlantic, Indian and Pacific Oceans; rare in subantarctic waters. Breeds Tristan da Cunha group, Gough Island, St Paul, Lord Howe (c 1,000 pairs), Kermadecs (c 1,000 pairs), Austral group, Rapa, Juan Fernandez. Total population a few thousand breeding pairs. Dispersal north to tropics after breeding, but movements poorly understood. Recorded Coral Sea and north of New Zealand and Tasman Sea, but few records Australia; recorded to 7°S in Atlantic and to 2°N in west Pacific.

WHITE-THROATED or POLYNESIAN STORM-PETREL

Nesofregetta fuliginosa L 25 cm (10 in), WS ?
Large, polymorphic, Pacific storm-petrel with broad and rounded wings and long forked tail.

IDENTIFICATION Normal flight sailing, using feet to kick from water surface, with changes of direction and variable flight speed. Dark above, with narrow white rump band, and variable below from white to sooty-brown. *Typical*: Head and hindneck blackish-brown, this extending from lower mandible below eye and ear-coverts, curling upwards towards nape and then across throat, isolating white chin. Mantle, back, scapulars and rump blackish-brown; uppertail-coverts white, forming conspicuous narrow band joining white of underparts. Tail blackish, long and deeply forked (feet project beyond tail in flight). Underparts: blackish-brown of hindneck extends across sides of neck and foreneck to form clearly demarcated upper breastband; lower breast and belly to vent white; undertail-coverts and undertail blackish-brown. Upperwing-coverts blackish-brown; inner greater coverts have whitish tips forming a short paler bar on inner wing; primary coverts, primaries and secondaries blackish. Underwing has central coverts white, with blackish-brown leading edge becoming broader at wing tips (primaries) and forming broad trailing edge across flight feathers, narrowing towards innermost secondaries. Bill blackish; iris dark brown; legs and feet blackish-grey. *Intermediates*: Upperparts as typical; 50% of Christmas Island birds show variable blackish-brown streaking on lower breast, belly and underwing-coverts. Phoenix and McKean Island populations show continuous gradation between pale and dark morphs. *Dark*: Samoan birds entirely sooty-brown, apart from pale upperwing bar and narrow white rump band. Care needed to distinguish from Tristram's Storm-petrel. White-throated is the largest storm-petrel, having broad wings with rounded tips and no angle (unlike *Oceanodroma*).

DISTRIBUTION AND STATUS Tropical Pacific Ocean. Breeds Gambier, Line (Christmas Islands), Phoenix and McKean Islands, Sala y Gomez; may breed Marquesas, possibly Samoa, Fiji, Vanuatu. Total population unknown but various islands hold several thousand pairs. Dispersal not known; believed to remain in warm Pacific waters along south Equatorial Current.

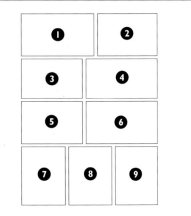

1 **Black-bellied Storm-petrel** (off Sydney, Australia, December)
2 **Black-bellied Storm-petrel** (in Tasman Sea)
3 **Black-bellied Storm-petrel** (off Sydney, Australia)
4 **White-bellied Storm-petrel** (Gough Island)
5 **White-bellied Storm-petrel** (off South Africa)
6 **White-bellied Storm-petrel** (Gough Island)
7 **White-throated (Polynesian) Storm-petrel**
8 **White-throated (Polynesian) Storm-petrel**
9 **White-throated (Polynesian) Storm-petrel**

STORM-PETRELS

BRITISH or EUROPEAN STORM-PETREL

Hydrobates pelagicus L 15 cm (6 in), WS 37 cm (15 in)
Small, dark, north Atlantic storm-petrel with fluttering bat-like flight.
IDENTIFICATION Flight weak and continually fluttering, interspersed with very short periods of gliding: noticeably bat-like, with wingbeats generally rapid. Patters with feet on water surface, but does not 'walk' on water as Wilson's Storm-petrel. Generally gregarious at sea. Will follow ships; attracted to trawlers. Plumage dark, with square white rump, barely visible paler greater coverts on upperwing, and diagnostic white stripe on central underwing. Head and hindneck sooty-black, slightly paler on forehead. Mantle, back and scapulars sooty-black, continuous with head colour; rump and uppertail-coverts white, conspicuous and square, extending marginally to upper sides of flanks only. Tail blackish, short and square-ended (feet do not project in flight). Underparts sooty-black from bill to undertail, slightly browner on belly and with chin slightly paler; extension of white rump onto lower flanks more extensive than on Leach's Storm-petrel, but less than on Wilson's Storm-petrel. Upperwing sooty-black, flight feathers darker than mantle, with whitish tips to greater coverts forming indistinct diagonal bar on inner wing. Underwing sooty-brown, with diagnostic white central stripe from axillaries to greater coverts. Bill black; iris dark brown; legs and feet blackish. From Wilson's Storm-petrel by smaller size, darker upperwing, whiter underwing, shape and extent of white rump, absence of projecting feet beyond tail. From similar Atlantic *Oceanodroma* species (Leach's and Madeiran Storm-petrels) by smaller size, wing and tail shape, upperwing and underwing patterns, and flight. Wing shape short and broad, without the carpal bend typical of *Oceanodroma* species.
DISTRIBUTION AND STATUS North Atlantic. Breeds (April-September) Norway, Faeroes, Iceland, British Isles, most Mediterranean countries, Canaries (southern limit), but not on Azores or Cape Verdes. Total population 130,000-290,000 breeding pairs. Dispersal southwards; Mediterranean population may be sedentary, while others move south to seas off Namibia and South Africa east to Natal and south to 38°S. Rare western north Atlantic. Some colonies have declined through human interference, rats and gulls.

LEAST STORM-PETREL

Oceanodroma microsoma L 14 cm (5.5 in), WS 32 cm (13 in)
Very small, dark storm-petrel of the American Pacific coast, the smallest storm-petrel.
IDENTIFICATION Normal flight swift and direct, with deep wingbeats, more rapid than that of Black Storm-petrel. Wings held in 'V' when feeding, often while sitting on water; splashes

forward breast first. Does not foot-patter. Very small size, with comparatively short rounded wings, and short wedge-shaped (not forked) tail which appears rounded at sea. Entirely blackish-brown on head, upperparts, underparts and tail, with greyish-brown greater coverts forming paler diagonal bar on inner upperwing from carpal joint to trailing edge. Upper mantle may be slightly paler greyish-brown. Feet do not extend beyond tail in normal flight. Bill blackish; iris dark brown; legs and feet blackish. From larger Ashy Storm-petrel by size, shorter wedge-shaped (not forked) tail, dark (not pale) underwing-coverts, and more fluttering flight with deeper wingbeats. From larger Black Storm-petrel by size, smaller wings, wedge-shaped (not forked) tail, faster wingbeats.
DISTRIBUTION AND STATUS North-east Pacific Ocean off American coast of Baja California and Gulf of California. Off the Pacific coast of Baja California breeds only on Islas San Benito (c 15,000 breeding birds). Most abundant seabird in Gulf of California, concentrated mainly on Cardinosa and Little Cardinosa islands. Probably breeds on all islands free from predators in Gulf of California. Population perhaps numbers millions of birds. After breeding, disperses south to Central America, extending south to Colombia, Ecuador and possibly Peru (status here needs clarification).

GALAPAGOS or WEDGE-RUMPED STORM-PETREL

Oceanodroma tethys L 19 cm (7.5 in), WS 37 cm (15 in)
Small to medium-sized, dark, eastern Pacific storm-petrel. Classified as Near-threatened.
IDENTIFICATION Normal flight direct and fast, often quite high, with deep full wingbeats accompanied by a lot of banking, wings usually bowed and held forward with noticeable angle at carpal joint. Feeding flight more bounding; dips from surface with trailing legs, not normally 'walking on surface'. Generally gregarious at sea. Occasional ship-follower. Unlike other storm-petrels, visits breeding colonies in daylight, and consequently suffers predation by Short-eared Owls. Plumage dark, with very large triangular-shaped area of white on rump and uppertail-coverts, extending laterally onto lower flanks and thighs. Head and neck sooty-blackish. Mantle, back and scapulars blackish-brown; rump and uppertail-coverts conspicuously white, forming large triangular shape from just below trailing edge of wing almost to central tip of tail, and extending laterally onto lower flanks and thighs (the most extensive white rump of any storm-petrel). Tail black, forked (feet do not extend beyond tail in flight). Underparts blackish-brown from chin to underside of tail, with white lower flanks and thighs (extension of rump colour). Upperwing-coverts blackish-brown, greater coverts paler and forming fairly conspicuous diagonal bar on inner wing from carpal joint to trailing edge; primary coverts, primaries and secondaries

blackish. Underwing blackish-brown with paler central wing-coverts. Bill blackish; iris dark brown; legs and feet blackish.
DISTRIBUTION AND STATUS Eastern Pacific Ocean. Breeds in Galapagos on Genovesa and San Cristóbal, with an estimated population of 200,000. Presumed breeding in Peru (San Gallan, 13°50'S), but numbers unknown; also Islas Pescadores off Ancón, possibly also Isla La Vieja, and Isla San Lorenzo off Lima. Both populations disperse north after breeding, reaching seas off Ecuador, Colombia and Panama; more rarely seas off Mexico. Vagrants north to California.

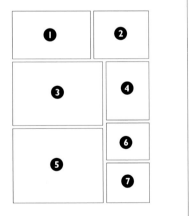

1 **British Storm-petrel** (at breeding site, Skomer Island, Wales)
2 **British Storm-petrel** (Merseyside, England)
3 **British Storm-petrel** (feeding flock, off Cornwall, England, August)
4 **Least Storm-petrel**
5 **Least Storm-petrel** (at breeding site)
6 **Galapagos (Wedge-rumped) Storm-petrel** (Galapagos Islands)
7 **Galapagos (Wedge-rumped) Storm-petrel** (Galapagos Islands)

STORM-PETRELS

MADEIRAN or BAND-RUMPED STORM-PETREL

Oceanodroma castro L 20 cm (8 in), WS 43 cm (17 in)
Medium-sized, dark, tropical Atlantic and Pacific storm-petrel.

IDENTIFICATION Normal flight buoyant, with relatively quick wingbeats interspersed with short shearwater-like glides on bowed wings: essentially intermediate between fluttering flight of British Storm-petrel and more erratic flight of Leach's Storm-petrel. Does not regularly patter on surface. Tends to be solitary at sea. Not a ship-follower. Dark-plumaged, with conspicuous white rump and pale diagonal upperwing bar, and longish forked tail. Head and neck blackish-brown. Mantle, scapulars and back blackish-brown; rump and uppertail-coverts white, narrow and conspicuous, extending slightly onto lower flanks. Tail blackish, quite long and slightly forked (feet do not extend beyond tail in flight). Underparts blackish-brown, browner than upperparts. Upperwing-coverts blackish-brown, greater coverts paler, greyish-brown, and forming pale diagonal bar on inner wing from carpal joint to trailing edge; primary coverts, primaries and secondaries blackish. Underwing blackish-brown, with variable paler central stripe across coverts. Bill black; iris dark brown; legs and feet blackish. Jizz and wing shape between Wilson's and Leach's Storm-petrels. From Leach's (same size) by shorter, broader wings, shallower tail fork, less noticeable pale upperwing-coverts, more extensive, whiter and more even rump, and rather smoother, more shearwater-like flight. From Wilson's by larger size, wing shape, forked tail without foot projection, less noticeable pale upperwing-coverts, and narrower white rump extending less onto lower flanks.

DISTRIBUTION AND STATUS Tropical and subtropical Atlantic and Pacific Oceans. In Atlantic, breeds Azores, Desertas, Porto Santo, Salvages (1,500+ pairs), Cape Verdes, Berlengas (50 pairs), Canaries, Ascension (c 1,500 pairs), St Helena (23 pairs), probably also in Gulf of Guinea; in Pacific, breeds on islands off Japan (25,000 pairs on Hide Island off Honshu), main Hawaiian islands, and Galapagos (c 15,000 pairs). Some populations suffer from mammalian predation and exploitation by fishermen. Atlantic dispersal not well known, but recorded Brazil, Cuba, Canada and eastern USA (which may indicate dispersal towards western north Atlantic), and vagrant Britain and Finland. Highly pelagic when not breeding. Pacific dispersal appears to be confined within subtropical and tropical waters. Vagrant Eilat (Israel).

LEACH'S STORM-PETREL

Oceanodroma leucorhoa L 20 cm (8 in), WS 46 cm (18 in)
Medium-sized, dark storm-petrel of the north Pacific and Atlantic Oceans.

IDENTIFICATION Normal flight fast and bounding, with deep wingbeats interspersed with short periods of gliding on bowed and slightly angled wings, often with rapid changes of direction and speed. Will patter on water surface, and may rest on sea. Does not follow ships. Dark-plumaged, with pale upperwing bar and variable white rump; long angular wings and forked tail. Head and neck blackish-brown, slightly darker on crown, and a greyer brown on forehead, lores and chin. Mantle, back and scapulars blackish-brown; usually white patch on lower rump and uppertail-coverts, partially divided centrally or with complete narrow blackish-brown central streak (some north-eastern Pacific birds have dark rump continuous with mantle colour). Tail blackish, long and forked (feet do not project beyond tail in flight). Underparts slightly browner than upperparts; white of rump (if present) usually extends marginally onto lateral undertail-coverts. Upperwing-coverts mainly blackish-brown, with pale whitish-grey tips to greater coverts forming conspicuous pale bar on inner wing from carpal joint to trailing edge; primary coverts, primaries and secondaries blackish. Underwing dark brown; no distinct white on coverts. Bill black; iris dark brown; legs and feet black. From Madeiran Storm-petrel by longer, more angular wings, more prominent upperwing bar, and more erratic flight. From smaller and darker Wilson's and British Storm-petrels by wing shape, rump, forked tail and flight. In north-eastern Pacific, dark-rumped birds resemble Ashy and Black Storm-petrels, differing mainly in flight, shape and jizz.

DISTRIBUTION AND STATUS North Pacific and Atlantic Oceans. In Pacific, breeds Hokkaido (2 million birds), Kuril Islands (350,000 birds), Sakhalin, Commanders, Aleutians (1,060,000 birds) and Gulf of Alaska (1,210,000 birds), giving Alaskan population of c 4 million birds – many former colonies now re-established; also British Columbia (1,100,000 birds) south to Los Coronados, San Benito, Isla Guadelupe and Rocas Alijos (Guadelupe may have three different populations). In Atlantic, breeds eastern North America (750,000+ pairs), with fewer in Westmann Islands, Faeroes, Norway, Scotland, Ireland. Total population perhaps 10 million birds. Dispersal south to tropical and subtropical waters in non-breeding season: regular South Africa, has reached Southern Ocean, occasionally Indian Ocean; vagrant Australia and New Zealand. Birds found in burrows New Zealand, and recently proved to breed off the South African coast.

SWINHOE'S STORM-PETREL

Oceanodroma monorhis L 20 cm (8 in), WS 45 cm (18 in)
Medium-sized, dark, mainly Pacific storm-petrel. Classified as Near-threatened.

IDENTIFICATION Flight fast and swooping, often with vertical leaping, similar to Leach's. Does not follow ships. Uniformly dark, with paler diagonal bar across upperwing-coverts; longish angled wings, forked tail. Head and hindneck dark brown. Mantle, back, scapulars and rump dark brown. Tail blackish-brown, with shallow fork which is difficult to see (legs do not project beyond tail in flight). Underparts dark brown, including undertail; chin slightly paler. Upperwing-coverts dark brown, greater coverts greyish-white and forming paler inconspicuous diagonal bar on inner wing from carpal joint to trailing edge; primary coverts, primaries and secondaries blackish, darker than upperparts. Underwing brownish, with greyer tinge on central underwing-coverts. Bill black; iris dark brown; legs and feet blackish. From larger Matsudaira's Storm-petrel by smaller size, narrower and more angled wings, and faster flight; unlike on Matsudaira's, white primary bases not normally visible at sea. From Tristram's Storm-petrel by smaller size, less obvious upperwing bar, less deeply notched tail, lack of greyish-blue cast to plumage.

DISTRIBUTION AND STATUS North-west Pacific Ocean. Breeds Sea of Japan, Russia on Verkhovsky (7,500 pairs), Karamzin (30-40 pairs) in Peter the Great Bay, with smaller colonies on the mainland coast; some evidence of recent decline. Also on islands off south-west Honshu, Shikoku and Kyushu (Okinoshima, 180 pairs; Kutsujima in Wakasa Bay, 500-600 birds) and on Oshima; may also breed on islands off northern Honshu, as well as Korea and China, but status there not well known. Dispersal south-westwards to Singapore and into northern Indian Ocean and Arabian Sea, west to Somalia; has reached Eilat (Israel). Recent spate of north Atlantic records (Salvages, Spain, Italy, France, England, Norway) may indicate undiscovered Atlantic colony.

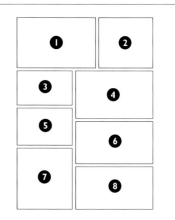

1 **Madeiran Storm-petrel** (at breeding site)
2 **Madeiran Storm-petrel** (at breeding site)
3 **Leach's Storm-petrel** (Lancashire, England)
4 **Leach's Storm-petrel** (at breeding site)
5 **Leach's Storm-petrel** (Lancashire, England)
6 **Swinhoe's Storm-petrel** (Tynemouth, England)
7 **Swinhoe's Storm-petrel** (Tynemouth, England)
8 **Swinhoe's Storm-petrel** (Tynemouth, England)

STORM-PETRELS

TRISTRAM'S STORM-PETREL

Oceanodroma tristrami L 24 cm (9.5 in), WS 56 cm (22 in)

Large and dark, central and western Pacific storm-petrel. Classified as Near-threatened.

IDENTIFICATION Normal flight strong, with fluttering wingbeats interspersed with steep banking arcs and periods of gliding; occasionally patters on water surface. Dark-plumaged, with conspicuous upperwing bar; long-winged, with deeply forked tail. Head and neck blackish-brown. Mantle, scapulars and back sooty-black, with greyish-blue cast in fresh plumage enhancing darker head and imparting 'hooded' appearance (in worn plumage, upperparts become browner); rump variable, generally dark, but some may show either narrow greyish area across rump or greyish-white sides to rump. Tail blackish and deeply forked (feet do not project beyond tail in flight). Underparts sooty-brown. Upperwing-coverts dark brownish-grey, greater coverts whitish and forming narrow but conspicuous pale diagonal bar on inner wing from carpal joint to trailing edge; primary coverts, primaries and secondaries blackish. Underwing dark sooty-brown with indistinct paler central coverts. Bill black; iris dark brown; legs and feet blackish. Markham's Storm-petrel also has greyish-blue cast to plumage, but ranges do not overlap. Matsudaira's Storm-petrel is browner in tone, with less prominent upperwing bar and with visible white shafts at base of outer primaries.

DISTRIBUTION AND STATUS Western and central Pacific. In western, breeds on Izu Islands north of Sofu Island, Hebijima and Onbase, but current status unknown; on Torishima large numbers bred until the early 1960s, but exterminated by cats and rats; previously bred in Bonins (Kita-iwojima), but current status unknown, though may breed Mukojima Islands. Decreasing population, breeding in small numbers where known. In central Pacific, breeds Hawaiian archipelago at Nihoa (2,000-3,000 pairs), Necker, French Frigate Shoals, Laysan (500-2,500 pairs), Pearl and Hermes Reef (1,000-2,000 pairs), and may also breed Lisianski and Kure. Dispersal poorly known; some move northwards to the seas east of Japan.

MARKHAM'S STORM-PETREL

Oceanodroma markhami L 23 cm (9 in), WS 52 cm (20 in)

Large, dark, eastern Pacific storm-petrel, very similar to Black Storm-petrel. Breeding ground recently discovered in Peru.

IDENTIFICATION Normal flight with shallow wingbeats interspersed with brief periods of gliding. Does not follow ships. Unlike Black Storm-petrel, prefers cool water. Dark-plumaged, with extensive paler upperwing-coverts; long wings, deeply forked tail. Head and neck blackish-brown. Mantle, scapulars, back and rump blackish-brown. (In fresh plumage shows slight bluish-grey cast, which fades to brown in worn plumage.) Tail blackish, long and deeply forked (feet do not project beyond tail in flight). Upperwing-coverts blackish-brown as mantle, greater coverts whitish and forming narrow but long pale diagonal bar on inner wing from carpal to trailing edge; primary coverts, primaries and secondaries blackish, darker than mantle. Underwing blackish-brown. Bill black; iris dark brown; legs and feet blackish. Size and jizz similar to Black Storm-petrel, from which normally distinguished by deeper fork to tail, more extensive upperwing bar almost reaching carpal joint, and generally browner tone to plumage, as well as more shallow wingbeats with longer periods of gliding.

DISTRIBUTION AND STATUS Eastern Pacific from Mexico to Chile. Recently found breeding Paracas Peninsula in Peru (14°S), probably also elsewhere along Peruvian desert coastline. Pelagic range not well known, probably disperses along Humboldt current between 15°N and 26°S; some remain off Peru all year.

MATSUDAIRA'S STORM-PETREL

Oceanodroma matsudairae L 24 cm (9.5 in), WS 56 cm (22 in)

Very large, long-winged, dark storm-petrel from Pacific and Indian Oceans.

IDENTIFICATION Normal flight slower than that of Swinhoe's Storm-petrel, with flap-and-glide progression with occasional periods of rapid acceleration; also longer, more continuous flapping flight. Feeds by landing on surface with wings raised. Readily follows ships. Dark-plumaged, with paler upperwing bar and diagnostic white forewing patch on leading edge of upperwing between carpal and wing tip; long-winged, with long, deeply forked tail. Head and neck dark brown. Mantle, back, scapulars, rump and uppertail-coverts dark brown. Tail blackish, long and deeply forked (feet do not project beyond tail in flight). Underparts dark brown. Upperwing-coverts dark brown, shading to paler buffish on greater coverts, which form pale diagonal bar on inner wing from carpal joint to trailing edge; primary coverts, primaries and secondaries blackish-brown, with whitish shafts of outer one to seven primaries forming small but diagnostic white patch on leading edge of wing between carpal joint and wing tip. Underwing dark brownish with no visible paler central wing-coverts. Bill black; iris dark brown; legs and feet black. From Tristram's Storm-petrel by white forewing patch, less obvious upperwing bar, and in addition lacks Tristram's greyish cast to plumage. From Swinhoe's Storm-petrel by larger size, broader-based wings, white forewing patch, and slower, more deliberate flight.

DISTRIBUTION AND STATUS North-western Pacific Ocean, dispersing to northern Indian Ocean. Breeds (January-June) North Volcano Island, Bonin Islands, south of Japan, in large numbers; reported to breed on Kita-iwojima in the Iwo Islands, but not recently visited; and many were known to breed in early 1980s on Minami-iwojima. Disperses south-west through Indonesian islands and Timor Sea to winter in northern Indian Ocean around Seychelles Islands, off Kenya and Somalia, generally within 5° of the Equator. Some may winter off north-east New Guinea. Vagrant to north Australia, no records New Zealand, has reached southwards to South Africa.

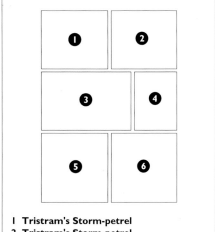

1 **Tristram's Storm-petrel**
2 **Tristram's Storm-petrel**
3 **Markham's Storm-petrel**
4 **Markham's Storm-petrel**
5 **Markham's Storm-petrel**
6 **Matsudaira's Storm-petrel** (off southern Japan)

BLACK STORM-PETREL

Oceanodroma melania L 23 cm (9 in), WS 48 cm (19 in)
Large, dark, long-winged storm-petrel of the north-eastern Pacific.

IDENTIFICATION Normal flight deliberate, with very deep wingbeats interspersed with occasional short glides and shallower wingbeats. Gregarious; occasionally follows ships. Very similar in appearance to Markham's Storm-petrel, but prefers warmer waters; see Markham's for further differences. Plumage blackish-brown, with paler upperwing-coverts; strongly forked tail. Head and neck blackish-brown. Upperparts from mantle and scapulars to uppertail-coverts blackish-brown. Tail blackish, long and deeply forked (feet do not extend beyond tail in flight). Underparts warm blackish-brown. Upperwing-coverts blackish-brown as mantle, greater coverts whitish and forming pale diagonal bar from carpal joint to trailing edge of wing (less extensive than that found on Markham's Storm-petrel); primary coverts, primaries and secondaries blackish, darker than mantle. Underwing blackish-brown with no definable paler central coverts. Bill black; iris dark brown; legs and feet (very long tarsus) blackish. From Ashy Storm-petrel by larger size, proportionately longer wings, browner cast to plumage, dark underwing-coverts, and deeper wingbeats.

DISTRIBUTION AND STATUS North-eastern Pacific Ocean. Breeds off Pacific coast of Baja California at Islas Los Coronados (c 200-300 birds) and Islas San Benito, where there are 'thousands or hundreds of thousands'; nests in old auklet burrows or in rock crevices, where heavily preyed on by cats and rats on some breeding islands. In the Gulf of California, the second most abundant seabird (after Least Storm-petrel). Also breeds in small numbers off the Californian Coast. Dispersal north to Point Reyes and Monterey Bay in warm-water years. Ranges south to seas off Ecuador and Galapagos Islands, but exact pelagic range not clear as must be separated from similar Markham's Storm-petrel, which is difficult.

ASHY STORM-PETREL

Oceanodroma homochroa L 20 cm (8 in), WS 42 cm (17 in)
Medium-sized, dark storm-petrel of the north-east Pacific Ocean. Classified as Near-threatened.

IDENTIFICATION Normal flight fluttering with generally shallow wingbeats, becoming deeper when accelerating. Gregarious at sea. Head and neck sooty-brown. Plumage sooty-brown, with paler upperwing-coverts and slightly paler central underwing-coverts; long wings and forked tail. Mantle, back, scapulars and rump blackish-brown. Tail blackish, forked (feet do not extend beyond tail in flight). Upperwing-coverts blackish-brown, greater coverts whitish and forming pale diagonal bar from carpal joint to trailing edge of wing; primary

coverts, primaries and secondaries blackish, darker than mantle. Underwing blackish-brown with indistinct paler central coverts. Bill black; iris dark brown; legs and feet blackish. From Black Storm-petrel by smaller size, shorter and more rounded wings, paler underwing-coverts, and flight.

DISTRIBUTION AND STATUS North-eastern Pacific Ocean. Population of c 5,000 pairs, majority of which breed on the Farallon Islands off California, also Channel Islands: breeding habitat protected, but foraging habitat is not and is threatened by oil development. A few breed farther south at Islas Los Coronados off north-west Mexico, where described as a very rare summer resident. Pelagic range not well known; dispersal to adjacent waters, with limited southward dispersal. Absent from Farallon Islands November and December.

HORNBY'S or RINGED STORM-PETREL

Oceanodroma hornbyi L 22 cm (8.5 in), WS ?
A large, distinctive, fork-tailed and grey-backed storm-petrel of the eastern Pacific, with breeding grounds uncertain.

IDENTIFICATION Normal flight consists of slow and deep wingbeats interspersed with erratic sailing glides, often with legs dangling. Often gregarious at sea. Grey above, with dark cap, pale face, dark tail and conspicuous white upperwing bars, and white below, with grey breastband. Crown and nape blackish to just below eye and extending across ear-coverts, with thin white collar across upper hindneck and extending onto sides of face, throat, chin and forehead. Hindneck dark greyish, this colour extending across upper breast as dark greyish-black breastband. Mantle, back, scapulars, rump and uppertail-coverts dark greyish (uppertail-coverts may show paler tips). Uppertail blackish, forked (feet do not extend beyond tail in flight). Underparts white from grey breastband to undertail. Inner wing-coverts dark greyish-brown, greater coverts whitish and forming conspicuous diagonal bar on upperwing from carpal joint to inner trailing edge; primary coverts, primaries and secondaries blackish, enhancing diagonal bar. Underwing dark greyish-brown with no definable paler central coverts. Bill black; iris dark brown; legs and feet blackish. Care required with phalaropes in non-breeding plumage resting on the sea, though in reasonably close views should be easily distinguishable as a storm-petrel by tubenose bill shape, general build, and plumage differences (phalaropes are generally paler-headed and most show a distinctive blackish eye patch).

DISTRIBUTION AND STATUS South-eastern Pacific Ocean. Breeding grounds remain undiscovered; believed to be in coastal deserts of Peru and northern Chile. Pelagic dispersal from c 35°S off Chile north to the Equator off Ecuador, where numerous August to

December. Very common off Chile and Peru July to November.

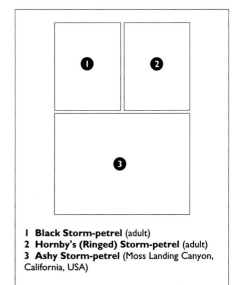

1 **Black Storm-petrel** (adult)
2 **Hornby's (Ringed) Storm-petrel** (adult)
3 **Ashy Storm-petrel** (Moss Landing Canyon, California, USA)

FORK-TAILED STORM-PETREL

Oceanodroma furcata L 22 cm (8.5 in), WS 46 cm (18 in)
Distinctive, medium-sized storm-petrel of the north Pacific Ocean, the only grey storm-petrel to occur in that region.
IDENTIFICATION Normal flight low, recalling Leach's Storm-petrel, but less erratic, with shallower wingbeats interspersed with stiff-winged gliding. Will follow ships, and can form rafts at sea. Largely grey, with darker forehead and eye mask, blackish underwing-coverts and forked tail. Forehead and lores blackish, this colour extending through and below eye to ear-coverts, forming dark facial mask; crown, nape and hindneck pale bluish-grey, extending to sides of neck. Mantle, back, rump and uppertail-coverts medium bluish-grey; longer scapulars have blackish-grey tips. Tail dark bluish-grey with variable whitish tips and edges (feet do not extend beyond tail in flight). Chin and throat whitish; sides of upper breast pale bluish-grey, becoming whiter towards lower belly and vent; undertail greyish. Marginal and lesser upperwing-coverts dark blackish-grey, forming dark leading edge to inner wing; greater coverts paler whitish-grey, forming pale centre to inner wing; primary coverts, primaries and secondaries dark greyish. Underwing-coverts and axillaries blackish, with variable whitish tips along centre of underwing; flight feathers bluish-grey below, with slightly darker narrow tips to primaries. Bill black; iris dark brown; legs and feet blackish. Care required with winter-plumaged phalaropes at a distance.
DISTRIBUTION AND STATUS North Pacific Ocean, from Bering Sea southwards to about 30°N from Japan to California. Breeds Kuril Islands (c 200,000 birds) and Commander Islands, possibly elsewhere in Sea of Okhotsk (formerly bred Sakhalin Island); also Aleutian Islands (880,000 birds), Gulf of Alaska (990,000 birds), with total Alaskan population c 5 million birds, and British Columbia (380,000 breeding birds). Has increased where there are no predators. Dispersal to southern Alaska, British Columbia, Washington, Oregon and northern California.

RED-BILLED TROPICBIRD

Phaethon aethereus L 98 cm (39 in), including tail-streamers of c 50 cm, WS 105 cm (41 in)
Largest tropicbird, with diagnostic adult pattern of red bill, barred upperparts and wing-coverts, blackish outer primaries, and long white tail; immatures consequently resemble adults more than in other tropicbirds.
IDENTIFICATION Flies high over ocean; wingbeats alternate with soaring glides. Feeds by hovering, and then plunging on half-closed wings. Can take flying fish-fish in flight. Floats on surface with tail cocked. Pelagic outside breeding areas, ranging far from land. Generally solitary at sea; occasionally follows ships.
Juvenile/immature Head white, with black eye-stripes joining across back of nape to form nuchal collar. Nape, hindneck, mantle, back, rump and wing-coverts to carpal finely and densely barred blackish-grey. Tail white with blackish tips, no streamers. Underparts white. Outer primaries and their coverts blackish, this decreasing inwards; inner primaries and secondaries white. Bill yellowish with black tip, becoming orange-red. **Adult** Head white, with blackish eye-stripes from lores to ear-coverts occasionally meeting on hind nape. Mantle, back and rump white with fine blackish-grey barring, this extending onto wing-coverts and more faintly onto hindneck. Tail white, with two long white central streamers which have black shafts. Underparts white; some grey mottling on flanks. Outer primaries and primary coverts blackish, this decreasing inwards; inner primaries and secondaries white. Underwing white, with inner secondaries greyish. Bill stout and decurved, bright red; iris blackish-brown; legs yellowish, feet black.
DISTRIBUTION AND STATUS Tropical and subtropical eastern Pacific (Gulf of California to Peru), Atlantic (Caribbean to Venezuela, Azores, Cape Verdes, Fernando Noronha, Ascension, St Helena) and north-western Indian Ocean, Red Sea, Persian Gulf and Arabian Sea. Probably the least numerous tropicbird with a total population of c 10,000 pairs, most on the coasts of Central America (Gulf of California c 1,000 pairs, Galapagos several thousand pairs and Caribbean over 1,600 pairs). Juveniles disperse up to 1,500 km; adults more sedentary. Vagrants north to Washington; possibly regular off eastern USA, Philippines. Some populations suffer from mammalian predation and persecution by fishermen.

RED-TAILED TROPICBIRD

Phaethon rubricauda L 78 cm (31 in), including tail-streamers of c 35 cm, WS 107 cm (42 in)
Medium-sized tropicbird with red bill and red tail-streamers; whiter body and wings than other tropicbirds, often with pinkish suffusion.
IDENTIFICATION **Immature** Head white, with black stripe from lores through eye to ear-coverts but not extending to hindcrown as on Red-billed Tropicbird. Lacks pinkish flush and tail-streamers of adult. Nape, mantle, back, rump and upperwing-coverts heavily and coarsely barred blackish-grey. Tail white, tipped black. Flight feathers white, with dark blackish shafts on outer primaries (less extensive than on other tropicbirds). Underparts white. Absence of barred secondaries on underwing. Bill blackish, becoming yellow from base. Transition to adult involves progressive decrease in upperpart barring probably over two to three years. **Adult** Head white, with black stripe from lores through eye to ear-coverts (not onto hindcrown). Entire upperparts and underparts white with variable pinkish suffusion. Upper surface of wings white, with black shafts on outermost primaries (but not primary coverts); inner secondaries and scapulars black with white edges (less black than other tropicbirds, and wings may have pinkish suffusion). Underwings white, sometimes dusky on inner secondaries, axillaries and onto flanks. Tail white with black shafts; two long, black-shafted red central streamers (these often broken). Bill stout, pointed and decurved, red; iris brown; legs bluish-grey, feet black. In flight, appears heavier-bodied and broader- and shorter-winged than other tropicbirds, with correspondingly heavier flight; has less black on upperwing surface.
DISTRIBUTION AND STATUS Tropical and subtropical Pacific and Indian Oceans; most numerous in Pacific (eg 12,000 pairs Hawaii). Generally in water of over 22°C. The most pelagic tropicbird with dispersal further north and south than other tropicbirds (c 40°N and 40°S). Vagrants California, South Africa, Japan, Bay of Bengal, New Zealand. Pacific populations can be adversely affected by *El Niño* as well as by human exploitation and rats.

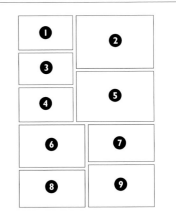

1 **Fork-tailed Storm-petrel** (Homer, Alaska)
2 **Fork-tailed Storm-petrel** (Homer, Alaska)
3 **Red-billed Tropicbird** (Senegal, April)
4 **Red-billed Tropicbird** (Galapagos Islands)
5 **Red-billed Tropicbird** (Galapagos Islands)
6 **Red-tailed Tropicbird** (adult at nest with chick, Lady Elliott Island, Coral Sea, March)
7 **Red-tailed Tropicbird**
8 **Red-tailed Tropicbird** (Kilauea Point, Hawaii)
9 **Red-tailed Tropicbird** (Philip Is., off Norfolk Island, Australia)

TROPICBIRDS & PELICANS

WHITE-TAILED TROPICBIRD

Phaethon lepturus L 78 cm (31 in), including long tail-streamers of *c* 40 cm, WS 92 cm (36 in)
The smallest tropicbird, with slender proportions and long angular wings with diagnostic bar on inner upperwing, black-based outer primaries, long white central tail feathers, and yellowish or orange bill. Occurs in two colour morphs, and in subtropical and tropical waters of all three oceans.
IDENTIFICATION Immature Head white, with reduced black eye-stripe not extending to hindneck (unlike on Red-billed). Generally similar to adult, but with nape, hindneck, mantle, back and rump barred with greyish-black. Underparts and underwing white, with faint spots on flanks. Upperwing-coverts barred greyish-black (as mantle), this extending to carpal joint and forming triangle on inner upperwing; rest of wing white, with black outer webs of outer four to five primaries. Tail white, no streamers, black tip. Bill dull yellow with black tip. Has more black on outer primaries than juvenile Red-tailed. Juvenile Red-billed has finer barring on upperparts, as well as darker nuchal collar. **Adult** Head white, with black stripe from lores extending through eye to ear-coverts. Upperparts white from head to tail, with scapulars tipped black. Underparts white with variable flush, flanks tipped black. Upperwing white with two black patches: outer webs of outer four to five primaries black (not reaching primary tips), and black diagonal mark on inner wing (black from median coverts to innermost secondaries). Tail pointed and white, with two long white central streamers which have black shafts. Bill stout, pointed and decurved, usually yellow or orange; iris dark brown; legs and feet yellowish with black webs. Christmas Island race (*P. l. fulvus*) has golden-apricot wash over white plumage.
DISTRIBUTION AND STATUS Tropical and subtropical Pacific, Atlantic and Indian Oceans. Breeds on many oceanic island groups. The most numerous tropicbird with over 10,000 pairs in the Caribbean, 3,000 pairs in the south Atlantic, 6,000-12,000 pairs on Christmas Island (Indian Ocean) with *c* 5,000 pairs elsewhere in the Indian Ocean and several thousand pairs in the Pacific. Some populations are seasonal (eg Bermuda). Regular Australia; vagrants Nova Scotia, Arizona, west coast North America, South Africa, New Zealand.

BROWN PELICAN

Pelecanus occidentalis L 114 cm (45 in), WS 203 cm (80 in)
The smallest pelican, found on both coasts of North and South America. Plumage generally grey, with blackish belly and flight feathers, yellow and white head with chestnut nape and hindneck. Adult plumage acquired in third year.
IDENTIFICATION Juvenile/immature Generally brown above and white below. Head and neck medium-brown; crown and neck become whiter with age. Complete upperparts

dull greyish-brown, this extending to upper breast and gradually merging into dull white underparts. Primaries and secondaries blackish, wing-coverts browner. Underwing dark, with whitish line along underwing-coverts. Tail black. Facial skin, bill and legs grey. **Adult non-breeding** As adult breeding, but head and neck mainly white, merging into yellowish on crown, or white continues onto crown. Bare parts generally duller. **Adult breeding** Forehead, crown and ear-coverts yellowish-white, more yellow on forehead, and merging into white on ear-coverts and sides of bill and continuing down sides of neck. Nape and hindneck dark chestnut-brown, merging into blackish on foreneck, with yellowish on upper breast. Upperparts silvery greyish-brown. Underparts blackish-brown, with grey streaking on breast sides and flanks. Flight feathers blackish, with white primary shafts; upperwing-coverts silvery greyish-brown. Underwing dark, whiter on coverts. Tail dark brownish-grey. Bare parts vary considerably with geographical race, age and season. From similar marine Peruvian Pelican by smaller size, smaller crest, duller bare parts, absence of pale upperwing patch, and darker belly.
DISTRIBUTION AND STATUS Both coasts of North and South America, from Washington south to Peru (including Galapagos) and from Maryland south through Caribbean to Brazil. Northern populations migratory; stragglers to British Columbia, Great Lakes, Great Plains, Idaho, Nova Scotia and Bermuda. Populations now recovering from decline, but sensitive at breeding localities; disturbance can lead to egg loss from Laughing and Heermann's Gull.

PERUVIAN PELICAN

Pelecanus thagus L 152 cm (60 in), WS 228 cm (90 in)
Huge-sized, and noticeably larger than Brown Pelican, which it closely resembles and of which it was previously regarded as a subspecies. Restricted to Humboldt region of South America. Adult plumage acquired in third year.
IDENTIFICATION Juvenile/immature Generally as juvenile Brown Pelican, with brown upperparts and white underparts, but is darker brown above. Noticeably larger than Brown Pelican. **Adult non-breeding** As adult breeding, but bare parts duller in colour. Head and neck generally white, more extensively so than on Brown Pelican; crown may be pale yellowish. Mantle, back and scapulars whitish with blackish tips (whiter than Brown Pelican). Winter plumage more variable and contrasting than Brown Pelican. **Adult breeding** Generally similar to Brown Pelican, but larger, with brighter bare parts. Head straw-yellow, with more developed occipital crest. Nape and hindneck darker brown than Brown Pelican, almost black as foreneck. Underparts blackish-brown, finely streaked with white, thus lighter than Brown Pelican. Flight feathers and inner wing (near carpal) generally darker than Brown Pelican, with pale rectangular patch near leading

edge of upperwing on coverts. Bill pale yellow at base, upper mandible with reddish tip, lower mandible greyish-blue; caruncles between culmen base and the eye. Other non-marine pelicans are mainly white, and the dark plumage of Brown and Peruvian Pelicans probably correlates with marine plunge-diving; they are the only pelicans to do this.
DISTRIBUTION AND STATUS Endemic to Humboldt Current of western South America off Peru and Chile. Breeds offshore islands from Peru south to 33.5°S in central Chile (Concon Island near Valparaiso); generally within 60 km of shore. Probably the most numerous pelican with *c* 620,000-1 million breeding birds in the Peruvian guano colonies. Non-breeders disperse south to Chiloé and more rarely to Tierra del Fuego. Population fluctuates with *El Niño*; also competes with local fishing and suffers from egg-collectors.

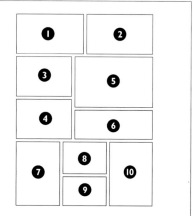

1 **White-tailed Tropicbird**, subspecies *P. l. fulvus* (Christmas Island, Indian Ocean)
2 **White-tailed Tropicbird** (adult, Spittal Pond, Bermuda, July)
3 **White-tailed Tropicbird** (juvenile, Aride Island, Seychelles, April)
4 **White-tailed Tropicbird** (adults)
5 **Brown Pelican** (adult, California, USA)
6 **Brown Pelican** (immature, Florida, USA)
7 **Brown Pelican** (immature, California, USA)
8 **Brown Pelican** (adult breeding, California, USA)
9 **Peruvian Pelican** (adult non-breeding, Chile, February)
10 **Peruvian Pelican** (immature, Chile, April)

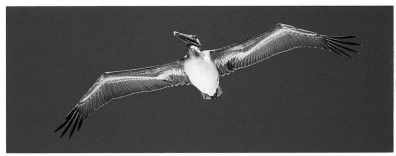

GANNETS & BOOBIES

ABBOTT'S BOOBY

Papasula abbotti L 71 cm (28 in), WS ?
Small and distinctive tree-nesting booby with black and white plumage. Juveniles resemble adult males, and bill colour separates the sexes; bill hooked unlike other sulids. Confined to Christmas Island (Indian Ocean). Classified as Vulnerable.

IDENTIFICATION Distinctive jizz: narrow body with heavy head and long neck, long and narrow wings, giving rakish appearance. Flight steady, with shallow wingbeats between long glides. Rarely recorded at sea. **Juvenile** Resembles adult male (unique among sulids), but with browner upperparts; buff edges to scapulars and wing-coverts. Bill blue-grey with no pinkish tinge. **Adult** Head and neck pure white. Mantle and upper back blackish, with narrow white line from hindneck to lower back with some blackish blotches; rump and uppertail-coverts white with large blackish spots. Tail feathers black with white tips. Underparts white from chin to abdomen, with irregular black patches on flanks and thighs, reaching undertail-coverts. Scapulars and wings deep blackish when fresh, fading to burnt-brown, with buff- or whitish-edged wing-coverts; thin whitish leading edge from carpal to body, conspicuous in flight; inner webs of outer primaries white. Underwing mainly white, with black tips along primaries. Bill blue-grey with black tip in male, deep rosy-pink with black tip (fading to dull pink) in female; iris brown with dark surrounding skin, making orbital region appear large; legs and feet grey, with black tips.

DISTRIBUTION AND STATUS Christmas Island and surrounding seas. Breeds in tops of trees on central plateau where open-cut phosphate-mining (pre-1987) and cyclone (1988), together with very low breeding success (average of one chick fledged per pair every 5 years) make this the rarest and most endangered sulid. Population 1,900 pairs (1989), c 3,000 pairs (1991) representing 5,000-8,000 birds. Dispersal not well known, but recently recorded from east Banda Sea (1994), representing known range eastward extension. Has bred Rodrigues, probably Assumption, possibly Chagos group.

NORTHERN GANNET

Morus bassanus L 93 cm (37 in), WS 172 cm (68 in)
Largest north Atlantic seabird and the biggest sulid, with cigar-shaped body.
IDENTIFICATION Steady flight, with shallow flaps and long glides; in high winds, wings angled and flight more undulating. Very gregarious; attracted to fishing vessels. Plunge-dives from 10 m above the surface. **Juvenile** Head and neck dark greyish-brown. Upperparts slaty greyish-black, but variable, with white spots of differing sizes; 'V'-shaped white patch on uppertail-coverts. Underparts paler, sometimes whitish, with darker breastband. Primaries and secondaries blackish-brown; upperwing-coverts brown with whitish spots. Underwing white

with brownish streaks. Tail blackish. Bill and iris dark. **Immature** (second-fourth year) Dark juvenile plumage progressively whitens with age: the white spots disappear, the forehead and hindneck become paler, producing a 'capped' effect, with a dark pectoral band. Underparts whiten: generally browner than juvenile. By second year, head, underparts and rump whiten: head may have golden hue on crown and nape; upperparts and wings become boldly patterned as speckling becomes more pronounced, especially on mantle, scapulars and back; primaries and primary coverts black, with dark speckling on greater coverts and secondaries. By third year, wings more white than dark, including white feathers in secondaries (not present on either Cape or Australasian Gannet). Fourth- and fifth-year variable but essentially as adult, with progressively fewer dark feathers in secondaries and tail. Occasional late-fifth-year birds may be fully adult. **Adult** Head, nape and upper neck vary from white to pale yellow to deeper buff: darkest in breeding season, almost white in winter. Body plumage, tail, secondaries, and greater, median and lesser coverts pure white. Primaries blackish-brown, paler on inner webs; primary coverts and alula black, lesser primary coverts along edge of wing white; rest of wings white. Underwing similar, but primary coverts white. Bill pale bluish-grey with black cutting edges; iris pale bluish-grey with cobalt-blue orbital ring; black facial skin extends onto throat as gular stripe; legs and feet black. Occasional albinos occur.

DISTRIBUTION AND STATUS North Atlantic. Breeds colonially eastern USA, Iceland, Faeroes, Norway, British Isles, Channel Islands, north-west France. Total population 263,000 breeding pairs (600,000 birds) with 60% in British waters (160,000 pairs). Dispersal south in winter. Recent expansion in numbers and range, *eg* breeding south France. Still taken for food off Scotland.

CAPE GANNET

Morus capensis L 85 cm (33 in), WS ?
Large seabird of southern Africa, with plumage sequences similar to those of larger Northern Gannet. Africa's only endemic sulid. Classified as Near-threatened.

IDENTIFICATION Similar to other gannets; flaps more between glides than Northern. **Juvenile and immature** As Northern, with similar progression of whitening, but adult plumage acquired in third to fourth year (variable): second-year birds may look like third-year Northern or like adult Cape. By second and third year, only wing-coverts show white; primaries, secondaries and tail remain wholly dark blackish-brown through all transitional plumage stages, with no white in lower secondaries as on Northern. Second-year probably indistinguishable from Australasian unless diagnostic longer black gular stripe seen; perhaps underparts paler on Australasian, also slight differences in behaviour, iris colour and voice. **Adult** Much as Northern, with white

body plumage but more extensive black on wings and tail. Primaries, primary coverts and secondaries black, thus dark trailing edge to wing which stops several centimetres short of body. Tail usually all black, whereas on Australasian only the four central tail feathers are dark (some, however, occasionally as Australasian, but lacking latter's symmetry). Head deep golden-buff, slightly darker than average Northern's. Long black gular stripe three to four times longer than on either Australasian or Northern; black facial skin as Northern. Bill light blue; iris silvery-cream, paler than on Australasian and darker than Northern's; legs and feet blackish. Call lower-pitched than that of Australasian, with which has successfully hybridized.

DISTRIBUTION AND STATUS Southern Africa. Breeds colonially on six islands off Namibia and South Africa. Population declined from c 166,000 pairs (1956) to c 80,000 pairs (1980) probably representing some 350,000 birds, but now appears stable. Post-breeding dispersal northwards to Gulf of Guinea, Natal and Mozambique, may overlap with Northern Gannet off West Africa. Vagrants western Sahara, Kenya, and possibly Bass Rock, Scotland. Recently, regular sightings from Amsterdam and St Paul Islands (Indian Ocean) and Australia.

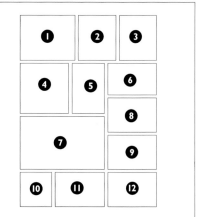

1 **Abbott's Booby** (adult at nest site, Christmas Island, Indian Ocean, May)
2 **Abbott's Booby** (Christmas Island, Indian Ocean, May)
3 **Abbott's Booby** (Christmas Island, Indian Ocean, May)
4 **Northern Gannet** (adult, Bass Rock, Scotland, July)
5 **Northern Gannet** (adult, Great Saltee Island, Southern Ireland, June)
6 **Northern Gannet** (adult, Bass Rock, Scotland, July)
7 **Northern Gannet** (breeding colony, Bass Rock, Scotland, June)
8 **Northern Gannet** (juvenile)
9 **Northern Gannet** (immature, Bass Rock, Scotland, July)
10 **Cape Gannet** (adult, Lambert's Bay, South Africa, November)
11 **Cape Gannet** (adult, Lambert's Bay, South Africa)
12 **Cape Gannet** (adult with juvenile, Lambert's Bay, South Africa)

GANNETS & BOOBIES

AUSTRALASIAN GANNET

Morus serrator L 84 cm (33 in), WS 170 cm (67 in)

Large seabird of Australasian region, with plumage more similar to Cape Gannet's than to Northern Gannet's, but with white outer tail feathers.

IDENTIFICATION Juvenile and immature Very similar to Cape and Northern Gannets, but slightly paler on head, neck and underparts. Progression of whitening of plumage from dark juveniles to pale adults as for Northern Gannet. Normal adult plumage acquired in third or fourth year. White spotting on back of juveniles is larger than on either Cape or Northern Gannet. Intermediate stages of immature plumage lack the bold, heavily speckled pattern of Northern Gannet, being more finely variegated on upperparts. Crown and nape start to show buffy-white coloration after *c* eight months (males). Iris dark brown; bill, facial skin, legs and feet slate-black. **Adult** Head and neck golden-buff, intensity varying with season, but generally deeper in colour than Northern Gannet. Body plumage white, essentially as Northern and Cape Gannets. Wings white, with black primaries, primary coverts and all but inner three secondaries, giving black trailing edge to wing (as Cape Gannet); innermost secondaries and tertials white, alula black. Underwing as upperwing, but with primary coverts white. Tail white except for four central feathers, which are blackish, but variable: inner three to ten may be blackish, but outer two always white. (Number of tail feathers may also be variable, thus altering appearance of tail pattern.) Bill bluish-grey; iris silver-grey, eye-ring blue; legs and feet blackish-grey, with greenish stripes on tarsus and toes. Facial skin and gular stripe blackish: gular stripe similar in length to Northern Gannet's (three to four times longer on Cape Gannet). Note that all adult gannets are separable from smaller boobies by yellowish-buff head.

DISTRIBUTION AND STATUS Australasia. Breeds colonially on islands off south-east Australia, Tasmania, North Island and South Island, Stewart Island and Norfolk Island. Total population (1980-81) 52,664 pairs (46,004 New Zealand; 6,660 Australia); probably stable or slightly increasing. Post-breeding dispersal west and north to Tropic of Capricorn along both east and west coasts of Australia. Vagrant Brazil, South Africa, Marion Island and Crozets.

BLUE-FOOTED BOOBY

Sula nebouxii L 80 cm (32 in), WS 152 cm (60 in)

Large, gregarious booby found on the Pacific coast of Central and South America, with brownish head, upperparts and wings, white underparts, and diagnostic bright blue feet.

IDENTIFICATION Inshore feeder; forages communally. **Juvenile** Head and hindneck plain dark brown, terminating at broad white patch on upper mantle starting at lower hindneck.

Lighter greyish-brown on throat and upper breast, clearly demarcated from white underparts; brown thigh patch. Lower mantle and back brown with broad white tips, giving scaly pattern; uppertail-coverts white, forming narrow horseshoe over rump. Tail blackish-brown with white shafts. Upperwing dark brown, duller and darker than adult's. Underwing brown, apart from diagnostic white rectangular axillary patch extending towards wing tip as two white stripes (pattern generally less well defined than on adult). Bill black, becoming horn; iris brown; legs grey. From juvenile Masked Booby by more brown on foreneck and upper breast, lack of white cervical collar, white rump, white axillary patch. From Brown Booby by white hindneck, white rump, white axillary patch. **Immature** Poorly documented. Much as adult, but head dull greyish-brown with faint white streaks merging into whiter chin and throat; scapulars have pale tips; underwing pattern less defined than adult's; eye lighter, bill bluish. Adult plumage acquired second to third year. **Adult** Head and hindneck pale cinnamon-brown, with dense white streaking terminating in broad white patch on hindneck/upper mantle. Chin and throat whiter and less streaked, merging into white of foreneck and underparts; brown thigh patch. Upperparts pale cinnamon-brown, with white tips extending from mantle and back onto scapulars, giving barred effect; rump white, conspicuous in flight; tail-coverts and tail dark brownish, with longest central tail feathers whitish. Upperwing uniform deep burnt-brown, but scapulars have white tips. Underwing brown, but with broad white rectangular axillary patch diagnostic and extending towards wing tip as two white stripes. Bill dark slate-blue; iris pale yellow; orbital ring and facial skin bluish-grey; legs and feet turquoise-bright blue.

DISTRIBUTION AND STATUS Subtropical and tropical American Pacific coast. Breeds colonially on islands, generally on flat ground, off Mexico, Ecuador, northern Peru and Galapagos. Population 25,000-40,000 pairs with strongholds in the Gulf of California and Peru. Disperses widely in *El Niño* years, north to California and south to northern Chile.

PERUVIAN BOOBY

Sula variegata L 74 cm (29 in), WS ?

Medium-sized, gregarious South American booby with brown upperparts and wings, white head and underparts, blackish-blue feet and greyish-black bill.

IDENTIFICATION Jizz as Blue-footed Booby. Joins with flocks of cormorants and pelicans in Humboldt Current. **Juvenile** Pattern much as adult's, but with narrower white tips to upperparts and wings imparting generally darker appearance. Head and neck finely streaked ash-grey. Wings and back duller and darker than adult; white down on rump may persist until fledging. Underparts buffish-grey with white margins which can look barred, and darker pectoral band extending from sides of

lower neck. Bill and face bluish; iris yellowish-grey; legs and feet lighter blue-grey than adult's. **Adult** Head and neck pure white. Upperparts brown with whitish tips, giving variegated pattern; uppertail-coverts white, forming narrow horseshoe. Tail brownish, with longer central feathers white. Underparts white, with upper thigh mottled brown. Upperwing with flight feathers warm darkish brown, coverts browner and tipped white as mantle and back. Underwing dark brownish with whitish central stripe, similar to Blue-footed Booby but lacking rectangular white axillary patch. Bill lead-blue to greyish-black, redder in breeding season; iris pale yellow; facial skin blackish-grey; legs and feet bluish-grey. From Blue-footed Booby by white head, black face mask, underwing pattern, dark feet, absence of white on hindneck/mantle.

DISTRIBUTION AND STATUS South America. Breeds colonially on cliffs or flat ground on islands from Point Pariñas (Peru) south to Concepcion (Chile). Normally sedentary, but in *El Niño* years moves north to northern Ecuador and south to Chiloé Island (Chile); in stable years a few regularly reach south-western Ecuador. Population in decline because of overfishing of anchovy and *El Niño* which has caused mass desertions (eg 2,700,000 birds 1981/82, 730,000 birds 1982/83, 1,160,000 birds 1985/86).

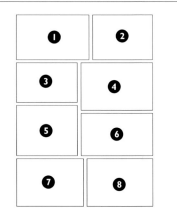

1 **Australasian Gannet** (breeding adult, Cape Kidnappers, New Zealand)
2 **Australasian Gannet** (juvenile, Cape Kidnappers, New Zealand)
3 **Australasian Gannet** (adult, Cape Kidnappers, New Zealand)
4 **Australasian Gannet** (breeding colony, Cape Kidnappers, New Zealand)
5 **Blue-footed Booby** (adult displaying, Galapagos Islands)
6 **Blue-footed Booby** (juvenile, Galapagos Islands, November)
7 **Peruvian Booby** (adults, Paracas, Peru)
8 **Peruvian Booby** (adults, Paracas, Peru)

GANNETS & BOOBIES

MASKED BOOBY

Sula dactylatra L 86 cm (34 in), WS 152 cm (60 in)

Largest and most robust booby, adults appearing brilliant white with blackish trailing edge to wing, black tail and dark face mask. Has hybridized with Brown Booby.

IDENTIFICATION Strong flight usually high and fast; generally dives vertically. Loosely gregarious; does not usually follow ships. **Juvenile** Head, neck, chin and throat greyish-brown, occasionally flecked white. Narrow white collar across lower hindneck and joining white of underparts on foreneck. Mantle, scapulars and back greyish-brown with whiter edges; narrow band of white across rump; tail blackish. Underparts white from foreneck, with some mottling on lower flanks; undertail blackish. Upperwing-coverts sandy greyish-brown with whiter edges; flight feathers dark brown, appearing blackish. Underwing with dark trailing edge (primaries and secondaries), white leading edge (coverts), and narrow dark brown band from carpal to axillaries. Bill yellowish-green; iris dark brownish; facial skin dark blue-grey; feet dark blue-grey. From adult Brown Booby by paler upperparts, white cervical collar, white foreneck and underwing pattern. From juvenile Blue-footed Booby by white foreneck, white cervical collar, dark uppertail-coverts and underwing pattern. **Immature** Much as juvenile, becoming progressively whiter: more extensive neck collar as head whitens; rump, back, upperwing-coverts and scapulars become tipped with white. Adult plumage acquired in third year. **Adult** Head and neck white. Mantle, back, rump and underparts white, except for black tips to longer scapulars. Tail black, occasionally white on centre and base of upper surface. Flight feathers blackish-brown right up to edge of body, with remainder of upperwings (including all coverts) entirely white: thus white leading edge, black trailing edge. Underwing as upperwing. Bill varies with season and locality, generally yellowish with variable greenish shades; iris yellow or dark brown, depending on subspecies; dark facial skin, with gular pouch bluish-grey – appears as a blackish mask at sea; legs and feet variable yellow, can be greyish or orange.

DISTRIBUTION AND STATUS Pantropical in all three oceans, breeding colonially on oceanic islands, atolls and cays usually far from mainland. Total population several hundred thousand birds. Distribution may be determined by occurrence of flying-fish, and requires cool upwellings of nutrient-rich water. Often seen far from land. Large foraging range preferring deeper water and taking larger prey than other boobies. Dispersal not well known; adults probably mainly sedentary while juveniles disperse; has reached Carolina and California.

RED-FOOTED BOOBY

Sula sula L 71 cm (28 in), WS 152 cm (60 in)

Gregarious, small, polymorphic and pantropical, tree-nesting booby with red feet and pink base of bill. Variable adult plumage, with largest eye of any booby, probably correlated with partially nocturnal habits.

IDENTIFICATION Wings held forward in flight, which is faster than that of other boobies, with much gliding. Smallest and lightest booby, gregarious and attracted to ships. Undertakes long foraging trips. **Juvenile** Dark brown upperparts streaked darker blackish. Tail and flight feathers blackish-brown. Underparts generally paler than upperparts, but streaked dark brown; palish lower belly, shading to white undertail-coverts. Underwing dark, with paler greater coverts. Bill dark brown; iris grey; facial skin dark grey or pinkish; legs and feet greyish-pink. **Immature** *White morph*: Plumage gradually whitens over two to three years. Head and neck mottled greyish-brown, paler on nape. Mantle, rump and some wing-coverts greyish-brown. Tail greyish. Throat greyish; breast and lower belly white. Last remaining brown feathers on back and thighs. *Dark morph*: Fairly uniform dark brown, but paler on back, rump, tail and vent, darker on head and flight feathers. Perhaps dark pectoral band. Underwing patchy, with no definite pattern. Bill purple-brown with pinkish base, eventually turning pale blue with pink base; facial skin and gular pale blue, later becoming pink; legs brownish-red. **Adult** *White morph* (most common): Head and body white with variable golden or apricot wash. Upperwing-coverts as body, and primaries and secondaries black. Underwing similar in pattern, but diagnostic black patch at carpal. Tail white (Galapagos birds have blackish-brown tail, could be confused with Masked Booby). Underparts white; some may have yellow wash. Bill pale blue or greenish-blue with pink base; iris dark brown; facial skin pink, with blue around eye; legs and feet orange-red to deep red. From Masked Booby by smaller size, bare-part colours, white scapulars, and black carpal patch on underwing (and Christmas Island birds have more extensive golden-apricot wash on upperparts). *White-tailed brown morph*: As brown morph (see below), but with lower back, rump, tail-coverts, tail and lower belly white or yellowish-white. Head and neck, mantle and upper back mid brown (on some, head and neck pale golden-brown). Upperwings mid brown, with darker flight feathers. Underparts mid brown, but lower belly to tail white. Bare parts as white morph. *Intermediates*: Varying amounts of white and brown; generally, the paler the plumage, the paler the underwing. Bare parts as white morph. (1) Similar to white-tailed brown morph, but paler body. (2) Brown, with pale or whitish scapulars. (3) White head and body, with dark brown or mottled back and brown wings. (4) Brown to brownish-grey, with pale head and neck (usually yellowish).

DISTRIBUTION AND STATUS Pantropical in all three oceans, in waters of above 22°C. One of the most widespread and abundant of all sulids, but breeding sites scattered widely over numerous small islands; distribution may be determined by occurrence of flying-fish and also by arboreal nesting habits. Population probably easily exceeds 1 million individuals, with 14,000 pairs Caribbean, 250,000 pairs Galapagos, 12,000 pairs Christmas Island (Indian Ocean), and 30,000 birds Cocos Keeling. Formerly numbered many more, but severely reduced over the last two centuries through human exploitation, and more recently by habitat destruction (especially western Indian Ocean), predation (especially by rats), and disturbance caused by tourism. Adults sedentary; juveniles dispersive.

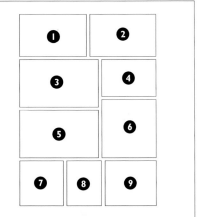

1 **Masked Booby** (adult breeding, Galapagos Islands)
2 **Masked Booby** (adult breeding, Galapagos Islands)
3 **Masked Booby** (immature)
4 **Masked Booby** (adult)
5 **Red-footed Booby** (adult breeding, brown morph, Galapagos Islands)
6 **Red-footed Booby** (adult breeding, white morph, Galapagos Islands)
7 **Red-footed Booby** (immature, Hawaii)
8 **Red-footed Booby** (adult, white morph, Hawaii)
9 **Red-footed Booby** (juveniles)

BOOBIES & CORMORANTS

BROWN BOOBY

Sula leucogaster L 75-80 cm (30-31 in), WS
141 cm (56 in)
Smallish, gregarious, pantropical booby, with
dark brown upperparts, wings, head and upper
breast sharply demarcated from white
underparts; bill and legs usually yellowish.
IDENTIFICATION Lighter flight than that of
other boobies. Can form large flocks; tends to
feed inshore with shallow plunge-dives. Can
perch in trees, but breeds on the ground;
rarely sits on water. **Juvenile** Generally
resembles adult in pattern, but upperparts
duller brown; head and neck darker brown
than back and scapulars, but paler than on
adult. Tail brown. Underparts from upper
breast (lower breast, belly, undertail-coverts)
greyish-brown, which progressively whitens to
adult plumage, though traces of brown may
remain on lower breast and belly until third
year. Underwing white centrally, but mottled
and merging into grey-brown; gradually loses
mottling to give adult's white centre with
contrasting dark margins. Bill and facial skin
grey-blue, bill lightening to adult colour; iris
variable, generally greyish; legs and feet orange-
grey. From immature Northern Gannet by
smaller size, lighter jizz, proportionately longer
tail, more rapid wingbeats, dark (not spotted)
upperparts, darker chin and throat. **Adult**
Head and neck to upper breast dark chocolate-
brown. Upperparts, including tail, uniform dark
brown. Underparts white, with sharp
demarcation on upper breast; undertail dark
brown. Upperwing blackish-brown. Underwing
white with brown margins. Bill bluish-grey; iris
silver; orbital ring blue in males, yellow in
females; facial skin deep blue; legs yellowish or
yellowish-green. *S. l. brewsteri* of eastern Pacific
has pale greyish-white head and chin, merging
into greyish-brown hindneck and breast, and
grey bill.
DISTRIBUTION AND STATUS Pantropical in all
three oceans; one of the most widespread and
common boobies. Total population probably
several hundred thousand birds, more evenly
spread than other pantropic boobies (large
numbers western Australia). Adults mainly
sedentary but juveniles and non-breeding birds
disperse widely. Has occurred New England
States, Nova Scotia, Azores, southern
Australia, New Zealand, Galapagos and
California.

CROWNED CORMORANT

Phalacrocorax coronatus L 50 cm (20 in), WS
85 cm (33 in)
Small, dark, marine cormorant of Namibia and
South Africa, with blackish crest from forehead,
long tail, yellowish bill, and red iris and facial
skin. The marine equivalent of Reed (Long-
tailed) Cormorant. Classified as Near-
threatened.
IDENTIFICATION Juvenile Browner than
juvenile Reed Cormorant, especially on
underparts. Chin and throat whitish; breast,

belly and abdomen dark brown. Upperparts
dark brown to blackish, mantle feathers with
paler fringes. Bill brownish to yellow-horn; iris
bluish-grey. **Adult non-breeding** Generally
similar to juvenile plumage. Mostly brown, with
paler chin and throat; lacks crest. **Adult
breeding** Head blackish with green gloss;
occasional white filoplumes behind eye; blackish
crest from forehead, longer than on Reed
Cormorant. Upperparts blackish with silvery-
purple gloss, generally darker than Reed
Cormorant and with narrower black tips to
scapulars and wing-coverts. Underparts
blackish with slight green gloss. Bill reddish-
orange to orange-yellow; gular skin orange-
yellow; iris and facial skin red. Closely
resembles Reed Cormorant, but marine in
habits. Differs in slightly smaller size, shorter
tail, longer legs; adults also have brighter red
facial skin, longer crest, and darker and more
uniform upperparts with concolorous wing-
coverts, lacking the patterned appearance of
Reed Cormorant; immatures have darker
underparts.
DISTRIBUTION AND STATUS Endemic to
Namibia and western South Africa. Strictly
marine, breeding in loose colonies on offshore
islands and cliffs, and foraging amongst inshore
kelp beds, rarely more than 10 km offshore.
Total population *c* 2,700 pairs, breeding at over
40 sites, representing some 7,000 birds with
about 1,700 pairs in South Africa. Small
population, but no evidence of reduction in
numbers. Probably vulnerable to human
disturbance and oiling. Sedentary; occurrence
in Angola not proven.

BRANDT'S CORMORANT

Phalacrocorax penicillatus L 85 cm (33 in), WS
118 cm (46 in)
Blackish, non-crested, marine cormorant of the
north-east Pacific Ocean, in summer with dark
facial skin, yellow-bordered sky-blue gular, and
white filoplumes on sides of head.
IDENTIFICATION Juvenile Crown and
hindneck blackish, shading to brown on rest of
head; paler on foreneck, with pale greyish-
brown border along gular. Upperparts blackish-
brown, shading to greyish or straw-brown
underparts, with a paler 'V' shape across
junction of foreneck and upper breast often
extending to belly. Upperwing blackish-brown,
with scapulars and coverts margined lighter
brown. Underwing and tail blackish-brown. Bill,
legs and feet dark brown to blackish. From
Double-crested Cormorant by greyish-brown
border to gular and less white on underparts.
Adult non-breeding Generally uniform dull
blackish plumage, with very faint greenish gloss
on head and rump. Lacks white filoplumes on
sides of head and sky-blue gular; border of
gular greyish-brown. From Double-crested
Cormorant by smaller size, flight profile (head
and neck held straight), more upright jizz,
shorter tail, greyish-brown gular border, lack of
bright orange facial skin, and more uniform
upperparts. **Adult breeding** Blackish plumage,

with purplish gloss on head and neck shading to
greenish gloss on back, rump and underparts.
Sides of upper back, coverts and scapulars
greenish with narrow blackish margins. Flight
feathers black. Whitish hair-like filoplumes on
sides of head, neck, scapulars and rump. Head
lacks crest. Bill slate-grey; cobalt-blue gular
with yellow border; dark facial skin; iris green
to blue; legs and feet black.
DISTRIBUTION AND STATUS North-east Pacific
Ocean. Most common cormorant of Pacific
coast of North America, breeding colonially on
islands and gently sloping hillsides from
southern Alaska to Baja California and the
Pacific coast of Mexico, with the bulk of the
population in California (*c* 65,000 birds).
Possibly increasing in numbers although suffers
periodic mortalities with *El Niño*. Mainly
sedentary, some range south in winter as far as
Mazatlan (Mexico).

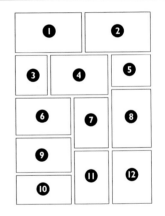

1 **Brown Booby** (adult breeding, Razo Island,
Cape Verdes, February)
2 **Brown Booby** (juvenile, Christmas Island,
Indian Ocean, October)
3 **Brown Booby** (adult)
4 **Brown Booby subspecies** *S.l. brewsteri*
(adults, Clipperton Island, east Pacific Ocean)
5 **Brown Booby** (adult, Razo Island, Cape
Verdes)
6 **Crowned Cormorant** (adult at nest)
7 **Crowned Cormorant** (juveniles)
8 **Brandt's Cormorant** (adult breeding,
California, USA)
9 **Brandt's Cormorant** (adult breeding,
California, USA)
10 **Brandt's Cormorant** (adult non-breeding,
California, USA)
11 **Brandt's Cormorant** (worn juvenile,
California, USA)
12 **Brandt's Cormorant** (worn juvenile,
California, USA)

CORMORANTS & SHAGS

FLIGHTLESS or GALAPAGOS CORMORANT

Phalacrocorax harrisi L 95 cm (37 in)
Large, dark, marine flightless cormorant confined to two islands in the Galapagos. Classified as Vulnerable.
IDENTIFICATION The only cormorant at the Galapagos. Swims low in the water, with large-headed appearance. Exclusively marine, but sedentary; returns from sea to roost on rocks. Male much larger than female, expanding range of foods taken, and reducing male/female competition. **Immature** Resembles adult, but uniform blackish-brown plumage is darker, with primaries and secondaries neater, lacking adult's frayed and ragged appearance; underparts lack adult's brownish tones. A few white filoplumes on the neck. Bill, legs and feet blackish-brown; iris dark grey. **Adult** Generally blackish-brown on upperparts when fresh, fading to tawny-brown: upperparts may show faint greenish gloss. Underparts lighter brown. White filoplumes on sides of head and neck, and small whitish base to lower mandible. Wings blackish-brown, reduced in size and number (nine primaries, 15 secondaries; fifth primary from outermost is longest); wing-coverts greyer. Bill black, paler at tip; gular skin purple-brown; facial skin dusky; iris emerald-green; legs and feet black.
DISTRIBUTION AND STATUS Restricted to *c* 370 km of coastline on Fernandina and Isabela in the Galapagos. Highly sedentary; never seen more than 1 km from breeding grounds and rarely more than 200 m offshore. Very restricted range a result of need for cold plankton-rich waters (for food), shallow seas with rocky bottoms (for foraging), and coastlines giving sheltered shores (with easy landing places). In 1970-71 700-800 pairs; thereafter stable until *El Niño* of 1982-83, when 50% decline. Recovered by 1986, and now again numbers 700-800 pairs in 112 colonies. Threats include feral dogs, Galapagos Hawk, disturbance from fisheries (especially if nets are used), tourism (if not controlled), and oil pollution.

BANK CORMORANT

Phalacrocorax neglectus L 76 cm (30 in), WS 132 cm (52 in)
Large, dull blackish cormorant restricted to Namibia and South Africa, with blackish bare parts but uniquely coloured iris and, in summer, whitish on rump. Classified as Near-threatened.
IDENTIFICATION Feeds in inshore kelp beds, either singly or in small parties, often roosting with other cormorants on rocks; tends to avoid flat land and beaches. **Juvenile** Complete plumage dull blackish-brown, with faint greenish sheen to head and faint bronze sheen on upperparts and wings; lacks white rump and white filoplumes on head and neck. Iris dark brown. By second year, sub-adults may have white filoplumes, and green iris; less iridescent

than adults. **Adult non-breeding** Browner and duller than adult breeding, without white filoplumes on head and neck, and no white on rump. Iris brown above, green below; other bare parts black. **Adult breeding** Plumage appears entirely dull blackish-brown, especially from a distance, but at closer range shows variable greenish sheen on head and underparts, and bronze sheen on upperparts and wings. Diagnostic white patch on rump present for short time only. Erectile feathers on forehead, appearing as small rounded crest; small white filoplumes on forehead and neck. Wing-coverts and scapulars bronzy-brown with narrow blacker margins; flight feathers darker blackish-brown. Iris orange-brown above, greenish below; rest of bare parts, including gular, black, but bill paler towards tip. Note that some birds show varying amounts of white on sides of head and foreneck.
DISTRIBUTION AND STATUS Namibia and western South Africa from Walvis Bay south to Cape Agulhas, with breeding from Hollamsbird Island (Namibia) to Quoin Rock (South Africa). Range wherever inshore kelp beds provide foraging. Nests colonially on marine islands and cliffs. Population *c* 18,000 adults (71% on Ichaboe and Mercury): recent decline in breeding success. Subject to Kelp Gull predation and human disturbance, but no conflict with fisheries at present; possible competition for nest sites with seals. Sedentary, but juveniles occasionally disperse outside breeding range.

BLACK-FACED CORMORANT

Phalacrocorax fuscescens L 65 cm (26 in), WS 107 cm (42 in)
Medium-sized, exclusively marine cormorant found on coasts of southern Australia and Tasmania, with black upperparts and white underparts, dark grey bill, and black facial skin, legs and feet.
IDENTIFICATION Most marine of Australian cormorants. **Juvenile** Much as adult non-breeding, but upperparts browner, cheeks and sides of face greyer, shading to brownish on foreneck and upper breast, all well demarcated from white underparts. Gular skin pink; facial skin pale buff-brown; iris brown; legs brown. From juvenile Pied Cormorant by smaller size, brown (not white) foreneck and upper breast, grey (not yellow) skin before eye. **Adult non-breeding** Crown, nape, hindneck, facial skin and gular black; rest of head and neck white, with demarcation below eye level but extending upwards onto ear-coverts. Upperparts blackish with steel-blue gloss, but duller and blacker than breeding plumage. Scapulars and wing-coverts glossed dull green, with narrow black borders; flight feathers blackish-brown with some green gloss. Underparts white, with black thighs; underwings and undertail black. Fewer white filoplumes than adult breeding. **Adult breeding** Pattern as non-breeding adult, but brighter upperparts with steel-blue gloss, and

white filoplumes on hindneck, rump and thighs. Bill dark grey; facial skin, pouch, legs and feet black; iris blue-green. Resembles more numerous Pied Cormorant, but smaller, with darker bill colour, no yellow-orange facial skin, black/white demarcation below eye (above eye on Pied), and different flight jizz with humpbacked appearance (head and neck held low).
DISTRIBUTION AND STATUS Breeds colonially on ledges, clefts and low cliffs in southern Australia from Hopetown and Recherche archipelago off Western Australia, east locally to South Australia, western Victoria, Bass Strait Islands and coastal Tasmania. Total population probably several tens of thousands of birds. Generally sedentary, with no proven interchange between the two distinct populations, though young birds disperse several hundred kilometres. Some persecution by fishermen – by shooting and usage as bait for crayfish.

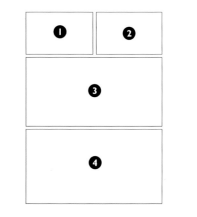

1 **Flightless Cormorant** (breeding pair at nest, Galapagos Islands)
2 **Flightless Cormorant** (adult, Galapagos Islands)
3 **Bank Cormorant** (adults at breeding colony)
4 **Black-faced Cormorant** (adult breeding and juvenile, Port Philip Bay, Australia)

NEOTROPIC CORMORANT

Phalacrocorax brasilianus
(formerly **OLIVACEOUS CORMORANT**
P. olivaceus)
L 56 cm (22 in), WS 95 cm (37 in)
Smallish, colonial and gregarious, dark cormorant occurring at marine and freshwater habitats from Texas through South America, with whitish tufts to the sides of the head in summer, and whitish border to gular pouch. **IDENTIFICATION** The only wholly dark cormorant in South America. Feeds by pursuit-diving, but can also plunge-dive – the only cormorant to do this. **Juvenile** Initially wholly brown in plumage, lacking white gular border, with flight feathers and tail darker brown. Bill and facial skin yellowish; gular skin yellow; iris brown. **Immature** Similar to juvenile, but paler underparts; white border to gular pouch. Brownish-white underparts become spotted with brown and black as adult plumage acquired. Bill and gular skin brownish; iris green; legs and feet black. **Adult non-breeding** Similar to breeding adult, but duller, browner, more olive plumage. Head blackish, lacking white sides of head, but white border to gular retained. Mantle and scapulars browner, with darker feather edges imparting scaly appearance. Flight feathers blackish; wing-coverts olive-brown, edged black. Underparts, including underwing and undertail, blackish. Bare parts less bright than adult breeding. **Adult breeding** Blackish, with blue-green sheen on head and body. White tufts to sides of head from behind eye, white border to gular, and variable scattered white filoplumes on neck, breast and mantle. Primaries brownish-black; secondaries, scapulars, wing-coverts and upper back more ashy. Bill horn to blackish; gular skin brownish to yellow-orange with diagonal narrow white border; iris blue to green; legs and feet black. Double-crested Cormorant is larger, short-tailed, more robust, and lacks white border to yellow gular.
DISTRIBUTION AND STATUS Breeds from southern North America (New Mexico, Texas, Louisiana), south through Central America, West Indies and all South America to Cape Horn: widespread and numerous (abundant Brazil). Broadest ecological and climatic range of any Western Hemisphere cormorant. Generally sedentary, but some movement of northern populations; stragglers Nevada, Colorado, Kansas and west to California. Numbers and range increased in USA since 1970s aided by construction of new reservoirs.

DOUBLE-CRESTED CORMORANT

Phalacrocorax auritus L 84 cm (33 in), WS 134 cm (53 in)
Medium-sized, blackish, marine and freshwater cormorant found throughout North America, with orange-yellow facial skin and gular pouch; in summer has a short crest on sides of head. **IDENTIFICATION Juvenile** Head dark brownish-grey, gradually shading to greyish-white on chin, throat and foreneck, with browner feather tips imparting a mottled appearance. Upperparts dark brownish-grey, with darker tips producing scaled appearance. Underparts variably mottled greyish-white and brown, becoming blackish-brown on lower belly and vent. Upperwing-coverts scaled as upperparts; flight feathers dark brownish-grey or blackish. Underwing black; undertail brownish-grey to black. Bill pale horn; gular skin dull yellow; iris brownish; legs and feet black. From juvenile Brandt's Cormorant by larger size, more scaled upperparts, paler underparts with brown mottling, yellow gular, longer tail, larger bill, and flight silhouette. **Immature** Much as juvenile, but with throat, foreneck and underparts mostly dull brown or whitish. Upperparts become increasingly glossed greenish. Some two-year-old sub-adults breed. **Adult non-breeding** Much as breeding adult, but generally browner, and with no crest or filoplumes; facial skin and gular skin yellow instead of orange. **Adult breeding** Plumage generally wholly black with variable greenish gloss. Upper back, scapulars and wing-coverts brownish-grey with wide blackish margins; flight feathers brownish-black to black. Short crest on sides of head from behind eye, white on western birds and black on eastern; additional variable filoplumes on crown and neck. Bill variably dark with greyish-yellow; facial skin and gular deep orange-yellow; iris emerald-green; legs and feet black.
DISTRIBUTION AND STATUS Breeds from Aleutians to Alaska, Canadian Prairies, Quebec and Newfoundland, southwards along Pacific coast, interior of USA and Atlantic coast, to Baja California, Mexico, Gulf of Mexico and Florida; also Islas Revilla Gigedo, Bahamas, Cuba and Isle of Pines. Dispersal southwards, especially of northern populations; vagrants to Guatemala, Belize and Europe. Most widespread North American cormorant and the only one to be seen on fresh water. After a long period of decline, resulting from pollutants, persecution, and disturbance (eg San Martin Island, Baja California: formerly held 1,800,000 birds, but now abandoned), the last decade has seen some increase and range expansion.

INDIAN CORMORANT

Phalacrocorax fuscicollis L 65 cm (26 in), WS ?
Medium-sized, dark, Asiatic freshwater and marine cormorant, with scaly upperparts and a long, graduated tail; in summer has a small tuft of white behind eye, pale green facial skin, yellowish gular and brownish bill. **IDENTIFICATION Immature** Much as non-breeding adult, but with whiter underparts. Head, hindneck, upperparts and wings duller and browner, lacking bronze sheen, but with slightly darker feather edges. Chin, throat, breast and underparts dingy whitish, with brown mottling on thighs and flanks. Iris brown. Underparts gradually become dark brown with white feather bases in later plumages, with soft parts changing colour. From non-marine Little (Javanese) Cormorant by larger size and slimmer jizz with longer neck and tail, scaly upperparts. **Adult non-breeding** Similar to breeding adult, but upperparts duller brownish-grey, lacking bronze gloss. Chin, throat and lower cheeks variably mottled with white. Lacks ornamental white head feathers. Facial skin and gular yellowish. **Adult breeding** Plumage blackish-bronze with darker feather edges, giving scaly pattern, especially on upper back, wing-coverts and scapulars (which can show greenish gloss). Flight feathers blackish. White stripe on each side of head starting behind eye, also scattered white filoplumes on the neck. Bill dark brown; facial skin variable; iris greenish-blue; legs and feet black.
DISTRIBUTION AND STATUS Found in both coastal and freshwater habitats, and breeding in trees, in Sri Lanka (3,820 birds 1991), and from the Indus Valley of Pakistan eastwards, south of the Himalayan foothills, to southern Indo-China, excluding the Malay Peninsula. Widespread in India (5,861 birds 1991) and Pakistan (18,879 birds 1991). Sedentary, with local movement according to local water conditions. A common and widely distributed species, but understudied.

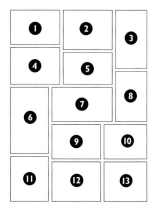

1 **Neotropic Cormorant** (adult)
2 **Neotropic Cormorant** (adult)
3 **Neotropic Cormorant** (juvenile)
4 **Neotropic Cormorant** (immature)
5 **Double-crested Cormorant** (adult breeding, Florida, USA)
6 **Double-crested Cormorant** (immature, USA)
7 **Double-crested Cormorant** (adults in flight, USA)
8 **Double-crested Cormorant** (adult breeding, Florida, USA)
9 **Double-crested Cormorant** (adult non-breeding, USA)
10 **Indian Cormorant** (adult non-breeding)
11 **Indian Cormorant** (adult at breeding colony, southern India)
12 **Indian Cormorant** (adults breeding at colony, southern India)
13 **Indian Cormorant** (near Colombo, Sri Lanka)

PIED CORMORANT

Phalacrocorax varius L 75 cm (30 in), WS 121 cm (48 in)

Large marine and freshwater cormorant of Australia and New Zealand.

IDENTIFICATION Most common Australian cormorant; gregarious. **Juvenile** Forehead, crown, nape, hindneck and upperparts brown. Chin and throat whitish, separated from grey-and-white-streaked upper breast by brownish foreneck; lower underparts dull white. Wings brown, as upperparts. Bill pinkish with dark culmen; facial and gular skin pale yellow-cream; iris dark brown; legs and feet blackish-brown. Similar to juvenile Black-faced Cormorant, but larger, with yellow facial skin. **Immature** Brown upperparts gradually become blacker, developing greenish sheen; brown on foreneck becomes mottled white then white. New Zealand immatures have all-brown underparts. Bill horn with dark culmen; gular skin pale pink; facial skin orange-yellow; iris green; legs and feet black. **Adult non-breeding** Much as breeding adult, but with duller and blacker upperparts. Bare parts also duller; bare patch in front of eye yellowish-buff. **Adult breeding** Crown, hindneck, lower back, rump, uppertail-coverts and thighs brownish-black, glossed dark green; upper back, wing-coverts and scapulars bronze-grey with slight green gloss, bordered black. Chin, throat, sides of head, neck and underparts white, with line of demarcation well above eye (thus appears 'paler-faced' than Black-faced). Flight feathers blackish-brown; underwing black. Tail black, paler at base. Bill dark horn; gular skin pinkish; yellow to orange facial skin in front of eyes; iris green, eye-ring dark blue; legs and feet black.

DISTRIBUTION AND STATUS Australia and New Zealand. Resident Australia, especially marine habitats in west; also Northern Territory east to Victoria and South Australia, fewer in interior, now absent from Tasmania. No population estimates but widespread. Most sedentary of Australian cormorants, limited post-juvenile dispersal; has reached Lord Howe Island. New Zealand population fewer than 100,000 birds, mostly North Island, especially east coast. Vagrants Snares Island. Less affected than other cormorants by habitat modification and has adapted to new reservoirs and introduced fish.

GREAT CORMORANT

Phalacrocorax carbo L 90 cm (35 in), WS 140 cm (55 in)

Large and dark, almost cosmopolitan, marine and freshwater cormorant.

IDENTIFICATION Juvenile Similar to adult non-breeding, but browner above, with off-white underparts. Head dull brown, shading to mottled fawn; white on sides of face, throat and foreneck. Upperparts brownish with darker edges, appearing; underparts variable from whitish to brownish. Wing-coverts dull bronze, edged darker; flight feathers brownish-black. Tail brownish-black. Bill dark brown; facial skin and gular greenish-yellow; iris grey-brown; legs and feet black. **Immature** Much as juvenile, but upperparts and belly become progressively darker; belly mottled brownish-white by second year, entirely dark by third year. Foreneck and upper breast mottled brown. Some may show whitish filoplumes on brownish sides of neck. Iris becomes green. Yellow facial skin bordered by diffuse whitish on chin and throat only. **Adult non-breeding** Much as breeding adult, but duller and browner. No white filoplumes or white thigh patch. Bare parts duller. **Adult breeding** Head and neck blackish with bluish or greenish gloss; erectile black crest behind middle of nape. Some whitish plumes on sides of head; whitish throat and forecheeks. Body blackish with bluish or greenish gloss, with white oval patch on thigh. Upper back, scapulars and wing-coverts dull bronze-brown, with darker edges forming scaly pattern. Flight feathers blackish-brown with slight greenish gloss. Underwing blackish-brown; tail blackish. Bill greyish-horn, yellow at base; facial skin variable, usually yellow or orange; iris emerald-green; legs and feet blackish. *P. c. sinensis* (most of Europe, Asia) has greener gloss, more white on throat and forecheeks, and whitish stripe on head from crown to sides of neck. *P. c. maroccanus* (north-west Africa) as *sinensis*, but with white throat extending to upper breast; greener gloss. *P. c. lucidus* (Africa) white from chin to breast, occasionally belly; gloss purplish.

DISTRIBUTION AND STATUS Widely distributed. From Scandinavia to British Isles east to China and Japan, south to North Africa, India, southern China, Africa south of the Sahara and Australasia; also Iceland, Greenland, eastern maritime Canada. Generally resident. Vagrants Louisiana, New Guinea, Indonesia, Christmas Island. Many populations unknown, but c 80,000 in western Europe and north Atlantic, and 5,400 birds in Canada. Generally protected, some populations expanding and re-colonizing (Europe), while others are declining (Japan).

JAPANESE CORMORANT

Phalacrocorax capillatus L 92 cm (36 in), WS 152 cm (60 in)

Very large Asiatic marine cormorant, similar to Great Cormorant in plumage.

IDENTIFICATION Juvenile: Upperparts wholly dark greyish-brown to dark chocolate-brown without any sheen, but with darker tips to feathers. Underparts brownish-white, with brownish spots on flanks; chin, throat and foreneck whiter. Bill yellow; legs and feet black. **Immature** Similar to juvenile plumage, but underparts show progressive darkening on breast and belly; chin, throat and foreneck whitish. Upperparts blackish-brown; wing-coverts and scapulars browner, with blackish tips imparting scaled appearance; flight feathers darker. Upperparts start to acquire metallic sheen. **Adult non-breeding** As breeding adult, but duller and browner, without short crest; lacks white filoplumes on sides of head and neck, and white thigh patch. Bare parts less bright. **Adult breeding** Head dark greenish-black, with white of cheeks and chin extending under lower mandible; narrow white filoplumes on sides of head and neck. Short dark crest. Mantle, scapulars, back and wing-coverts greenish with darker, blackish fringes. Flight feathers blackish. Tail black. Underwing black. Underparts blackish-green, with white thigh patch. Bill yellowish-horn; gular skin yellow; facial skin orange-yellow; iris green; legs and feet blackish-brown. From slightly smaller Great Cormorant by exclusively marine habitats (does not perch in trees), more white and less yellow on sides of face, greener (not bronze-brown) gloss on upperparts, more conspicuous white filoplumes on sides of neck and head.

DISTRIBUTION AND STATUS Breeds along rocky coasts and promontories in central and northern Japan, South Kuril Islands, Okinoshima, coastal China and Korea, Siberia's maritime territory, and Sakhalin. Winter dispersal to coastal Korea, China, and Japan (especially Honshu and northern Kyushu); has occurred Taiwan. A recent census gave 1,199 birds in Japan with 3 colonies each holding several hundred pairs, 825 in South Korea, and under 16,000 birds in Siberian Russia. Population appears stable, previously persecuted and may still suffer from sport fishermen.

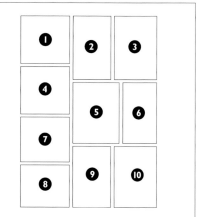

1 Pied Cormorant (adult breeding, Athenzee, New Zealand, March)
2 Pied Cormorant (juvenile, Miranda, New Zealand, May)
3 Great Cormorant, subspecies *P. c. carbo* (breeding adult at nest with chick, Craigleith, Scotland, June)
4 Great Cormorant, subspecies *P. c. carbo* (adult non-breeding, Kent, England)
5 Great Cormorant, subspecies *P. c. sinensis* (adult at breeding colony, Netherlands)
6 Great Cormorant, subspecies *P. c. lucidus* (White-breasted) (adult, Lake Nakuru, Kenya)
7 Great Cormorant (immature, Islay, Scotland)
8 Great Cormorant (immature, Kent, England, November)
9 Japanese Cormorant (adult at nest, Moyururi Island, Japan)
10 Japanese Cormorant (adult with chicks at nest, Moyururi Island, Japan)

CORMORANTS & SHAGS

SOCOTRA CORMORANT

Phalacrocorax nigrogularis L 80 cm (31 in), WS 106 cm (42 in)

Large, blackish, highly gregarious, exclusively marine cormorant found only in the Arabian Sea and Persian Gulf. Breeding adults show a purple sheen on head and neck, with a whitish eye-stripe and variable white flecking on throat and neck. Classified as Near-threatened.

IDENTIFICATION Juvenile Generally brownish upperparts, whiter underparts. Greyish-brown crown and hindneck, shading to whitish on chin, throat and foreneck. Upperparts and wings greyish-brown, with indistinct paler feather edges and darker centres on wing-coverts; flight feathers darker. Tail brown. Underparts dirty-white, variably washed brown. Underwing brown. Bill greyish; facial skin yellowish; iris grey; legs and feet brownish. **Immature** Much as juvenile, but mantle and scapulars more spotted (dark centres and paler edges); underparts browner, with darker spotting on throat and breast. Bare parts may take three or four years to assume adult coloration. **Adult non-breeding** Much as breeding adult, but duller and browner. Usually lacks white stripe behind eye and whitish streaking on the rump; less whitish streaking on neck and body. From Great Cormorant by smaller size, dark facial skin, lack of white on gular, head and thigh. **Adult breeding** Entirely blackish plumage. Head and neck glossed purple, with whitish streak starting behind eye over ear-coverts, and variable white flecking on neck and throat. Upperparts blackish with deep slate-green sheen, and darker feather centres giving spotted appearance. Wing-coverts as upperparts; flight feathers blackish-green. Underwing black; tail blackish-green. Underparts blackish with purple gloss; white flecking on rump. Bill greyish-black with greenish base; facial skin and gular blackish; iris green; legs and feet black.

DISTRIBUTION AND STATUS Breeds in large dense colonies on level offshore islands and islets, mainly in the Persian Gulf, with some in the Arabian Sea. Possibly breeds in the Gulf of Aden (Yemen, and on Socotra), but at present unproven. Dispersal south to Gulf of Aden and southern Red Sea; vagrants Somalia, Ethiopia, and western India. Shy, and sensitive to human disturbance. Adversely affected by Gulf War and subsequent oil pollution in the Persian Gulf, with a reduction of colonies from 28 to 11, and a total World population estimated at between 500,000 and 1 million pairs.

CAPE CORMORANT

Phalacrocorax capensis L 63 cm (25 in), WS 109 cm (43 in)

Small, blackish, gregarious marine cormorant of Namibia and South Africa, with bright yellow facial skin, green iris, blackish bill, legs and feet, and comparatively short tail.

IDENTIFICATION Very gregarious cormorant, breeding colonially and foraging in larger flocks than other South African cormorants. Coastal species, generally not found beyond 70 km from shore. Jumps clear of water when diving. **Juvenile** Similar to non-breeding adult, but with browner and duller upperparts, whiter underparts. Forehead, crown, nape and hindneck dark brown, merging into whiter sides of face, chin, foreneck and upper breast. Upperparts dull blackish-brown, with slightly darker feather edges on scapulars and wing-coverts; darker flight feathers. Tail blackish-brown. Underparts whitish. Facial skin dull brown; iris grey; legs blackish-brown. **Adult non-breeding** Plumage dull blackish-brown, much as juvenile, but with paler greyer-brown chin, foreneck and upper breast. Upperparts show reduced greenish and bronze iridescence, but no white filoplumes. Facial skin dull yellowish-brown; iris grey to greenish; legs brownish-black. **Adult breeding** Plumage uniform blackish, with strong greenish gloss on head and body, and greenish-bronze gloss on wings. No crest; head and neck may show scattered white filoplumes. Upper back, scapulars and wing-coverts have darker edges, imparting scaled appearance. Flight feathers blackish with some greenish gloss. Tail strongly graduated, giving short-tailed appearance. Bill, legs and feet blackish; gular skin orange-yellow; iris green.

DISTRIBUTION AND STATUS Breeds on steep slopes, rock outcrops, mainland cliffs and guano platforms in Namibia and western South Africa. Some dispersal north and east, with vagrants to mouth of Congo River and Mozambique; regular Angola. Most abundant South African cormorant; however, population in decline, expecially in north of range. 1 million birds in the early 1970s were reduced to 277,000 pairs in the late 1970s and further to 120,000 pairs by the mid 1980s. Pilchards were an important food until the 1970s crash after which anchovy became the main food. Population reduction can further be correleated with breeding failure and mass mortality induced by abnormal oceanographic conditions.

GUANAY CORMORANT or SHAG

Phalacrocorax bougainvillii L 76 cm (30 in), WS ?

A large marine cormorant of South America, with dark head and upperparts, whitish underparts and chin, red facial skin and, in summer, a crest on the crown, whitish tufts over the eye and yellowish bill.

IDENTIFICATION Immature Much as non-breeding adult, but bare parts duller, upperparts duller brown, lower underparts brownish-white. **Adult non-breeding** Generally duller and browner than breeding adult, without dark crest, white tuft over eye or white filoplumes. Head, hindneck and foreneck brown with a dull greenish gloss; whitish chin. Upper back, wing-coverts and scapulars brownish-bronze with less apparent gloss and inconspicuous darker feather margins. Wings and tail brown. Underparts from breast whitish, with browner flanks, lower breast, thighs and undertail-coverts. **Adult breeding** Head and foreneck blackish, glossed with steel-blue; crest and top of head dark green; small white tuft over eye and scattered white filoplumes on neck; chin white. Lower back, rump and uppertail-coverts dark bluish-green. Wing-coverts and scapulars dull bronze-green with narrow margins of darker greenish-blue; rest of wings brownish-black. Underparts from base of foreneck white; thighs glossed dark bluish-green. Bill horn-yellow to brownish; facial skin and gular skin red; iris dark brown, orbital ring olive-green; legs and feet pinkish. From Rock Shag by smaller size, dark foreneck and lighter bill colour.

DISTRIBUTION AND STATUS Breeds colonially in vast colonies on islands and headlands along the Pacific coast of South America from Macabi and Guanape islands, Peru, south through Chura and Lobos islands to Chile south to Concon island (near Valparaiso); formerly bred Mocha Island; also on Atlantic coast between Puerto Deseado and Santa Cruz, Chubut, Argentina. Probably the World's most numerous cormorant; however, population declining from c 30 million birds in the 1960s to c 3 million birds in 1981 and c 1,380,000 birds 1985–86 (with c 900,000 in Peru). Decline related to the anchovy crash of 1972 from overfishing, to guano extraction and to the failure, from abnormal oceanographic conditions (*El Niño*), of the food supply which results in breeding failure and mass mortality. Dispersal north to Ecuador and south to Valdivia (Chile), but in *El Niño* years moves further, north to Colombia and Panama and south to southern Chile, as well as following rivers inland.

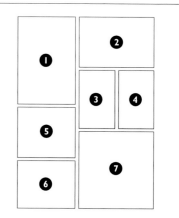

1 **Socotra Cormorant** (juvenile, Abu Ali, Saudi Arabia, April)
2 **Socotra Cormorant** (adult on nest, Hawar Island, Bahrain)
3 **Socotra Cormorant** (juvenile, Abu Ali, Saudi Arabia, April)
4 **Cape Cormorant** (adult, Strandfontein, South Africa)
5 **Cape Cormorant** (adult breeding, Kommetjie, South Africa)
6 **Guanay Cormorant** (juvenile)
7 **Guanay Cormorant** (adult breeding)

CORMORANTS & SHAGS

KERGUELEN SHAG

Phalacrocorax verrucosus L 65 cm (26 in), WS 110 cm (43 in)

Smallest of the blue-eyed shags, confined to Kerguelen. Generally similar to *P. albiventor* Imperial Shag.

IDENTIFICATION Flight heavy and laboured. Feeds close to the coastline. Gregarious when roosting or breeding; does not spread wings when perched. **Juvenile/immature** Upperparts dark brown, underparts variable brown and white; no caruncles. With increasing age, metallic sheen appears on upperparts, and underparts become whiter. **Adult non-breeding** Much as adult breeding, but plumage duller and faded; caruncles less developed, dull yellow. Eye-ring blue, no forehead crest. **Adult breeding** Front and sides of head steel-blue; back of head and hindneck steel-blue with purple gloss; black erectile crest on forehead. Line of dark/white demarcation on head runs from chin, below eye, to ear-coverts, giving dark-faced appearance. Back, upperwing-coverts, scapulars and tail metallic dark green (white forewing and back patches only rarely present). Throat, foreneck and underparts white, line of demarcation extending below bill to chin; thighs blue-black. Underwing brown. Bill shorter than on other island shags, brownish; yellow to orange caruncles above base of bill; gular pouch dark brown; iris dark brown, eye-ring ultramarine; legs and feet variable, brown to pinkish. Bare parts less bright than in *albiventor* Imperial. Differs from other blue-eyed shags in having more black on cheeks.

DISTRIBUTION AND STATUS Kerguelen Island, where 6,000-7,000 pairs breed. Population apparently stable. Not adversely affected by humans or introduced mammals, although eggs are taken by skuas, sheathbills and gulls. Has been observed up to 80 km from land on Kerguelen continental shelf. Population considered sedentary, although the presence of some birds with white wing bars and dorsal patch in eastern Kerguelen may represent arrivals from the Crozets or Heard hybridizing with local birds. Individuals seen Heard Island and western Australia probably ship-assisted.

IMPERIAL SHAG

Phalacrocorax atriceps L 72 cm (28 in), WS 124 cm (49 in)

Widespread insular subantarctic shag, black above and on head and white below, with geographically variable forewing bar and dorsal patch. Taxonomy here follows Sibley and Monroe, with *atriceps*, *albiventor*, *nivalis*, *purpurascens* and *melanogenis* included in Imperial, and *verrucosus*, *bransfieldensis* and *georgianus* treated as separate species.

IDENTIFICATION Juvenile Pattern of plumage much as non-breeding adult, but upperparts duller and browner, with greenish sheen; lacks crest and caruncles. Forewing bars, if present, are mottled pale brownish-white. Underparts white. Bill dark grey; gular violet; iris brown;

legs and feet grey to brown. **Adult non-breeding** Much as breeding adult, but crest lacking, caruncles shrunken in size and duller, bare parts less bright. White forewing bars and dorsal patch reduced or totally absent. **Adult breeding** Crown, nape and hindneck blackish with bluish sheen; small crest on nape; some white filoplumes on sides of head. Lower cheeks, chin, throat and foreneck white, with line of demarcation variable (level with eye or just below). Upperparts bluish-black, with variable white patch on middle back and variable white stripe on forewing. Flight feathers blackish. Uppertail blackish with blue sheen. Underparts white; thighs black. Underwing black. Bill grey to olive; caruncles bright orange to yellow; lores and gular sooty; facial skin blue-grey; iris brown, orbital ring blue; legs and feet pink. *P. a. atriceps*: Line of demarcation separating black and white on head level with eye; median white patch on middle back and white alar stripes on anterior margins of wings (appear at time of egg-laying). Some Patagonian birds resemble *albiventor*. *P. a. albiventor*: Demarcation between black and white on head is lower on cheeks, approximately at level of gape; white tuft of filoplumes above and behind eye; white forewing stripes but no white dorsal patch; caruncles yellow-orange, more strongly developed than in *atriceps*. *P. a. melanogenis*: Black/white demarcation similar to *albiventor*, with black of cheeks extending below level of ear; white filoplumes above and behind eye; white forewing stripes on some; rarely, white scapular; no white on back. *P. a. nivalis*: Similar to *atriceps*, but generally larger in size (77 cm), with black extending lower down on cheeks and only scattered white feathers in forewing region; some white normally present in scapulars; white dorsal patch in breeding season, but scapular and forewing markings may be reduced or absent. *P. a. purpurascens*: Similar to *albiventor*, with black of crown extending down cheeks to below ear level; white forewing and scapular patches prominent on some but reduced or lacking on others; back lacks white patches.

DISTRIBUTION AND STATUS *P. a. atriceps*: Mocha Island (Chile) south to Tierra del Fuego, Straits of Magellan, Beagle Channel, north in Argentina to Punta Tombo, Chubut with many large and dense colonies. Common in Chile despite some egg-collecting. Vagrants north to Uruguay. *P. a. albiventor*: Falklands. *P. a. melanogenis*: Prince Edwards (400 pairs), Crozets (815 pairs). Vagrants may reach Kerguelen. *P. a. nivalis*: Heard Island (600-1,000 birds). *P. a. purpurascens*: Macquarie Island (760 pairs).

ANTARCTIC SHAG

Phalacrocorax bransfieldensis L c 77 cm (30 in), WS ?

The only shag on the Antarctic Peninsula. Very large, black and white, marine species with prominent white forewing and dorsal patches and white ear-coverts.

IDENTIFICATION After penguins, the most

numerous bird around Antarctic Peninsula. Head held below body in normal flight; does not perch with spread wings. Gregarious; can form large rafts. Very similar in appearance to *atriceps* Imperial, but with larger caruncles. **Juvenile/immature** Pattern as non-breeding adult, but upperparts are dull brown; no caruncles. **Adult non-breeding** Much as breeding adult, but upperparts duller and faded, bare parts duller; caruncles yellow. No crest. **Adult breeding** Forehead, crown, nape and hindneck blackish-blue, with short recurved black crest on crown. Lower cheeks, ear-coverts, throat and foreneck white: line of demarcation arches across cheek, leaving ear-coverts white. Upperparts blackish-blue with white dorsal patch. Tail black. Upperwing-coverts blackish-blue with conspicuous white bar. Underparts white, with black thighs. Underwing blackish. Bill greyish-black; caruncles bright orange-yellow; eye-ring bright blue; legs and feet pinkish-flesh. Other blue-eyed shags have less white on face, are smaller (except race *nivalis* of Imperial), and do not penetrate south to Antarctic Peninsula.

DISTRIBUTION AND STATUS Breeds on north-facing slopes (where snow melts early) or on small rocky islets and stacks on Antarctic Peninsula (10,000 pairs in 56 colonies), South Shetlands (700 pairs in 21 colonies), Elephant Island (205 pairs in 14 colonies), with smaller colonies on islands off the Peninsula. Breeding success linked to availability of food. Generally sedentary, but in winter may be forced northwards to forage in ice-free open water.

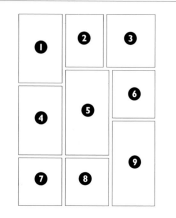

1 Kerguelen Shag (adult breeding, Kerguelen Island)
2 Kerguelen Shag (adult breeding with juvenile, Kerguelen Island)
3 Kerguelen Shag (adult breeding with immature, Kerguelen Island)
4 Imperial Shag (immature and adult breeding)
5 Imperial Shag (adult breeding, Falkland Islands)
6 Imperial Shag (adult, Tierra del Fuego)
7 Antarctic Shag (adult breeding, Antarctic Peninsula)
8 Antarctic Shag (juvenile)
9 Antarctic Shag (adult breeding, Aitcho Islands, Antarctica)

CORMORANTS & SHAGS

SOUTH GEORGIA SHAG

Phalacrocorax georgianus L 72 cm (28 in), WS 120 cm (47 in)

Black and white shag of Scotia Arc islands, very similar to *atriceps* Imperial Shag, but caruncles larger and deep chrome-yellow; black/white demarcation crosses ear opening; white patches on wings and back may be prominent, reduced or lacking. Birds from South Sandwich and South Orkneys previously regarded as Antarctic Shag or *atriceps* Imperial Shag.

IDENTIFICATION Immature Brown upperparts, white underparts; no caruncles; eye-ring deep blue. **Adult non-breeding** Much as breeding adult, but upperparts more faded in colour, bare parts duller, no crest. **Adult breeding** Forehead, crown and hindneck blackish-blue; black crest on forehead; white filoplumes above and behind eye. Border with white underparts starts at eye and passes through ear-coverts, thus intermediate between *atriceps* Imperial (white cheeks) and *albiventer* Imperial (black cheeks), similar to *P. a. nivalis*. Upperwing-coverts and scapulars black with greenish sheen; mantle has bluish sheen, distinct from greenish on wings and scapulars. White patches on wings and back generally prominent, but may be reduced or absent; back patches may be obscured by wings. Tail black. Bill dark brown; yellow caruncles above base of bill in front of eyes; skin of face and throat blackish-brown to purple; eye-ring blue; legs and feet pinkish. Closely resembles Imperial Shag of race *nivalis* (Heard Island), but demarcation of light and dark at side of neck passes across ear opening, whereas above ear on *nivalis* (and on Antarctic Shag); caruncles larger and bill shorter. Dries wings in typical cormorant fashion.

DISTRIBUTION AND STATUS Islands of Scotia Arc, including South Georgia (4,000 pairs), Shag Rocks (1,000 pairs), South Sandwich (100-1,000 pairs), South Orkney (2,000 pairs), Laurie (2,500 pairs) and Signy (830 pairs). Mainly resident; some movement towards open water in places where sea ice is too prevalent. Taken historically by whalers for food, but no immediate threats at present.

CAMPBELL or CAMPBELL ISLAND SHAG

Phalacrocorax campbelli L 63 cm (25 in), WS 105 cm (41 in)

Medium-sized, black and white shag restricted to Campbell Island, with variable white forewing bar, whitish chin, and black of head and hindneck extending onto foreneck. Classified as Vulnerable.

IDENTIFICATION In flight, head held below body line. Highly gregarious species; congregates in large rafts offshore, foraging together; dives clear of water. Groups attract other seabird species. **Juvenile** Pattern as adult non-breeding, but upperparts and head to foreneck dark brown; no white chin and no white forewing patch. Bill pinkish, orange at base and gape; iris grey-brown; legs and feet flesh-coloured. From vagrant (non-marine) Little Pied Cormorant by plumage pattern and foot colour. **Adult non-breeding** As breeding adult, but upperparts duller with less sheen, and bare parts duller; lacks crest and filoplumes; no white dorsal patch. **Adult breeding** Head and whole of neck blackish with blue sheen; blackish forehead crest, and white filoplumes on side of head; chin white. Upperparts blackish with blue sheen. Underparts white from lower foreneck; thighs black. Upperwing-coverts and scapulars purple-grey with greenish sheen and narrow black borders; white forewing stripes (sometimes absent); no white on scapulars or back. Underwing black. Tail blackish with white shafts. Bill black-brown, yellower at base; no nasal caruncles, but line above gape and spot at base of lower mandible orange; gular purple to red; facial skin variable purple; iris dark brown; legs and feet dull pink. Resembles Auckland Shag (more white on foreneck and orange eye-ring) and Bounty Shag (larger, white foreneck), but ranges do not overlap.

DISTRIBUTION AND STATUS New Zealand. Breeds usually colonially on seaward-facing cliffs, ledges etc, also in sea caves or amongst tussock at Campbell Island and its adjacent stacks, rocks and islands. Population estimated at 8,000 birds and 2,000 nests in 1975 (van Tets 1980). Impact of introduced mammals (rats, cats, sheep, cattle) is small, though some eggs are lost to skuas. Sedentary, but either this species or Bounty Shag may have reached Antipodes (800 km). No major threats at present.

ROUGH-FACED or (NEW ZEALAND) KING SHAG

Phalacrocorax carunculatus L 76 cm (30 in), WS ? Large, black and white, marine shag of New Zealand, with white dorsal patch and two white bars on upperwing. Very restricted range. Classified as Vulnerable.

IDENTIFICATION Does not spread wings to dry, and does not perch in trees. **Juvenile** Pattern as adult non-breeding, but head and upperparts mid brown with some green sheen, with indistinct or no buffish forewing bar and dorsal patch. Underparts dirty white; thighs dark. Lacks caruncles. Upper mandible brown, lower white; facial skin and legs whitish-flesh. **Immature** As juvenile but darker, with more noticeable greenish gloss to upperparts; underparts clearer and cleaner white. Bare parts brighter than juvenile. **Adult non-breeding** Similar to adult breeding, but lacks crest on forehead; upperparts duller, bare parts duller and faded, white forewing bar and dorsal patch reduced or absent, facial skin dark reddish-brown; yellow caruncles smaller and less intense in colour. **Adult breeding** Head and hindneck black with metallic bluish-green sheen (black starts at sides of chin under lower mandible, so head predominantly dark); black crest on forehead at start of breeding season.

Chin, throat and foreneck white. Mantle, scapulars and upperwing-coverts dark purple-brown with greenish sheen and darker black borders; white stripe on inner median coverts and white scapular patches variable in extent; variable white patch(es) on upper back; lower back, rump and uppertail-coverts black with metallic bluish-green sheen. Tail black with whitish shafts. Flight feathers blackish. Underparts from chin white, but dark blackish-blue thigh patch. Underwing black, with white leading edge on inner wing. Bill greyish-pink; prominent orange-yellow caruncles above base of bill; facial skin and gular blue-grey; iris hazel-grey; legs and feet greyish-pink. From Pied Cormorant by darker face, white patches on upperwing and back, pink (not black) legs.

DISTRIBUTION AND STATUS Very rare, endangered, and restricted to five or six colonies of up to 80 pairs on rocky slopes and stacks in Marlborough Sound, Cook Strait. Population below 600 birds (192 in 1965). Protected since 1924, but suffers from historical egg-collecting, illegal killing (by fishermen) and human disturbance (by boats and scuba divers) at colonies and subsequent gull predation. Sedentary, occasional records on South Island away from Cook Strait.

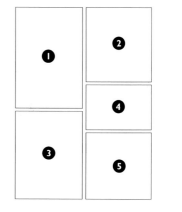

1 **South Georgia Shag** (adult breeding)
2 **South Georgia Shag** (immatures)
3 **Campbell Island Shag** (adult breeding, Campbell Island)
4 **Campbell Island Shag** (adult)
5 **Rough-faced Shag** (breeding adult on nest)

CORMORANTS & SHAGS

BRONZE or STEWART ISLAND SHAG

Phalacrocorax chalconotus L 68 cm (27 in), WS ? Large, dimorphic marine shag similar to Rough-faced Shag in plumage (pied morph), but with richer greener gloss on upperparts, only one bar on upperwing, and smaller white dorsal spot. Classified as Vulnerable.
IDENTIFICATION Occurs in two basic morphs. **Juvenile** Similar to non-breeding adult, but duller. Upperparts dark brown glossed with green; some (pied morph?) show indications of white forewing stripes and dorsal patches, but generally absent. Underparts dark brown (bronze morph), white (pied morph), or mixture of brown and white. Bill sandy-grey with dark culmen; facial skin dark brown with some yellow at gape; iris pale brown; legs and feet flesh-coloured. **Immature** Similar to juvenile, but brighter. Bronze morph slightly glossy black on upperparts and underparts; pied morph variably white on underparts. Bare parts brighter than in juveniles. Breeding occurs in third year. **Adult non-breeding** Both morphs similar to respective breeding plumage, but duller, lacking crest and white filoplumes; bare parts less bright. **Adult breeding** *Bronze morph*: Plumage entirely black, with upperparts and head glossed dark bluish-green, wings and back glossed more brassy or bronze-green. Bare parts and white filoplumes as for pied morph. Rarely, intermediates occur with white spotting on lower breast and belly or, more rarely, complete white underparts. *Pied morph*: Plumage pattern resembles that of Rough-faced Shag. Head and hindneck black with bluish sheen; black forehead crest; white filoplumes in tufts on sides of crown, also on head and neck. Upperwing-coverts, mantle and scapulars dark brown with greenish sheen and darker blackish borders; white patches on upperwing, scapulars and upper back variable (usually single dorsal patch). Flight feathers blackish. Lower back, rump, uppertail-coverts and thighs black with bluish sheen. Tail black. Underparts white from chin to undertail-coverts, but thighs dark. Underwing dark. Bill variable, but dark culmen; red-orange caruncles above base of bill; facial skin variable, purple-grey; gular reddish; iris golden-brown, blue eye-ring; legs and feet pink.
DISTRIBUTION AND STATUS New Zealand, where sedentary. Breeds colonially on rocky headlands and islands off Stewart Island and adjoining islands (eg Codfish) of Foveaux Strait, and southern tip of South Island: 11 known colonies. Population estimate 3,000 birds, but probably 5,000-8,000, perhaps 10,000. Trend unclear. Threats include human disturbance, predators, and gill-net fishing.

CHATHAM or CHATHAM ISLAND SHAG

Phalacrocorax onslowi L 63 cm (25 in), WS ? Black and white marine shag with plumage much as Rough-faced Shag, but smaller, with brighter red facial skin and gular, larger white dorsal patch, and deeper black upperparts with more iridescence. Classified as Vulnerable.
IDENTIFICATION Juvenile Pattern as adult non-breeding, but upperparts dark brown with green gloss. Mantle feathers blackish near tips, edged buffish; some have white forewing patches; dull white underparts may have a brown breastband. Bill yellowish-horn with darker culmen; no facial caruncles; facial skin brown; gular skin yellowish; iris greyish-blue, blue eye-ring; legs and feet pink. **Adult non-breeding** No crests or filoplumes. Upperparts and bare parts duller and faded; facial caruncles yellow, no orange-red at base of lower mandible. Blue eye-ring. **Adult breeding** Head and hindneck black with metallic blue sheen; black forehead crest, and white filoplumes on neck. Upperwing-coverts, scapulars and mantle dark greyish-brown with metallic green sheen and darker, blacker tips; white forewing and dorsal patches present but variable; some show white on scapulars. Flight feathers blacker. Lower back, rump, uppertail-coverts and thighs black with purple-blue sheen. Tail black. Underparts from chin white. Underwing dark (with white on leading edge). Bill greyish-brown; orange-red caruncles above base of bill; gular pouch and skin at base of lower mandible orange-red; iris brown, eye-ring purple-blue; legs and feet pink. From Great Cormorant and Spotted Shag (at Chathams) by white underparts and pink feet and presence of caruncles. From Rough-faced Shag by smaller size and orange-red base to lower mandible when breeding.
DISTRIBUTION AND STATUS New Zealand. Endemic to Chathams, where sedentary, breeding colonially on exposed rocks on tops of headlands and small islands off Chatham Island, Rabbit Island (near Pitt Island) and Star Keys. Population fewer than 5,000 birds (Robertson 1988), but no recent complete survey. BirdLife International (1994) states that population is estimated at fewer than 1,000 birds. Threat from humans, particularly since, when disturbed at colonies, birds stampede which results in egg loss and subsequent gull predation; also perhaps from farm stock on Chatham Island and increasing competition for nest sites with fur seals.

AUCKLAND or AUCKLAND ISLAND SHAG

Phalacrocorax colensoi L 63 cm (25 in), WS 105 cm (41 in)
Medium-sized, black and white shag found only at Auckland Islands. Much as Campbell Shag, but generally has less white on chin and throat. Classified as Vulnerable.
IDENTIFICATION Juvenile Pattern as adult non-breeding, but upperparts and head dark brown, including chin, throat and foreneck, although variable; some may show only a dark band or spots across foreneck. Forewing and scapular stripes, if present, pale sandy. Bill brownish-horn, pinker at tip; iris and bare facial skin brown. **Adult non-breeding** Upperparts duller and browner than adult breeding; no crest, and white forewing bar and dorsal patch absent; bare parts duller. **Adult breeding** Head and hindneck black with blue sheen; long recurved black crest on forehead. Upperparts black with blue sheen; some males have white dorsal patches. Upperwing-coverts dark purple-grey with green sheen and narrow blacker borders; white forewing patches vary from absent to prominent; occasionally white on scapulars. Tail black with whitish shafts. Underparts from chin white, foreneck varying from thin white vertical stripe joining chin and breast to complete broad blackish band which may be spotted; thighs black with blue sheen. Underwing black. Bill blackish, with orange tip to lower mandible; no caruncles at bill base, but orange line from upper mandible to gape, lower mandible with orange skin at base; facial skin dark purple; gular pouch orange-red; iris dark purple-brown, eye-ring violet-purple; legs and feet pinkish.
DISTRIBUTION AND STATUS New Zealand. Breeds colonially on grass tussocks with overhanging rocks or trees on Auckland, Enderby and Cape Crozier. Total population c 5,000 birds, no evidence of decline. Sedentary. The threat on Auckland is from feral pigs and possibly cats. In addition, nests are occasionally washed away by storm waves.

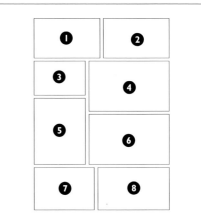

1 **Bronze Shag** (breeding adults, bronze and pied morph)
2 **Bronze Shag** (breeding adults, bronze morph, New Zealand, February)
3 **Bronze Shag** (breeding adult at nest, bronze morph, Codfish Island, New Zealand)
4 **Chatham Island Shag** (adult breeding, Chatham Islands)
5 **Chatham Island Shag** (adult breeding at nest, Chatham Islands)
6 **Chatham Island Shag** (juveniles, Chatham Islands)
7 **Chatham Island Shag** (breeding adult, Chatham Islands)
8 **Auckland Island Shag** (breeding adult, Enderby Island)

BOUNTY or BOUNTY ISLAND SHAG

Phalacrocorax ranfurlyi L 71 cm (28 in), WS ?
Large, black and white shag confined to Bounty Islands. Plumage much as Campbell Shag but larger, with more white on chin and throat and more pronounced white bar on upperwing. Classified as Vulnerable.

IDENTIFICATION The only shag at Bounty Islands. **Juvenile** Upperparts, including head, back and wings, dark brown with glossy blackish-green tips and brownish fringes; no white forewing patch. Chin, throat and underparts white, but dark brown thighs; some brown spots on foreneck, or brown extends across foreneck as a band. Bill pale brown; facial skin brown, gular grey; iris brown; legs and feet brownish-flesh. **Adult non-breeding** Much as adult breeding, but lacks crest. Upperparts and bare parts duller. **Adult breeding** Head and hindneck black with blue sheen; long recurved black crest on forehead. Chin, throat, foreneck and underparts white, but thighs blackish-blue. Scapulars, mantle and upperwing-coverts dark brown with green sheen and indistinct black borders; white forewing stripes present, but variable in extent; no white on scapulars, but some show small white dorsal patch. Back black with blue sheen; lower back, rump and uppertail-coverts blackish-blue. Tail black. Bill brown or pinkish, with darker culmen, paler tip; no caruncles at base of bill; gular orange-red; facial skin red to orange-purple; iris light brown; legs and feet pinkish. Most similar to Auckland Shag, which is smaller and has variable black foreneck.

DISTRIBUTION AND STATUS New Zealand. Restricted to Bounty Islands, where it breeds colonially on ledges and alcoves of coastal cliffs of rocky islands. Total population fewer than 1,000 pairs in 1978. BirdLife International (1994) gives fewer than 1,200 individuals in the 12 known colonies. Sedentary, but may have reached Antipodes. The Bounty Islands are nature reserves and are predator-free; however, competition for nest spaces with fur seals, penguins and albatrosses may limit breeding success.

ROCK SHAG

Phalacrocorax magellanicus L 66 cm (26 in), WS 92 cm (36 in)
Medium-sized South American shag with blackish head and upperparts, white underparts from lower breast, with black thighs, bright red facial skin, red iris and black bill.

IDENTIFICATION Immature Polymorphic and geographically variable. Head, neck, upper breast and upperparts blackish-brown with some greenish gloss; scattered and variable paler feather edges to back, mantle and scapulars. Tail blackish-brown. Underparts from breast to undertail variable from almost white, through increasingly darker streaking to completely dark. Rasmussen (1987) has shown that birds from Chile are predominantly white-bellied, or white-bellied with minimal dark

streaking, whereas those from the Falklands and Argentina are predominantly dark-breasted; between these two extremes, birds from Tierra del Fuego are more variable but none has pure white underparts. This polymorphism had previously been interpreted as two distinct sequential immature plumages. Some birds may have a white chin, independent of underparts colour. Iris brown, but variable; legs and feet blackish. From Neotropic Cormorant by smaller size, more slender jizz with thinner neck and smaller head, dark bill and facial skin, and lacks that species' hunched flight profile. **Adult non-breeding** Plumage much as adult breeding, but lacks forehead crest and white ear tuft. Some show scattered white filoplumes on throat and neck (as Bank Cormorant), creating a mottled appearance on foreneck: this feature generally found in the Argentine and Falkland populations, more rarely in Chile populations, and unknown from Tierra del Fuego populations. **Adult breeding** Head, upper breast and foreneck blackish with green or violet gloss; wispy greenish crest on nape and nuptial crest on forehead. Chin and tuft on side of head white, but some show more highly developed filoplumes on head, back, wing-coverts and thighs. Upper back, scapulars and wings dark greenish-black, primaries blacker; lower back, rump and tail blackish. Lower breast and belly white, usually sharply demarcated at pectoral from dark head; undertail-coverts and thighs blackish. Bill blackish; facial skin red, bordered with black; gular red; iris variable; legs and feet flesh-coloured.

DISTRIBUTION AND STATUS Breeds colonially on exposed sea cliffs in southern South America from about Valdivia, Chile, and Punta Tombo, Argentina, south to Tierra del Fuego; also a sedentary population on Falklands. General distribution reflects a preference for colder Atlantic Ocean water rather than the warmer Pacific Ocean side of South America. Dispersal northwards after breeding to Santiago, Chile, and the Valdez Peninsula, Argentina. Vagrants have reached Uruguay. Some of the Tierra del Fuego population moves to Patagonia for the winter.

RED-FACED CORMORANT or SHAG

Phalacrocorax urile L 84 cm (33 in), WS 116 cm (46 in)
Medium-sized, dark, north Pacific marine cormorant with, in summer, a double crest, red facial skin enclosing eyes and meeting above upper mandible, and white oval patch on flanks.

IDENTIFICATION Juvenile Plumage uniformly dark brown, slightly glossed purplish on upperparts; underparts slightly paler. Bill variable, greyish to yellowish; facial skin brownish, joining over bill; iris light brown; feet blackish. Similar to juvenile Pelagic Cormorant but larger, with bigger head, longer bill, thicker neck; and brighter facial skin extending above upper mandible. **Adult non-breeding** Much as adult breeding, with duller, less glossy

plumage; lacks double head crest, white thigh patch, and white filoplumes on sides of neck. Upperwings browner than in breeding plumage, and bare parts duller, with facial skin dull reddish. **Adult breeding** Head blackish with rich violet or greenish gloss; scattered white filoplumes on sides of neck; two crests, one on crown, the other on nape. Upperparts and underparts blackish with violet or greenish gloss; white oval thigh patch. Upperwing and tail blackish-brown without dark margins and lacking greenish or violet gloss, thus contrasting with iridescent body. Bill greyish-yellow (some blue at base); facial skin bright orange to red, encloses eye and extends above upper mandible; iris light brown.

DISTRIBUTION AND STATUS North Pacific. Breeds colonially on steep inaccessible slopes and offshore islands from Nemuro Peninsula, Hokkaido, Japan (very few) north and east in the Bering Sea to the Commander, Pribilof, Nunivak and Aleutian Islands, east to the Shumagins and Kodiak Island; also coastal Alaska from the tip of the Alaska Peninsula, north-east to Bristol Bay and Cape Nowenham, east along the southern coast to Prince William Sound. Population increasing, at least in Alaska. Generally winters in open water within breeding range; vagrant British Columbia.

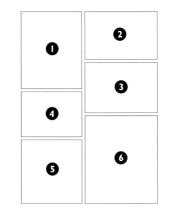

1 **Bounty Island Shag** (adult breeding, Bounty Island, November)
2 **Rock Shag** (adult on nest, Falkland Islands)
3 **Rock Shag** (adult breeding and juvenile, Kidney Is., Falkland Islands)
4 **Red-faced Cormorant** (adult breeding, St Paul Island, Alaska, June)
5 **Red-faced Cormorant** (sub-adult pair, Homer, Alaska, USA, August)
6 **Red-faced Cormorant** (adult breeding pair, Commander Islands, Bering Sea, June)

CORMORANTS & SHAGS

PELAGIC CORMORANT or SHAG

Phalacrocorax pelagicus L 68 cm (27 in), WS 96 cm (38 in)
Small, blackish, north Pacific cormorant with strong purplish and greenish gloss, reddish facial skin not joining across upper mandible, and, in summer, double crest and white oval patch on flank.
IDENTIFICATION Exclusively marine; usually, but not always, colonial, but less gregarious than other Pacific cormorants. Most of body submerged when swimming; flies with head and neck straight and with fast wingbeats. **Juvenile** Plumage generally uniformly dark brown: upperparts blackish with slight dull green gloss; wing-coverts and flight feathers blacker; underparts slightly paler, greyer and duller, but not showing distinct dark upperparts/light underparts contrast of young Brandt's or Double-crested Cormorant. Bill blackish; facial skin ashy-flesh, with pink gular; iris brownish; legs and feet blackish. From similar juvenile Red-faced Cormorant by smaller size, less extensive facial skin. **Adult non-breeding** Plumage black with variable greenish and violet gloss (less gloss than breeders); no crests and no white oval patch on flanks. Bill variable, from greyish to yellowish; facial skin and gular pouch dull brownish-orange. **Adult breeding** Head and neck black, with strong purple gloss on neck; small recurved blackish crest from forehead and a second blackish crest from nape; scattered white filoplumes on neck. Body rich blackish-green, with conspicuous white oval patch on flanks; wings and tail blackish-green. Bill brownish with orange-yellow base (unlike Red-faced Cormorant, no blue at all at base); iris variable green; facial skin red, enclosing eye, but not joining across upper mandible. Appears smaller, more delicate and smaller-headed than Double-crested and Brandt's Cormorants, and in flight has different profile (head and neck held straight) and faster wingbeats.
DISTRIBUTION AND STATUS North Pacific. Breeds on narrow inaccessible cliffs from northern Japan (Hokkaido and northern Honshu), Sea of Okhotsk, Siberia, Sakhalin, Kurils, Aleutians, Bering Sea, Alaska, British Columbia, and Pacific coastal states south to Baja California (Coronado Islands). Winters (especially northern populations from Alaska and Siberia) from northern limit of open water, south to southern Japan, China, Taiwan, Baja California (Cape San Lucas). Vagrant Hawaii. Less numerous than Double-crested Cormorant, with North American population estimated at *c* 130,000 birds, largest colonies Kuril Islands (50,000-60,000 birds).

EUROPEAN SHAG

Phalacrocorax aristotelis L 72 cm (28 in), WS 97 cm (38 in)
Small, dark, Palearctic cormorant, wholly black with strong and variable bronze-green gloss, and with a yellow-based darkish bill, bright green iris and, in summer, a dark recurved forehead crest.
IDENTIFICATION Juvenile Head dull brown, gradually shading to whitish on chin, throat and foreneck. Upperparts dull brown with faint greenish gloss, darker feather edges giving scaled effect. Underparts brown, with variable white on upper breast and belly (whitest in Mediterranean race). Wing-coverts dull brown with slight greenish gloss and edged buff; flight feathers dull blackish. Underwing and tail blackish-brown. Bill pinkish-yellow; facial skin yellowish-flesh; iris yellow-white; legs and feet brownish-black. **Immature** Much as non-breeding adult, but upperparts duller and browner. Chin pale buff; throat, foreneck and belly brown, speckled with white. Facial skin bright yellow (second-summer); iris yellow-green. **Adult non-breeding** Plumage much as adult breeding, but generally duller and browner, with less gloss. Lacks crest on forehead and white neck filoplumes; yellowish gape reduced. **Adult breeding** Plumage overall blackish, with strong greenish gloss on head and neck shading to bronze-green on rest of body; upper back, wing-coverts and scapulars glossed purplish-bronze, narrowly margined greenish-black; flight feathers greenish-black to black. Long, wispy, recurved dark crest on forehead. Bill greyish, with yellowish gape and base (mostly yellow in Mediterranean race); iris emerald-green; legs and feet blackish (brown with yellow webs in Mediterranean race). From Great Cormorant by exclusively marine habitat, smaller size, darker plumage (with no white on head, throat or thigh), wispy crest, thin yellow gape, finer bill, smaller head, thinner neck, and, in flight, quicker wingbeats; does not perch in trees.
DISTRIBUTION AND STATUS Breeds from Kola Peninsula (Russia) to Gibraltar, including Iceland, Faeroes, British Isles, Mediterranean, Black Sea, coast of Morocco. Some southward dispersal from northern areas by young birds. Estimated population of *c* 100,000 pairs; increasing in parts of range eg Britain (*c* 47,000 pairs), Norway and France. Much less common in Mediterranean (*c* 10,000 pairs). Accidental to Israel, Egypt, Iraq and central Europe.

RED-LEGGED CORMORANT

Phalacrocorax gaimardi L 76 cm (30 in), WS 91 cm (36 in)
Large, distinctive, silver-greyish South American cormorant having white patch on side of neck, whitish wing-coverts, red legs and red-based yellow bill. Classified as Near-threatened.
IDENTIFICATION Less gregarious than other South American cormorants; does not perch with wings spread. **Juvenile** Much as non-breeding adult, but with browner-grey upperparts. Underparts with thin whitish chin, greyish-brown breast, and white belly and lower underparts. Atlantic birds are very pale, whereas Pacific birds are more variable from pale to dark. Bill yellow with orange-red base; gular skin, legs and feet variable in colour.

Adult non-breeding Similar to adult breeding, but with upperparts slightly darker, and no white filoplumes on crown. Bare parts probably duller. **Adult breeding** Head dark silvery-grey, with conspicuous white patch on side of neck; crown has scattered white filoplumes. Upperparts dark silvery-grey, with silver-grey edges on mantle and back. Underparts grey, but paler than upperparts, whiter on lower breast and belly. Flight feathers dark greyish-black, with wing-coverts and scapulars silvery-grey: in flight, whitish-silver on upperwing-coverts forms a pale forewing patch contrasting with flight feathers. Bill orange-red at base, with yellowish-horn tip; iris pale green; legs and feet red. Distinguished from all other South American cormorants by grey plumage, red legs, and bright yellow to orange bill; white patch on side of neck is larger and further down on the neck than on Rock Shag.
DISTRIBUTION AND STATUS South America. Resident and breeds along Pacific coast from Macabi Islands, Peru, south to Chiloé Island, Chile; and along Atlantic coast from Puerto Deseado to Santa Cruz, Argentina. More common on Pacific coast with up to 10,000 breeding birds in Peru, less common and declining in Chile. Widespread, but nowhere abundant. No evidence of regular dispersal of either population, but has reached southern Ecuador and the Magellan Straits.

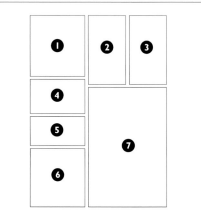

1 **Pelagic Cormorant** (adult at nest, Commander Island, June)
2 **Pelagic Cormorant** (adult non-breeding preening, California, USA)
3 **European Shag** (adult non-breeding, Great Saltee Island, Southern Ireland)
4 **European Shag** (first winter, Bangor, Northern Ireland, January)
5 **European Shag** (adult breeding, Morocco, April)
6 **European Shag** (adult breeding, Craigleith, Scotland, June)
7 **Red-legged Cormorant** (adults in breeding colony)

CORMORANTS, SHAGS & FRIGATEBIRDS

SPOTTED SHAG

Phalacrocorax punctatus L 69 cm (27 in), WS 95 cm (37 in)

Medium-sized, colourful and distinctive shag of New Zealand, occurring in two forms, both of which have greenish-black head and neck with a white dividing stripe, and black-spotted greenish-grey upperparts.

IDENTIFICATION Slender jizz; spreads wings to dry them; jumps clear of water when diving. Gregarious, can form large feeding flocks. **Juvenile** Head greyish-brown, becoming paler on chin and throat. Upperparts greyish-brown with a few small white filoplumes and black tips, giving spotted appearance. Tail brown. Chin, throat and breast dull fawn to pale grey; belly and flanks brownish, thighs and undertail-coverts blackish-brown. Upperwing-coverts greyish-brown with black tips, giving spotted appearance; flight feathers dark brownish. Underwing brown. Bill, facial skin, legs and feet brownish-yellow; iris brown. **Adult non-breeding** Similar to adult breeding, but lacks double crest and white filoplumes on head, neck, back and rump; lacks white stripe on side of head. Black of top of head and chin to foreneck becomes light brownish-grey. Bill brownish-yellow; facial skin and gular medium blue (gular sea-green in *oliveri*); legs and feet pale yellowish. **Adult breeding** Top of head to hindneck black with greenish-blue gloss, and with double crest (forehead and nape); scattered white filoplumes on hindneck; whitish stripe from base of upper mandible, above eye and down sides of neck to shoulder (narrower in *oliveri*). Chin, throat and foreneck black with greenish gloss. Upperparts greyish-green with black tips, giving spotted appearance to mantle, back, scapulars and wing-coverts; lower back, rump and uppertail-coverts black with greenish-blue gloss. Flight feathers darker and browner than upperparts and wing-coverts. Underparts whitish-grey from foreneck, shading to blackish with green-blue gloss on flanks, lower belly, thighs and undertail-coverts. Bill yellowish-brown; iris hazel; orbital ring and facial skin blue-green; legs and feet bright orange-yellow.

DISTRIBUTION AND STATUS New Zealand. Breeds colonially on cliff ledges, alcoves, etc along headlands and rocky shores of North Island, South Island and Stewart Island. *P. p. punctatus*: North Island and east coast of South Island (population c 50,000-100,000 birds). *P. p. oliveri*: West coast of South Island, Foveaux Strait islands and Stewart Island (population c 10,000-50,000 birds); some winter dispersal, has reached northern New Zealand. Threat of human interference at breeding colonies, mainly from persecution and shooting, also from recreational boating and fishing.

PITT ISLAND or PITT SHAG

Phalacrocorax featherstoni L 63 cm (25 in), WS ? Colourful marine cormorant confined to Chathams; much as Spotted Shag (formerly treated as a subspecies), but smaller and darker. Classified as Vulnerable.

IDENTIFICATION Juvenile Crown to hindneck dark blackish-brown with greenish gloss; filoplumes, but no crests. Foreneck and upperparts blackish-brown with greenish gloss. Breast and upper abdomen paler brown; thighs and undertail-coverts blackish-brown. Wing-coverts dark brown with greenish gloss and darker blackish-green tips; flight feathers blackish-green to dark brown. Bill grey-brown with darker culmen; facial skin and gular greyish-yellow; iris greyish-brown; legs and feet yellow. **Adult non-breeding** As adult breeding, but crests smaller or absent; lacks white filoplumes on hindneck. Gular green. **Adult breeding** Head, hindneck and upper foreneck bluish-black, with black crests on forehead and on nape; white filoplumes mainly on hindneck, also a few on head and neck. Mantle, scapulars and upperwing-coverts dark olive-brown, glossed green, with black terminal spots. Flight feathers darker, blackish. Back, rump and uppertail-coverts glossy bluish-black; tail black. Lower foreneck, breast and belly medium grey; flanks, undertail-coverts and underwing bluish-black. Bill black with light brown tip, and cream bar at base of lower mandible; facial skin and orbital ring green; iris red-brown; legs and feet orange.

DISTRIBUTION AND STATUS New Zealand. Breeds colonially on rocky coasts and cliff ledges on Chathams (Chatham, Pitt, Mangere, Little Mangere, Star Keys, Pyramid Rock and Rabbit Island). Population estimated at under 1,000 birds. Sedentary; no records outside Chathams. Few data on population trends or threats.

MAGNIFICENT FRIGATEBIRD

Fregata magnificens L 101 cm (40 in), WS 238 cm (94 in)

Largest, longest-billed, and least pelagic frigatebird, found in tropical Pacific and tropical Atlantic Oceans, with variable white on head and underparts dependent on age and sex.

IDENTIFICATION Juvenile Head white. Mantle and back dark blackish-brown; upperwing similar, with paler bar on inner wing. Tail blackish. White of head continues to white lower belly patch, latter nearly isolated by incomplete dark breastband (dark spurs); flanks, vent and undertail blackish-brown. Underwing blackish-brown. **Immature** Dark wedge-shaped spurs on sides of breast whiten, giving fuller white underparts; then head becomes duskier (especially on nape), this extending across throat as narrow collar. Brown spotting on breast may form partial breastband. Flanks and vent black. Axillaries narrowly edged white, forming indistinct spur on underwing. **Sub-adult male** Head and underparts become more uniformly dark, glossier on upperparts, with upperwing bar less pronounced. Narrow white horseshoe mark on breast extends onto axillaries (reverse shape to that on sub-adult Great Frigatebird). **Sub-**

adult female Head becomes blackish-brown; underparts dusky white, divided by blackish band across lower breast; blackish spotting on white underparts. Whitish axillaries. **Adult male** Red gular pouch. Wholly black plumage glossed purple and green, usually without pale inner wing bar. Probably indistinguishable from Ascension Frigatebird. **Adult female** Head, including chin and throat, blackish, ending in a 'V' at upper breast; nape and hindneck greyer, forming collar. Mantle and back blackish-brown, glossed purple-green. Underparts white on upper breast, extending upwards onto flanks and axillaries as wavy lines; lower breast to tail blackish. Upperwing dark brownish, with pale bar on inner wing.

DISTRIBUTION AND STATUS Tropical Pacific and tropical Atlantic Oceans with a total population of several hundred thousand birds. Breeds colonially in mangroves or occasionally on the ground, from Baja California to Ecuador (with c 60,000 pairs western Mexico), including Galapagos, and from Florida through Caribbean (c 8,000 pairs: slow decline) to southern Brazil where common; very few also breed on Cape Verdes. Generally sedentary, but some dispersal of juveniles and non-breeders, occasionally displaced by hurricanes. Vagrants Canada (Newfoundland and British Columbia), Europe, Oregon, Gulf of Alaska, south to Argentina. Threats are human disturbance, direct persecution and habitat destruction.

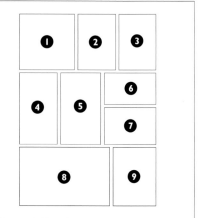

1 **Spotted Shag** (adult breeding, New Zealand, April)
2 **Spotted Shag** (adult breeding, New Zealand)
3 **Spotted Shag** (adult non-breeding, New Zealand)
4 **Pitt Island Shag** (adult breeding)
5 **Pitt Island Shag** (juvenile, Chatham Islands)
6 **Magnificent Frigatebird** (immature, Galapagos Islands)
7 **Magnificent Frigatebird** (male, adult breeding with gular pouch inflated, Galapagos Islands)
8 **Magnificent Frigatebird** (immature and juvenile, Galapagos Islands, November)
9 **Magnificent Frigatebird** (adult male, Florida, USA)

FRIGATEBIRDS

ASCENSION FRIGATEBIRD

Fregata aquila L 91 cm (36 in), WS 198 cm (78 in)

Large frigatebird, confined to Ascension. Classified as Critical.

IDENTIFICATION Juvenile Head white. Mantle and back blackish-brown. Underparts white, continuing from head; lower flanks and vent black. Upperwing blackish-brown, with paler bar on inner wing. Underwing blackish, with small whitish patches on coverts and white axillary spur. Gradually develops dark brownish band across upper breast, separating whitish head from whitish belly. **Immature** Definitive transitional plumages from juvenile to adult unclear: some breeding males and females with white breasts may either represent paler morphs or be a stage of progressively darkening adult plumage. Head darkens to blackish on males, browner on females, with paler nape and hindneck. Upperparts and wings become blacker, glossed green; variable whitish lower breast which may be streaked black (male?), with upper breast, flanks and vent blackish. Underwings blackish, with white axillary spurs. **Adult male** Red gular pouch. Plumage black, strongly glossed greenish on head, upperparts and upperwing-coverts; paler bar on inner upperwing. Underwing blackish. Probably indistinguishable from Magnificent. **Adult female** The only all-dark female frigatebird. Plumage blackish, with lighter brown on nape and hindneck which continues across upper breast to form indistinct breastband; pale bar on inner upperwing. No white on underparts.

DISTRIBUTION AND STATUS Tropical Atlantic. Now breeds biennially only at Boatswainbird Islet off Ascension Island on the ground in loose colonies where 2,500 birds and 1,000 nests counted (1988). Feeds on fish, baby green turtles, and Sooty Tern chicks. Formerly bred on Ascension in 'huge' numbers until the arrival of cats; declined to 8,000-10,000 breeding adults in 1950s (Stonehouse and Stonehouse 1963); 5,000 birds in 1976. Risk of disturbance has increased since the Falklands conflict of 1982. Rarely strays more than 150 km from Ascension. Vagrant West Africa.

GREAT FRIGATEBIRD

Fregata minor L 93 cm (37 in), WS 218 cm (86 in)

Large frigatebird found in the tropics of all three oceans.

IDENTIFICATION Gregarious; follows ships. In flight, broader wings and shorter tail than Magnificent. **Juvenile** Head, throat and upper neck rusty-brown (white in some populations, eg Galapagos). Partial or complete brownish breastband enclosing white belly patch; flanks, vent, axillaries and underwing black; upperwings blackish-brown, with whitish-brown bar across coverts. Breastband fades to produce white-breasted and tawny-breasted forms, the latter more numerous. (Similar-stage Magnificent has white head and upper breast; white birds not distinguishable until white spurs appear on axillaries of Magnificent.) Bill pale grey; eye-ring brown; legs brownish-grey. **Immature to sub-adult male** Initially as juvenile, before breastband disappears, followed by darkening of head, chin, throat. Inverted whitish horseshoe on lower breast and flanks becomes mottled black, then fully black. Black axillaries separate it from male Magnificent and Lesser. **Immature to sub-adult female** Breastband disappears; cap and mottled white belly patch gradually turn black. **Adult male** Red gular pouch. Black plumage with metallic-green and purple gloss. Upperwing glossy black, sandy-brown bar across inner coverts. Bill greyish; iris dark brown, eye-ring blackish-brown; legs pink. **Adult female** Forehead, crown, nape and hindneck black, forming dark cap demarcated from grey on chin and throat. Upperparts blackish. Upperwing blackish-brown, with sandy-brown bar across inner coverts. Grey of chin and throat merges into white of upper breast, flanks and upper belly; black abdomen, vent and tail. Underwing wholly black, axillaries black. Bill greyish-blue; eye-ring pink; iris, legs and feet as male.

DISTRIBUTION AND STATUS Pan-tropic in waters above 22°C. Breeds colonially in mangroves or bushes, occasionally on the ground and on small islands. Total population estimate 500,000-1 million birds. In the Atlantic, breeds only at Trinidade and Martin Vaz; in the Indian several thousand pairs; most in the Pacific (eg 64,000 birds breed Hawaii, and large numbers on the Galapagos, Line and Phoenix islands). Some dispersal of juveniles and non-breeders. Vagrants north-east USA, South Africa, New Zealand, Philippines, Japan, Siberia. Threats from direct persecution, disturbance, and habitat destruction. As with Lesser Frigatebird, *El Niño* may cause partial or total breeding failure of some Pacific populations.

LESSER FRIGATEBIRD

Fregata ariel L 76 cm (30 in), WS 184 cm (72 in) Smallest frigatebird, found in the tropics of all three oceans. Size difference apparent only when seen with other frigatebirds.

IDENTIFICATION Gregarious; follows ships. **Juvenile** Head, throat and upper neck reddish-brown. Mantle, back and wings blackish-brown, with paler bar on inner upperwing (paler than on adult females). Reddish of head separated from white underparts by blackish breastband, usually complete and thinnest at centre of breast; belly to legs white, extending as white spurs onto axillaries; vent and undertail blackish. **Immature male** Loses blackish breastband, followed by darkening of chin and throat. Central abdomen and mid breast turn darker, becoming mottled black and white, and then acquire black of adult male, with thin white spurs eventually separated from central breast. **Immature female** Loses blackish breastband, followed by darkening of head, chin, throat and abdomen until adult plumage acquired. White spurs on axillaries. **Adult male** Red gular pouch. Head, mantle and back black with metallic-green and purple gloss. Upperwings glossy black, with slightly browner greater coverts forming indistinct bar across inner wing. Underparts black, with narrow white stripe on each side of abdomen extending from flanks onto axillaries as white spur. Bill greyish-black; iris brown, orbital ring black; legs and feet reddish-brown to black. **Adult female** No pouch. Head, throat and foreneck black, forming dark hood separated from mostly black mantle and back by white nuchal collar. Upperwings blackish, with pale buffish bar across inner wing. Dark hood extends in a 'V' shape to middle of upper breast, contrasting sharply with white breast and flanks which continue onto axillaries to form white spurs. Underwing, lower abdomen, vent and undertail black. Bill variable, pinkish to greyish; iris brown, orbital ring variable; legs and feet pink to red.

DISTRIBUTION AND STATUS Pantropic in waters above 22°C. Breeds colonially in mangroves, bushes, and on the ground on small islands. Total population estimate several hundred thousand birds. In the Atlantic only at Trinidade and Martin Vaz; widespread in the Indian and west and central Pacific. Dispersal of juveniles and non-breeders within the tropics – vagrants north-east USA, South Africa, New Zealand, Japan, Siberia and Hawaii.

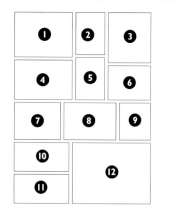

1 **Ascension Frigatebird** (adult female on nest, Ascension Island)
2 **Ascension Frigatebird** (juvenile, Ascension Island)
3 **Great Frigatebird** (juvenile, Galapagos Islands)
4 **Great Frigatebird** (adult male on nest, red gular pouch inflated, Galapagos Islands)
5 **Great Frigatebird** (juvenile, Galapagos Islands)
6 **Great Frigatebird** (juvenile, Galapagos Islands)
7 **Great Frigatebird** (adult female on nest, Galapagos Islands)
8 **Great Frigatebird** (adult male, Galapagos Islands)
9 **Lesser Frigatebird** (adult female, Lady Elliott Island, Coral Sea, March)
10 **Lesser Frigatebird** (juvenile, Lady Elliott Island, Coral Sea, March)
11 **Lesser Frigatebird** (male, Lady Elliott Island, Coral Sea, March)
12 **Lesser Frigatebird** (male, Lady Elliott Island, Coral Sea, March)

FRIGATEBIRDS & SKUAS

CHRISTMAS ISLAND FRIGATEBIRD

Fregata andrewsi L 94 cm (37 in), WS 218 cm (86 in)

Large frigatebird breeding only at Christmas Island in tropical Indian Ocean. Classified as Vulnerable.

IDENTIFICATION Gregarious; follows ships. **Juvenile** Head pale fawn, paler on nape, darker on crown and throat. Upperparts dark blackish-brown. Upperwing brownish, with whitish bar on inner wing. Whitish upper breast separated from white lower underparts by broad black breastband extending from breast sides, band narrowest on mid breast and often incomplete; lower breast down to legs white, with white spurs on axillaries; flanks, vent and undertail blackish. Underwing blackish-brown. **Immature** Head fawn to tawny-yellow, darkest on throat. By second year, head and throat become white. Some birds appear to retain blackish breastband (males?), while others lose central part of breastband. By third year, black on head and other areas appears, depending on sex. Sub-adult male has lower breast scaled black and white, before turning black. **Adult male** Red gular pouch. Upperparts entirely black, with glossy green and purple sheen on head, mantle and back. Upperwing black, with paler brown lesser coverts giving pale diagonal bar across inner wing to carpal. Underparts black, except for single white patch on lower abdomen and vent; no white spurs. Underwing all black. Bill and legs blackish; iris brown, orbital ring blackish. **Adult female** No pouch. Head, including throat and foreneck to upper breast, blackish, forming black hood, with nape and hindneck narrowly white and forming whitish nuchal collar. Upperparts blackish-brown, with metallic-green sheen on back. Upperwing blackish, with broad whitish bar across wing-coverts to carpal (paler than on male). Underparts mainly white from foreneck down, except for blackish sides of breast extending as short dark spurs on upper breast (white also extends as white spurs onto underwing); flanks, vent and undertail-coverts black. Tail black. Bill pinkish; iris brown, orbital ring pink; legs pinkish.

DISTRIBUTION AND STATUS Tropical Indian Ocean, preferring warmer water than other frigatebirds. Breeds biennially in loose colonies in trees in lee of prevailing south-east trade winds, only at Christmas Island (approximately 1,600 pairs). Poachers and local mining activities have contributed to decline over the years, but species is now protected. Potential recovery, however, will inevitably be slow, as it takes 18 months to rear a single chick. Pelagic range not well known, although dispersal of juveniles and non-breeders to Indonesia, Timor Sea, Borneo and south-west Thailand. Vagrants Kenya, and possibly India, northern Australia, Hong Kong, China and the Solomon Islands.

GREAT SKUA

Catharacta skua L 58 cm (23 in), WS 150 cm (59 in)

Largest and strongest skua of the north Atlantic. Broad wings, heavy body and short tail impart heavy, gull-like jizz.

IDENTIFICATION Flight strong and direct, with full downstroke; not unduly affected by strong winds, when wings become angled back; often flies quite high above surface. Readily attracted to ships and trawlers, and will attack gannets. **Immature** Much as adult, but generally duller and more uniform. Blackish cap less distinct; hindneck and throat lack golden shaft streaks of adult. Upperparts and coverts more uniform brown, paler feather edges lacking golden tone of adult; white primary flash sometimes less conspicuous. Underparts may be more tawny-brown, and with increasing age may become paler through wear and bleaching. From South Polar Skua by absence of pale nuchal collar, by warm tone to underparts (unlike the colder greyish tone of South Polar, which contrasts with dark underwings), by absence of pale area around longer bill, and by larger head and generally bulkier jizz. **Adult** Head with variable blackish cap from gape to crown, when present visible at long distance; nape, hindneck, sides of neck and throat brownish with variable golden and rufous shaft streaks. Mantle, scapulars and wing-coverts variable brown, with golden and rufous fringes imparting speckled appearance, especially on older birds, which contrasts with more uniform blackish-brown flight feathers. Tail blackish-brown, short and slightly wedge-shaped. Underparts more uniform warm brown than upperparts, with variable cinnamon or buffish markings. On upperwing, primaries show whitish bases decreasing inwards and forming conspicuous white wing flash visible at considerable distance. Underwing mainly dark brown, not contrasting with underparts, but showing even more conspicuous wing flash than on upper surface. Bill blackish-grey, sometimes paler grey with dark tip; iris brown; legs and feet blackish.

DISTRIBUTION AND STATUS North Atlantic. Breeds loosely colonially Iceland (5,400 pairs), Scotland (7,900 pairs), with fewer Spitsbergen, Finnmark, Bear Island, Faeroes, Orkney. Total population 13,600 pairs, increasing since 1900 and range expansion in north of range. Disperses south to Mediterranean, north-west Africa, east coast of USA (probably Icelandic birds). Recorded from northern South America.

ANTARCTIC or SOUTHERN SKUA

Catharacta antarctica L 63 cm (25 in), WS ?
Now split from more widespread Brown Skua as separate species consisting of two subspecies, *antarctica* and *hamiltoni*.

IDENTIFICATION **Juvenile** Much as Great Skua, but generally darker and more variable, from dark brown to reddish-brown. Mantle, back, scapulars and wing-coverts brownish with buffish streaking and edging. Tail blackish-brown. Underparts variable brown. Wings blackish-brown, with whitish flash at base of primaries as adult. Young *hamiltoni* has mantle and back more heavily streaked, and paler and more rufous-brown underparts. **Adult** Head brownish, usually with ill-defined darker cap from gape to crown. Nape, hindneck and sides of neck show variable yellow streaking, which may extend onto upper breast. Mantle, back and scapulars dark brown with variable paler buffish streaking. Tail blackish-brown. Underparts lighter, greyer and more uniform than upperparts. Primaries and secondaries blackish-brown, with whitish wing flash at base of primaries. Underwing dark brown, with primary flash more conspicuous than on upperwing; some birds may show rufous on underwing-coverts. Adult *hamiltoni* shows more prominent paler edges to mantle and back, producing paler saddle that contrasts more with upperwings. Bill, legs and feet blackish-grey; iris pale brown. From South Polar Skua by larger size, absence of pale nuchal collar, lack of contrast between underparts and underwing, and general warm tone to plumage.

DISTRIBUTION AND STATUS *C. a. antarctica* breeds coastal southern Argentina from Chubut to Tierra del Fuego, and on Falklands with a total population of 3,000-5,000 pairs; hybridizes with Chilean Skua. *C. a. hamiltoni* breeds Gough Island (2,500 pairs) and Tristan da Cunha group (c 200 pairs); may prove to be a separate species. Dispersal at sea southwards towards Antarctica, and northwards to Brazil, South Africa and New Zealand.

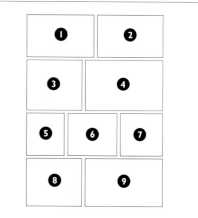

1 **Christmas Frigatebird** (breeding adult male, Christmas Island, Indian Ocean, May)
2 **Christmas Frigatebird** (juvenile, Christmas Island, Indian Ocean, November)
3 **Christmas Frigatebird** (adult female, Christmas Island, Indian Ocean)
4 **Great Skua** (adult displaying, Shetland Islands, Scotland, June)
5 **Great Skua** (adult, Shetland Islands, Scotland)
6 **Great Skua** (adult, Shetland Islands, Scotland)
7 **Antarctic Skua** (New Island, Falkland Islands)
8 **Antarctic Skua subspecies C. a. hamiltoni** (Gough Island)
9 **Antarctic Skua** (adult displaying, New Island, Falkland Islands)

SKUAS

BROWN SKUA

Catharacta lonnbergi L 63 cm (25 in), WS ?
Large, dark brown skua, breeding on many
Southern Ocean islands and the Antarctic
Peninsula. Previously included as a subspecies
of the more restricted Antarctic Skua.
IDENTIFICATION Juvenile Dark brown and
much as adult, but upperparts warmer brown,
more uniform, with fewer lighter spots and
streaks. Underparts brownish, with variable
chestnut-brown flecking (including on sides of
neck). Tail blackish-brown. Wings blackish-
brown, with whitish flash at base of primaries
(often reduced on younger birds). Bill blackish,
weaker than that of adult; legs and feet blackish
with some grey mottling. **Adult** Head uniform
blackish-brown, lacking dark-capped
appearance. Nape and hindneck paler, often
with whitish-golden streaking. Upperparts
blackish-brown with occasional whitish-golden
streaking; some birds may show rufous-brown
on mantle. Underparts brown with variable
yellowish or golden streaking; some
populations (eg Kerguelen) are more distinctly
reddish-chestnut; with wear (by February),
back and breast become lighter. (Brown of
upperparts and underparts noticeably warmer
in tone than that of smaller South Polar Skua.)
Wings blackish-brown, with whitish flash at
base of primaries. Bill, legs and feet blackish-
grey; iris pale brown.
DISTRIBUTION AND STATUS Circumpolar in
Southern Hemisphere. Breeds Antarctic
Continent to at least 65°S, also South Georgia
(1,000 pairs), South Sandwich, South Orkneys,
South Shetlands (420 pairs), Bouvet, Prince
Edwards (460 pairs), Crozets (400-1,000 pairs),
Kerguelen (1,000-2,000 pairs), Heard,
Macquarie (550 pairs), south coast of South
Island (New Zealand) and Stewart Island; also
New Zealand subantarctic islands (Campbell,
Auckland, Snares, Antipodes, Bounty and
Chathams). Total population *c* 7,000 pairs.
Dispersal not well known, but northwards
towards the tropics in all three oceans. In the
Atlantic has reached Guadeloupe (Leeward
Islands).

CHILEAN SKUA

Catharacta chilensis L 58 cm (23 in), WS ?
Large, dark skua of southern South America,
with cinnamon underparts and underwing-
coverts, dark grey cap, and blackish-brown
upperparts with white wing flashes on both
surfaces of wings.
IDENTIFICATION Juvenile Similar to adult, but
dark cap less pronounced and greyer. Mantle
and scapulars blackish-brown, with variable
cinnamon barring extending to rump. Tail
blackish-brown with short, blunt central
projections. Underparts from chin and sides of
neck brighter cinnamon than adult. Upperwing
blackish-brown, with white bases to primaries.
Underwing-coverts tawny-cinnamon; flight
feathers darker, with white primary flash.
Adult Brownish-grey cap from gape to crown,
merging into cinnamon of chin and underparts;
ear-coverts greyer. Nape and sides of neck
lightly streaked whitish, this extending to upper
breast. Scapulars, mantle and back blackish-
brown with indistinct rufous-brown streaking.
Tail blackish-brown. Underparts uniform
cinnamon, becoming paler with age, some
showing darker breast. Upperwing as juvenile.
Underwing-coverts cinnamon, contrasting with
blackish-brown flight feathers, primaries of
which have conspicuous white bases. Bill short,
pale blue with dark tip (unlike other *Catharacta*
skuas); iris brown; legs and feet blackish. Note:
will hybridize with Antarctic Skua in southern
Argentina: hybrids appear viable.
DISTRIBUTION AND STATUS South America.
Unlike other skuas breeds colonially, and
generally is non-aggressive to human intruders
within breeding territory. Breeds on remote
coasts and islands of southern Chile from about
Aruco to Cape Horn, Tierra del Fuego, and
southern Argentina. Total population unknown,
but probably several thousand pairs. Dispersal,
mainly of juveniles, northwards along both
coasts of South America, certainly to Peru and
probably to the tropics.

SOUTH POLAR SKUA

Catharacta maccormicki L 53 cm (21 in), WS
127 cm (50 in)
The smallest *Catharacta* skua, breeding on
Antarctic Continent and Antarctic Peninsula.
Most forms differ from other southern
Catharacta skuas in smaller size, comparatively
smaller head and bill, a pale nuchal collar
contrasting with uniform upperparts, and a
dark underwing contrasting with (generally)
paler underparts.
IDENTIFICATION Polymorphic. **Juvenile**
Variable from light to dark. Light birds similar
to pale adults, but with head variable grey, with
paler chin and throat; hindneck pale greyish-
buff, forming pale nuchal collar; mantle,
scapulars and wing-coverts greyer, with
variable paler feather edges; underparts
generally greyer than adult. Some show less
prominent white wing flashes. Darker birds
similar to dark adults, often showing blacker
head giving hooded appearance. Bill bluish with
dark tip; iris dark brown; legs and feet bluish.
Adult Polymorphic, from light to dark, with
intermediates. *Light*: Head variable greyish,
bordered on sides of neck and upper nape by
variable buffish or golden suffusion. Hindneck
pale greyish, forming uniform nuchal collar.
Upperparts uniform blackish-brown, some
showing scattered paler fringes. Tail blackish.
Underparts pale greyish; undertail blackish.
Wings fairly uniform blackish-brown on both
surfaces, with conspicuous white flash at base
of primaries on upperwing and underwing;
underwing thus contrasts with paler
underparts. *Intermediate*: Much as pale birds,
but with head, hindneck and underparts buffish-
brown. Uniform pale nuchal collar retained.
Dark: Head dark brown with paler nape and
sides of neck, enhancing hooded effect, with
indistinct paler nuchal collar; some may show
pale at base of bill. Upperparts and wings
uniform blackish-brown with a few paler
fringes. Whitish primary flash. Tail blackish.
Underparts brownish, generally paler than
upperparts. Bill and legs blackish-grey.
DISTRIBUTION AND STATUS Breeds on snow-
free sea coasts and mountains of the Antarctic
Continent, Antarctic Peninsula and the South
Shetland Islands. Total population 5,000-8,000
pairs with most (2,000-6,000 pairs) in the Ross
Sea. Northward dispersal, especially of
juveniles, in all three oceans, reaching Alaska,
Greenland, northern Indian Ocean. Dark birds
predominate on northern part of Antarctic
Peninsula, pale birds elsewhere on the
Continent. At South Shetlands South Polar and
Brown Skuas overlap, and *c* 10% of pairs are
mixed or hybrids.

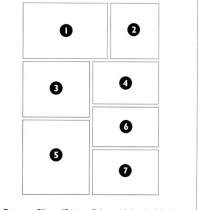

1 **Brown Skua** (Prince Edward Islands, May)
2 **Brown Skua** (Prince Edward Islands, May)
3 **Chilean Skua**
4 **Chilean Skua** (Chile, February)
5 **South Polar Skua**
6 **South Polar Skua** (Antarctica)
7 **South Polar Skua** (Cooverville Island,
Antarctica)

SKUAS

POMARINE SKUA or JAEGER

Stercorarius pomarinus L 56 cm (22 in), WS 124 cm (49 in)

Large and heavy polymorphic *Stercorarius* skua, almost circumpolar in the Northern Hemisphere. Larger size, heavy chest, broad wings and slower, more purposeful flight help distinguish from Arctic Skua.

IDENTIFICATION Will investigate ships and trawlers. **Juvenile** Less variable than Arctic or Long-tailed Skua: *c* 90% are dark to medium, with fewer paler-headed and very dark individuals. Head uniform dark greyish-brown, with darker area near base of bill (generally lacks Arctic's paler hindneck). Upperparts dark brown, with narrow pale sandy to rusty-brown fringes on wing-coverts; uppertail-coverts barred, often forming paler patch contrasting with dark upperparts. Upperwing dark, much as mantle, with pale shafts to outermost three to eight primaries. Underparts brown to greyish-brown with darker barring; some may show darker barred breastband with paler belly; undertail-coverts barred on all but darkest birds (generally more distinct than on Arctic). Underwing barred on axillaries and underwing-coverts; bases of greater primary coverts pale, contrasting with dark tips, and together with pale primary bases form conspicuous pale double patch visible at up to 500 m (more conspicuous than that found on pale and intermediate Arctics Skuas, though less noticeable on dark Pomarines). **Immature** Generally similar to non-breeding adult with some juvenile features (eg barred axillaries and underwing-coverts), but highly variable. **Adult non-breeding** As breeding adult, but tail projections shorter (often lacking completely during moult); pale and intermediate birds barred on both uppertail- and undertail-coverts, with some pale edges on upperparts, and neck and breast region usually dirtier and appearing obscurely barred (dark cap less clear-cut). **Adult breeding** Polymorphic: majority are pale birds, 5-10% are dark, and a few intermediates occur. *Pale*: Blackish cap extends to base of lower mandible and further down ear-coverts than on Arctic or Long-tailed. Hindneck and chin deeper and warmer yellow than on Arctic or Long-tailed, shading to white on throat. Mantle and back blackish-brown, this extending to rump and uppertail-coverts. Tail blackish, with twisted long central feathers (up to 11 cm) which are often broken. Underparts whitish, with variable dark spotted breastband and barred flanks (though both may be absent); undertail-coverts dark. Upperwing blackish-brown, with whitish shafts on outer three to eight primaries; underwing dark, with basal half of primaries pale (as Arctic, but not Long-tailed). *Dark*: Generally uniform dark brown, with indistinct yellowish-brown cheeks. Whitish flashes on primaries on both upperwing and underwing. *Intermediate*: May show traces of a breastband. Characteristic heavy jizz and steady flight separate this species from Arctic Skua; large hooked bill has dark tip

and browner base, while bill of both Arctic and Long-tailed appears more uniform.

DISTRIBUTION AND STATUS Almost circumpolar north of Arctic Circle breeding in the tundra of northern Canada, northern Russia and northern Alaska. Breeding depends on lemming abundance. Total population estimated at several tens of thousands of pairs, probably stable, but data scarce; some loss of eggs and chicks to Arctic foxes and Snowy Owls. Dispersal south to pelagic habitat in all three oceans where immature birds summer. Returning birds in May migrate in flocks, as do Long-tailed Skuas.

ARCTIC SKUA or PARASITIC JAEGER

Stercorarius parasiticus L 45 cm (18 in), WS 117 cm (46 in)

Medium-sized polymorphic *Stercorarius* skua, circumpolar in the Arctic. Intermediate between Long-tailed and Pomarine Skuas, less dependent on rodent populations, and breeds further south.

IDENTIFICATION Juvenile Variable from pale to dark; dark juveniles may become pale-morph adults. Pale birds have brownish-grey cap contrasting with greyer head and paler hindneck, which may be tinged rusty or even orange. Upperparts dark brown, with broad and paler whitish, orange or rusty fringes to coverts, often with pale leading edge to wings; barred uppertail-coverts generally more wavy-patterned than on Pomarine (less noticeable on darker birds). Primaries blackish, pale shafts on generally outer three to eight; pale tips to primaries (more noticeable than on Pomarine Skua). Underparts variable, brown to greyish-brown or rusty-brown with darker barring; barred darker breastband with paler belly often present; barred undertail-coverts (more wavy and less distinct than on Pomarine Skua). Underwing with barring on axillaries and underwing-coverts warmer brown than on Pomarine Skua and contrasting less with body colour (some intermediates and dark birds appear darker). Pale and intermediate morphs may show pale double patch on underwing, but less conspicuous than on Pomarine Skua. **Immature** Extremely variable: generally resembles non-breeding adult but with some juvenile features (eg barred axillaries and underwing-coverts). Second-winter dark-morph birds similar to adult. **Adult non-breeding** Similar to breeding adult, but with shorter tail projections (often lost completely during moult); pale and intermediate birds barred on uppertail- and usually also undertail-coverts, with some pale edges on upperparts, and obscure barring around neck and breast area (dark cap less clear-cut). **Adult breeding** Polymorphic. Dark morph predominates in southern populations, but pale more common further north; a few intermediates. *Pale*: Dark blackish-brown cap to base of cutting edge of bill; chin and hindneck pale yellowish (less deep than on Pomarine Skua), with pale patch at base of upper mandible (not present on

Pomarine or Long-tailed Skua). Upperparts dark greyish-brown. Tail blackish, with central feathers pointed and extending 8-14 cm. Underparts usually completely whitish, with dark undertail-coverts; some may show variable unspotted breastband; flanks never barred as on Pomarine Skua. Upperwing uniform dark brownish; shafts of outer primaries three to eight whitish. *Dark*: Generally uniform dark greyish-brown plumage, with darker cap, yellowish-brown cheeks and hindneck, and whitish wing flashes. *Intermediate*: Variable between pale and dark, usually with a breastband (not found on Long-tailed Skua). Bill greyish-black; legs blackish-grey. Arctic Skua differs from Pomarine in being smaller-headed, with more slender body and narrower wings; flight less laboured.

DISTRIBUTION AND STATUS Circumpolar in the Arctic from 57°N to 80°N. Breeds further south than Pomarine or Long-tailed Skua (eg Aleutians and Scotland). The most numerous skua with a total population of probably several hundreds of thousands of pairs, most in Canada, Russia and Alaska. Smaller and therefore less able than Pomarine Skua to fight off Arctic foxes and Snowy Owls. Disperses south in winter to pelagic habitat off South America, South Africa and Australasia.

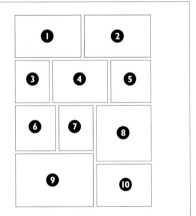

1 **Pomarine Skua** (breeding adult, pale morph, Siberia, June)
2 **Pomarine Skua** (adult non-breeding, pale morph, Netherlands)
3 **Pomarine Skua** (adult breeding, pale morph, Siberia, June)
4 **Pomarine Skua** (juvenile, Lancashire, England)
5 **Pomarine Skua** (immature, Australia, December)
6 **Arctic Skua** (breeding adult, dark morph, Shetland Islands, Scotland, June)
7 **Arctic Skua** (breeding adult, pale morph, Shetland Islands, Scotland, June)
8 **Arctic Skua** (breeding adult, pale morph, Manitoba, Canada, June)
9 **Arctic Skua** (juvenile, Netherlands)
10 **Arctic Skua** (adult breeding, pale morph, Shetland Islands, Scotland, June)

SKUAS & GULLS

LONG-TAILED SKUA or JAEGER

Stercorarius longicaudus L 54 cm (21 in), including tail-streamers of 15-24 cm, WS 111 cm (44 in) Smallest *Stercorarius* skua but with the longest tail. Circumpolar in Northern Hemisphere. **IDENTIFICATION** Attracted to trawlers in Southern Hemisphere non-breeding grounds; less piratical than other skuas. Juveniles variable, adults invariably pale. **Juvenile** Variable from pale ash-grey with white head to more uniform blackish-brown, but always cold and never rusty as Arctic Skua. Cold grey hindneck may contrast with both mantle and head. Upperparts noticeably greyer and colder than Arctic Skua, with paler edges; uppertail-coverts barred, less noticeable on dark birds. Upperwing contrast between greyish-brown coverts and darker flight feathers in pale and intermediate birds (more noticeable than on either Pomarine or Arctic Skua); pale tips to coverts and scapulars broader than on Arctic or Pomarine; blackish primaries show only one to two pale shafts (three to eight on Pomarine and Arctic Skuas). Underwing barred on axillaries and wing-coverts, with basal primaries pale (less extensive than on Arctic or Pomarine); no double pale patch as on Pomarine. Underparts variable: some have dark grey breastband contrasting with paler, whitish breast and belly; others more uniformly barred dark below, especially on undertail-coverts. More extensive dark bill tip than either Arctic or Pomarine. **Immature** Extremely variable: more or less as juvenile but with some features of non-breeding adult; retains juvenile barring on axillaries and underwing-coverts. **Adult non-breeding** Similar to breeding adult, but with shorter tail projections (often absent during moult), barred tail-coverts, and diffuse barring on neck and breast area (dark cap less clear-cut). **Adult breeding** Invariably pale although sooty grey dark morph may occur Greenland. Head with small blackish cap; chin and hindneck faintly greyish-yellow. Mantle and back cold greyish-brown, contrasting with darker flight feathers (more so than on Arctic or Pomarine Skua), with one to two pale shafts on outer primaries; uppertail-coverts slightly paler than mantle. Tail blackish-brown; central streamers may extend 25 cm, but often broken. Underparts variable, but no breastband: generally whitish, becoming progressively darker on belly and undertail-coverts; some have white extending to undertail-coverts. Underwing more uniformly dark than on either Arctic or Pomarine Skua, lacking pale basal primaries; underwing-coverts all dark. Bill and legs dark. Jizz and flight help separate Long-tailed from Arctic. **DISTRIBUTION AND STATUS** Circumpolar in high Arctic. Breeds further inland than Arctic Skua and dependent on lemming abundance. Total population probably several hundreds of thousands of pairs though few data; most in Canada, Russia and Alaska. Some predation by Arctic foxes. Dispersal southwards to winter at sea, mainly in Atlantic and Pacific Oceans; more pelagic than either Pomarine or Arctic Skua.

DOLPHIN GULL

Larus scoresbii L 44 cm (17 in), WS 104 cm (41 in)
Medium-sized, dark-mantled gull of southern South America, adult plumage acquired in third year.
IDENTIFICATION A handsome gull, but an opportunistic scavenger along coasts; urban areas in winter, seal and seabird colonies in summer. **Juvenile** Head brownish, becoming paler on hindneck and foreneck; chin and throat whitish. Saddle and rump dark brownish, shading to white on uppertail-coverts. Upper breast brownish, shading to white underparts. Primaries blackish, becoming browner on rest of upperwing; white trailing edge to upperwing from inner primaries. White tail with black subterminal band. Underwing greyish; primaries and secondaries browner, with white trailing edge. Bill black; iris dark; legs brownish-grey. **First-year** Similar to juvenile, but pink base to bill; sooty-grey head, becoming dark grey with brownish mottling in summer. Underparts become whiter, with brownish mottling on sides of breast. **Second-year** Similar to first-year, but bill red at base with black subterminal bar; legs reddish-brown, iris paler. Head sooty-grey in winter, becoming greyer in summer. Saddle deep grey, rump white. Underparts pale greyish. Upperwing slate-brown, inner primaries and secondaries with white tips forming white trailing edge. Tail white with some remaining dark tips. **Adult non-breeding** (third-winter) Head dusky grey, giving hooded appearance. Saddle slate-black, rump white, underparts pale grey. Upperwing slaty-black with white trailing edge; tail white. **Adult breeding** Head whitish-grey, otherwise as non-breeding adult. Pale iris with crimson orbital ring; crimson-red bill and legs.
DISTRIBUTION AND STATUS Southern South America. Breeds colonially in southern Chile (north to Chiloé Island), southern Argentina (north to Punta Tombo, Chubut) and southwards to Tierra del Fuego. Also a sedentary population (1,000 pairs) at the Falklands. Total population not known but probably in the low 10,000s; most common in southern Chile and Tierra del Fuego. In winter disperses north to c 35°S in Chile and to c 42°S in Argentina.

PACIFIC GULL

Larus pacificus L 62 cm (24 in), WS 147 cm (58 in)
An Australian and Tasmanian endemic gull with huge red-tipped yellow bill. Adult plumage acquired in fourth year.
IDENTIFICATION Has the largest bill of any gull. Can dive for food, and is predatory on seabirds to the size of young gannets. Exclusively marine; generally solitary outside breeding season.
Juvenile Resembles young Kelp Gull, but large pink bill with dark tip diagnostic. Head brownish with whitish tips; forehead and throat whiter. Saddle brown with buffish tips and

darker mottling, becoming paler on rump. Underparts brown with whitish tips (darker than corresponding Kelp Gull). Primaries and their coverts blackish; secondaries blackish with white tips; rest of wing (coverts) brownish with buffish tips. Underwing mainly white. Tail blackish-brown with narrow lighter tip. Iris dark; legs flesh-brown. **First-year** As juvenile, but upperparts greyer; by summer, head, rump and underparts whiter. Wings and tail faded and unmoulted. **Second-year** As first-year, but head and rump becoming whiter, underparts white. Mantle and saddle becoming increasingly slate-coloured. **Third-year** Head white with brownish streaks in winter; streaks absent by summer. Mantle and saddle blackish-brown; rump whitish. Underparts white, with brownish streaking on breast. Outer primaries black; rest of wing slate-black with whitish trailing edge. Tail white, with emerging dark subterminal band. Bill, iris and legs resemble those of adult. **Adult breeding** Head and underparts white. Saddle slate-black; rump white. Upperwing black with broad white trailing edge. Underwing has black primaries, grey secondaries and whitish coverts. Tail white with full black subterminal band. Bill yellow with red tip; iris white; legs yellow. Bare parts duller in winter (non-breeding).
DISTRIBUTION AND STATUS Breeds in loose colonies on islands and headlands from Western Australia eastwards through South Australia to Victoria and Tasmania. Total population c 10,000 pairs. Some immature dispersal; has occurred northern Australia.

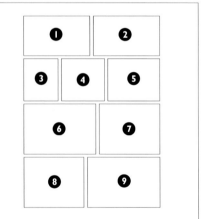

1 **Long-tailed Skua** (adult breeding, Oxfordshire, England)
2 **Long-tailed Skua** (juvenile, dark intermediate type, Somerset, England, October)
3 **Long-tailed Skua** (adult breeding, Norway, June)
4 **Long-tailed Skua** (adult breeding, Victoria Island, Canada, June)
5 **Dolphin Gull** (adult non-breeding, Falkland Islands)
6 **Dolphin Gull** (adult breeding, Falkland Islands)
7 **Pacific Gull** (second winter, Victoria, Australia, March)
8 **Pacific Gull** (adult breeding, Australia)
9 **Pacific Gull** (juvenile, Batemans Bay, Australia)

GULLS

BAND-TAILED or BELCHER'S GULL

Larus belcheri L 51 cm (20 in), WS 124 cm (49 in)

A medium-sized to large, black-backed gull with a black subterminal band on the white tail, a yellow bill with black band and red tip, and upperwings lacking mirrors or white spots. Adult plumage acquired in third year. Previously regarded as conspecific with Olrog's Gull.

IDENTIFICATION Exclusively marine, but does not follow ships; associates with cormorants, and predatory on guano-producing birds. **Juvenile** Dark brown hood extends to breast; paler forehead. Mantle and scapulars greyish-brown, becoming browner on back, all with buffish edges; uppertail-coverts whitish. Brownish breast with whitish edges, becoming white on undertail-coverts. Primaries and secondaries blackish-brown, secondaries edged white; coverts brown, edged buffish. Underwing buff-brown, with darker primaries. Tail blackish, with narrow whitish tip. Bill pale yellow (variable) with black tip; legs greyish. **First-year** As juvenile, but head darker in winter, becoming mainly white by summer. Edging on mantle fades and becomes greyer; breast and belly also greyer. **Second-year** Brownish of head extends onto breast and sides of neck, with hindneck whitish; hood becomes white by summer. Saddle and upperwings become browner. **Adult non-breeding** (third-winter) Brownish-black hood; hindneck, rump and underparts white. Saddle and mantle slaty-black. Upperwing slaty-black, with whitish trailing edge not extending to outer primaries. Underwing greyish, with blacker primaries. Tail white with black subterminal band. Legs yellow. **Adult breeding** Head completely white; otherwise as third-winter/adult non-breeding. From larger Kelp Gull by banded tail, bill colour, lack of white tips on outer primaries. From Olrog's Gull by structural differences and eye-ring colour.

DISTRIBUTION AND STATUS Humboldt Current. Breeds colonially on Pacific coast and islands from northern Peru to Chile as far as Coquimbo (30°S). Total population under 100,000 pairs with most at San Gallan Island – more numerous in Peru than Chile. Occasional birds recorded north to Panama and south to central Chile. May have occurred naturally Florida. Vulnerable to *El Niño*.

OLROG'S GULL

Larus atlanticus L 56 cm (22 in), WS 135 cm (53 in)

A large, black-backed, crab-eating and scavenging gull of the South American Atlantic coast, previously considered a subspecies of Band-tailed Gull. Very similar to Band-tailed, but 20-30% larger, with longer wings and heavier bill, as well as other differences in plumage and breeding biology. Classified as Vulnerable.

IDENTIFICATION Juvenile Much as Band-tailed

Gull, but generally lighter in colour. Lacks Band-tailed's solid dark brown head and breast, which instead are whitish, with greyish-brown streaking and mottling on lower hindneck and upper breast. Head mainly white, especially forehead and throat. Tail blackish with narrow whitish tip. **First- and second-years** Always lack the dark hood and upper breast of Band-tailed, but otherwise similar. Neck, upper back and underparts progressively whiten, losing brownish-grey streaking. Mantle and scapulars darken, losing whitish edges to become slaty greyish-black. Tail may be all dark, or may assume adult's white tail with blackish subterminal band. **Adult non-breeding** Head white with brownish-grey mottling, never forming demarcated hood and breast as on Band-tailed (therefore resembles Kelp Gull in winter, whereas winter Band-tailed resembles hooded Dolphin Gull). White rump; dark subterminal tail band. **Adult breeding** Head white. Mantle, scapulars, back and upperwings jet-black, as Kelp Gull (unlike the brownish-black upperparts of Band-tailed). Outer primaries have no white mirrors (unlike Kelp Gull); inner primaries tipped white, secondaries with larger whitish tips forming whitish crescent on trailing edge of wing (unlike the grey of Band-tailed). Hindneck, upper back and breast white, lacking the pearl-grey tone of Band-tailed. Rump white. Tail white, with glossy black subterminal band narrower than on Band-tailed and not reaching outer feathers. Bill larger than Band-tailed's, yellowish-orange with black subterminal band (larger than on Band-tailed) and red tip; iris light brown, eye-ring red (yellow on Band-tailed); feet yellowish-green.

DISTRIBUTION AND STATUS South America. Breeds discontinuously along the Argentine coast on islands from Isla Brightman (Buenos Aires) to Islas Vernaci (Chubut), with a total population of *c* 1,300 pairs. The six known colonies are vulnerable to both deliberate and accidental disturbance and destruction; egg-collecting takes place. Post-breeding dispersal in winter north to Uruguay (vagrant Brazil) and south along the Argentinian coast (vagrant Tierra del Fuego).

BLACK-TAILED or JAPANESE GULL

Larus crassirostris L 47 cm (19 in), WS 120 cm (47 in)

Medium-sized, dark-backed gull of the north-west Pacific, lacking white spots or mirrors on the primaries, but having a prominent black subterminal band on the tail, and a yellow bill with a black band and red tip. Adult plumage acquired in third year.

IDENTIFICATION The only dark-mantled Japanese gull with a black subterminal tail band. **Juvenile** Head brownish-white, lighter on forehead and chin, darker on nape, hindneck and sides of neck. Saddle brownish with buffish-grey edges, becoming whitish-grey on rump. Underparts white with light brown mottling. Primaries and secondaries brownish-black, secondaries with whitish tips; coverts brownish

with buffy-grey edges. Tail blackish-brown with small buff tip. Bill pinkish-flesh with dark tip; iris dark; legs pinkish. **First-year** As juvenile, but head becomes whiter, with darker grey streaking on crown; underparts become whiter, with some darker streaking on throat. Saddle and uppertail-coverts start to become slate-grey. **Second-year** Resembles adult plumage, but slate-grey on saddle with brownish tips; head becomes white with darker crown; underparts whiter. Upperwing brownish-black with white trailing edge; wing-coverts have brownish tips. White rump and dark tail band contrast. Bill becomes yellow with black subterminal tip. **Adult non-breeding** (third-winter) As breeding adult, but grey crown, and bare parts duller. **Adult breeding** Head and underparts white. Saddle blackish-grey; rump white. Primaries black; rest of upperwing blackish-grey, white tips on secondaries forming trailing edge. Underwing with primaries blackish, secondaries greyish, coverts white. Tail white, with black subterminal band and narrow white tip. Bill develops red tip; legs yellowish. Slaty-backed Gull overlaps in range, but is larger and darker and has white spots on the primaries, as well as different bare parts and tail pattern.

DISTRIBUTION AND STATUS North-west Pacific. Breeds colonially on islands and coasts of Sea of Japan including China, Korea, Japan, Sakhalin, eastern Siberia and the Kuril Islands). Total population *c* 350,000 pairs, with most in Russia and Japan (the commonest gull). Dispersal in winter north to Sea of Okhotsk (vagrant Aleutians and California) and south to Hong Kong with most around the East China Sea and Korean Strait.

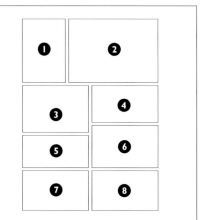

1 **Band-tailed Gull** (adult breeding, Chile)
2 **Band-tailed Gull** (adult breeding, Chile)
3 **Band-tailed Gull** (second winter, Chile, February)
4 **Olrog's Gull** (juvenile, Bahia San Blas, Argentina, December)
5 **Black-tailed Gull** (adult breeding, Sakhalin, June)
6 **Black-tailed Gull** (adult non-breeding, China, October)
7 **Black-tailed Gull** (juvenile moulting to first winter, China, October)
8 **Black-tailed Gull** (second winter, China, October)

GULLS

GREY GULL

Larus modestus L 46 cm (18 in), WS ?
Medium-sized, dark gull of western South America. Adult plumage acquired in third year.
IDENTIFICATION Can form large seasonal flocks on sandy beaches and around trawlers; avoids stony beaches; feeds among waders at the shoreline, mainly on mole crabs. **Juvenile** Head brownish-grey, paler on forehead and chin, darker on nape. Saddle and mantle brownish-grey with buffish edges. Underparts brownish-grey with narrower buffish edges. Primaries and secondaries blackish-brown; coverts brownish-grey with buffish edges, forming paler patch on closed wing. Underwing with primaries blackish, otherwise brownish-grey. Tail blackish-brown, narrowly tipped buffish. **First-year** As juvenile, but nape darker brown; upperparts lose buffish edges and become greyer. Forehead and face sides whiter in summer. **Second-year** Dark brown hood in winter. Saddle greyish-brown, with paler rump and underparts. Wing-coverts greyer. Tail with dark subterminal band. In summer, hood whitish-grey, saddle becoming progressively greyer. **Adult non-breeding** (third-winter) Brown hood; saddle becoming clearer grey. **Adult breeding** Whitish-grey hood to nape and throat, well demarcated from greyish-brown upperparts and underparts. White trailing edge of upperwing visible on closed wing.
DISTRIBUTION AND STATUS Breeds colonially on inland coastal deserts of northern Chile and probably southern Peru; forages at sea along sandy coastal beaches, flying through the night. Total population c 100,000 pairs. Can suffer from egg-collecting and birds do not breed in severe *El Niño* years. Chicks grow more slowly than other gull chicks. Winters on sea coasts of Peru and Chile, with post-breeding dispersal north to Ecuador (especially May-November) and occasionally Colombia, southwards to Valparaiso (Chile), and has occurred at Falklands.

HEERMANN'S GULL

Larus heermanni L 49 cm (19 in), WS 130 cm (51 in)
Medium-sized, distinctive dusky-mantled gull of the Pacific coast of North America. Adult plumage acquired in third year.
IDENTIFICATION Juvenile Plumage generally dark sooty-brown, with paler fringes to mantle, scapulars and wing-coverts giving scaly pattern. Underparts paler and greyer. Primaries and secondaries dull blackish-brown, coverts with paler edges. Tail dull blackish with narrow buff tip. Bill pink at base, with dark tip; legs blackish-grey. **First-year** First-winter as juvenile, but more uniformly dusky brown, with paler wing-coverts; head and body slightly greyer in tone. Bill yellow-flesh with black tip; legs blackish. By summer, bill base becomes pink; head has whitish tips on forehead and chin which can form partial hood; mantle and underparts become greyer. Wings and tail unmoulted and

faded. **Second-year** Plumage resembles non-breeding adult, except head darker (streaked hood), upperparts browner, and underparts with brownish tips. Upperwing-coverts browner; some may show white primary coverts; narrow white trailing edge to wing. Tail dark with narrow whitish tip. Bill base becomes orange-red. By summer, has partial whitish hood. **Adult non-breeding** (third-winter) Similar to breeding adult, except dusky greyish-brown hood peppered with white, and forehead, chin and nape whiter. **Adult breeding** Head white, merging into grey body. Upperparts uniform dark grey, paler on rump and uppertail-coverts. Tail blackish with narrow white border. Underparts and underwing pale grey. Above, blackish primaries and secondaries, with white trailing edge from inner primaries inwards, contrast with grey upperwing-coverts.
DISTRIBUTION AND STATUS Breeds colonially on remote rocky coasts and islands mainly in the Gulf of California (especially Isla Raza with c 90% of the total population), also Baja California, western Mexico, and irregularly north in California to San Francisco Bay. Total population c 150,000 pairs in the eight known colonies. Disperses north to central California, occasionally British Columbia, and south to Guatemala. Vagrants Arizona and Great Lakes.

WHITE-EYED GULL

Larus leucophthalmus L 39 cm (15 in), WS 108 cm (43 in)
Medium-sized, dark-hooded gull (summer), confined to north-west Indian Ocean. Adult plumage acquired in third year. Classified as Vulnerable.
IDENTIFICATION Juvenile Head brown, whitish on face and throat, with dusky ear-coverts; whitish crescents above and below eye. Mantle and scapulars grey-brown with paler fringes; back and upper rump greyish, lower rump and uppertail-coverts white. Breast brownish, this extending to flanks; belly and undertail-coverts white. Primaries and secondaries blackish, with narrow white trailing edge from inner primaries; tertials and coverts grey-brown with paler fringes. Underwing grey-brown. Tail black with narrow white terminal fringe. Bill black, browner at base; iris dark brown; legs greenish-grey. **First-year** As juvenile, but blackish mask from eye to nape; eye crescents more pronounced. Mantle, scapulars, breastband and flanks uniform grey-brown. By summer, wings and tail very worn and faded. **Second-year** In winter as adult winter, except hood and bib browner; mantle, scapulars, breastband and flanks mostly greyish-brown. Outer primaries, primary coverts, alula and secondaries blackish, shading to greyer inwards; narrow white trailing edge from seventh primary inwards; inner wing-coverts browner. Tail white, with variable blackish subterminal band. Bare parts duller than adult. By summer, wings and tail unmoulted and faded. **Adult non-breeding** (third-winter) As adult breeding, but hood and bib have white flecking, and white half-collar less

defined. Primaries and primary coverts black, shading inwards to uniform dark grey coverts; secondaries and tertials blackish, with white tips extending to third or fourth primary; thin white leading edge to inner wing (lacking on Sooty). Tail white. **Adult breeding** Glossy black hood extends to upper breast as a bib; white eye crescents, and white half-collar on hindneck. Mantle, scapulars and back dark grey (no brownish tone as on Sooty); rump and uppertail-coverts white. Breastband and flanks pale grey; belly white. Wings as non-breeding adult. Bill bright red, black at tip; iris dark brown; legs yellowish.
DISTRIBUTION AND STATUS North-west Indian Ocean. Breeds loosely colonially on inshore islands in the Red Sea from the Gulf of Suez and Gulf of Aqaba to the Gulf of Aden with most in Egypt (1,000-2,000+ pairs); fewer Sudan, Eritrea, Saudi Arabia, Yemen; status off Somalia needs clarification. Total population not well known, probably 4,000-6,500 pairs. Adults mainly sedentary in Red Sea, occasionally reaching south-east Mediterranean. Vagrant Kenya. At risk from oil pollution and oil exploration, collection of both eggs and chicks, and disturbance from tourism developments.

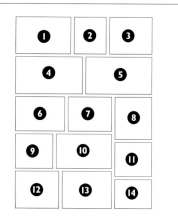

1 **Grey Gull** (adult breeding, worn, Antofagasta, Chile, February)
2 **Grey Gull** (adult non-breeding, Chile)
3 **Grey Gull** (adult breeding, worn)
4 **Heermann's Gull** (adult breeding, California, USA)
5 **Heermann's Gull** (adult non-breeding, California, USA)
6 **Heermann's Gull** (second winter, California, USA)
7 **Heermann's Gull** (second winter, California, USA)
8 **Heermann's Gull** (adult breeding, California, USA)
9 **Heermann's Gull** (first winter, California, USA)
10 **White-eyed Gull** (adult breeding, Gulf of Suez, June)
11 **White-eyed Gull** (juvenile, Egypt, October)
12 **White-eyed Gull** (first summer moulting to second winter, Egypt, December)
13 **White-eyed Gull** (first summer moulting to second winter, Egypt, October)
14 **White-eyed Gull** (adult moulting into non-breeding, Egypt, October)

GULLS

SOOTY GULL

Larus hemprichii L 45 cm (18 in), WS 112 cm (44 in)

Medium-sized, heavily built gull confined to north-west Indian Ocean. Dark-hooded in summer; has a long yellow bill with black subterminal band and red tip, greenish-yellow legs, and brownish-grey wings and upperparts. Adult plumage acquired in third year. From White-eyed Gull by larger size, different jizz, broader, less pointed wings, thicker bill with different colour and browner, less grey plumage.

IDENTIFICATION Juvenile Head pale brownish-grey, paler than mantle; whiter on chin and face, browner on nape. Mantle, scapulars and back brown, with paler buff fringes forming scaly pattern (unlike White-eyed Gull); rump and uppertail-coverts pale greyish-brown. Underparts whitish from belly to undertail; breast and flanks pale brown with some mottling. Outer primaries, primary coverts and secondaries blackish, with narrow white trailing edge from third to fourth primary inwards; inner primaries paler; inner wing-coverts pale brown, fringed whitish, forming scaly pattern. Underwing greyish-brown. Tail mainly black, with thin white subterminal. Bill greyish, tipped black; iris dark brown; legs dark grey. **First-year** As juvenile, but breastband and flanks grey-brown. Mantle and scapulars grey-brown; rump and uppertail-coverts whitish. By summer, wings and tail worn and faded, fewer paler fringes on coverts and tertials. **Second-year** As adult winter, except head as first-year; mantle, scapulars, breastband and flanks browner and patchy, less uniform grey-brown. Broader black secondary bar, with white trailing edge to wing reduced. Tail white, with variable black subterminal. Bare parts as first-year. By summer, partial to full brownish-grey hood, bill becoming yellower. **Adult non-breeding** (third-winter) As adult breeding, except paler brown hood, with white cervical collar reduced or lacking. Primaries, primary coverts and alula blackish, shading to blackish-brown inwards; secondaries and tertials blackish-brown with white tips; broad trailing edge from third to fourth primary outwards; inner wing-coverts dark grey-brown. **Adult breeding** Dark brown hood extending to upper breast; white crescent above eye, smaller one below; whitish half-collar on lower hindneck and sides of neck borders hood. Mantle, scapulars and back brownish-grey; rump, uppertail-coverts and tail white. Breastband greyish-brown, extending to flanks; rest of underparts white. Wings as adult winter, faded browner. Bill yellow, with blackish subterminal band and red tip.

DISTRIBUTION AND STATUS North-west Indian Ocean. Breeds usually colonially on coasts and islands in the Red Sea, Gulf of Aden, Persian Gulf, Gulf of Oman, east to Pakistan, and south to northern Kenya. No full documentation of total population, but likely to be between 50,000 and 100,000 breeding pairs; two colonies off Arabian coast each hold 5,000 pairs. Main threat within rather limited breeding range is human interference, including egg-collecting and oil spills. Dispersal mostly south to Kenya, Tanzania (occasionally to north Mozambique), west coast of India and Pakistan, north occasionally to Eilat (Israel); many remain in Red Sea throughout year.

MEW or COMMON GULL

Larus canus L 43 cm (17 in), WS 120 cm (47 in)

Medium-sized, grey-mantled gull, almost circumpolar in the Northern Hemisphere, with yellowish-green bill and legs, the blackish primaries having large whitish mirrors at their tips. Adult plumage acquired in third year.

IDENTIFICATION Juvenile Forehead, chin, throat and nape whitish; grey-brown streaking on crown and ear-coverts forms partial hood on darker birds. Saddle, back and scapulars buff with paler edges; rump and uppertail-coverts white with dark arrowhead bars. Underparts white, with grey-brown mottling on hindneck, flanks and breast. Upperwing with outer three to five primaries, primary coverts and alula blackish-brown, inner primaries grey-brown with blackish tips; secondaries blackish-brown, forming secondary bar; greater coverts grey-brown, forming pale mid-wing panel; brown carpal bar on remaining coverts. Tail white, with broad black subterminal band. Bill black with pink base; legs pinkish. **First-year** As juvenile, but saddle, mantle and scapulars uniform bluish-grey; head, rump and underparts whiter. By summer, brown and grey in wings and tail very faded, primary tips faded and browner, thus pale wings contrast with fresh blue-grey saddle. **Second-year** Head and body as first-year, but less streaking on breast, flanks and rump; uppertail-coverts white. Upperwings as adult, but black extends to eighth primary and along leading edge of forewing onto primary coverts and alula; two small mirrors on outer primaries. Tail white. Bill greyish-green with dark tip; legs greyish-flesh. By summer, head and breast sides white and blackish on upperwing faded to brown. **Adult non-breeding** (third-winter) Head white, streaked greyish-brown, heaviest on lower hindneck. Mantle, scapulars and back blue-grey; rump and tail white. Underparts white, with greyish-brown streaks on sides of breast and flanks. Primaries one to six blackish, this decreasing inwards, with small whitish tips and two large mirrors on outer two primaries; rest of wing uniform blue-grey, with thin white leading edge and thicker white trailing edge. Bill yellowish with dark subterminal band; iris dark; legs yellowish (but variable). **Adult breeding** As adult non-breeding, but head and sides of breast white, white primary tips reduced, bill yellowish-green. *L. c. brachyrhynchus* (Alaska and Canada): Shorter-winged than nominate *canus*. **First-year** Wings paler and browner, tail darker, head and underparts more uniform brownish-grey. **Second-year** Upperparts darker, retains immature markings on wings and tail. **Adult** More white in wing tip, darker on mantle.

DISTRIBUTION AND STATUS Almost circumpolar in Northern Hemisphere. Breeds usually colonially near the sea and inland, not necessarily close to water, in Alaska, British Columbia, north-west Canada, Iceland, north-west and central Europe, Russia, Siberia. Total population probably 1,000,000+ pairs, but not comprehensively documented – most birds probably in Fenno-Scandinavia. European populations increasing and expanding range. Dispersal in winter southwards as far as California, north Africa, Persian Gulf, Japan and Taiwan. Some predation of eggs and chicks by mammals and larger birds.

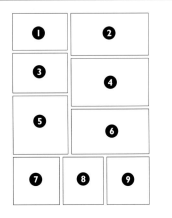

1 **Sooty Gull** (adult breeding)
2 **Sooty Gull** (adult non-breeding and first winter, Egypt, December)
3 **Sooty Gull** (second winter, Egypt, October)
4 **Mew Gull** subspecies *L. c. brachyrhynchus* (adult non-breeding, USA)
5 **Mew Gull** subspecies *L. c. brachyrhynchus* (adult breeding)
6 **Mew Gull** (non-breeding adult showing 'hood' effect)
7 **Mew Gull** (juvenile, Netherlands, July)
8 **Mew Gull** (first winter, Norfolk, England, March)
9 **Mew Gull** (adult non-breeding, Norfolk, England, March)

GULLS

AUDOUIN'S GULL

Larus audouinii L 50 cm (20 in), WS 127 cm (50 in)

Large, grey-mantled, coastal gull breeding only in the Mediterranean. Resembles Herring Gull (15% smaller), but with red bill and olive-grey legs, and more prominent blackish on the outer wing (without white mirrors). Adult plumage acquired in fourth year.

IDENTIFICATION At rest has distinctive slim and elegant shape, lacking heavy-chested appearance, with elongated rear end, long sloping forehead peaking behind eye, and long legs. Flight is graceful, and feeds by plunging, dependent on discard of pelagic clupeid fish from fishing fleet. **Juvenile** Much as juvenile Herring Gull. Head and neck uniform grey-brown, shading to whitish around bill and crown. Mantle grey-brown; scapulars and tertials dark brown, with broad pale fringes giving scaly pattern; back and central rump grey-brown, barred darker; lower rump and uppertail-coverts white, contrasting with black (whitish-tipped) tail and dark centre of upper rump. Underparts grey-brown, especially on breast sides, darker on rear flanks; belly white. Primaries and primary coverts blackish, without paler window on inner primaries, and secondaries blackish with white fringes, thus double dark bar across wings in flight (as Lesser Black-backed Gull). Underwing has pale central area. Bill black; iris dark brown; legs long and greyish. **First-year** In winter as juvenile, but upperparts less scaly, being uniform dark brown; head whiter, with streaked hindneck. By summer, head and underparts whiter, mantle, scapulars and back clear grey and paler; wings and tail worn and faded, with greyish inner wing panel (greater and median coverts). Bill paler blackish-grey. **Second-year** In winter head white, with dusky ear-coverts, and streaking on hindneck. Mantle, back, scapulars and most coverts clear silvery-grey; rump and underparts white. Outer primaries blackish with white tips (except on first and second outermost), inner primaries clear grey; secondaries blackish-brown subterminally, forming secondary bar; greater coverts grey with brown tips. Tail white, with variable black subterminal band. Bill base reddish. By summer, head white, wings faded and browner, inner wing-coverts clearer grey. **Third-year** As adult non-breeding, but more extensive black on primary coverts and alula; outer five primaries black with small white tips, and usually one mirror on outer primary (may be lacking). Tail may have dark subterminal marks. **Adult non-breeding** (fourth-winter) Head white, faintly streaked on crown and nape; hindneck greyer (from mantle). Mantle, scapulars and back pale grey, merging into white rump. Underparts white, breast sides greyer. Outer primaries black (more extensive than on Herring Gull), black decreasing inwards to subterminal spots on fifth and sixth, all tipped white, with white mirror on first larger; primary coverts and alula white; rest of upperwing pale grey, with narrow white leading and trailing edges. Tail white. Bill deep red, with black subterminal band and yellowish or orange tip; iris brown; legs olive. **Adult breeding** As adult non-breeding, but head white, and white primary tips reduced or lacking.

DISTRIBUTION AND STATUS Mediterranean. Breeds colonially on rocky offshore islands and sandy beaches with 90% of the population in Spain (60% of this Ebro Delta: 10,300 pairs) and 3,500 pairs at the Chafarinas Islands off north-east Morocco, with fewer in Tunisia, Italy, Cyprus, the Aegean Sea and southern Turkey. Total population *c* 17,000 pairs at 30+ colonies. Population increasing with strict conservation measures introduced by Spain in 1987 however, breeding productivity can be low. Dispersal around the Mediterranean and past Gibraltar to winter on the north-west African coast south to Senegambia, regular Canaries in winter. Occasionally recorded south-east Mediterranean countries with vagrants northern France, Switzerland, Czech Republic, Black Sea, and Turkey. Threats: egg-taking in the eastern Mediterranean, predation by Yellow-legged Gull.

RING-BILLED GULL

Larus delawarensis L 45 cm (18 in), WS 124 cm (49 in)

Medium-sized, grey-mantled North American Gull, very similar to Mew Gull. Adult plumage acquired in third year.

IDENTIFICATION Juvenile Head dull white with crown streaked brown, becoming spotted on nape and hindneck. Mantle and scapulars grey-brown with buff edges; rump and uppertail-coverts white, spotted brown. Underparts dull white, with grey-brown spotting from hindneck extending to throat, breast and flanks. Upperwing has outer four to five primaries, alula and primary coverts blackish-brown; inner primaries pale grey, subterminally black; secondaries blackish-brown, thus dark trailing edge; coverts pale grey, except for brownish carpal and diagonal bar. Tail white with black subterminal band. Bill black with pink base; legs flesh-pink. **First-year** First-winter as juvenile, except head whiter, with distinct blackish spots on lower hindneck. Mantle, scapulars and back pale grey with a few brown feathers. Wings and tail unmoulted and faded. By summer, bill and legs yellowish, with black subterminal band on bill; head whiter, with faint spots on nape; brown and grey areas of wings and tail faded to whitish, black areas faded to brown. **Second-year** As first-year, except spotting on nape and hindneck. Outer four to five primaries blackish, with one white mirror on outer primary; primary coverts and alula edged black; rest of upperwing pale grey with white trailing edge; some retain dark secondary bar. Tail may have partial dark tail band. By summer head whiter, with light spots on hindneck; wings and tail further faded. **Adult non-breeding** (third-winter) Head white, with dark spots on nape and hindneck. Upperparts pale grey; rump and underparts white. Outer four primaries mainly black, fifth and sixth subterminally black, all tipped white, with mirror on outer two primaries; the rest pale grey. Bill greenish-yellow with black subterminal band; iris pale yellow; legs greenish-yellow. **Adult breeding** As adult non-breeding, except head white, white primary tips reduced or lacking, bare parts brighter yellow.

DISTRIBUTION AND STATUS North America. Breeds colonially on islands in freshwater lakes and in meadows from northern California across the prairie provinces to the Great Lakes (500,000 pairs) and the maritime provinces of the east coast. Total population 1,500,000-2,000,000 pairs, steadily increasing. Winters south to Gulf Coast, Central America, Lesser and Greater Antilles. Vagrants Hawaii, Trinidad, Panama, also north to Alaska and Yukon. Now recorded annually western Europe, especially Britain and Ireland (where regular in small numbers).

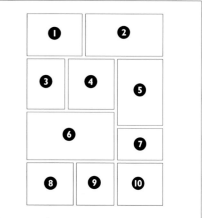

1 Audouin's Gull (adult breeding, Mallorca, May)
2 Audouin's Gull (two birds with dark legs) (first winter, accompanying Yellow-legged and Lesser Black-backed Gulls, Morocco, April)
3 Audouin's Gull (adult breeding, April)
4 Audouin's Gull (second summer, Mallorca, May)
5 Ring-billed Gull (adult breeding, Florida, USA)
6 Ring-billed Gull (adult non-breeding, California, USA)
7 Ring-billed Gull (second winter, California, USA)
8 Ring-billed Gull (first winter)
9 Ring-billed Gull (adult non-breeding, Florida, USA)
10 Ring-billed Gull (juvenile moulting to first winter, Cape Cod, USA)

GULLS

CALIFORNIA GULL

Larus californicus L 54 cm (21 in), WS 137 cm (54 in)

Large western North American gull resembling Herring Gull. Adult plumage acquired in fourth year.

IDENTIFICATION Juvenile Head greyish-brown, streaked silvery. Mantle and back greyish-brown with silvery fringes; rump and uppertail-coverts whiter. Underparts whitish with greyish-brown barring and mottling; forehead, throat and upper breast whiter. Outer primaries and primary coverts blackish; inner primaries paler, forming indistinct window; secondaries dark brown with paler fringes; coverts greyish-brown with paler fringes. Tail dark brown. Bill pink with well-defined black tip; legs pinkish. **First-year** As juvenile, but greyer, less silvery on upperparts; upper breast whiter. By summer, head whiter, underparts white and saddle has grey tips. Upperparts more uniform than on Herring. **Second-year** In winter, head greyish-white with brownish streaks, these strongest on nape and hindneck. Mantle and scapulars grey; rump whitish with little barring. Underparts whitish with brownish mottling, especially on breast. Wings as first-year, but paler inner window more pronounced, coverts becoming greyish, outermost primary may have white mirror. Head and breast whiter in summer. Bill greyish-blue with black tip; legs greyish. **Third-year** As adult, but bill and legs duller; primary coverts, alula, greater coverts edged blackish, thus wing tip less defined. Partial tail band. Some dark may remain in secondaries. Head whiter in summer. **Adult non-breeding** (fourth-winter) Much as breeding adult, but head as second-winter. Blackish subterminal band bordering red gonydeal spot more extensive; bill base greenish-yellow. **Adult breeding** Head, rump, tail and underparts white. Upperparts and wings dark bluish-grey, darker than on Mew, Herring or Ring-billed Gull; conspicuous white trailing edge. Outermost primaries black, decreasing inwards, all with apical spots; white mirror on outer two primaries Bill yellow with black subterminal band, red gonydeal spot, yellow tip; iris dark brown; legs yellow or greenish-yellow.

DISTRIBUTION AND STATUS Breeds colonially on islands in lakes and inland marshes of western North America. Total population c 200,000 pairs, increasing and expanding with protection. Dispersal south-west to the Pacific coast, occasionally recorded Atlantic coast and Alaska. Vagrants Hawaii, Japan.

GREAT BLACK-BACKED GULL

Larus marinus L 75 cm (30 in), WS 160 cm (63 in)

Large, non-hooded, black-backed gull of north Atlantic. Adult plumage acquired fourth year.

IDENTIFICATION Juvenile Head white with greyish-brown streaks. Mantle, scapulars and back blackish-brown with whitish edges, giving chequered pattern; rump whitish, streaked darker. Underparts whitish, strongly streaked grey-brown on breast sides and belly. Primaries and secondaries blackish-brown, sometimes with paler window on inner primaries; coverts blackish brown with white edges, less chequered than saddle. Tail whitish at base with diffuse dark subterminal band. Bill black; iris dark brown; legs dull flesh-coloured. **First-year** In winter as juvenile, but head and underparts whiter; mantle and scapulars strongly barred in chequered pattern. By summer, head and underparts whiter, and upperparts more uniformly dark with less chequered pattern; dark wing and tail areas worn and faded paler; bill may have pale base. **Second-year** In winter head white, with light streaking on hindneck. Mantle, scapulars and back dark grey with brown and white bars. Underparts with dark streaking on breast sides and flanks. Primaries and secondaries blackish-brown, inner primaries slightly paler; coverts brownish; blackish secondary bar. Tail whitish with dark subterminal band. Iris may become pale. By summer, head and underparts white, mantle and scapulars mainly uniform blackish, and wings and tail worn and faded, especially inner wing (which may be whitish). Bill becomes yellowish. **Third-year** In winter as adult non-breeding, except black on wing tip less demarcated, with less white; brownish on inner wing. Mantle and scapulars blackish with some brown fringes. Tail white with faint subterminal band. By summer, head and underparts white, upperparts brownish, and reduced white primary tips. **Adult non-breeding** (fourth-winter) Dusky head streaks, uniform blackish upperparts and wings, with darker wing tip, large mirrors on first and second primaries and white trailing edge. Tail white. Bill yellow; legs flesh-coloured. **Adult breeding** As adult non-breeding, but head pure white, wings faded to brownish tone, and white primary tips reduced.

DISTRIBUTION AND STATUS Breeds solitarily or loosely colonially on islands, sand dunes, and buildings around North American east coast, southern Greenland, Iceland, Faeroes, coastal Europe and Spitsbergen. Total population c 200,000 pairs increasing and expanding southwards. Winter dispersal south; occasionally reaches Morocco.

KELP GULL

Larus dominicanus L 58 cm (23 in), WS 135 cm (53 in)

Large Southern Hemisphere black-backed gull. Adult plumage acquired in fourth year.

IDENTIFICATION The only large black-backed and white-tailed gull that breeds in the Southern Hemisphere. A gregarious forager, found inland and at sea; follows ships and trawlers. **Juvenile** Head mid brown, paler on forehead and chin, with nape and ear-coverts darker. Saddle brownish with buff edges and darker barring; rump and uppertail-coverts brownish, barred white. Underparts mottled brown and white, darker on belly. Primaries and secondaries blackish, secondaries with whitish tips; coverts brownish with buffish edges. Underwing-coverts brownish, primaries and secondaries dusky greyish-white, with whitish tips to secondaries. Tail blackish-brown. Bill blackish; iris black; legs pink-brownish. **First-year** As juvenile, but whiter head with brown streaks. Upperparts become greyer, with slaty tips on saddle. Chin and throat becoming whiter, breast paler. **Second-year** Whitish head with some brownish streaks; saddle brownish, becoming increasingly darker and slaty. Underparts progressively whiter. Upperwing darker than first-year. Whitish base to tail. Bill and legs olive by summer. **Third-year** White head has light brown streaking on crown, nape and sides of breast. Underparts white with some light brown streaks. Upperwing blackish-brown with white trailing edge. Underwing greyish; primaries and secondaries darker with whitish tips. Tail white. **Adult breeding** Head, underparts and rump white; saddle and mantle blackish. Upperwing blackish, with variable white spot on outer primary separated from white trailing edge. Underwing with black primaries and grey secondaries. *L. d. vetula* of southern Africa has darker eye than nominate *dominicanus*.

DISTRIBUTION AND STATUS Circumpolar in Southern Hemisphere. Breeds usually colonially. Total population unknown, but large and increasing. Has bred Senegal.

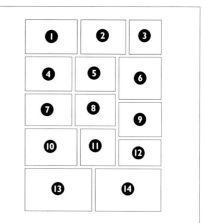

1 **California Gull** (first winter, California, USA)
2 **California Gull** (adult breeding, worn)
3 **California Gull** (adult non-breeding, California, USA)
4 **California Gull** (adult non-breeding, worn, California, USA)
5 **California Gull** (adult non-breeding, fresh, California, USA)
6 **Great Black-backed Gull** (adult breeding and second summer, Cape May, USA)
7 **Great Black-backed Gull** (second winter, Scotland)
8 **Great Black-backed Gull** (second winter, New York, USA)
9 **Great Black-backed Gull** (third winter, Scotland)
10 **Great Black-backed Gull** (adult carrying clam, USA)
11 **Kelp Gull** (first winter, Wellington, New Zealand)
12 **Kelp Gull** (adult breeding, Falkland Islands, December)
13 **Kelp Gull** (breeding pair, Falkland Islands)
14 **Kelp Gull** (first summer, Falkland Islands)

GULLS

GLAUCOUS-WINGED GULL

Larus glaucescens L 65 cm (26 in), WS 147 cm (58 in)

Large non-hooded, grey-mantled gull of north Pacific. Adult plumage acquired fourth year. **IDENTIFICATION Juvenile** Head buffish-grey; hindneck whiter. Mantle, scapulars and back buffish-grey, mottled paler; rump and uppertail-coverts whiter, usually distinctly barred. Underparts buffish-grey. Primaries and secondaries buffish-grey with darker subterminal tips and paler fringes; coverts as upperparts. Underwing and tail pinkish-grey. Bill black. **First-year** As juvenile in winter, but paler, whiter, bleached and worn. By summer, bill base pinkish, and plumage generally silvery-grey with brownish mottling on coverts; primaries almost white. **Second-year** In winter, mantle and scapulars pale grey, and rump and uppertail white, barred grey-brown. No pale barring on wing-coverts. Underparts and wings generally paler than first-year. Bill has more extensive dark tip than on Glaucous Gull. **Third-year** Head white, nape streaked. Upperparts pale grey; rump and tail white. Underparts white, with some grey on breast. Upperwing as adult, but primaries slightly browner with smaller apical spots, mirror on outer primary often lacking; wing-coverts with brownish wash. Bill yellowish with dark subterminal band, which reduces by summer, when head and underparts are white. **Adult non-breeding** As breeding adult, but head as third-winter. **Adult breeding** Head white; upperparts pale grey, with rump white; underparts white. Upperwing pale grey; outer four to five primaries have darker grey subterminal tips (but variable), outermost primary with one white mirror, and all primaries have white apical spots increasing inwards and joining white-tipped secondaries to form white trailing edge to wing. Underwing white. Tail white. Bill yellow with red gonydeal spot; iris brown; legs pink. Hybridizes with Western, Herring and Glaucous Gulls, providing identification problems.

DISTRIBUTION AND STATUS Breeds colonially or solitarily in a variety of habitats (including roofs) from the Commander Islands eastwards to Aleutians, Pribilofs, South Bering Sea, southern Alaska to British Columbia and Oregon: presently extending range to the interior of North America and Canada. Total population probably 250,000-300,000 pairs, with 135,000+ pairs in Alaska. Most birds disperse south in winter. Has reached China. Vagrants Hawaii, Canaries, Morocco and Switzerland.

WESTERN GULL

Larus occidentalis L 64 cm (25 in), WS 137 cm (54 in)

Large and stocky, non-hooded, dark-mantled gull of the Pacific coast of North America. Adult plumage acquired in fourth year. **IDENTIFICATION Juvenile** Heavy structure, all-black bill, and dark general colour, especially darker, more uniform sooty-grey on head and underparts. Pale markings on mantle, scapulars and wing-coverts. Dark outer greater coverts form dark bar in flight; lacks obvious pale window on primaries. Whitish, dark-barred rump and uppertail-coverts contrast with dark tail. **First-year** In winter, head and underparts uniform, sooty grey-brown. By summer, head and body generally whiter, wing-coverts faded to whitish, and primaries, secondary bar and tail much faded. **Second-year** Mantle and scapulars clear blackish-grey; dark saddle. Wing and tail as first-year, but coverts plainer, paler grey-brown with whitish fringes. By summer, all wing-coverts faded to whitish. Tail often fades to pale brown by second summer. Head, body and rump whiter, especially by second summer. Bill becomes pale at base. **Third-year** As adult, except upperwing-coverts brown-washed; white tips on outermost primaries smaller or lacking; mirror on first primary small or lacking. Tail with narrow subterminal row of spots. Bill has dark tip. **Adult** From Slaty-blacked Gull by different wing-tip pattern, being blacker above and below: underside of outer primaries black (grey on Slaty-backed), lacks mirror on second primary, and lacks white dividing spots on primaries three to six. Narrower white trailing edge to inner wing and heavier structure, especially bill. From Yellow-footed Gull by pink (not yellow) legs, paler upperparts (only nominate *occidentalis*), and grey-streaked head in winter (*occidentalis*). Bill yellow, paler in winter; iris yellow-white. *L. o. occidentalis* (northern paler-backed subspecies) larger, with darker eye; adults have grey on head in winter. *L. o. wymani* (southern darker-backed subspecies) smaller, with paler eye and darker upperparts; adults usually white-headed in winter.

DISTRIBUTION AND STATUS Breeds colonially on rocky islands from Washington south through California to Baja California. Total population c 32,000 pairs of which 13,000 pairs on southeast Farallon Island. Dispersal both north and south, vagrants to Alaska, and to Baja California, and occasionally Mexico. Adversely affected by oil pollution, *El Niño*, human disturbance and destruction, and hybridization with Glaucous-winged Gull.

YELLOW-FOOTED GULL

Larus livens L 69 cm (27 in), WS 152 cm (60 in)

Large non-hooded, dark-mantled gull, restricted to Gulf of California. Formerly regarded as a subspecies of Western Gull, but acquires adult plumage in third year (Western in fourth year). Distinguished from Western Gull by darker mantle and bare-part differences. **IDENTIFICATION Juvenile** Similar to juvenile Herring Gull: head and upperparts greyish-brown, upperparts edged paler, rump and uppertail-coverts barred whiter, with contrasting blackish-brown tail; underparts mottled greyish-brown, with belly and undertail-coverts whitish. Outer five to six primaries and coverts blackish-brown; inner primaries paler, forming indistinct window; secondaries blackish-brown, tipped white. Bill and iris black; legs pink. **First-year** In winter, head (with dark-streaked hindneck) and underparts whitish; mantle and scapulars a mix of faded brown and new blackish-grey feathers; wing-coverts faded grey-brown, thus juvenile contrast lost. Pale flesh base to bill, and legs yellowish-flesh. By summer, mantle and scapulars blackish and contrast with faded and whitish wing-coverts. Legs yellowish, thus resembling second-summer Western Gull, but has black tail. **Second-year** Adult-like, but brownish upperwing-coverts; wing-tip pattern less developed, with smaller white tips and no mirror on outer primary. Tail mainly black. Resembles third-year Western Gull, but more black on bill and tail, and yellow legs. **Adult non-breeding** As adult breeding, lacking head streaks of Western Gull. **Adult breeding** Plumage and bare parts much as Western Gull, except legs bright yellow.

DISTRIBUTION AND STATUS North-west Mexico. Breeds usually colonially on islands in the Gulf of California. Total population probably 3,600 pairs in 11 colonies: not well known and little studied within restricted range. Some dispersal to the Salton Sea (south-east California), more rarely on the Californian coast, and also southwards to Mexico.

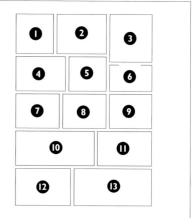

1 **Glaucous-winged Gull** (adult breeding, Homer, Alaska, June)
2 **Glaucous-winged Gull** (adult non-breeding, California, USA)
3 **Glaucous-winged Gull** (adult non-breeding eating starfish, California, USA)
4 **Glaucous-winged Gull** (first winter, USA)
5 **Western Gull** (first winter, bathing, USA)
6 **Western Gull** (adult breeding, California, USA)
7 **Western Gull** (adult breeding scavenging on dead seal, California, USA)
8 **Western Gull** (juvenile/first winter, California, USA)
9 **Western Gull** (first summer, California, USA)
10 **Western Gull** (sub-adult eating clam, California, USA)
11 **Yellow-footed Gull** (first year)
12 **Yellow-footed Gull** (first year)
13 **Yellow-footed Gull** (adult breeding, worn, moulting, California, USA)

GULLS

GLAUCOUS GULL

Larus hyperboreus L 71 cm (28 in), WS 158 cm (62 in)

Large white-winged gull, circumpolar in the Northern Hemisphere, with yellow bill and pink legs when adult; white wing tips diagnostic at all ages (except for eliminating Iceland Gull, which is smaller and structurally different). Adult plumage acquired in fourth year. Hybridizes with Glaucous-winged Gull in Alaska, and maybe with Herring Gull in Iceland.

IDENTIFICATION Juvenile Head biscuit-white with fine brownish-grey streaking. Mantle and scapulars pale buff with brownish barring; rump barred. Underparts buff (darkest on belly), barred on breast sides and flanks, usually darker than upperparts. Primaries and secondaries buffish with whitish tips; rest of wing as mantle, darkening gradually inwards. Tail buff with variable barring. Bill pink with black tip; iris brown; legs flesh. **First-year** In winter as juvenile, but head and underparts paler; mantle and scapulars whiter, but still coarsely barred. By summer, head and body whitish with faint mottling, mantle and scapulars whitish with sparse brown barring, and wings and tail worn and faded (whitish). **Second-year** In winter, plumage generally whiter or paler buff, more uniform and less barred than first-year; head and underparts may be coarsely streaked darker; less barring on wing-coverts; tail paler, with fainter barring. Tip of bill pale, with reduced black, base may be yellowish; iris may become pale. By summer, head and underparts pale buff to whitish, mantle and scapulars whitish-grey, and wings and tail whitish or pale buff (worn and faded). **Third-year** In winter, head streaked; underparts white with some brownish mottling; mantle and scapulars pale grey, rump white; tail white, with darker tip. Wings grey as adult, but some brownish mottling. Bare parts as adult, bill blackish subterminally. By summer, head and underparts white, and brownish areas on wings and tail reduced and faded. **Adult non-breeding** (fourth-winter) Head white, streaked. Upperparts and upperwing pale grey, with whiter primaries and secondaries; thin white leading edge and broader white trailing edge to wing. Underparts, rump and tail white. Bill yellow with orange gonydeal spot; iris pale yellow; legs pinkish. **Adult breeding** As adult non-breeding, but head white, bare parts brighter.

DISTRIBUTION AND STATUS Circumpolar in Northern Hemisphere. Breeds colonially or solitarily on cliffs and offshore islands in Arctic regions of Alaska (15,000+ pairs) to Canada, Greenland (10,000-100,000 pairs but decreasing), Iceland, Jan Mayen, Spitsbergen, Taymyr Peninsula to Bering Sea and Pribilofs. Total population over 100,000 pairs with c 20,000 pairs in the western Palearctic (most on Spitsbergen) and 10,000–50,000 pairs in the Eastern palearctic. Variable dispersal southwards from the ice edge to both coasts of North America occasionally reaching California,

Florida, Cuba and Bermuda; also southwards to north-west Europe, China, Japan, with many more recorded in southern parts of winter range in some years than in others. Most of west Siberian population remains within breeding range throughout year. Vagrant Hawaii.

ICELAND GULL

Larus glaucoides L 61 cm (24 in), WS 140 cm (55 in)

Large white-winged gull of the north Atlantic, with yellow bill and pink legs when adult; generally like a small Glaucous Gull, with similar plumage stages. Adult plumage acquired in fourth year. Controversial taxonomy with *thayeri*, variably assigned to *glaucoides* or *argentatus*.

IDENTIFICATION Juvenile As juvenile Glaucous Gull, except general coloration greyer, less buff; barring on mantle, scapulars, wings and tail-coverts denser; white terminal tail band more distinct; bill base pinkish, remaining half blackish. **Further plumage stages** As for Glaucous Gull, except orbital ring of adult summer usually red (not yellowish); bill of third-winter onwards greenish-yellow (Glaucous Gull lacks greenish tone). Iceland Gull is generally smaller than Herring Gull, whereas Glaucous is generally larger. Iceland has a comparatively shorter bill than Glaucous, being less than one-half the head length, whereas Glaucous has a larger and more massive bill (over one-half the head length). Iceland has a more rounded forehead and crown, which together with the smaller bill give a gentle expression (unlike the fiercer expression of Glaucous). Iceland is larger-eyed and has a slimmer jizz, without the full-chested appearance of Glaucous. Primary projection is comparatively longer on Iceland, which has relatively longer and slimmer wings. Iceland has proportionately shorter legs. First-year Iceland has much more black on the bill (Glaucous has just a dark tip); by third year the bill is greenish (Glaucous never has greenish tinge). *L. g. kumlieni* is almost identical to nominate *glaucoides* in size, structure, and immature plumages, but has a slightly larger bill and immatures are less barred than *glaucoides* and have darker primaries; adults have frosted grey or brown on outer five primaries, decreasing inwards and appearing as dark outer webs and subterminal bars (visible from below), but very variable (in *kumlieni* colonies, some birds have wing tips all white and others have primaries almost uniform pale grey). *L. g. thayeri* (sometimes treated as a subspecies of Herring Gull, but now often considered a full species) has darker grey upperparts than *kumlieni*, plus dark iris (but iris yellow with brown flecks in northernmost part of range) and deep pink legs; adult pattern of dark on the outer primaries is similar to that of *kumlieni*, but more extensive, reaching to the sixth primary, and only black tips are visible from below as black is confined to the outer web of each feather (note that markings are black, not grey, when fresh, thus

darker than *kumlieni*). Subspecies *kumlieni* and *thayeri* often hybridize where their ranges overlap, in north Hudson Bay and east Baffin Island, identification of hybrids being extremely difficult.

DISTRIBUTION AND STATUS North Atlantic. Breeds colonially or solitarily on cliffs and offshore islands. Total population figures not well known, possibly under 100,000 pairs with perhaps 10,000-100,000 pairs in Greenland. Dispersal southwards of northern populations with young birds moving further than adults; some populations are resident, eg southern Greenland. *L. g. glaucoides* breeds Greenland (occasionally Iceland?); some birds resident, but most winter south mainly to Iceland and Faeroes, with some reaching north and north-west Europe and occasionally further south. *L. g. kumlieni* breeds north-east Canada; winters south to eastern North America, mostly from Labrador to Great Lakes and Virginia, occasionally Florida, with odd individuals north-west Europe. *L. g. thayeri* breeds arctic Canada and west Greenland; winters on Pacific coast from British Columbia to Baja California (probably also elsewhere but overlooked), rare north-east North America and recorded only very rarely north-west Europe. Breeding population in Greenland heavily hunted, with over 20% taken for food every year.

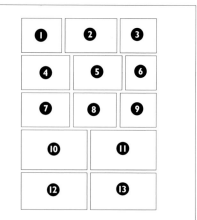

1 **Glaucous Gull** (adult breeding, Siberia, June)
2 **Glaucous Gull** (adult non-breeding, Norfolk, England)
3 **Glaucous Gull** (first winter)
4 **Glaucous Gull** (first summer, Florida, USA)
5 **Glaucous Gull** (first winter, Co. Donegal, Ireland, March)
6 **Glaucous Gull** (adult breeding, June)
7 **Iceland Gull** (presumed) subspecies *L. g. thayeri* (first winter, Co. Cork, Ireland, February)
8 **Iceland Gull** subspecies *L. g. kumlieni* (first summer, Canada, May)
9 **Iceland Gull** (first winter, Norfolk, England, January)
10 **Iceland Gull** subspecies *L. g. kumlieni* (adult non-breeding)
11 **Iceland Gull** (first winter, Scotland, January)
12 **Iceland Gull** subspecies *L. g. thayeri* (adult breeding)
13 **Iceland Gull** (adult, Co. Donegal, Ireland, March)

GULLS

HERRING GULL

Larus argentatus L 61 cm (24 in), WS 147 cm (58 in)

Large grey-mantled gull, almost circumpolar in the Northern Hemisphere, with white head and underparts, yellow bill with red spot, pinkish legs, and blackish primary tips with two white mirrors. Adult plumage acquired in fourth year.

IDENTIFICATION Juvenile Head streaked greyish-brown. Mantle, scapulars and back greyish-brown with paler fringes; rump and uppertail-coverts slightly paler. Underparts streaked greyish-brown. Primaries and secondaries dark brown, paler inner primaries forming pale window; wing-coverts streaked greyish-brown. Tail base whitish, merging into blackish-brown subterminal band. Bill black, pinkish at base; iris dark brown; legs dull flesh-coloured. **First-year** In winter as juvenile, but head and underparts whiter, upperparts less scaly. By summer progressively paler, wings and tail worn and faded, and clear grey scapulars appear. **Second-year** In winter, head white with strong brown streaking. Mantle, scapulars and back progressively greyer; rump and underparts white. Outer primaries and secondary bar blackish, with inner primaries greyish, thus window more conspicuous; coverts greyer with variable brown barring. Black tail band less extensive than first-year. By summer, head and underparts whiter and mantle and back clearer grey; wings and tail faded and worn, contrast with grey saddle. Bill becoming yellowish with dark subterminal band; iris pale. **Third-year** As adult non-breeding, but more extensive black on wing tips reaching to primary coverts and alula, and no mirrors; variable brown on inner wing-coverts and tail. Black subterminal band on bill. By summer, head white, wings and tail faded, white primary tips reduced or lacking. **Adult non-breeding** Head white, heavily streaked brown, especially on nape. Mantle, scapulars and back clear grey; rump and underparts white. Wings grey with white trailing edge; black on outer primaries clear cut, decreasing inwards to sixth primary, all primaries tipped white and with white mirror on outer two. Bill yellow with red gonydeal spot; iris yellow; legs flesh-coloured (yellowish on some birds from north-east Europe). **Adult breeding** Head white, reduced white primary tips, bare parts brighter. Four races currently recognized: *argenteus* is smallest, with pale mantle; nominate *argentatus* and *smithsonianus* larger and generally darker above, with less black in wing tips, young *smithsonianus* also being much darker overall; and *vegae* (probably a separate species) is big, with powerful bill, very dark mantle and more black in primaries. (Note that relationships within '*L argentatus* complex' unclear, controversial and inconsistent: all 'forms' variously treated as subspecies or as separate species; some considered subspecies of Lesser Black-backed Gull. Variables include size, darkness of plumage, pattern of wing tip,

and bill and leg colours. See Grant 1986 for comprehensive treatment, including hybrids.)

DISTRIBUTION AND STATUS Almost circumpolar in Northern Hemisphere. Breeds usually colonially in a wide variety of habitats including roofs in North America, Europe, and north-east Asia. Total population unknown but very large with over 1,000,000 pairs in the Palearctic and over 150,000 pairs in eastern North America. Populations now stabilizing after rapid expansion throughout the first half of this century; now considered a pest. *L. a. argentatus*: Scandinavia, Finland and south-east Baltic east to White Sea. *L. a. argenteus*: Iceland, Faeroes, British Isles, north-west France, Netherlands, and Belgium. *L. a. vegae*: northern Siberia. *L. a. smithsonianus*: North America. Most northern populations disperse south in winter reaching Central America, Iberian Peninsula and the South China Sea. Vagrants south to Venezuela, Kenya, South Africa, Thailand.

ARMENIAN GULL

Larus armenicus L 60 cm (24 in) WS 140 cm (55 in)

Breeds on the Armenian lakes. Formerly included within Yellow-legged Gull, but differs in plumage and soft parts. Adult plumage acquired in fourth year.

IDENTIFICATION First-year In winter, head white, with fine brownish-grey streaking on face and crown, coarser brownish-grey streaking on nape and hindneck (less extensive than on Herring Gull). Mantle and scapulars white or pale greyish with dark grey bars. Underparts whitish, with brownish-grey spotting on breast sides and flanks. Outer primaries and secondaries blackish-brown, usually with paler window on inner primaries (Herring Gull has paler wings with more pronounced window); wing-coverts paler than primaries. Tail has solid blackish-brown band contrasting with white rump and tail base (less defined on Herring Gull). Bill all black; legs dull grey-flesh. Generally 'cleaner' than Herring Gull: whiter-headed and whiter-bodied. **Second-year** Head white, with faint greyish-brown face streaking; hindneck coarsely streaked, giving collared effect. Mantle and scapulars variable, but generally plain ash-grey. Outer wing and secondaries dark brown, contrasting with lighter coverts and pale window on inner primaries. Bill variable, some having yellow base. **Third-year** Head white, with greyish-brown on hindneck. Mantle and scapulars ash-grey as adult; wings as adult, with some dark markings on coverts. Bill deep yellow with black tip or subterminal band; legs yellowish. **Adult** Head and underparts white, in winter with light brownish marks on face and crown and more coarsely marked on nape and hindneck (Herring Gull more heavily marked, but Yellow-legged similar). Upperparts ash-grey, darker than Herring Gull (but paler than Lesser Black-backed) and slightly darker than Yellow-legged. Black triangle on outer seven

primaries (more than on Yellow-legged or *argenteus* Herring Gull), each with small white tip; small white mirror on outer primary; grey bases of secondaries give clear subterminal band on underwing. Bill in winter deep yellow, with black subterminal band and indistinct red gonydeal spot; by spring bill more orange, with reduced subterminal, but red spot more noticeable. (Other members of 'Herring Gull complex' generally have paler yellow bill.) Legs yellow (paler on Yellow-legged, flesh-coloured on most Herring Gulls). Iris generally dark (unlike others of complex).

DISTRIBUTION AND STATUS Breeds Armenian lakes, eastern Turkey, north-west Iran. Breeds colonially on islands in Armenian mountain lakes at Lake Sevan (4,000 pairs) and Lake Arpilich (4,000+ pairs), with a total population of probably less than 10,000 pairs. However, few data available – low numbers and very restricted range. Some birds sedentary, others disperse in winter to the south-east Black Sea, the eastern Mediterranean and the northern Red Sea. Vagrant Bahrain.

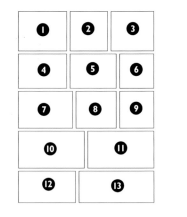

1 Herring Gull subspecies *L. a. argenteus* (adult breeding, Craigleith, Scotland, June)
2 Herring Gull subspecies *L. a. argenteus* (adult non-breeding, Scotland, January)
3 Herring Gull subspecies *L. a. smithsonianus* (juvenile, USA)
4 Herring Gull subspecies *L. a. argenteus* **or** *L. a. argentatus* (second winter, England)
5 Herring Gull subspecies *L. a. smithsonianus* (adult breeding, USA)
6 Herring Gull subspecific identity uncertain (adult breeding, Yemen, March)
7 Herring Gull subspecies *L. a. smithsonianus* (second winter, California, USA)
8 Herring Gull subspecific identity uncertain (adult non-breeding, Hong Kong, April)
9 Herring Gull subspecies *L. a. argenteus* (third summer, Scotland, July)
10 Herring Gull subspecific identity uncertain (apparently third winter, Mai Po, Hong Kong, February)
11 Armenian Gull (first winter, Tel Aviv, Israel)
12 Armenian Gull (adult breeding, Israel)
13 Armenian Gull (adult non-breeding, Israel, December)

GULLS

SLATY-BACKED GULL

Larus schistisagus L 64 cm (25 in), WS 147 cm (58 in)

A large white-headed, dark-mantled gull of the north-west Pacific Ocean, with yellow bill and pink legs, conspicuous white trailing edge to wing, and the blackish tips to the outer primaries usually separated from slate-grey upperwing by a whitish band. Adult plumage acquired in fourth year.

IDENTIFICATION Juvenile Head whitish, streaked brownish-grey. Mantle, scapulars and back greyish-brown, fringed paler grey; rump and uppertail-coverts whitish, barred brown. Underparts uniform greyish-brown, becoming brown-barred whitish on belly. Outer primaries, alula, primary coverts, secondaries and secondary coverts dark brown; inner primaries paler, forming window. Tail brownish, whiter at base. Bill blackish; legs pink. **First-year** In winter as juvenile, but head, upperparts and underparts paler; wings and tail faded. By summer, further fading: head whitish; saddle pale greyish-white, spotted brown; rump white. Bill pink at base. **Second-year** Head progressively whiter. Saddle becomes slate-blackish, contrasting with faded and whitish inner wing; rump and underparts white, tail dark. Primaries and secondaries blacker; coverts have whitish fringes. **Third-year** Similar to adult, but black wing tip more extensive and less well demarcated, extending to primary coverts, alula and secondary coverts; saddle browner than adult's, tail white with dark subterminal band, and underparts with light brown streaking. By summer, head whiter and mantle and coverts clearer slate-grey. Bill pink with dusky subterminal band. **Adult non-breeding** (fourth-winter) As breeding adult, but grey-brown streaking on nape and hindneck. **Adult breeding** Head white; saddle deep slate-grey; rump and underparts white. Upperwing deep slate-grey with conspicuous white trailing edge; blackish on outer primaries decreasing inwards, with one mirror on outermost two primaries; usually shows pale (whitish) band separating black primary tips from slaty rest of upperwing. From below, outer primaries appear grey, not black. Bill yellow with red spot near gonys; iris yellow; legs reddish-pink.

DISTRIBUTION AND STATUS North-west Pacific Ocean. Breeds colonially on islands, sea cliffs and cliff tops in north-east Siberia from Cape Navarin and Kamchatka south to Japan (Hokkaido, north-east Honshu) and Vladivostok. Total population c 100,000 pairs (Kamchatka estimates vary from 47,000 to 110,000 pairs). Some disperse into Bering Sea and Sea of Japan, others move south as far as China and Taiwan. Vagrants Aleutians, Pribilof Islands, Alaska and British Columbia.

YELLOW-LEGGED GULL

Larus cachinnans L 60 cm (24 in), WS 150 cm (59 in)

Essentially similar to Herring Gull, but with yellow legs; differs also in vocalizations and displays. Five subspecies in Europe and Asia.

IDENTIFICATION Differs structurally from Herring Gull in having long wings extending well past the tail, relatively longer legs, a flatter-topped, angular head profile and a very long-looking neck, appearing much slimmer and lighter than Herring Gull. Although leg colour normally differs from that of Herring Gull, some populations of Yellow-legged Gull (eg north-west Spain) contain small numbers of birds having legs pinkish or partly pink. **L. c. atlantis**: Size equal to or slightly larger than Herring Gull of race *argenteus*. Adult breeding has larger red gonydeal spot, prominent red eye-ring, and bright yellow legs; grey upperparts and upperwings are darker in tone, intermediate between *argenteus* and race *graellsii* of Lesser Black-backed Gull, with more black in primaries and only one mirror on outer primary. In winter, head often heavily streaked. First-year birds much darker and browner than Herring, with darker tail and darker inner primaries (window faint or lacking) and greater-covert bar (thus resembling Lesser Black-backed Gull). Bill brownish with paler base; iris dark; legs and feet brownish-pink. (The brown iris colour of immature Yellow-legged Gull is retained for a relatively long period, sometimes even into adult plumage.) **L. c. michahellis**: Bigger than *atlantis*, with upperparts and wings paler (only slightly darker than European Herring Gull) and with less black in primaries, but the white mirror on the first primary is large, and usually shows a white mirror also on second primary; inner webs of primaries somewhat paler than the mantle. In winter, head usually more or less unstreaked. First-years paler than *atlantis*, with paler inner primaries (window). Immatures more contrasty-looking than same-age Herring Gulls: darker (black-brown) outer primaries, darker tail band, but almost pure white uppertail-coverts, and much paler head and underparts. **L. c. cachinnans**: Averages larger than *argenteus* Herring; structural features as for other races of Yellow-legged, but even more pronounced. Adults have plumage much as *michahellis*, but grey upperparts and upperwings slightly paler, with less black and more white in wing tip. Immatures similar to *michahellis*, but even paler overall (and mainly white below). **L. c. barabensis and L. c. mongolicus**: These two Asian races have mantle colour generally similar to or darker than nominate and *michahellis*.

DISTRIBUTION AND STATUS Breeds colonially on islands, beaches, cliffs and occasionally roofs, from the Azores to Mongolia. *L. c. atlantis*: eastern Atlantic islands (Azores, Madeira, Canaries, possibly Cape Verdes, c 6,500 pairs), and perhaps Iberian Peninsula. *L. c. michahellis*: southern Europe, Mediterranean (under 100,000 pairs), western France, Morocco. *L. c. cachinnans*: Black Sea and Caspian Sea east to Kazakhstan. *L. c. barabensis*: central Asian steppes. *L. c. mongolicus*: east Altai to Lake Baikal and Mongolia. Total population unknown at present but large. Many populations currently increasing and expanding in range, even though egg-collecting regular at some colonies, especially in east of range. Some are culled in Spain to help protect Audouin's Gull. Some populations resident, but many move to coasts in winter: in west, many disperse to Mediterranean, Red Sea and Persian Gulf, also to Atlantic coast, while eastern races migrate to Indian Ocean and China Sea. In recent years, increasing numbers from colonies in south-west Europe and Mediterranean have dispersed north after breeding, *michahellis* regularly reaching North Sea (Britain, English Channel), while some nominate winter in south Baltic region and southern North Sea.

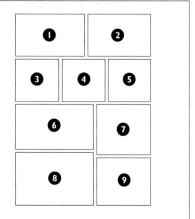

1 **Slaty-backed Gull** (left) (adult breeding, Commander Island, Bering Sea, June)
2 **Slaty-backed Gull** (adult breeding, Commander Island, Bering Sea, June)
3 **Slaty-backed Gull** (second summer, north Pacific Ocean, June)
4 **Slaty-backed Gull** (first summer, north Pacific Ocean, June)
5 **Yellow-legged Gull** subspecies *L. c. michahellis* (first summer, Morocco, April)
6 **Yellow-legged Gull** subspecies *L. c. michahellis* (adult breeding, Lesbos, Greece, May)
7 **Yellow-legged Gull** subspecies *L. c. michahellis* (second summer, Mallorca, March)
8 **Yellow-legged Gull** subspecific identification uncertain (first summer, worn)
9 **Yellow-legged Gull** subspecies *L. c. michahellis* (adult breeding, Morocco, April)

GULLS

LESSER BLACK-BACKED GULL

Larus fuscus L 56 cm (22 in), WS 140 cm (55 in)
Large non-hooded, black-backed gull of the
north-east Atlantic and north Siberia, with
yellow bill and yellow legs; upperpart colour
varies from blackish (northern *fuscus*) to slate-
grey (western *graellsii*). Adult plumage acquired
in fourth year.

IDENTIFICATION Juvenile Head brownish-
white, paler on forehead and chin, with darker
ear-coverts and eye crescent. Mantle, scapulars
and back dark brown, edged white (darker than
on Herring Gull and more contrast, especially
with whitish rump). Underparts greyish-white,
with blackish mottling on breast sides and
flanks; belly paler. Primaries and their coverts,
secondaries and greater coverts blackish,
forming broad dark trailing edge to wing; no
pale window on inner primaries; forewing-
coverts dark brown, edged white. Tail whitish
with contrasting blackish subterminal band. Bill
black; iris dark brown; legs dull flesh. **First-
year** In winter as juvenile, except ear-coverts
less prominent; mantle and scapulars more
uniformly dark, less scaly. Upperparts darker
than on either Herring or Great Black-backed
Gull. Head and underparts may become whiter.
By summer, head and underparts whiter,
mantle, scapulars and upperwing more uniform
and browner; old coverts faded to pale brown.
Second-year In winter, head white with
extensive dark streaking. Mantle and scapulars
with grey developing; rump white. Underparts
white, with blackish mottling on breast sides
and flanks. Outer wing and secondaries
blackish; coverts brown with paler fringes. Tail
white with narrower subterminal band. Bill pale
with dark tip, but variable; legs flesh-coloured.
By summer, head and underparts whiter,
mantle and scapulars clear slate-grey, blackish
wing areas faded to brown, and bill and legs
yellowish. **Third-year** In winter, head as
second-winter; underparts white with dark
streaking; rump white, mantle and scapulars
dark slate-grey. Wings as adult, but black on
outer wing more extensive and less well
demarcated, white primary tips smaller, only
one mirror; brown on inner wing. Tail white,
with subterminal band faint. Bill may have dark
subterminal band. By summer, head and
underparts white and upperwing faded. **Adult
non-breeding** (fourth-winter) Head and body
as third-winter; dark slate-grey upperparts and
wings, latter with white trailing edge; clear-cut
black wing tip with one or two mirrors, and
white tips to primaries; tail white. No black on
bill. **Adult breeding** Head and underparts
white; white primary tips reduced or lacking.
Bill and legs bright orange-yellow. *L. f. fuscus*
(Baltic and northern Norway to White Sea):
Adult's upperparts as dark as Great Black-
backed Gull, with little contrast with black wing
tips, and usually only one mirror; winter adults
have whiter head. *L. f. intermedius* (southern
Norway, Sweden, Denmark and north-east
Spain): Adult's upperparts between *fuscus* and
graellsii. *L. f. graellsii* (Iceland, British Isles,

Faeroes, Netherlands, France and Spain):
Upperparts dull smoky-grey (darker than most
Herring Gulls, but lacking blackish tone of
fuscus and *intermedius*), showing contrast with
black wing tip. *L. a. heuglini* (north-west Russia:
from Kola Peninsula to Taymyr Peninsula):
Upperparts similar to *graellsii*.
DISTRIBUTION AND STATUS Breeds colonially
on vegetated sea coasts, cliffs, islands and roofs
in the north-east Atlantic, from Scandinavia to
Spain, also northern Siberia. Total population
probably 250,000-300,000 pairs, with 175,000
pairs in the western Palearctic (88,700 pairs
British Isles). Population increasing since the
1940s and range expansion into North
America. Disperses south in winter to north-
east USA, western Europe, west Africa,
occasionally southern Africa, north-eastern
populations moving to area from Black and
Caspian Seas south to east Africa, and also
north-west India. Vagrant Pacific coast of
North America.

GREAT BLACK-HEADED GULL

Larus ichthyaetus L 69 cm (27 in), WS 160 cm
(63 in)
Large, distinctive Asian gull, with a full black
hood in breeding plumage, yellow bill with
black subterminal band and red tip, and yellow
legs; grey mantle and wings with black
subterminal primary tips. Adult plumage
acquired in fourth year.

IDENTIFICATION Juvenile Head white, with
dusky eye crescents; hindneck streaked. Mantle
and scapulars rich brown with paler edges,
imparting scaly impression; rump white.
Underparts white, with brownish-streaked
breast sides joining hindneck. Outer primaries,
coverts, alula, carpal bar and secondaries
brownish-black, with pale mid-wing panel. Tail
white with blackish subterminal band. Bill grey
with dark tip; iris dark; legs grey. **First-year** In
winter, mantle and scapulars clear pale grey,
sometimes brown; streaked hindcrown and
breast sides. Wings and tail unmoulted and
paler, especially mid-wing panel; brownish
coverts and dark secondary bar; broad tail
band. Bill may be yellowish with dark tip. By
summer, may acquire partial or full hood, wings
and tail faded, often with whitish wing panel,
and carpal bar reduced. **Second-year** In
winter, head as first-winter; upperparts mainly
grey, rump and underparts white. Wings mainly
grey; outer primaries and primary coverts
blackish, this decreasing inwards; secondaries
and lesser wing-coverts may be brownish. Tail
white with thinner black subterminal band. Bill
yellowish with black subterminal band; legs
greenish. In summer, partial or full hood
acquired, white primary tips reduced or lacking.
Bill and legs yellowish. **Third-year** As adult
winter, but more extensive black on outer
primaries and less white at tips; subterminal tail
band reduced. By summer acquires full hood,
while white primary tips reduced or lacking.
Adult non-breeding Head as first-winter.
Mantle and back grey; rump and underparts

white. Upperwing paler grey than mantle, with
white leading edge from carpal to primary tips,
and a subterminal black crescent across
primaries one to six; broad white trailing edge
along secondaries. Tail white. Bare parts as
second-winter. **Adult breeding** As non-
breeding adult, except full black hood with
white crescents above and below eye. White
primaries reduced through wear. Bill yellow,
with black subterminal band and red tip; iris
dark brown; legs yellow.
DISTRIBUTION AND STATUS Asia. Breeds
colonially on barren islands in lakes and inland
seas, with a preference for saline soils,
discontinuously from the Black Sea to Lake
Balkhash, north-west Mongolia and possibly
northern China and Tibet. Total population
unknown at present, but large with *c* 25,000
pairs in Russia, being especially numerous
around the northern Caspian Sea. Disperses
south in winter to eastern Mediterranean, Red
Sea, southern Caspian Sea, Middle East,
northern Indian Ocean coast. Increasingly
recorded in Europe, vagrants Madeira,
Canaries, Kenya, Japan.

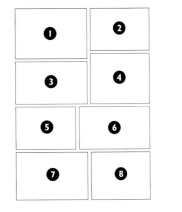

1 Lesser Black-backed Gull subspecies *L. f.
graellsii* (adult breeding, Craigleith, Scotland,
June)
2 Lesser Black-backed Gull subspecies *L. f.
graellsii* (adult non-breeding, Norfolk, England,
January)
3 Lesser Black-backed Gull (third winter or
fourth winter with still growing primaries,
Liverpool, England)
4 Lesser Black-backed Gull subspecies *L. f.
graellsii* (first summer moulting to second
winter, Cornwall, England, August)
5 Lesser Black-backed Gull subspecies *L. f.
graellsii* (adult breeding, Skokholm Island,
Wales, May)
6 Great Black-headed Gull (first winter and
second winter, India, January)
7 Great Black-headed Gull (first summer,
Eilat, Israel, April)
8 Great Black-headed Gull (adult breeding,
Israel, March)

GULLS

BROWN-HEADED GULL

Larus brunnicephalus L 42 cm (17 in), WS ?
Medium-sized Asiatic hooded gull. Adult plumage acquired in second year.
IDENTIFICATION Juvenile Head white; crown, nape and ear-coverts brownish-grey. Saddle and mantle brownish-grey with paler edges; rump and underparts white. Primaries and secondaries blackish-brown, forming broad dark trailing edge; brownish carpal bar and median coverts, otherwise greyish. Tail white with brownish subterminal band. From similar-aged Black-headed Gull by larger size, heavier bill, dark trailing edge to wing and no mirrors. **First-year** As juvenile but head whiter, developing partial brown hood in summer. Saddle and mantle becoming clearer grey; wings and tail faded (unmoulted). Bill and legs become redder. **Adult non-breeding** (second-winter) Head white, with dusky lower nape, ear-coverts, and eye crescent. Saddle and mantle pale grey; rump and underparts white. Tail white. Primaries blackish at tip, with white mirror on the two outermost, black decreasing inwards, with small white tips; outer primary bases white, becoming greyer inwards to mantle (thus similar pattern to Grey-headed Gull). Underwing grey, blackish primaries with visible mirrors. **Adult breeding** Pattern and plumage as adult non-breeding, except for chocolate-brown hood. From Black-headed Gull by pale iris, heavier bill, larger size, and upperwing pattern recalling Grey-headed Gull.
DISTRIBUTION AND STATUS Breeds colonially on islands in mountainous lakes and adjacent marshes of central southern Asia in Turkestan, northern India, Tibet, China and southern Mongolia. Total population unknown at present with few data available, but not rare *eg* 1,000 pairs breeding in Pamirs (Tadjikistan). Dispersal southwards towards coasts of southern Asia from Arabian Peninsula, coastal India and Sri Lanka eastwards to coastal Indo-China where common; some winter inland in Nepal.

GREY-HEADED GULL

Larus cirrocephalus L 42 cm (17 in), WS 102 cm (40 in)
Medium-sized, grey-hooded gull of South America and Africa. Adult plumage acquired in third year.
IDENTIFICATION Juvenile Head whitish, with grey-brown partial hood separated from mantle by white hindcollar. Mantle, scapulars and back brownish with paler feather edges; rump pale grey. Underparts white; breast sides greyish-brown (from mantle). Outer two or three primaries blackish-brown; inner primaries greyer with blackish tips and white bases, which with white primary coverts form white patch in middle of outer wing; dusky secondaries form dark trailing edge with inner primaries; greater coverts grey, tipped brown, median coverts browner. Underwing dusky, with primaries darker. Tail white with narrow black subterminal band. Bill yellow-flesh with dark tip;

iris brown; legs dull flesh. **First-year** In winter as juvenile, but head white, with dusky ear spot and greyish-brown mottling on crown. Mantle and scapulars uniform grey. Wing and tail unmoulted, blackish and brown areas faded. By summer similar to first-winter, but with partial grey hood; dark of wings and tail further faded (especially carpal bar). **Second-year** In winter resembles non-breeding adult, but bare parts duller, more black than white on outer primaries, mirrors on outer primaries smaller, and secondaries dusky, forming indistinct trailing edge to wing. By summer, acquires full or partial grey adult hood; bare parts much as breeding adult, but iris dark. **Adult non-breeding** (third-winter) Head as first-winter or with ghost image of hood. Mantle and scapulars uniform grey. More white than black on outer primaries, with white mirrors on outer two primaries; small white tips to primaries three to eight. Underwing dusky. Tail white. Pale iris. **Adult breeding** As adult non-breeding, but full dove-grey hood from nape to throat, with darker rear border. Whitish crescents above and below eye and whitish iris contrast with red orbital ring. White hindneck; mantle grey, rump and tail white; underparts white, occasionally with pinkish flush. Outer primaries black, black decreasing inwards, outer two with white mirrors; bases of inner primaries, primary coverts and alula white, forming white leading edge to outer wing; rest of wing grey (whitish tips on primaries reduced or lacking). Bill and legs crimson. Nominate *cirrocephalus* of South America is larger than African *poiocephalus*, and has paler saddle and upperwings and larger wing mirrors.
DISTRIBUTION AND STATUS Breeds colonially on rocky islands, dunes and marshes in South America and Africa. Total population probably under 50,000 pairs but not well known: most in central Africa. Most populations sedentary or disperse only a short distance to coasts. *L. c. cirrocephalus*: Coastal Ecuador and Peru (c 1,000 pairs), Brazil, Argentina, Uruguay, Bolivia and Paraguay (eastern South American population c 10,000 pairs). *L. c. poiocephalus*: Coastal and inland rivers of west Africa, also discontinuously from Ethiopia along Rift Valley lakes to Malawi and southern Africa, also Madagascar. Vagrants Panama, Spain, northern Red Sea.

HARTLAUB'S or KING GULL

Larus hartlaubii L 38 cm (15 in), WS 91 cm (36 in)
Medium-sized, pale-headed gull of southern Africa. Adult plumage acquired in second year.
IDENTIFICATION A scavenging species found on the coast, at dumps and occasionally inland; follows ships and trawlers. Has adapted to breeding on buildings. **Juvenile** Head white. Saddle and mantle brown with darker centres and buffish fringes; rump and underparts white. Primaries tipped black, black decreasing inwards, with white apical spots; inner primaries and secondaries grey, with darker trailing edge; coverts as saddle, primary coverts

brown. Tail white with narrow blackish tip. Bill blackish; iris dark; legs brownish-red. **First-year** As juvenile, but saddle becomes clearer grey, wings and tail faded (unmoulted). From corresponding Grey-headed Gull by thinner blackish bill, whiter head and tail, and shorter legs. **Adult non-breeding** (second-year) Head white, saddle pale grey, rump and underparts white. Outer three or four primaries blackish, black decreasing in extent inwards, with two white mirrors on outer primaries; rest of wing pale grey, except for distinctive white leading edge on outer primaries. Tail white. **Adult breeding** As non-breeding adult, but with pale lavender hood with darker necklace. Iris dark, but variable. From Grey-headed Gull by smaller, darker bill, shorter, darker legs and generally dark iris, as well as smaller size.
DISTRIBUTION AND STATUS Breeds colonially on low flat islands in sewage lagoons and salt works, occasionally on buildings and inland, from Swakopmund (Namibia) to Dyer Island (Cape Province, South Africa). Total population c 12,000 pairs (possibly 15,000 pairs) with 28% at Robben Island, off Cape Town, and only 12% in Namibia. Essentially sedentary, vagrant east to Durban. Population increased from 1950s to late 1970s especially around Cape Town. Often suffers breeding failure and may be displaced by larger Swift Terns. Vulnerable to human disturbance at breeding sites and to some predation. Range overlaps with that of Grey-headed Gull, with which it occasionally hybridizes.

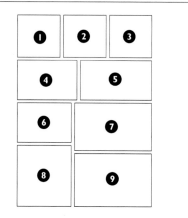

1 Brown-headed Gull (adult non-breeding, India)
2 Brown-headed Gull (adult acquiring breeding plumage, Thailand, March)
3 Brown-headed Gull (adult non-breeding, Sri Lanka, March)
4 Brown-headed Gull (adult acquiring breeding plumage, Sri Lanka, March)
5 Grey-headed Gull (adult non-breeding)
6 Grey-headed Gull (adult breeding, Kenya, March)
7 Grey-headed Gull (adult breeding, Gambia, November)
8 Hartlaub's Gull (adult non-breeding)
9 Hartlaub's Gull (adults moulting from breeding to non-breeding, South Africa)

GULLS

SILVER GULL

Larus novaehollandiae L 41 cm (16 in), WS 93 cm (37 in)
Medium-sized, white-headed gull of Australia, with red bill and legs, grey mantle and wings, and black primary tips with white mirrors. Adult plumage acquired in second year.
IDENTIFICATION The only small gull in Australia; well adapted to urbanization and inland foraging, considered a pest at airports. **Juvenile** Head white. Saddle and mantle brown with darker centres and buffish fringes; rump and underparts white. Primaries tipped black, this decreasing inwards, with white apical spots; inner primaries and secondaries grey, with darker trailing edge; wing-coverts as saddle, primary coverts brown. Tail white, with narrow black subterminal tip. Bill blackish; iris dark; legs brownish-red. **First-year** As juvenile, but saddle becomes clearer grey, wings and tail unmoulted and faded. Bill blackish. **Adult non-breeding** (second-year) Head white, saddle pale grey, rump and underparts white. Outer three or four primaries blackish, this decreasing in extent inwards, with two white mirrors on outer primaries; rest of wing pale grey, except for distinctive white leading edge to primaries. Underwing dusky grey with white mirrors. Tail white. **Adult breeding** As non-breeding adult, but with brighter red bill and legs. Iris white with red orbital ring.
DISTRIBUTION AND STATUS Australasia. Breeds colonially (occasionally solitarily) on small offshore islands and on brackish and freshwater lakes in Australia, Tasmania, New Caledonia, and the Loyalty Islands. Total population unknown but over 500,000 pairs at 200 sites in Australia – Australian population increasing especially in the south. Limited dispersal towards and around the Australian coast.

RED-BILLED GULL

Larus scopulinus L 37 cm (15 in), WS 89 cm (35 in)
Medium-sized, white-headed gull with crimson bill and legs, pale grey mantle and upperwings, and black wing tips with a single mirror on first and second primaries. Previously placed with Silver Gull, but New Zealand birds smaller in wing length, culmen, tail and tarsus, with smaller wing mirrors.
IDENTIFICATION Mainly coastal, rarer inland; predominantly a scavenger. Similar to larger Australian Silver Gull, but has two smaller wing mirrors (Silver can have three); basal white tongue on first three primaries longer and broader than on Silver Gull; may have pinkish breast. **Juvenile** Much as Silver Gull. Head white. Mantle brown, feathers subterminally darker brown with buff fringes; rump and underparts white. Primaries have black tips with white apical spots and two small mirrors; secondaries grey, with darker trailing edge; wing-coverts as mantle. Tail white with narrow dark subterminal band. Bill, legs, iris and eye-ring dark brown. From Black-billed Gull by white head, heavier thicker dark bill, larger size, different wing pattern. **First-year** As Silver Gull; similar to juvenile, but saddle becomes clear grey. From Black-billed Gull by white head without dark crown and ear spot, heavier thicker bill, larger size, and upperwing pattern. **Adult non-breeding** (second-winter) Head white. Mantle and back pale grey, rump and underparts white. Outer three or four primaries mainly black, black decreasing inwards to subterminal marks by seventh or eighth, with white apical spots; mirrors on first and second primaries; white leading edge to outer wing from primary coverts; rest of wing pale grey. Tail white. Bill, orbital ring, eyelids and feet scarlet; iris white. **Adult breeding** Bare parts brighter; otherwise as adult non-breeding. Red legs and bill and distinctive upperwing (black primary tips) separate it from Black-billed Gull. Has bred with latter, and fertile hybrids between the two have bred with Red-billed Gulls.
DISTRIBUTION AND STATUS New Zealand. Breeds colonially or solitarily on islands, rocky beaches, and occasionally inland lakes on both North and South Island with most on the east coasts; also Stewart, Chathams, Snares, Bounties, Auckland, and Campbell Islands. Total population probably over 500,000 pairs. Despite low breeding productivity has increased dramatically this century. Vagrant Kermadecs.

BLACK-BILLED GULL

Larus bulleri L 36 cm (14 in), WS ?
Medium-sized, non-hooded, very pale gull of New Zealand, with black bill and variable dull red or blackish legs; adult upperwing pattern recalls Black-headed Gull. Adult plumage acquired in second year.
IDENTIFICATION Juvenile Head white, with greyish-brown mottling on crown, lower nape, hindneck and ear-coverts. Saddle and mantle grey with brownish spots and paler edges, shading to pale grey on rump and whitish on uppertail-coverts. Underparts white. Primaries and secondaries greyish-white, with narrow blackish tips and some black shafts on outer primaries; wing-coverts with brownish tips forming dark carpal bar. Underwing greyish, primaries blacker. Tail white, occasionally darker on central feathers. Bill pink or orange with dark tip; iris brown; legs flesh-pink. **First-year** As juvenile, but paler, with whiter head, saddle becoming clearer grey and losing brownish. Head and wing patterns differ from those of Red-billed Gull. **Adult non-breeding** (second-year) May have faint grey wash over crown, giving slight hooded effect; greyish wash on breast. **Adult breeding** Head, underparts and tail white. Saddle pale pearl-grey; rump and uppertail-coverts white. Outer primaries and primary coverts white, with small blackish tips to primaries; rest of upperwing pale silver-grey (as Black-headed Gull). Underwing greyish; primaries darker, with small white mirrors visible. Bill blackish with reddish base; iris pale; legs variable from blackish to brownish-red. From Red-billed Gull by generally paler plumage, smaller size and daintier jizz, thinner black bill, and different upperwing pattern more reminiscent of Black-headed Gull.
DISTRIBUTION AND STATUS New Zealand. Breeds colonially almost exclusively inland on islands in rivers and along shores of lakes mainly in South Island with fewer in North Island. Although the total population of *c* 100,000 pairs has historically increased, it is vulnerable at many colonies. Main threat is habitat deterioration from alien vegetation overgrowth. Limited dispersal to larger estuaries and coasts mainly either side of the Cook Strait. Vagrants Stewart Island, Snares Islands. Occasionally hybridizes with Red-billed Gull. Formerly taken for food by Maoris.

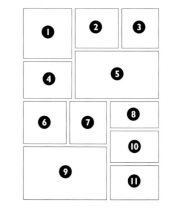

1 **Silver Gull** (adult breeding, Brisbane, Australia, January)
2 **Silver Gull** (first summer, Brisbane, Australia, January)
3 **Silver Gull** (adult, Queensland, May)
4 **Silver Gull** (juvenile, Victoria, Australia, February)
5 **Red-billed Gull** (adult breeding, New Zealand, November)
6 **Red-billed Gull** (juvenile, New Zealand, January)
7 **Red-billed Gull** (sub-adult, New Zealand)
8 **Red-billed Gull** (adult breeding, New Zealand, November)
9 **Black-billed Gull** (adult breeding, New Zealand, November)
10 **Black-billed Gull** (adult breeding, New Zealand)
11 **Black-billed Gull** (second year, New Zealand, March)

GULLS

BROWN-HOODED GULL

Larus maculipennis L 37 cm (15 in), WS ?
Medium-sized South American gull, dark-hooded in summer plumage, with red bill and red legs and an upperwing pattern recalling Black-headed Gull. Adult plumage acquired in second year.

IDENTIFICATION Resembles Black-headed Gull in size, jizz and wing pattern. **Juvenile** Head white, with brownish-grey on crown, nape and ear-coverts. Saddle and mantle greyish-brown with darker centres and buff edges; rump and underparts white. Outer two primaries blackish-brown, with white mirrors near tip; inner primaries greyish-white, with decreasing blackish tips inwards; secondaries blackish-brown, forming darkish trailing edge; tertials edged brown, and coverts grey with brownish edges. Underwing greyish, primaries darker. Tail white with black subterminal band. Bill reddish with black tip; iris brown; legs orange-brown. From corresponding Grey-headed Gull by white mirrors on outer primaries, and paler head. **First-year** As juvenile, but head whiter with more conspicuous dark ear-coverts, becoming partial hood by summer; upperparts become clearer grey, bill and legs more red, and tail may lose subterminal band. **Adult non-breeding** (second-winter) Head as first-year. Saddle pale grey, rump white. Outer five or six primaries white, forming white leading edge to wing with variable narrow black tips; rest of upperwing pale grey. Underwing whitish, coverts darker. Tail white. **Adult breeding** As non-breeding adult, but with chocolate-brown hood, white eye crescents; bill and legs dark crimson-red. From Andean and Grey-headed Gulls by smaller size, different wing pattern, and chocolate-brown (not dark brown or grey) hood in summer.

DISTRIBUTION AND STATUS South America. Breeds usually colonially mainly on freshwater and alkaline lakes, also marshes, beaches and inland from c 40°S in Chile and c 33°S in Uruguay southwards through Argentina to Tierra del Fuego. Also breeds Falklands (600 pairs) and possibly also southern Brazil. Total population probably 50,000-100,000 pairs but few data; common in Chile and Argentina. Relatively sedentary with limited dispersal to larger rivers and coastal areas, reaches northern Chile and eastern Brazil.

BLACK-HEADED GULL

Larus ridibundus L 38 cm (15 in), WS 104 cm (41 in)
Small European and Asian gull with brown (not black) hood in summer which extends only onto nape; pale grey above, with prominent white leading edge to outer wing and blackish tips to first six to eight primaries, red legs and red bill. Adult plumage acquired in second year.

IDENTIFICATION **Juvenile** Chin, throat and hindcollar white, separating partial ginger-buff hood from mantle. Mantle, scapulars, lower hindneck and breast sides rich ginger-brown,

with paler feather edges giving scaled appearance; rump and underparts mainly white. Outer webs of outer three or four primaries blackish-brown, with whitish inner webs; remaining primaries grey with blackish tips, joining with blackish secondaries to form dark trailing edge to wing; greater coverts grey, forming pale mid-wing panel, with brown carpal bar on fore coverts. Tail white, with narrow blackish-brown subterminal band. Bill yellowish-flesh with blackish tip; legs yellow-flesh. **First-year** Much as juvenile, but by winter head whiter, with blackish ear spot; mantle and scapulars uniform pale grey, extending to breast sides; brown and blackish-brown on wings faded. In summer, has variable blackish-brown hood; wings and tail further worn and faded, and legs and bill become more orange. **Adult non-breeding** (second-winter) Head and body much as first-year, head with two dusky bands across crown. Primaries and primary coverts whiter than first-year, with black outer web of first primary and black tips to up to six to eight primaries; rest of upperwing pale grey, with thin white leading and trailing edges. Underwing with dark primaries, but not secondaries. Tail all white. Bill red with dark tip; legs dark red. **Adult breeding** As adult non-breeding, except blackish-brown hood to nape, with white crescents above and below eye; some show pinkish flush on underparts. Bare parts brighter.

DISTRIBUTION AND STATUS Breeds colonially mainly inland on freshwater lakes and marshes, moors, sand dunes and beaches in north-east North America, southern Greenland, Iceland, most of Europe, Asia to Kamchatka, south-east Russia and north-east China. Total population c 2,000,000 pairs with a western Europe estimate of 1,500,000-1,800,000 pairs (300,000 pairs Sweden, 200,000 pairs British Isles). Rapid population increase and range extension this century (Iceland 1911, Greenland 1969, Canada 1977). Dispersal southwards especially of northern populations wintering west and east Africa (occasionally South Africa), Red Sea and Persian Gulf, India and Indo-China. Vagrants California, West Indies.

SLENDER-BILLED GULL

Larus genei L 43 cm (17 in), WS 105 cm (41 in)
Medium-sized Eurasian and north African white-headed gull, with red bill and legs, an upperwing pattern recalling Black-headed Gull, but at all ages distinguished by characteristic shape of bill, head and neck giving distinctive jizz. Adult plumage acquired in second year.

IDENTIFICATION **Juvenile** Head white, with buff and grey markings on crown and hindneck, indistinct ear spot. Mantle, scapulars and sides of breast grey-brown (not ginger-brown as on Black-headed Gull); rump and underparts white. Upperwing with white on outer primaries, primary coverts and alula more extensive than on Black-headed Gull, but less black on inner primary tips; carpal bar paler brown than on Black-headed. Tail white with blackish subterminal band. Bill and legs orange-flesh; iris

brown, becoming pale. **First-year** Head white, with variable dark eye crescent and ear spot. Mantle and scapulars pale grey. Wings as juvenile, but blackish and brown areas faded paler; carpal bar pale brown. By summer, ear spot lacking, browns on upperwing further faded (carpal bar hardly noticeable). Bill and legs orange-flesh; iris pale. **Adult non-breeding** (second-winter) Wing and tail patterns as adult breeding. Eye crescent and ear spot usually lacking. Underparts may have pink flush. Wings and tail as adult Black-headed Gull, but more white on outer primaries. Bill dark red; iris variable but pale; legs orange-red. **Adult breeding** Head white; underparts white with pinkish flush. Upperparts pale grey; rump and tail white. Wings pale grey, with white leading edge to outer wing and black tips to outer six or seven primaries (similar to Black-headed Gull). Bill dark red with blackish tip; iris pale (white to yellow or greenish); legs red.

DISTRIBUTION AND STATUS Breeds colonially in coastal and inland seas, and Asian steppe lakes discontinuously from Senegal and Mauritania, south and east Iberia, Mediterranean and Black Seas, Asia Minor and Middle East, to Kazakhstan, Afghanistan, Pakistan and north-west India. Total population 75,000-125,000 pairs with most around the Black Sea (up to 50,000 pairs), Europe 2,000-3,000 pairs. Some populations sedentary, others disperse southwards.

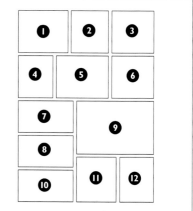

1 **Brown-hooded Gull** (adult breeding)
2 **Brown-hooded Gull** (adult breeding)
3 **Brown-hooded Gull** (adult non-breeding)
4 **Black-headed Gull** (probably second winter, Kent, England, October)
5 **Black-headed Gull** (adult breeding at nest, Norfolk, England, June)
6 **Black-headed Gull** (juvenile, England)
7 **Black-headed Gull** (first winter, Merseyside, England)
8 **Black-headed Gull** (adult non-breeding, Sussex, England, October)
9 **Black-headed Gull** (adult breeding, feeding frenzy, Norfolk, England, June)
10 **Slender-billed Gull** (adults breeding)
11 **Slender-billed Gull** (atypical adult or possibly second summer, Israel, April)
12 **Slender-billed Gull** (first summer, North Yemen, March)

GULLS

BONAPARTE'S GULL

Larus philadelphia L 31 cm (12 in), WS 82 cm (32 in)

Small tree-nesting North American gull, dark-hooded in summer, with black bill and red legs; wing pattern generally similar to Black-headed Gull's. Adult plumage acquired in second year.

IDENTIFICATION **Juvenile** Head white, with crown, eye crescent and ear spot blackish (less brown than Black-headed Gull). Mantle, scapulars, back and breast sides brown, lacking ginger tone of Black-headed. Rump and underparts white. Outer webs of outer three or four primaries blackish, inner webs white; inner primaries pale grey, tipped black, with small white spots at tip from third primary inwards; secondaries blackish, and with dark primary tips form dark subterminal trailing edge to wing; coverts grey, with blackish-brown carpal bar, and blackish outer primary coverts. Underwing shows translucent wedge on outer primaries (different from Black-headed). Tail white with blackish subterminal band. Bill black; iris dark brown; legs pale flesh. **First-year** Head as juvenile, but pale dusky crown and grey nape. Mantle, scapulars and back uniform grey, this extending to breast sides. Wings and tail as juvenile, unmoulted and faded. By summer, acquires partial blackish-grey hood, loses grey on nape and breast sides; wings and tail further faded and worn. **Adult non-breeding** (second-winter) Head and body as first-year; underparts may have pinkish flush. Upperwing grey, with prominent white leading edge to outer wing and with blackish tips to outer six to nine primaries. Underwing shows blackish tips (unlike Black-headed) to six to nine primaries only. Secondaries wholly white. Tail white. Black bill may have red base. **Adult breeding** As non-breeding adult, but with full blackish-grey hood from nape to throat, with white crescents above and below eye; pinkish flush on underparts; whitish tips to primaries reduced or lacking. Bill black; legs orange-red.

DISTRIBUTION AND STATUS North America. Breeds non-colonially in spruce and tamaracks in lakes and ponds in the coniferous forest belt from Alaska south to British Columbia and east to Hudson Bay and possibly Maine. Total population 85,000-175,000 pairs. Dispersal in flocks (sometimes very large) ahead of the winter freeze southwards to the Pacific coast and south to Mexico, and on the Atlantic coast south to Florida and the northern Caribbean; regular Bermuda. In mild winters less dispersive. Vagrant Japan, Hawaii, Europe.

SAUNDERS'S GULL

Larus saundersi L 32 cm (13 in), WS ?
Small Chinese gull, hooded in summer, with stubby black bill, dark red legs and diagnostic blackish patch on underwing. Adult plumage acquired in second year. Classified Endangered.

IDENTIFICATION Small size and underwing pattern diagnostic; saddle darker than on other hooded Asian gulls, and small bill recalls that of Gull-billed Tern. **Juvenile** Head brownish-grey, with darker ear-coverts and hindcrown; forehead, chin and throat white. Saddle and mantle brownish-grey with browner edges; rump and underparts white. Outer two primaries blackish, becoming whiter on three to five, remainder darkish-grey; secondaries darkish grey, with browner trailing edge to wing; brownish tip to coverts form 'M' across upperwing. Tail white with narrow black subterminal band, outer feathers white. Bill stubby, blackish; legs brownish-red. **First-year** Head as juvenile but whiter, with greyish-brown crown and darker ear-coverts, becoming partial hood by summer. Saddle becomes clear darkish grey. **Adult non-breeding** Head as first-year. Saddle clear dark bluish-grey; rump, tail and underparts white. Outer four or five primaries and primary coverts white, forming white leading edge to wing, with small black subterminal tips on primaries two to five; remainder of upperwing dark bluish-grey, secondaries with narrow white trailing edge. Underwing greyish-white, with diagnostic black wedge on outer primaries and translucent inner primaries. **Adult breeding** As non-breeding adult, but blackish hood sharply demarcated from nape to throat.

DISTRIBUTION AND STATUS Coastal China. Discovered breeding only in 1984, colonially in coastal salt marshes in four Chinese provinces (Liaoning *c* 600-700 pairs, Hebei *c* 25 pairs, Shandong *c* 200 pairs, Jiangsu 300-750 pairs) with a total population of under 5,000 birds and probably nearer 3,000 birds. All of the 7 known colonies are either being developed or are planned for development. Oil exploration and land reclamation have further reduced available salt marsh habitat elsewhere. Further threats include egg-collection, general human disturbance causing colony desertion, and pollution. Unless breeding habitat is protected extinction seems likely in the next decade. Dispersal after breeding to coastal eastern China, southern Japan, South Korea, Hong Kong, Taiwan and northern Vietnam.

ANDEAN GULL

Larus serranus L 48 cm (19 in), WS ?
Medium-sized to large South American gull, black-hooded in summer, with dark red bill and legs, and grey mantle and wings, latter with diagnostic pattern above and below. Adult plumage acquired in second year.

IDENTIFICATION Large for a hooded gull, with robust jizz and heavy body and broader and more rounded wings, as well as diagnostic wing pattern. **Juvenile** Head greyish-brown, with darker ear-coverts and paler forehead and nape. Mantle and saddle greyish-brown with whitish edges; rump grey; tail white with narrow black subterminal band. Underparts white, with greyish-brown sides to breast. Outer primaries and primary coverts blackish, joining with dark secondaries to form dark trailing edge to wing; coverts greyish-brown with whitish edges, forming open 'M' across back. Bill and legs blackish. **First-year** As juvenile, but head whiter, saddle becomes grey, wing-coverts become greyer, and partial hood develops by summer. Primaries and secondaries have blackish tips, three outer primaries showing white mirrors at tip; whitish wedge on outer wing developing. Upperwing pattern separates it from Grey-headed, Franklin's and Laughing Gulls. **Adult non-breeding** (second-winter) Head white, with brownish-grey ear-coverts, eye crescent and occasionally crown. Saddle grey; rump, tail and underparts white. Blackish primary tips have white mirrors on outer three, separated from white forewing, which contrasts with grey secondaries, coverts and mantle. Underwing pale greyish with black primaries, outer three of which show white mirrors. Bill and legs dark. **Adult breeding** As adult non-breeding, but with dark brown hood sharply demarcated from nape to throat; underparts may be rosy. Bill and legs dark red.

DISTRIBUTION AND STATUS Breeds colonially or solitarily on riverbanks and marshes, or on islands in Altiplano lakes, from northern Ecuador through Peru to northern Chile, and from western Bolivia to northern Argentina. Total population unknown but possibly fewer than 50,000 pairs, with most in southern Peru and northern Chile. Some birds sedentary but most disperse to large river mouths on the Pacific coast southwards to *c* 46°S and very occasionally on the Atlantic coast.

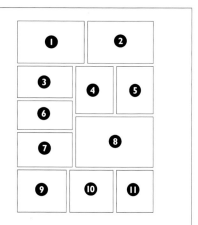

1 **Bonaparte's Gull** (adult breeding, Great Slave Lake, Canada)
2 **Bonaparte's Gull** (adult non-breeding, USA)
3 **Bonaparte's Gull** (first winter, USA)
4 **Bonaparte's Gull** (first winter, USA, December)
5 **Bonaparte's Gull** (adult acquiring breeding plumage, California, USA)
6 **Saunders's Gull** (adult breeding, Mai Po, Hong Kong, April)
7 **Saunders's Gull** (adult breeding, Mai Po, Hong Kong, April)
8 **Saunders's Gull** (extremely worn first summer, Mai Po, Hong Kong)
9 **Saunders's Gull** (first summer, Mai Po, Hong Kong)
10 **Andean Gull** (adult breeding, Chile, December)
11 **Andean Gull** (adult breeding, Junin, Peru, April)

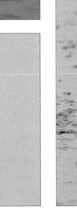

GULLS

MEDITERRANEAN GULL

Larus melanocephalus L 40 cm (16 in), WS
106 cm (42 in)
Medium-sized European gull, with black hood in summer, unmarked very pale grey wings and mantle, and red bill and legs. Adult plumage acquired in third year.
IDENTIFICATION Juvenile Head white with buff wash; ear-coverts and rear crown brownish-grey, blackish eye crescent. Lower hindneck, mantle and scapulars brownish-grey with paler feather edges, giving scaly pattern; rump white. Underparts white, with buff or brownish band across breast extending to flanks. Outer five or six primaries and primary coverts blackish, inner primaries grey with black tips, and secondaries blackish, completing dark trailing edge to wing; greater coverts paler grey, forming mid-wing panel contrasting with brownish forewing-coverts. Tail white with blackish subterminal band. Bill and legs blackish.
First-year As juvenile, but head white with blackish eye crescent and ear-coverts (occasionally extending to crown); mantle, scapulars and back uniform pale grey; faded carpal bar. Wings and tail unmoulted. By summer, has partial black hood, carpal bar further reduced. Bill and leg colour variable.
Second-year As adult non-breeding, but head as first-winter, and outer three to six primaries with variable black subterminal marks (also occasionally on primary coverts and alula); bare parts dull reddish-black. By summer, hood fully developed, white primary tips reduced, bill and legs as adult breeding. **Adult non-breeding** (third-winter) Head and body as first-winter. Wings and tail as adult breeding, pale grey, becoming white on primary tips; first primary has thin black line on outer web. Bill and legs variable. **Adult breeding** As adult non-breeding, but with full black hood from nape to throat, with white eye crescents. Bill scarlet, with dusky subterminal band and yellow tip; legs scarlet.
DISTRIBUTION AND STATUS Breeds colonially (occasionally solitarily amongst other species) in coastal lagoons and salt marshes, steppe lakes and marshes of the Black Sea and Aegean, with fewer westwards throughout Mediterranean Europe to Spain, and north to southern England and northern Germany; also central Europe. Total population 300,000-370,000 pairs, 90% of these on the Black Sea. Some range extension west in the last 50 years and more recently east to Azerbaijan (western Caspian Sea). Easily disturbed when breeding resulting in low productivity. Dispersal westwards mainly to the Mediterranean (especially Spain), also the north-west African coast to Mauritania. Some remain on the Black Sea. Occasionally reaches northern Red Sea, Senegal and Gambia.

RELICT GULL

Larus relictus L 44 cm (17 in), WS ?
Medium-sized Asiatic hooded gull with dark red bill and legs, rediscovered breeding in 1970. Recalls both larger Great Black-headed Gull and smaller Mediterranean Gull; most similar to second-summer Mediterranean, but with more extensive black wing tips. Classified as Near-threatened.
IDENTIFICATION Much as larger Great Black-headed Gull, with similar wing and head patterns but different jizz. **Juvenile** Head white. Nape, mantle and back reddish-brown with white fringes; rump and uppertail-coverts white. Tail white, all but outer two feathers with blackish-brown spots forming dark subterminal band. Underparts white. Upperwing-coverts reddish-brown with white fringes; black on primaries more extensive than on adult, with primaries two and three black, black decreasing inwards to subterminal band on seven and eight; white on inner webs of primary four inwards becomes more extensive, with inner primaries and secondaries white with small dark subterminal spots; primary tips white. Underwing-coverts white. Bill black, lighter at base; legs and feet dark grey. **First-year** Head white, with indistinct grey crescent in front of eye; hindneck with dense small dark spots. Upperparts pale grey; rump and uppertail-coverts white; tail white, central feathers with narrow black subterminal band. Underparts white; may retain some light brown juvenile feathers on flanks. Upperwing-coverts pale grey, variably mottled brown; tertials with blackish centres and very broad white fringes; outer five primaries largely black, tipped white, some with white on inner web; inner primaries and secondaries pale grey, tipped white, with variable dark subterminal marks. Underwing white, with dark outer primaries forming prominent dark wedge on leading edge of outer wing. Bill short, all black or with paler base; iris dark; legs and feet black. **Second-year** Similar to non-breeding adult, but apparently with dark-centred tertials as first-year. Bill black with red base. **Adult non-breeding** As breeding adult, but with distinct black patch on ear-coverts and streaked hindcrown (head pattern recalls adult winter Mediterranean Gull); hindneck often lightly streaked. Bill red, with paler tip and narrow grey subterminal band. **Adult breeding** Hood chocolate-brown on forehead and base of bill, becoming sooty-black posteriorly and extending to hindcrown and onto throat; white eye crescents above and below eye (larger than on Mediterranean Gull and similar to Great Black-headed Gull); nape white. Mantle, back and rump pearl-grey. Tail white. Underparts white. Upperwing-coverts pearl-grey; primaries and outer secondaries silvery-grey, with blackish on primaries two to seven forming variable subterminal crescent decreasing inwards; primary tips white. Underwing white, with blackish on primaries as on upper surface. Bill and legs blood-red. Call 'ka-ka, ka-ka, kee-aa', recalling Great Black-headed Gull. From Mediterranean Gull (including second-year) by more extensive blackish crescent on primaries, larger size and longer wings, longer legs, larger bill, and different colour and extent of hood. From Saunders's and Brown-headed Gulls by larger size, and upperwing and underwing patterns.
DISTRIBUTION AND STATUS Asiatic. Breeds highly colonially on shores or on islands in saline montane lakes of central and eastern Asia discontinuously in Russia, China and Mongolia. Total population unknown but probably under 2,000 pairs. One known colony in the Ordos Highlands of Inner Mongolia holds c 600 pairs, and unknown colonies may exist. Population has declined in Kazakhstan. Colonies are prone to flooding during storms, and heavy predation by Yellow-legged Gulls can wipe out entire colonies. Extremely sensitive to any form of disturbance. Should perhaps be classified as Vulnerable rather than, as at present, Near-threatened. Dispersal not fully known, but recorded in winter in South Korea and Vietnam as well as Hong Kong and Japan; possibly winters in East and South China Seas.

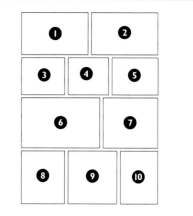

1 **Mediterranean Gull** (adult breeding, Kent, England, May)
2 **Mediterranean Gull** (adult non-breeding, Kent, England, December)
3 **Mediterranean Gull** (adult acquiring breeding plumage)
4 **Mediterranean Gull** (first summer moulting to second winter, July)
5 **Mediterranean Gull** (first winter, North Shields, England)
6 **Relict Gull** (adult breeding, nesting colony)
7 **Relict Gull** (adult breeding, Kazakhstan, June)
8 **Relict Gull** (adult breeding, Kazakhstan, June)
9 **Relict Gull** (first winter, China, October)
10 **Relict Gull** (first winter, China, October)

GULLS

LAVA GULL

Larus fuliginosus L 53 cm (21 in), WS ?
Large, scavenging, dusky gull with dark bill and legs, found only at the Galapagos. Adult plumage acquired in third year. Classified as Vulnerable.

IDENTIFICATION Unmistakable at Galapagos, where keeps to sandy shores (rarely on water); tame. Feeds on beach crustaceans, but a major scavenger. **Juvenile** Plumage uniformly sooty-brown, becoming greyer on mantle, rump, belly and vent; paler edgings to feathers of saddle, mantle, scapulars and wing-coverts. Head darker than mantle; uppertail-coverts whitish. Bill and legs blackish; iris brown. **First-year** As juvenile, but greyer on saddle, mantle, scapulars and underparts. Head becomes sooty-grey by summer, and wings and mantle become greyer. **Second-year** As non-breeding adult, but browner on head and body, becoming greyer. Uppertail-coverts white; tail grey with darker subterminal band. Wings as first-year. **Adult non-breeding** (third-winter) As breeding adult, but with greyer eye crescents and duller bill and legs. **Adult breeding** Hood sooty-brown, well demarcated from grey hindneck and throat; white eye crescents. Saddle and mantle mouse-grey, with greyish-white rump and uppertail-coverts. Chin brown, contrasting with grey throat; breast dusky grey, becoming whitish on lower belly. Outer primaries and primary coverts blackish; inner primaries and secondaries dusky grey as saddle. Tail dusky grey in centre (as saddle), whiter on outer feathers. Bill black with reddish tip; iris lemon-yellow; legs black.

DISTRIBUTION AND STATUS Breeds solitarily on sandy beaches and low outcrops near saline lagoons. Spread widely but sparsely throughout the islands (avoids cliffs). Total population under 400 pairs – the World's rarest gull. Largest numbers found at Academy Bay, Santa Cruz. Sedentary. No threats at present but population very low.

LAUGHING GULL

Larus atricilla L 40 cm (16 in), WS 103 cm (41 in)
Small but rakish, grey-backed American gull with extensive dark hood in summer; blackish wing tips without apical spots, dull red bill and legs. Adult plumage acquired in third year.

IDENTIFICATION **Juvenile** Head greyish-brown, paler on forehead, chin, lores and throat, darker on ear-coverts and hindcrown. Mantle and scapulars dull brown, with paler fringes giving scaly appearance; back uniform greyish. Hindneck, breastband and flanks uniform grey-brown; rest of underparts dull white. Primaries, their coverts and alula dull blackish-brown; secondaries blackish, fringed white; secondary coverts brown with paler edges. Dark diagonal bar on underwing. Tail whitish with blackish terminal band. Bill and legs blackish; iris dark. **First-year** In winter as juvenile, except partial greyish-brown hood on ear-coverts, nape and hindneck; mantle and scapulars uniform dark grey; wings and tail unmoulted and faded. By summer, some show less grey on head, nape and breast; brown coverts of inner wing faded to pale brownish. **Second-year** In winter head white, with variable partial grey hood from ear-coverts to nape and hindneck. Mantle and scapulars uniform dark grey; rump white. Underparts white, with grey wash on breast and flanks. Outer primaries and primary coverts blackish, remainder dark grey; secondaries and inner five or six primaries tipped white, forming trailing edge. Tail white; may show black subterminal spots (as can secondaries). By summer, acquires blackish hood which may be complete; breast and flanks whiter; bill and legs dusky red. **Adult non-breeding** (third-winter) As second-year, but grey confined to breast sides only. Upperwing dark grey, with clear-cut black wing tip extending to fifth or sixth primary; all except outer two primaries have white tips, increasing in extent inwards to form whitish trailing edge with secondaries (visible from above and below). Tail white. **Adult breeding** As adult non-breeding, but slaty-black hood from hindneck to throat, with white eye crescents; complete white underparts; white primary tips reduced or lacking. Bill and legs dull red.

DISTRIBUTION AND STATUS Breeds colonially on vegetated sandy beaches, rocky islands, and salt marshes from southern California to western Mexico and from Nova Scotia to Florida, Texas and eastern Central America, also the West Indies to Venezuela. Total population c 400,000 pairs, has increased this century: considered a pest near airports. Southward dispersal to Peru, Chile, and northern Brazil. Vagrants Greenland, Europe, Australia and numerous Pacific islands.

FRANKLIN'S GULL

Larus pipixcan L 35 cm (14 in), WS 90 cm (35 in)
Small grey-backed American gull; blackish wing tips outlined with white enable separation from similar Laughing Gull. Unusual in moulting in both spring and autumn, and adult plumage acquired in second year.

IDENTIFICATION **Juvenile** Head has partial dark brown hood. Hindneck, mantle, scapulars and back brownish, scapulars fringed paler and giving scaly pattern; rump and underparts white, breast sides washed brown. Outer primaries and primary coverts black, black decreasing inwards to subterminal band on sixth or seventh; inner primaries greyer and secondaries dark greyish-brown, all with white tips forming white trailing edge; coverts brownish-grey, carpal bar brownish. Tail pale grey, with black subterminal band not reaching whiter outer feathers. Bill and legs blackish. **First-year** In winter similar to juvenile, except half-hood blackish-brown to below eye level, with whitish eye crescents. Hindneck, mantle and scapulars clear dark grey. Blackish primaries, secondary bar and tail band; brown on inner wing-coverts.

By summer, has partial hood, grey inner wing, white trailing edge to secondaries and inner primaries; outer five or six primaries and their coverts blackish, this decreasing inwards; primaries have white tips. **Adult non-breeding** (second-winter) As first-winter, but wing pattern as adult breeding. Bare parts redder, but variable. **Adult breeding** (second-summer) Full slate-black hood from hindneck to throat, with white eye crescents. Body as first-summer, with pinkish flush on underparts. Upperwing as second-winter, but black on primaries reduced, with larger white primary tips, and area of white separating black from grey of rest of upperwing.

DISTRIBUTION AND STATUS Inland North America. Breeds highly colonially at inland lakes and marshes, from British Columbia and Alberta south-east through Montana, the Dakotas to Minnesota, with fewer in the Rockies and Great Basin. Total population c 350,000 pairs with increasing numbers and range expansion westwards. Dispersal south in flocks to Gulf Coast and Mexico continuing to Peru and Chile. Vagrants western Europe, Madeira, Tristan da Cunha, southern Africa, Hawaii.

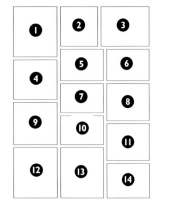

1 **Lava Gull** (adult breeding, Galapagos Islands, November)
2 **Lava Gull** (adult non-breeding, Galapagos Islands)
3 **Lava Gull** (sub-adult, Galapagos Islands, November)
4 **Lava Gull** (sub-adult, Galapagos Islands)
5 **Lava Gull** (adult breeding, Galapagos Islands, November)
6 **Laughing Gull** (adult breeding, USA)
7 **Laughing Gull** (adult non-breeding with Blowfish, Florida, USA)
8 **Laughing Gull** (juvenile, Cape May, USA)
9 **Laughing Gull** (adult breeding pair in territorial dispute at nest, USA)
10 **Laughing Gull** (adult moulting to breeding plumage, Florida, USA)
11 **Laughing Gull** (adult non-breeding, Texas, USA, February)
12 **Laughing Gull** (juvenile moulting to first winter, Cape May, USA)
13 **Franklin's Gull** (adult breeding, USA)
14 **Franklin's Gull** (first winter, New York, USA)

GULLS

LITTLE GULL

Larus minutus L 27 cm (11 in), WS 64 cm (25 in)
The World's smallest gull. Adult plumage acquired in third year.

IDENTIFICATION Juvenile Head white, with blackish-brown eye crescent, ear spot, crown and hindneck. Saddle, mantle and scapulars blackish-brown, with whitish edges giving scaly pattern. Rump and underparts white, with blackish-brown patches on breast sides. Blackish outer webs of outer five to seven primaries decrease in extent inwards, while blackish primary coverts and alula form dark leading edge to outer wing; inner primaries and secondaries pale grey (blackish centres can form dark bar on rear edge of inner wing); coverts pale grey, with broad blackish-brown carpal bar, thus completing 'M' on upperwings. Underwing white, tips of outer five to seven primaries blackish. Tail white with narrow subterminal band. Bill black; iris blackish; legs flesh to reddish. **First-year** As juvenile, but head whiter; markings become greyer, less brown. Saddle, mantle and scapulars become pale grey, and sides of breast also grey. By summer, acquires partial or complete hood, and grey hindneck and grey breast sides lost; carpal bar faded to pale brown; subterminal tail band faded to pale brown and often broken in centre. **Second-year** As adult non-breeding, but outer web of outer two to six primaries with subterminal blackish marks (variable); sometimes blackish on primary coverts, alula. Underwing pattern variable, but never uniformly black as adult. By summer, usually develops full hood, and blackish on wing tips reduced; legs dull red. **Adult non-breeding** (third-winter) Head as first-year; body much as first-year, with greyish sides to breast. Upperwing uniform pale grey, with all primaries and secondaries tipped white and forming prominent trailing edge to wing. Underwing mostly blackish (axillaries and coverts greyer), with corresponding prominent white trailing edge. Tail white. Bill blackish; legs dull red. **Adult breeding** As adult non-breeding, but full black hood from nape to throat; underparts may have pinkish flush. Bill reddish-brown; legs scarlet.

DISTRIBUTION AND STATUS Breeds generally colonially mainly inland at freshwater lakes and marshes, occasionally on coastal lagoons in North America (Canada 1962, USA 1975), western and central Europe with the bulk of the population western Russia, western and eastern Siberia. Total population unknown but large: few data for Siberia. Dispersal southwards to winter coastally.

IVORY GULL

Pagophila eburnea L 43 cm (17 in), WS 110 cm (43 in)
Medium-sized, pigeon-like gull confined to high-arctic seas. Distinctive at all ages. Adult plumage is completely white, and acquired in second year.

IDENTIFICATION An opportunistic scavenger in the Arctic; at rest, high crown, plump body and short legs reinforce pigeon-like appearance. Flight buoyant and graceful. **Juvenile** Head white, with variable blackish markings on forehead, lores and chin giving dark face; crown, nape, hindneck and ear-coverts lightly spotted with blackish. Upperparts and underparts white, with variable black spotting on mantle, scapulars (most) and, rarely, breast; uppertail-coverts may have black spots. Upperwing white, with black tips to primaries decreasing in size inwards; outer secondaries, tertials, alula and coverts tipped black. Underwing white, with blackish tips to primaries and secondaries. Tail white, with narrow subterminal bars forming broken tail band. Bill blackish at base, with yellow tip; legs blackish. **First-year** Resembles juvenile, but fewer blackish tips on head and upperparts. By summer, black of face reduced to base of bill and chin; upperpart spotting reduced or lacking. Bill colour as adult. **Adult non-breeding** (second-winter) Whole plumage uniformly white with very faint ivory tone. Straw-yellow shafts to primaries and tail feathers. Bill yellowish, with greyish-green base, and with orange tip to lower mandible; iris brown, orbital ring red; legs blackish. **Adult breeding** Plumage as non-breeding adult, but brighter orbital ring and bill. (It is essential to note bill and leg colours so as to eliminate all-white albinistic gulls.)

DISTRIBUTION AND STATUS Almost circumpolar in High Arctic. Breeds usually colonially on sea and inland cliffs and icefields in northern Canada, Greenland, Spitsbergen, Franz Josef Land, Novaya Zemlya, Severnaya Zemlya and New Siberian Islands. Total population unknown, but estimates vary from 9,000-25,000 pairs. Dispersal southwards usually only to ice-edge, occasionally Nova Scotia, Massachusetts, north-west Europe and Japan.

ROSS'S GULL

Rhodostethia rosea L 31 cm (12 in), WS 84 cm (33 in)
Small, distinctive high-arctic gull with black bill and red legs, pale grey upperparts and pinkish underparts, and a white wedge-shaped tail; adult in summer has a narrow black neck ring. Adult plumage acquired in second year.

IDENTIFICATION Juvenile Head white, with blackish-brown eye crescent, ear-coverts, crown and hindneck. Saddle, mantle, upper rump and scapulars blackish-brown, edged buff or golden; lower rump white. Underparts white, with blackish-brown breast sides. Outer three primaries mainly blackish, black decreasing inwards, remaining primaries and secondaries whitish, and outer primary coverts, alula and diagonal bar across coverts blackish-brown, forming 'M' across upperwings; remaining coverts pale pearl-grey. Underwing mainly grey. Tail wedge-shaped, white, central feathers with black subterminal tip. Bill blackish; iris black; legs brownish. **First-year** As juvenile, but head whiter, with dusky ear-coverts, and

greyish on crown, nape and hindneck, often extending to breast sides. Uniformly pale grey scapulars, saddle, mantle and upper rump; lower rump white. By summer, has partial or full neck ring; some acquire pinkish cast on underparts, losing grey breast sides; carpal bar fades to brownish. Tail faded, with brownish subterminal band. **Adult non-breeding** (second-winter) Head as first-year, but dark eye crescent and ear-coverts may be lacking. Partial or full neck ring. Underparts often with pinkish cast. Upperwing pale grey, with black outer web to first primary; whitish tips increase from sixth primary and with all-white secondaries form whitish triangular trailing edge to wing. Underwing grey with white trailing edge. Tail white or pinkish-white. Legs may be red. **Adult breeding** As adult non-breeding, but full neck ring (thickest on nape). Crown may have greyish wash, and head otherwise white or pinkish-white. Underparts white, with pinkish wash of variable intensity; rump may also be washed pink. Legs red or orange-red.

DISTRIBUTION AND STATUS High Arctic. Breeds in loose colonies in marshy tundra and small lakes near alders and willows, sparsely in Canada, Greenland and Spitsbergen, with most in north-east Siberia. Total population unknown with estimates varying from 10,000 to 50,000 pairs. Dispersal generally to edge of pack-ice in Arctic Ocean, occasionally Pribilof Islands, British Columbia, eastern USA, western Europe and Japan. Recent annual vagrant to British Isles.

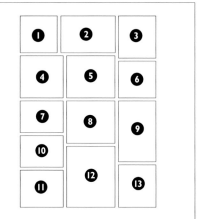

1 **Little Gull** (adult breeding, Merseyside, England)
2 **Little Gull** (adult non-breeding, Merseyside, England)
3 **Little Gull** (juvenile, Merseyside, England)
4 **Little Gull** (first winter, Merseyside, England)
5 **Little Gull** (first winter, Merseyside, England)
6 **Little Gull** (juvenile, Merseyside, England)
7 **Ivory Gull** (adult breeding, Spitsbergen, June)
8 **Ivory Gull** (first winter, Netherlands, February)
9 **Ross's Gull** (adult non-breeding, Fraserburgh, Scotland)
10 **Ross's Gull** (first winter, Cornwall, England)
11 **Ross's Gull** (adult breeding, Manitoba, Canada, June)
12 **Ross's Gull** (adult breeding, displaying, Manitoba, Canada, June)
13 **Ross's Gull** (adult non-breeding, Fraserburgh, Scotland)

GULLS

SABINE'S GULL

Larus sabini L 34 cm (13 in), WS 89 cm (35 in)
Small and distinctive circumpolar high-arctic gull.
Adult plumage acquired in second year.
IDENTIFICATION Juvenile Head brownish-grey,
with whiter forehead, chin and throat. Saddle,
mantle and scapulars brownish-grey, with paler
fringes giving scaly appearance, especially on
scapulars; rump and underparts white, with
extensive brownish-grey breast sides. Outer six
primaries, primary coverts and alula mostly
black, inner primaries and outer secondaries
mostly white, and inner wing-coverts brownish-
grey as mantle, thus producing tricoloured
wings. Underwing whitish, with variable dusky
bar on inner underwing. Tail forked, white with
black subterminal band. Bill black; iris brown;
legs greyish-flesh. **First-year** Saddle and inner
wing-coverts become clear grey. In winter head
as non-breeding adult, while in summer has
incomplete and variable or blackish hood.
Wings and tail faded and worn before moult.
Second-year (second-winter) Much as first-
summer, but head pattern as non-breeding
adult. Only those showing signs of immaturity in
wings and tail separable from adults. **Adult
breeding** (second-summer) Grey hood from
nape to throat, blacker on lower edge and
clearly demarcated from mantle. Saddle, mantle
and scapulars uniform grey; rump and
underparts white. Tricoloured upperwing
pattern: black outer five or six primaries, alula
and primary coverts, white inner primaries and
secondaries, grey inner wing-coverts and
innermost secondaries. Underwing whitish, with
variable dusky bar on inner wing. Tail forked,
white. Bill black with yellow tip; legs blackish-
grey. **Adult non-breeding** (third-winter) As
adult breeding, except head white with variable
blackish-grey on nape and upper hindneck,
sometimes extending to ear-coverts, crown and
sides of neck. Outer primaries browner, lacking
white tips. Legs may be flesh-grey.
DISTRIBUTION AND STATUS Breeds colonially
and solitarily in brackish water near coasts in
Alaska, Arctic Canada, Greenland, Spitsbergen,
Arctic Russia and Siberia. Total population
unknown, probably under 100,000 pairs.
Dispersal southwards in flocks to Benguela and
Humboldt upwellings, occasionally 'wrecked' en
route. Vagrants Florida, Sinai, Japan.

SWALLOW-TAILED GULL

Creagrus furcatus L 57 cm (22 in), WS 131 cm
(52 in)
Large hooded, fork-tailed and nocturnal foraging
South American gull. Adult plumage acquired in
second year.
IDENTIFICATION Long, broad wings enable
buoyant flight with deep wingbeats; forages
widely, primarily at night. **Juvenile** Head white,
with brownish ear spot, eye crescent and nape.
Upperparts greyish-brown with broad white
fringes, rump paler. Underparts white. Outer
primaries and primary coverts white, with dark
brown outer webs and tips forming dark wing

tip; inner primaries and secondaries white;
entire coverts to carpal joint greyish-brown
with white fringes (same as saddle). Underwing
whitish, with darker primaries. Tail strongly
forked, with broad blackish subterminal band.
Bill black; legs flesh-pink. **First-year** As juvenile,
but head becomes whiter in winter and acquires
partial brownish-grey hood in summer; saddle
and mantle become grey; wings and tail as
juvenile. **Adult non-breeding** Head white,
with black eye crescent and dark eye imparting
large-eyed appearance. Partial light grey
breastband; otherwise as breeding adult. **Adult
breeding** Dark blackish-grey hood from nape
to throat, white at bill base. Upperparts grey;
rump white. Underparts light grey below hood,
shading to white on breast and belly. Upperwing
of three contrasting colours, not dissimilar to
adult Sabine's Gull: outer primaries and primary
coverts white, with blackish outer webs and tips
forming dark wing tip; inner primaries and
secondaries white; coverts grey, as saddle and
mantle. Tail white. Bill black, with lighter
greenish tip; legs pinkish. From initially similar
Sabine's Gull by larger size and longer bill.
DISTRIBUTION AND STATUS Breeds loosely
colonially or solitarily on gravel beaches and cliff
slopes on most Galapagos islands, and Malpelo
Island (50 pairs) off Colombia. Total population
10,000-15,000 pairs. Dispersal east after
breeding to Ecuador and Peru, occasionally
Chile. Vagrant Panama, an occurrence in
California may have been ship assisted. Suffers
periodic food shortages.

BLACK-LEGGED KITTIWAKE

Rissa tridactyla L 41 cm (16 in), WS 91 cm
(36 in)
Medium-sized, almost circumpolar pelagic gull of
the Northern Hemisphere. Adult plumage
acquired in second year.
IDENTIFICATION Pelagic, especially in winter,
attending trawlers; opportunistic scavenger.
Flight variable with wind conditions. **Juvenile**
Head white, with blackish ear spot and black
collar across lower hindneck. Saddle, mantle
and scapulars uniform darkish grey; rump and
underparts white. Outer four or five primaries,
primary coverts and most wing-coverts blackish,
forming conspicuous 'M' across upperwing;
inner primaries and secondaries paler whitish-
grey; median coverts greyish. Underwing white,
with blackish tips to primaries. Tail white with
black subterminal band. Bill and legs blackish.
First-year Winter plumage as juvenile, except
for greyer hindneck and black cervical collar
reduced or becoming dark grey; blackish carpal
bar less extensive (very occasionally lacking
altogether). By summer variable, but generally
head whiter, 'M' pattern on upperwing faded to
pale brown, subterminal tail band reduced or
absent; bill becomes yellowish-green. **Adult
non-breeding** (second-winter) As adult
breeding, but with rear crown and hindneck
pale grey and merging with dark ear spot, which
can extend upwards to rear of crown. Some
may retain small dark marks on outer primary

coverts. **Adult breeding** Head, rump, tail and
underparts white. Saddle, mantle and scapulars
dark grey. Upperwing dark grey, shading to
silvery-white on primaries and secondaries;
black wing tip formed by outer web of first
primary and tips of first four primaries, with
subterminal black tip on fifth primary and
occasionally sixth. Underwing white with black
tip. Very occasionally has reddish legs. *R. t.
pollicaris* of north Pacific has darker grey
upperparts and more extensive black on outer
primaries than nominate *tridactyla*.
DISTRIBUTION AND STATUS Breeds in large,
sometimes huge colonies, often with auks,
usually on narrow cliff ledges in the Canadian
Arctic, northern North America, Greenland,
west and northern Europe, northern Russia.
Also in north Pacific from north-east Siberia,
Kuril Islands, Sea of Okhotsk and Kamchatka to
Alaska. Total population six to seven million
pairs with most in eastern Kamchatka (c
1,600,000 pairs) and large numbers Alaska and
Greenland. Population increase and range
expansions this century – the most abundant
gull. Dispersal south to winter pelagically in
north Atlantic and north Pacific. Vagrants Gulf
of Mexico, Senegal, South Africa, Caspian Sea,
Baluchistan, Oman, Japan, and Baja California.

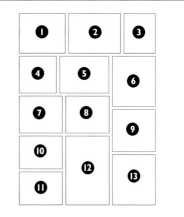

1 **Sabine's Gull** (adult breeding, Victoria Island,
Canada, June)
2 **Sabine's Gull** (probably first summer)
3 **Sabine's Gull** (adult breeding, Victoria Island,
Canada, June)
4 **Sabine's Gull** (first summer, Lancashire,
England, September)
5 **Sabine's Gull** (juvenile, USA)
6 **Swallow-tailed Gull** (adult breeding,
Galapagos Islands)
7 **Swallow-tailed Gull** (adult breeding,
Galapagos Islands)
8 **Swallow-tailed Gull** (breeding pair
copulating, Galapagos Islands)
9 **Swallow-tailed Gull** (juvenile, Galapagos
Islands)
10 **Black-legged Kittiwake** (juvenile, England)
11 **Black-legged Kittiwake** (juvenile, Dover,
England, July)
12 **Black-legged Kittiwake** (first winter,
England)
13 **Black-legged Kittiwake** (adult breeding,
Merseyside, England, May)

183

GULLS &TERNS

RED-LEGGED KITTIWAKE

Rissa brevirostris L 38 cm (15 in), WS 85 cm (33 in)
Medium-sized pelagic gull of the north Pacific. Adult plumage acquired in second year. Classified as Vulnerable.

IDENTIFICATION Juvenile Head white, with darker ear spot and cervical collar. Saddle dark grey; rump and underparts white. Outer four or five primaries and primary coverts black with grey inner webs, primary coverts black, inner primaries grey with white tips; secondaries whiter; wing-coverts dark grey with white tips. Underwing grey, primaries and secondaries darker, outermost four or five primaries with black tips. Tail white. Bill black; legs blackish-brown. From Black-legged Kittiwake by lack of carpal bar on upperwing, no black on tail and paler hindcollar. **First-year** As juvenile, but dark cervical collar reduced; wings and tail unmoulted. Bill base becomes yellow; legs brownish-yellow, red by summer. **Adult non-breeding** (second-winter) As breeding adult, except for dusky grey eye crescent, ear spot and nape to hindneck. **Adult breeding** Head white. Saddle dark grey; rump and underparts white. Outer four or five primaries have blackish tips, otherwise dark grey; inner primaries and secondaries dark grey with whitish tips. Underwing grey, with blackish primary tips. Tail white. Bill yellow; legs red. From larger Black-legged Kittiwake by darker, more uniform grey wings, with less black at tips, absence of silvery bases to primaries, wider white trailing edge to wing, greyer underwings, and red legs.

DISTRIBUTION AND STATUS Breeds colonially on narrow cliff ledges, often with other seabirds including Black-legged Kittiwake, at the Commander Islands (c 17,000 pairs), the Aleutians (Buldir c 6,600 birds and Bogoslof c 200 birds) with most at the Pribilof Islands (St George 57,000 pairs, also St Paul). Total population c 100,000 pairs recently decreased from c 150,000 pairs, possibly attributed to lack of food from increased commercial trawling. Breeding totally fails in some years, some fox predation human exploitation at Pribilofs. Dispersal southwards in winter ahead of ice. Vagrants Japan, Yukon, Oregon, Nevada.

GULL-BILLED TERN

Gelochelidon nilotica L 39 cm (15 in), WS 94 cm (37 in)
Medium-sized, pale and non-crested tern, superficially resembling Sandwich Tern; widespread, but not pelagic.

IDENTIFICATION Flies with shallow wingbeats, without up-and-down body movement of smaller terns; feeds from the surface by dipping, with only occasional plunge-dives. Perched birds heavier and more aggressive in appearance than Sandwich Tern, with shorter dark bill with curved upper mandible, more rounded head which lacks drooping nape crest of Sandwich, longer black legs, and overall more compact appearance than the more slender lines of

Sandwich Tern. **Juvenile** Similar to adult winter, but with pale sandy-brown wash on crown and nape, darker brownish tips to saddle and upperwing-coverts, and darker grey primaries. Tail white with brown tip. **First-winter** As juvenile, but reduction of brownish tips to saddle and upperwing-coverts. **Adult non-breeding** Much as adult breeding, but head white, with variable dusky area on ear-coverts (as Forster's Tern or Mediterranean Gull) which can extend from eye to eye across nape. Outer webs of outer primaries darker than on breeding adult. **Adult breeding** Uncrested black cap until August, then lost uniformly (not from bill backwards towards nape as on Sandwich Tern); sides of face, chin, throat and underparts white. Upperparts including rump and tail uniform silver-grey, slightly darker than Sandwich Tern and without latter's contrast between back and tail/rump. Upperwing as upperparts, except for dusky grey inner webs to outer six to eight primaries, these tipped blackish and forming dark trailing edge to outer wing (Sandwich has dark wedge on outer three to four primaries). Underwing mainly white, with darker primary tips (can recall Caspian Tern on darkest individuals). Bill, legs and feet black; iris dark brown. Less marine than Sandwich Tern; coastal, but more regularly on fresh water, mudflats and fields.

DISTRIBUTION AND STATUS Breeds usually colonially in salt marshes, salt works, coastal dunes, islands and freshwater lagoons in southern North America, the Caribbean, South America, Europe, Asia, Australia and northern Africa. Total population c 55,000 pairs with most in Asia (c 40,000 pairs). Widely distributed but nowhere common, European population (6,800–16,000 pairs) declining mainly through loss of habitat. Dispersal southwards, especially of northern populations, reaching Peru, southern Africa, Japan and New Zealand.

CASPIAN TERN

Sterna caspia L 54 cm (21 in), WS 134 cm (53 in)
The largest tern with massive red bill and very pale upperparts.

IDENTIFICATION Forages with bill pointing downwards, and hovers momentarily before diving vertically from up to 20 m. At rest, angular head and conspicuous dark-tipped red bill (as long as the head) impart a heavy powerful impression; long dark legs and general bulk make perched birds stand taller than other terns. **Juvenile** Resembles adult non-breeding. Large blackish cap, forehead and crown flecked with white. Upperparts pale grey, back and scapulars with dark brown 'V'-shaped markings; rump unmarked greyish-white. Tail has dark terminal band. Underparts white. Upperwing much as adult, but with faint carpal bar, brownish tips on coverts, dusky secondaries. Legs pale, but soon become blackish. **First-winter** Saddle becomes clearer grey, dark secondary wing bar, outer primaries and primary coverts darker. Dark tip to tail. First-

summer similar. **Second-year** Much as adult non-breeding, with whitish spots in cap and darker outer primaries. Tail tip may be dark. **Adult non-breeding** Forehead and crown streaked white; otherwise as adult breeding. **Adult breeding** Black cap with short crest. Upperparts pale grey, but rump and tail white; underparts white. Upperwing pale grey; inner webs of outer primaries darker; secondaries tipped white. Underwing mainly white, with diagnostic blackish outer primaries decreasing inwards (unlike any other large tern; recalls Lesser Black-backed Gull). Summer plumage retained longer than that of Royal Tern. Bill blood-red, blackish distally, often with yellow orange or white tip; iris black. Separated from smaller Royal Tern by size, broader wings, bill bulk and colour, shorter tail fork, less prominent crest, and dark (not pale) under surface of primaries.

DISTRIBUTION AND STATUS Widespread. Breeds colonially or solitarily on beaches, rocky islands, and occasionally salt marshes in North America, Baltic Europe, Black and Caspian Seas, eastwards through Asia to Siberia, Africa, Madagascar and Australasia. Total population c 50,000 pairs with most in Asia (15,000 pairs). Widely distributed but nowhere common; sensitive to disturbance, and some populations now declining. After breeding, dispersal southwards, especially of juveniles, from northern populations to Mexico and the Caribbean, central Africa and the Middle East.

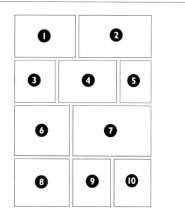

1 **Red-legged Kittiwake** (breeding adult at nest, Bering Sea, June)
2 **Red-legged Kittiwake** (adult breeding, Commander Island, Bering Sea, June)
3 **Red-legged Kittiwake** (adult non-breeding, Commander Island, Bering Sea, June)
4 **Gull-billed Tern** (adult breeding)
5 **Gull-billed Tern** (adult breeding, China, May)
6 **Gull-billed Tern** (adult non-breeding, Sri Lanka, March)
7 **Caspian Tern** (juvenile and adult breeding, USA)
8 **Caspian Tern** (adult non-breeding, Florida, USA)
9 **Caspian Tern** (adult non-breeding, Florida, USA)
10 **Caspian Tern** (adult breeding, California, USA)

TERNS

ROYAL TERN

Sterna maxima L 48 cm (19 in), WS 109 cm (43 in)

The second largest tern (the size of a smallish gull), a tropical and subtropical marine species, noticeably paler-winged than Caspian Tern and lacking latter's blackish primaries on underwing. **IDENTIFICATION** In flight, slow wingbeats can recall a slim Caspian Tern, but proportions are those of a crested tern; when foraging, plunges from several metres, but also dips to obtain food from the surface. Perched birds again recall a slim Caspian Tern, but Royal has shorter legs and the wing tips reach the tail or just beyond (Caspian's wings go well beyond the tail). Most adults have a white forehead by June, and in winter plumage the facial mask is less extensive than on Elegant Tern. **Juvenile** Partial black cap and eye mask larger than on non-breeding adult; forehead and crown whiter than juvenile Caspian Tern. Upperparts greyish-cream with yellowish-brown centres to feathers. Tail dark grey. Underparts white. Outer four to six primaries blackish, with inner primaries and secondaries slate-grey; marginal and lesser coverts slate-grey, forming conspicuous carpal bar. **First-winter** As juvenile, but saddle clearer grey. Pale creamy-white mid-wing panel, dusky grey secondary bar and slate-grey carpal bar. **Second-year** Dark lesser coverts; dark secondaries forming dark trailing edge. Primaries darker than on breeding adult. **Adult non-breeding** Much as breeding adult, except black cap reduced to dark streaks extending backwards from each eye and meeting on nape. Outer primaries dark, and contrast with rest of wing. Tail greyer, lacking streamers. **Adult breeding** Black cap, with crest which droops on nape (full cap present for short period only: forehead white by June); sides of face, chin, throat and underparts white. Upperparts pale grey; tail deeply forked, white. Upperwing with pale grey outer webs of outer four to five primaries, and most primary tips blackish; secondaries darker grey, forming slightly darker trailing edge to wing. (The upperparts are the palest grey of any of the crested terns, with darker outer primaries.) Underwing mainly white; outer primaries have blackish-grey tips forming dark outer trailing edge (as Crested, Lesser Crested and Sandwich Terns, but unlike Caspian Tern). Bill rich orange, tending to reddish-orange (occasionally entirely red) in the nominate American subspecies and to yellowish-orange in the west African race *albididorsalis*, always without dusky subterminal tip; iris black; legs and feet black. From west African race of Lesser Crested Tern by larger size, heavier appearance, broader bill, longer legs, paler upperparts and whiter rump and tail. From Elegant Tern by larger size, broader and shorter bill, longer legs, shorter crest, heavier flight, and less contrast between mantle and rump/tail.

DISTRIBUTION AND STATUS Central America and west Africa. Breeds in densely packed colonies on sandy beaches, coral islands and salt marsh islands near bays and rivers from southern California to Mexico and from Maryland to Texas, the Caribbean and South America: French Guiana, Brazil and Patagonia. In west Africa from Mauritania to Guinea and possibly further south. Total population unknown but large, although declining in some parts eg California. North American east coast population c 34,000 pairs, Africa c 25,000 pairs, South American population unknown. American population disperses to Pacific coast south to Peru and Atlantic coast from South Carolina to Argentina. African populations move north to Morocco and Mediterranean and south to Gulf of Guinea. Vagrants south to Namibia and north to north-west Europe.

ELEGANT TERN

Sterna elegans L 41 cm (16 in), WS 86 cm (34 in)

Medium-sized, pale, North American marine tern with crest and orange bill; white rump and tail separate it from Lesser Crested Tern, which it most resembles, although ranges do not overlap. Classified as Near-threatened. **IDENTIFICATION** In flight, appears very slim and pale, with the outer four to five primaries being darker than the rest of the wing. Adult's crest is the longest of any tern's. **Juvenile** Resembles juvenile Royal and Lesser Crested Terns. Brown scaly appearance on back, scapulars and wing-coverts. Bill greyish yellow-orange, shorter than adult's. **First-year** Less brown than juvenile, with darker secondaries and lesser coverts. Outer primaries dark. **Adult non-breeding** White forehead merging into black mask (which is broader and more triangular than on Royal, Crested and Lesser Crested Terns). Greyer inner half of upperwing than first-year; no secondary bar. Outer primaries dusky. **Adult breeding** Black cap with long crest. Sides of face, chin and throat white. Upperparts with saddle pale bluish-grey, rump white; tail white, deeply forked. Underparts white, may show pinkish suffusion (unlike other reddish-billed crested terns). Upperwing pale bluish-grey, with outer webs of outer three primaries dusky. Underwing white; outer primary tips dusky. Bill usually longer than the head length, droops at tip, yellowish-orange to red, becoming paler at tip; iris black; legs and feet black. From Royal Tern by smaller size, slimmer and less powerful jizz, proportionately longer and finer, more drooping bill, proportionately longer crest, shorter legs, lighter flight, and differences in voice and underwing pattern.

DISTRIBUTION AND STATUS Pacific coast of North America. Breeds in densely packed colonies on sandy beaches and low-lying islands from central California to Baja California, and in the Gulf of California. Total population probably 30,000-50,000 breeding pairs; in some years 90% of these nest on Raza in Gulf of California, where almost eliminated by egg-collectors until the island given protected status in 1964; Raza population estimated at c 80,000 pairs in early 1980s, but only 22,500 pairs ten years later. Population possibly declining; main threats include direct and indirect human disturbance (especially ecotourism). Post-breeding dispersal north to northern California (occasionally British Columbia), but winters mostly from Guatemala south to central Chile (most in Peru and north Chile); accidental Texas. Has wandered to western Europe (Netherlands, Ireland, Spain, France).

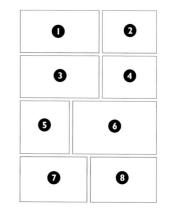

1 **Royal Tern** (adult breeding, Florida, USA)
2 **Royal Tern** (adult non-breeding, USA)
3 **Royal Tern** (first winter, Cape May, USA)
4 **Royal Tern** (adult non-breeding, California, USA)
5 **Royal Tern** (adult non-breeding, California, USA)
6 **Elegant Tern** (adult breeding pair, California, USA)
7 **Elegant Tern** (adult non-breeding, Chile, December)
8 **Elegant Tern** (adult non-breeding)

TERNS

LESSER CRESTED TERN

Sterna bengalensis L 40 cm (16 in), WS 92 cm (36 in)

Marine tern of the south-west Pacific and Indian Oceans. The smallest of the crested yellow/orange-billed terns.

IDENTIFICATION A distinctly marine species. Has a slower and more graceful flight than Sandwich Tern, but forages in a similar manner, making dives from a height and also picking food from the surface. Recalls Sandwich Tern in size and shape, but both body and tail appear longer, while the wings are longer and more slender. **Juvenile** Resembles small juvenile Royal Tern. Head as non-breeding adult. Upperparts grey, with brownish tips to saddle; rump pale grey; tail pale grey with brownish terminal band. Underparts white. Upperwing grey, with darker brown bars on lesser coverts, greater coverts and secondaries; dark brownish outer primaries. Lacks carpal bar of juvenile Swift Tern. Bill yellowish-grey. **First-year** Becomes greyer than juvenile, and more resembles non-breeding adult. Cap may be tinged with brown. Outer primaries dark brownish; some brownish edges to wing-coverts remain; brownish secondary bar. Bill duller than adult's. **Adult non-breeding** Forehead and most of crown white to behind peak of crown (thus whiter than Swift Tern); blackish eye mask extends to hindcrown; lores, sides of face, chin and throat white. Plumage otherwise as breeding adult. Bill yellowish-orange. **Adult breeding** Black cap extends from base of upper mandible to nape; sides of face, chin, throat and underparts white. Upperparts pale bluish-grey (deeper steel-grey in *S. b. torresii*); rump and tail pale bluish-grey. Upperwing pale blue-grey; primaries more silvery-grey, becoming darker gradually. Underwing white, with outermost primary tips greyer. Bill bright orange; iris dark brown; legs and feet black. The uniform grey upperparts help distinguish Lesser Crested from Sandwich, Royal and Elegant Terns (all of which show more contrast between the back and the rump/tail); the orange bill is the size and shape of Sandwich Tern's (but broader-based), more slender than that of Royal and shorter than that of Elegant. The impression is of an orange-billed Sandwich Tern, whereas Royal is more like a Caspian Tern with a white rump and tail (unlike Lesser Crested). For differences from Swift Tern, see that species.

DISTRIBUTION AND STATUS Breeds in dense colonies on low-lying sandy and coral islands as well as sandbanks in Libya, Red Sea, Persian Gulf, Laccadive and Maldive Islands, New Guinea and northern Australia. Total population c 225,000 pairs with over 100,000 pairs in Australia and 50,000-60,000 pairs in the Middle East. Northern populations disperse southwards. Vagrants north to British Isles.

SWIFT or CRESTED TERN

Sterna bergii L 46 cm (18 in), WS 104 cm (41 in)
Large marine tern of the Indian and Pacific Oceans (absent from the Americas). The third largest tern after Caspian and Royal.

IDENTIFICATION Slimmer than the similar-sized Royal Tern, with long and slender scythe-like wings usually held backwards, giving a powerful flight with very full wingbeats; forages by steep dives from several metres, but will also dip to collect food from the surface. Perched birds look front-heavy, with a powerful bill, and shape recalling a slim Royal Tern rather than Lesser Crested. **Juvenile** Head as adult non-breeding, but sides of face with darker streaking; lores, chin, throat and underparts white. Upperparts show grey saddle with brownish tips, rump generally paler; tail darker than rump, with variable darker tip. Upper primaries and their coverts blackish-brown; secondaries dark brown with whitish tips; greater and median coverts pale greyish-brown with whitish tips, forming pale mid-wing panel; lesser coverts and carpal brownish. Underwing as adult. Bill duller than adult's, with variable darker tip. **First-year** Much as juvenile, but saddle becomes uniformly grey with fewer brownish tips. Bill as non-breeding adult. **Adult non-breeding** Much as adult breeding, but with duller bill. Forehead and crown mainly white; blackish eye mask extends to hindcrown and nape (may show whitish streaks). Upperparts paler than breeding adult, and outer primaries darker grey. **Adult breeding** White forehead; glossy black cap with long crest; sides of face, chin, throat and underparts white. Upperparts with saddle grey, rump and deeply forked tail whitish. Upperwing pale grey, primaries silvery with duskier inner webs; secondaries have whitish tips forming narrow trailing edge to wing. (Primaries are paler than the rest of the wing, while the white rump and tail are generally paler than the back, though upperpart colour varies geographically from the darker grey of race *velox* to the paler *thalassina*.) Underwing white, primaries with greyish tips. Bill greenish-yellow, occasionally with orange tinge; iris dark brown; legs and feet black. From Lesser Crested Tern by larger, bulkier size, proportionately longer wings, longer legs, blunter heavier bill being greenish-yellow rather than orange, and generally lacking Lesser Crested's finer and more delicate lines.

DISTRIBUTION AND STATUS Indian and Pacific Oceans. Breeds colonially on offshore islands, lagoons and salt pans. Total population unknown, but c 500,000 pairs in Australia and c 50,000 pairs elsewhere, including c 33,000 pairs in the Middle East. Some populations disperse after breeding. *S. b. velox* breeds Red Sea, east Africa, Arabian Sea, Persian Gulf, north Indian Ocean; largest and darkest race. *S. b. thalassina* breeds east Africa and central Indian Ocean; smallest and palest race. *S. b. bergii* breeds South Africa and Namibia, *S. b. enigma* Mozambique and Madagascar, *S. b. cristata* Australia, southeast Asia, China, north to Japan and east to Fiji.

CHINESE CRESTED TERN

Sterna bernsteini L 38 cm (15 in), WS ?
Little-known medium-sized, black-crested tern with grey upperparts, whiter underparts, and black-tipped yellow bill and black legs. Classified as Critical. Possibly extinct.

IDENTIFICATION Resembles Swift Tern. **Juvenile/first-year** Undescribed; possibly resembles Swift Tern, but smaller. **Adult non-breeding** As adult breeding, but forehead and crown white, top of crown with black streaks extending onto black nape. Bill yellow with black subterminal bar. **Adult breeding** Full black cap extending to base of bill, and forming crest on nape; sides of face, chin, throat and underparts white. Upperparts with saddle pale pearl-grey, rump white; tail white, deeply forked with long streamers. Upperwing mainly pale pearl-grey as saddle, with outer webs of outer three to five primaries blackish, secondaries narrowly tipped white. Underwing mainly white. Bill yellow with broad black tip; iris dark brown; legs and feet black. The grey of the saddle is a shade lighter than that found on Swift Tern, compared with which Chinese Crested is also smaller, with a proportionately longer, more deeply forked tail, a full black crest (reaching bill base) in summer plumage, a black tip to the bill, and a clearer whitish underwing.

DISTRIBUTION AND STATUS Breeding grounds unknown, but believed to be on the north-east coast of China near the Yellow River delta in Shandong where probably sighted in September 1991. Winter records from Indonesia, Malaysia, Philippines and Thailand, where last reliably recorded July 1980. Habitat requirements and threats remain unknown.

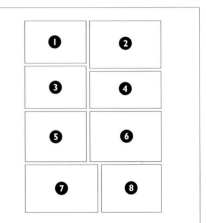

1 **Lesser Crested Tern** (breeding pair at nest, Karan, Saudi Arabia)
2 **Lesser Crested Tern** (adults at breeding colony, Karan, Saudi Arabia)
3 **Lesser Crested Tern** (adult non-breeding, Australia)
4 **Swift (Crested) Tern** (adult non-breeding, Queensland, Australia)
5 **Swift (Crested) Tern** (adult in transitional plumage, Australia)
6 **Swift (Crested) Tern** (adults at breeding colony, Christmas Island, Pacific Ocean)
7 **Swift (Crested) Tern** (moulting adults, Fraser Island, Australia, January)
8 **Swift (Crested) Tern** (juvenile, Queensland, Australia)

TERNS

SANDWICH TERN

Sterna sandvicensis L 40 cm (16 in), WS 92 cm (36 in)

Widespread, medium-sized to large, very pale and slim crested tern with a long and slender yellow-tipped black bill and black legs. More marine than Gull-billed Tern, which it superficially resembles.

IDENTIFICATION Powerful flight, with flat crown and downward-pointing bill when foraging; can dive from c 6 m. **Juvenile** Head as non-breeding adult, but browner, with paler streaks on crown; forehead, sides of face, chin, throat and underparts white. Upperparts show grey saddle with dull blackish barring, most pronounced on scapulars; rump white; tail greyish-white with black tip. Upperwing much as non-breeding adult, but with blackish 'V'-shaped barring on wing-coverts and primary tips. Bill dark, thicker and shorter than adult's (more like that of Gull-billed Tern). **First-winter** Much as juvenile, but saddle becomes clear grey; upperwing-coverts show reduced barring. Yellow tip to bill appears. **Adult non-breeding** Similar to breeding adult, but whitish forehead and lores, blackish crown and nape streaked with white (paler birds can resemble Forster's Tern). **Adult breeding** Black cap from base of bill to nape, with blackish crest on nape; sides of face, chin, throat and underparts white. Upperparts pale grey, with rump and tail white. Upperwing pale silvery-grey, inner webs of outer three to six primaries slightly darker grey, becoming progressively darker through breeding season. Underwing white, with dusky tips to outermost four or five primaries. Bill black with yellow tip; iris dark; legs and feet black. Superficially resembles Gull-billed Tern, which see for comparative differences (note that Sandwich is distinctly tern-like rather than gull-like, with long narrow wings usually with dark wedge on outer three to six primaries). **Cayenne Tern** of South America, currently regarded as a race of Sandwich (*S. s. eurygnatha*), has similar plumage phases but bare parts are variable: bill ranges from yellow to orange, to black with a yellow tip, and legs vary from yellow to black. Crest is longer and more shaggy than Sandwich Tern's and upperparts are a darker grey; inner secondaries have darker centres, which can form a faint secondary bar. Resembles Elegant Tern, but smaller, with usually pale yellow (not orange) bill.

DISTRIBUTION AND STATUS Breeds in dense colonies on low-lying, unvegetated sand, mud and gravel in eastern North America through the Antilles to the Caribbean; in South America (*S. s. eurygnatha*), from the north of the continent south to Brazil and Argentina (c 20,000 pairs); and in Europe east to the Caspian Sea. Total population at least 100,000 pairs with c 45,000 pairs eastern North America and c 40,000 pairs in Europe; however, Caspian Sea and other Russian populations may be equally as large. General post-breeding dispersal south to South America, Africa and northern Indian Ocean.

ROSEATE TERN

Sterna dougallii L 39 cm (15 in), WS 78 cm (31 in)

Medium-sized, widespread and pale marine tern having a black bill with reddish base, black cap, red legs, and long tail-streamers which extend well beyond the rear end at rest.

IDENTIFICATION Almost exclusively marine. Flight is steadier and more purposeful than that of Arctic Tern, with more even upstrokes and downstrokes; foraging birds dive from 8-12 m. **Juvenile** Crown, nape and ear-coverts sooty brownish-black, forehead often paler; chin, throat, hindneck and underparts white. Upperparts with saddle rich buffish-grey with blackish barring, producing scaly effect; rump, uppertail-coverts and tail white (no streamers). Upperwing mainly pale grey, with whitish tips to primaries and secondaries forming narrow white trailing edge to wing; darker sooty-brownish colour of outer primary coverts extends narrowly over carpal and along leading edge of wing. Underwing white, without dark primary tips. Bill and legs black. **First-year** Forehead becomes whiter, 'V'-shaped barring on saddle becomes greyish, and dark carpal bar becomes reduced. By summer, much as adult non-breeding; similar to pale Common Tern. **Adult non-breeding** Forehead and crown white; blackish eye mask extending onto nape and hindcrown; sides of face, chin, throat and underparts white (some may show pinkish on belly). Upperparts pale grey; tail-streamers retained. Upperwing pale grey, with blackish outer webs to outer two or three primaries forming dark leading edge to outer wing. Bill black; legs brownish-orange. **Adult breeding** Glossy black cap (retained until autumn) from base of bill to nape; sides of face, chin and throat white. Upperparts pale pearl-grey, rump white, and tail white with long streamers (but little contrast between back and rump/tail). Underparts white, often with pinkish tinge. Upperwing pale grey, as adult non-breeding (the outer upper primaries become darker by late summer, but there is no dark wedge). Underwing white, with no dark trailing edge to primaries, even when worn (unlike Common, Arctic or Forster's Tern). Bill dark with reddish base; iris blackish-brown; legs and feet dark red. From Common Tern at rest by longer-legged appearance, tail-streamers extending beyond wing tip, longer bill (as long as the head), and the white border to the hand formed by white inner webs of the primaries (unlike Common or Arctic Tern, more like Sandwich); in flight, Common Tern shows longer wings and a shorter tail.

DISTRIBUTION AND STATUS Breeds colonially, sometimes very densely, on sand, rock or coral islands with or without vegetation in eastern North America, West Indies, Central America, Venezuela, Azores, north-west Europe, west, east and southern Africa, Arabian Sea, west Indian Ocean, Sri Lanka, India, Andaman Islands, Burma, east to south New Guinea, Solomons, New Caledonia (possibly also Fiji) and Australia, also east China, Taiwan and Ryukyus. Total population c 50,000 pairs. North American and European populations (excluding Ireland) have declined severely, now considered endangered. Wintering grounds incompletely known. Northern populations disperse south in winter: American breeders may winter largely in central Atlantic, although some on north coast of South America; east Atlantic and European populations winter west African coast (mainly between Guinea and Gabon). Egg-collecting and the capture of birds for food in wintering areas may help explain population decline.

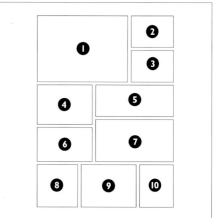

1 **Sandwich Tern** (breeding colony, Norfolk, England, June)
2 **Sandwich Tern** (adult breeding, Florida, USA)
3 **Cayenne Tern subspecies** *S. s. eurygnatha* (adult, Bahia San Blas, Argentina, December)
4 **Sandwich Tern** (adult non-breeding, Florida, USA)
5 **Sandwich Tern** (adult non-breeding, Florida, USA)
6 **Sandwich Tern** (juvenile, England)
7 **Roseate Tern** (non-breeding adult and first winter, roosting flock, Tema, Ghana)
8 **Roseate Tern** (adult breeding, USA)
9 **Roseate Tern** (juvenile, Southern Ireland, July)
10 **Roseate Tern** (adult breeding, Long Island, USA)

TERNS

WHITE-FRONTED TERN

Sterna striata L 41 cm (16 in), WS 76 cm (30 in)
Medium-sized, very pale, capped Australasian marine tern.

IDENTIFICATION Flight is buoyant and graceful; generally forages along the surf line, diving for food from up to 10 m. Tends to roost on rocks and shingle rather than on sand. **Juvenile** Forehead white, merging into brownish cap extending from eye to lower nape; chin, throat, sides of face and underparts white. Upperparts with grey saddle heavily edged with brown, rump white; tail white with brownish tips, no streamers. Upperwing with outer primaries and their coverts dark grey, subterminally brown with white tips, becoming greyer on innermost primaries; lesser and median coverts grey, tipped brown, forming dark carpal bar. Underwing white, with dusky grey outer primary tips. Bill and legs blackish-grey. **First-year** Much as adult non-breeding, but head darker and primaries have pronounced brownish carpal bar. **Adult non-breeding** As adult breeding, but with whiter crown and no tail-streamers. From Roseate Tern by whiter forehead and dark legs. From Common Tern by larger and heavier bill, white underwing, blacker lores and paler upperparts. **Adult breeding** Black cap from eye to lower nape, with contrasting white forehead; sides of face, chin, throat and underparts white (underparts may show pinkish tinge). Upperparts with saddle pearl-grey, rump white; tail white, deeply forked (streamers), with outer web of outer feather blackish. Upperwing pale pearl-grey, outer web of outermost primary black. Underwing whitish, with blackish outer primary; outer primary tips duskier. Bill black; iris brown; legs and feet dark brownish-black. Appears very white in flight, recalling Roseate Tern.

DISTRIBUTION AND STATUS Breeds usually colonially on beaches and riverine shingle islands on the Furneaux Group off north-east Tasmania; North, South and Stewart Island (New Zealand), also Chathams, Auckland and possibly Snares Islands. Total population *c* 500,000 pairs almost totally in New Zealand. Dispersal of adults northwards within New Zealand, while juveniles disperse to winter south-east Australia. Vagrant Campbell Island.

BLACK-NAPED TERN

Sterna sumatrana L 31 cm (12 in), WS 61 cm (24 in)
Small, very pale, uncapped tropical Indian and Pacific Ocean tern.

IDENTIFICATION Flight is generally stronger and more direct than that of most smaller terns; forages as noddies, snatching food from low over the surface with occasional flops into the water. Adult looks white at a distance, but the upperparts and wings are a pale grey, with black outer web on first primary visible in flight and at rest. **Juvenile** Greyish-brown eye mask from eye over ear-coverts backwards to lower nape; forehead whitish, crown becoming streaked darker; chin, throat and underparts white. Upperparts with saddle brownish, edged buff and grey; rump and uppertail-coverts whitish; tail greyish, with brown subterminally and white tip, rounded (not forked). Outer primaries dark grey, subterminally brown, with white tips; rest of upperwing paler grey, with buffish-brown tips to coverts and tertials. Underwing white. Bill greyish-yellow, soon turning black; legs black. **First-year** Much as adult, but with white crown showing darker brownish streaks. Saddle pale grey with a few scattered brownish tips. Upperwing mainly pale grey; tertials and some coverts show variable pale brownish tips. Tail becomes white (lacking streamers). Bill and legs black. **Adult** Head mainly white, with triangular black spots before each eye continuing narrowly over ear-coverts, broadening and meeting on lower nape. Upperparts very pale grey; rump, uppertail-coverts and deeply forked tail white. Underparts white (may show pinkish tinge). Upperwing uniformly pale grey (as upperparts), with outer web of outermost primary black. Underwing white, outermost primary with dark outer web. Bill slightly decurved, black (tip occasionally paler); iris dark brown; legs and feet black. Differs from non-breeding Roseate Tern in smaller size, black legs and whiter upperparts. From similar immature Little and Fairy Terns by larger size and jizz, longer bill, and pinkish flush on breast at close range; also stronger flight.

DISTRIBUTION AND STATUS Breeds colonially, usually on sand or gravel in the Indian Ocean at Seychelles, Chagos, Maldive, Andaman and Nicobar Islands, south-east Asia and north-east Australia; in the Pacific on numerous island groups east as far as Tokelau. Total population unknown but many thousands in the Pacific. Widespread, some populations dispersive. Vagrants Oman, South Africa, Line Islands.

SOUTH AMERICAN TERN

Sterna hirundinacea L 42 cm (17 in), WS 85 cm (33 in)
Medium-sized, black-capped South American marine tern.

IDENTIFICATION Often forages in flocks, plunge-diving for food from up to 5 m; also hovers and dips, snatching food from the sea surface. **Juvenile** Darkish cap extends from lores through eye to ear-coverts, broadening to reach lower nape and rear crown (brownish-black); forehead whitish-brown, becoming darker on crown; chin and throat buffish-brown, becoming whiter on hindneck. Upperparts have grey saddle with strong brownish-black barring; rump and uppertail-coverts white; tail greyish, with brownish barring on outer feathers. Underparts whitish, but buffish-brown of chin and throat extends to sides of breast. Outer four to six primaries dark greyish (outer web of first primary black); inner primaries and secondaries grey with whitish tips; coverts grey with strong brownish-black barring. Underwing white, outer primary tips slightly greyer. Bill blackish; legs and feet dull orange-brown. **First-winter** Eye mask, ear-coverts, hindcrown and nape blackish; forehead, lores, chin, throat and underparts white. Upperparts with saddle pale greyish with some brown tips; rump and uppertail-coverts white; tail greyish with reduced brownish tips. Wings much as juvenile, but median and greater coverts become grey; lesser coverts and carpal darker, forming dark carpal bar. Bill black; legs and feet become dull red. **Adult non-breeding** Much as breeding adult, but forehead and forecrown white, underparts mainly white. Bill and legs duller red. **Adult breeding** Black cap from upper mandible through and above eye to lower nape; whitish from bill base narrowly to ear-coverts, merging into greyish chin, throat and sides of lower face. Upperparts with saddle pale pearl-grey; rump, uppertail-coverts and tail white, tail deeply forked with long streamers. Underparts very pale grey, becoming whiter on vent. Upperwing pale pearl-grey, with darker outer primaries (darker outer webs to primaries one to six); tips of inner primaries and secondaries whitish. Underwing white, with slightly darker primary tips. Bill, legs and feet bright red. From Antarctic Tern by longer drooping bill, paler grey upperparts with darker outer primaries, and whiter underparts. From Common and Arctic Terns by larger size, heavier, longer and more curved bill.

DISTRIBUTION AND STATUS Breeds in dense colonies usually on sandy and rocky beaches from *c* 15°S in Peru and *c* 25°S in Brazil southwards to Tierra del Fuego and the Falkland Islands. Total population unknown, but very common Argentina. In winter disperses north to Ecuador and to *c* 12°S in Brazil.

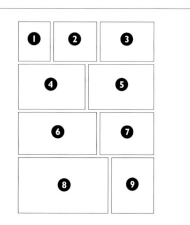

1 **White-fronted Tern** (adult non-breeding, New Zealand)
2 **White-fronted Tern** (adult non-breeding, New Zealand)
3 **White-fronted Tern** (juvenile, New Zealand, March)
4 **White-fronted Tern** (adult breeding, New Zealand, March)
5 **Black-naped Tern** (adult, Barrier Reef, Australia, October)
6 **South American Tern** (juvenile)
7 **South American Tern** (adult non-breeding)
8 **South American Tern** (adult breeding)
9 **South American Tern** (adult breeding, Falkland Islands)

TERNS

COMMON TERN

Sterna hirundo L 36 cm (14 in), WS 80 cm (31 in)

Medium-sized, widespread, marine and freshwater tern with black-tipped red bill, black cap, red legs, grey upperparts and paler grey underparts.

IDENTIFICATION Flight is slower and more gull-like than that of Arctic Tern, and against the light only the inner primaries are translucent (on Arctic all are translucent), forming a dark wedge on the outer primaries. **Juvenile** Ear-coverts, crown and nape sooty-brownish; ginger-brown forehead of fledgling becomes white by autumn; chin, throat and underparts white. Mantle, scapulars and back pale greyish-brown with brown and white scaling; rump greyish; tail greyish-white with darker outer web of outer feather. Upperwing mainly pale grey, with blackish carpal bar on forewing, blackish secondaries and primary tips. Underwing as adult. Bill black with pinkish or orange base; legs orange. **First-year** Much as adult non-breeding, but with duskier crown. Wings show dark carpal bar on inner forewing and dark secondaries (much more prominent than on either Roseate or Arctic Tern). Dark outer primaries contrast with lighter inner primaries. **Adult non-breeding** As adult breeding, but forehead and forecrown white. Underparts white. Tail lacks streamers. Bill blackish. **Adult breeding** Black cap from bill base to lower nape; faint whitish stripe from gape to ear-coverts (less pronounced than on Arctic Tern), merging into whitish-grey chin and throat. Upperparts mid grey, rump paler grey; tail white with long streamers, outer web of outer feather black. Underparts variable: generally whitish on breast and merging into greyer belly, which is paler than upperparts. Upperwing mid grey, with darker wedge on outer five or six primaries (more obvious in summer). Underwing whitish, with blackish-grey tips to outer five to six primaries. Bill orange-red with black tip; iris blackish; legs red. From Arctic Tern by longer bill, with longer, flatter crown (with the highest point behind the eye), longer legs, and wings never shorter than the tail, together with paler underparts and a wider black border along primaries on underwing; the head, neck and bill look more powerful and has a more angular shape than Arctic, with more uniformly broad and shorter wings giving more of a 'small gull' impression, a heavier body, and shorter and broader tail.

DISTRIBUTION AND STATUS Widespread. Breeds colonially and solitarily, both coastally and inland on sandy beaches and dunes, islands in lakes and estuaries, and artificial rafts from North America through the Caribbean to Venezuela, north Atlantic islands, north and west Africa, Europe through the Middle East to north-east Asia (including Kashmir, Tibet, Mongolia and China). Total population *c* 250,000-500,000 pairs with most in Asia and *c* 140,000 pairs in Europe. Disperses to Southern Hemisphere: American populations to Peru and Argentina; European populations mostly to west and South Africa; Asian populations largely to Indian Ocean and south Australia. Most first-winter birds remain in Southern Hemisphere throughout their first summer (and sometimes longer). Some populations now declining from human predation and loss of habitat.

ARCTIC TERN

Sterna paradisaea L 36 cm (14 in), WS 80 cm (31 in)

Medium-sized, northern circumpolar, marine tern with red bill, black cap and red legs, and medium grey upperparts with whiter rump and tail; underparts are a similar shade of grey to the upperparts, thus darker than either Common or Roseate Tern.

IDENTIFICATION Wingbeats are deeper than Common Tern's, with the body moving up and down in flight. Forages more efficiently in a wind than Common, with vertical plunges, diving more at an angle in calmer conditions. **Juvenile** Ear-coverts, crown and nape sooty-brownish; forehead, hindneck, chin, throat and underparts white. Upperparts dark grey, with less ginger-brownish tone than Common or Roseate Tern, usually without scaling; rump and tail pure white, latter without streamers and with outer web of outer feather greyish. Upperwing dark grey, with faint dark carpal bar on inner forewing; primaries have narrow dark tips; secondaries whiter, forming whitish triangle on hindwing. Underwing as adult. Bill blackish with variable dull orange base; legs and feet orange-red. **First-year** Much as non-breeding adult, except for indistinct carpal bar on inner forewing. Upperparts paler and greyer than juvenile. White rump and whitish secondaries help to distinguish it from Common Tern. **Adult non-breeding** As breeding adult, but forehead and underparts white. Bill blackish; legs blackish-red. **Adult breeding** Black cap from bill base to lower nape; whitish stripe from gape to ear-coverts, merging into greyish chin and throat. Mantle and back grey, contrasting with white rump and white tail, latter with long streamers. Underparts mainly medium grey, whiter on vent and undertail-coverts. Upperwing mainly uniform grey; outer seven to eight primaries have narrow dark tips, secondaries whitish tips. Underwing white, with narrow black tips on outer primaries forming thin dark trailing edge; primaries translucent. Bill, legs and feet red; iris blackish. Adults in flight have a characteristic appearance, with grey underparts, white underwing and long tail. Wings are narrower than Common Tern's, with longer, more pointed hand, and appear set more forward on the body, this enhanced by the shorter head and bill and the long tail; the primaries are translucent at all ages (thus lacking wedge of Common Tern), and the black rear edge to the outer seven to eight primaries is prominent on the underwing. Perched birds, compared with Common, look 'neckless' and have shorter body, deeper breast, longer tail (usually extending beyond wing length), very short legs, more evenly rounded crown (with the highest point above the eye), and normally a shorter, slimmer and narrower bill.

DISTRIBUTION AND STATUS Circumpolar in arctic and subarctic regions. Disperses south to Antarctica. Breeds usually colonially on shingle beaches, tundra, islands in lakes and artificial structures in North America and Canada, Greenland and Iceland, Europe south to France, and across northern Asia to Alaska. Total population *c* 500,000 pairs with most in Asia; some populations have declined and others insufficiently known. Long range dispersal south to the Antarctic pack ice, usually well offshore where first and second year birds remain.

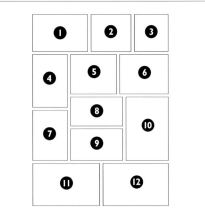

1 **Common Tern** (adult breeding)
2 **Common Tern** (adult breeding, USA)
3 **Common Tern** (first summer, Merseyside, England)
4 **Common Tern** (first winter, Kent, England, September)
5 **Common Tern** (juvenile, Merseyside, England)
6 **Common Tern** subspecies *S. h. longipennis* (adult breeding, New Zealand, April)
7 **Arctic Tern** (adult acquiring breeding plumage, Merseyside, England, May)
8 **Arctic Tern** (adult breeding, Manitoba, Canada)
9 **Arctic Tern** (first summer, Zeeland, Netherlands, August)
10 **Arctic Tern** (adult breeding, Manitoba, Canada)
11 **Arctic Tern** (juvenile, Netherlands, September)
12 **Arctic Tern** (adult breeding pair, Manitoba, Canada)

TERNS

ANTARCTIC TERN

Sterna vittata L 41 cm (16 in), WS 79 cm
(31 in)
Medium-sized Southern Hemisphere marine tern, with a black cap, red bill and legs, mainly grey upperparts and wings, with darker outer primaries and white rump, tail and underwing; variable greyish underparts, with correspondingly variable whitish facial streak.
IDENTIFICATION Generally forages in kelp beds and the surf zone, where birds hover up to 10 m above the sea and feed by dipping; will also forage on the ground inland on oceanic islands. **Juvenile** Forehead brownish, mottled with white, becoming darker blacker-brown with white mottling on crown and nape; chin, throat and sides of face white. Upperparts have greyish-buff saddle with black barring and white rump; uppertail-coverts white, barred dark brown; tail white, with darker grey outer webs and brownish tips. Underparts whitish, with brownish wash on breast sides extending to flanks. Primaries dark grey, subterminally tipped brown and fringed white; secondaries grey; coverts as saddle. Underwing white. Bill and legs black. **First-year** Much as non-breeding adult, but crown darker. Upperparts and upperwings have scattered brownish tips, with dark carpal bar on inner forewing. Bill and legs blackish. **Adult non-breeding** As breeding adult, but lores, forehead and crown white, merging well behind eye level into blackish nape and hindcrown, blackish extending over ear-coverts to reach eye and forming dark eye mask. Lower breast may be darker grey. Bare parts duller than adult breeding. **Adult breeding** Black cap from bill base to hindneck; whitish facial streak from gape to ear-coverts, extending to hindneck; chin and throat grey. Upperparts with saddle mid grey, contrasting with white rump and deeply forked white tail. Underparts variably greyish from chin and throat, becoming whiter on vent and undertail-coverts. Upperwing grey, outer webs of outermost primaries slightly darker. Underwing white, with narrow blackish trailing edge to primaries (much as Arctic Tern). Bill bright red; iris blackish; legs and feet dark reddish. Generally resembles a large Arctic Tern, which is in non-breeding plumage from October to April when in the Southern Hemisphere, but Antarctic Terns are in breeding plumage at this time. Summer-plumaged Antarctic differs from the slightly larger South American Tern in darker grey upperparts and underparts and proportionately smaller bill. From smaller Kerguelen Tern by lighter grey underparts, paler upperparts, white (not grey) underwing, larger and thicker bill, and more forked whiter tail. From similar, but smaller White-cheeked Tern (though ranges do not overlap) by white rump. In winter plumage resembles Arctic and Common Terns, but larger size imparts a heavier jizz, generally with darker plumage, whiter lores and a stronger, heavier bill which can be blackish or reddish.
DISTRIBUTION AND STATUS Almost circumpolar on islands in the Southern Ocean. Breeds colonially or solitarily on gravel and rocky beaches, stacks and cliffs on Antarctic Peninsula, South Shetlands, South Orkneys, South Sandwich, South Georgia, Bouvet, Tristan da Cunha and Gough, Prince Edward Islands, Crozets, Amsterdam and St Paul, Heard and Macquarie. Also Stewart Island, Snares, Auckland, Bounty, Antipodes and Campbell Islands. Total population unknown, but at least 50,000 pairs with 35,000 pairs in the South Shetlands. Some populations sedentary, others disperse to southern South America and South Africa (where birds moult) in austral winter. Vagrant Australia.

KERGUELEN TERN

Sterna virgata L 33 cm (13 in), WS 75 cm
(30 in)
Small, oceanic but sedentary, black-capped tern of the southern Indian Ocean, with reddish bill and legs, predominantly dark grey upperparts and underparts, white facial stripe, and a shortish, slightly forked grey tail. A little-studied species, classified as Vulnerable.
IDENTIFICATION Flight is graceful and buoyant, with a jizz reminiscent of a marsh tern; appears to forage at sea, generally within the kelp zone, and inland on crater lakes. Highly gregarious. **Juvenile** Forehead, crown and nape brownish-black; chin, throat and sides of face whitish with browner tips. Upperparts with saddle dark grey, barred darker brownish, rump whitish, and uppertail-coverts grey, barred brownish; tail grey with brownish tip. Underparts white, with brownish barring from chin and throat extending to breast sides and flanks; lower belly and vent progressively whiter. Upper primaries grey, brown subterminally, with tan fringes; secondaries grey; coverts as saddle. Underwing white. Bill and legs black. **First-year** Much as non-breeding adult, but with brownish tips to mantle, and brownish upperwing tips from dark carpal bar. Underwing white. **Adult non-breeding** Similar to breeding adult, but forehead and forecrown white with blackish streaking. Bill black; legs dark red. **Adult breeding** Black cap from bill base to lower nape; white facial streak from gape extending narrowly below eye onto hindcrown; chin and throat dark grey. Upperparts with saddle dark grey, contrasting with white rump; tail grey (whitish inner webs not normally visible). Underparts dark grey from chin and throat, becoming paler on vent and undertail-coverts. Upperwing dark grey, outer primaries darker. Underwing grey (no dark outer primary tips). Bill reddish; legs dark red. In summer plumage resembles a small Antarctic Tern, but darker grey both above and below (so the white rump and the white facial stripe are more conspicuous), with reddish bill smaller and thinner, underwing greyer and tail shorter and less forked; the outer web of the first primary is blackish (visible on perched birds at close range), while in flight the outer primaries are darker than the rest of the wing.

DISTRIBUTION AND STATUS Southern Indian Ocean. Breeds colonially, occasionally solitarily on partly vegetated flat ground, often close to both boulder beaches and inland water at the Prince Edward Islands (c 125 pairs), Crozets (150-200 pairs) and Kerguelen (up to 2,000 pairs). Total population c 2,400 pairs – one of the world's rarest terns. The main threat is from feral cats on Kerguelen; however, the introduction of salmonid fish in to the Kerguelen rivers should provide an additional food source. Sedentary, not recorded away from the few breeding islands.

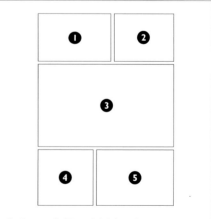

1 **Antarctic Tern** (adult breeding, Antarctic Peninsula)
2 **Antarctic Tern** (adult non-breeding)
3 **Antarctic Tern** (adult in transitional plumage, South Africa)
4 **Antarctic Tern** (first winter, South Africa)
5 **Kerguelen Tern** (adult breeding)

TERNS

FORSTER'S TERN

Sterna forsteri L 36 cm (14 in), WS 80 cm (31 in)

Medium-sized, pale, freshwater and marine North American tern with red bill, black cap and red legs.

IDENTIFICATION Flight is strong, and foraging birds plunge vertically or obliquely from up to 10 m; when hawking for insects over inland marshes, however, employs a slower, more graceful flight. **Juvenile** Forehead, crown and nape sooty-brown, becoming whiter from forehead backwards; lores and ear-coverts blacker, providing contrast with white of chin, throat and hindneck. Upperparts with saddle pale grey, tipped buffish-brown, providing contrast with white rump; tail pale grey, with whiter outer feathers and narrow black inner border. Underparts white (sides of breast may be brownish). Upperwing pale grey; darker outer primaries contrast with whiter inner primaries and outer secondaries; brownish tips to greater and median coverts. Bill blackish, occasionally with red base; legs orange. **First-year** Like adult non-breeding, but with more extensive dark eye patches meeting across greyer lower nape. Outer primaries darker, with mottling on carpal, tertials and inner secondaries. By summer, base of bill reddish with whitish tip. **Adult non-breeding** Much as adult breeding, but head mainly white, with blackish eye patches not meeting across pale greyish nape. Bill blackish (base may be reddish); legs orange-red. **Adult breeding** Black cap from bill base to lower nape; chin, throat, sides of face and underparts white. Upperparts with saddle pale grey, rump greyish-white; tail deeply forked (streamers), greyish-white with white outer web of outer feather. Upperwing mainly pale grey; outer three to five primaries darker, contrasting with paler silvery-white inner primaries; secondaries pale grey. Underwing greyish-white, with dusky grey tips to outer primaries and outer web of first primary. Bill and legs red. Species most resembles Common Tern, but has shorter wings, larger head, longer and heavier bill and longer legs and tail; usually white-headed, apart from adults in summer. In flight also recalls Common Tern, but has a more cigar-shaped body which (with larger head) looks more front-heavy; only the inner primaries are translucent. White-headed non-breeders can also recall a small Sandwich Tern in flight, with similar head pattern and pale plumage, while at rest Forster's Tern looks like a long-legged Common with paler primaries.

DISTRIBUTION AND STATUS North America. Breeds in loose colonies (occasionally solitarily) in freshwater lakes, inland and coastal marshes, and salt ponds from southern British Columbia across the prairie provinces to Ontario, the Great Lakes and Indiana, New York to North Carolina, and along the Gulf Coast from Alabama to New Mexico. Total population unknown but at least 14,000 breeding pairs in the USA with *c* 6,000 pairs of these on the Atlantic coast; Canadian and Mexican populations are not known. Range extension northwards in recent years. Disperses south in winter to southern California, Central America to Panama, the Atlantic Gulf coast and the Caribbean, with birds being decidedly more maritime in winter. Vagrant to Iceland and the British Isles.

TRUDEAU'S TERN

Sterna trudeaui L 33 cm (13 in), WS 77 cm (30 in)

Medium-sized, uncapped South American tern of fresh and salt water, with pale whitish-grey plumage, yellow bill with black tip, reddish-orange legs, and blackish eye patches which contrast against the white head.

IDENTIFICATION Juvenile Dusky eye crescent and black streak through ear-coverts, not extending across nape; forecrown, lores, chin, throat and underparts white; crown white with faint brownish mottling, upper nape white, lower nape and hindneck white with brownish-grey mottling. Upperparts with saddle pale grey with brownish tips, rump whitish; tail grey with brownish tips and white fringes. Primaries and primary coverts dark grey with whitish inner webs; innermost primaries and secondaries whiter with greyish centres; coverts pale grey with indistinct brownish tips, heaviest on tertials (no dark carpal bar). Underwing mainly white. Bill black with yellowish-brown base; legs dull yellow. **First-year** Much as non-breeding adult, but with darker blackish-grey outer webs to outer three primaries, and some greyish-brown mottling on alula and primary coverts. **Adult non-breeding** As adult breeding, but eye patch greyer (may show some grey on nape), underparts white; whiter outer primaries. Bill blackish with yellow tip. **Adult breeding** Head white, with conspicuous black eye patch extending to ear-coverts but not to nape. Saddle pale grey, rump white; tail greyish-white and forked, but no streamers. Underparts greyish-white. Upperwing pale grey, primaries more silvery-white; secondaries pale grey with narrow white edges. Underwing white (no dark primary tips). Bill yellow with blackish subterminal band; iris blackish; legs and feet reddish-orange. Flight, jizz and general appearance (especially non-breeding adults) can also suggest Forster's, but ranges do not overlap, and Trudeau's Tern is smaller, with a comparatively shorter tail, more uniformly pale upperparts and a different bill colour.

DISTRIBUTION AND STATUS Southern South America. Breeds loosely colonially in vegetated lagoons mainly in marshes, but also dykes and islands in saline lagoons from Uruguay (and probably south Brazil) to Patagonia, also in southern Chile (Aconcagua to Llanquihue) where less common. Total population unknown, but most in Patagonia; said to be abundant in March on Uruguayan coast and around mouth of Rio de la Plata. Dispersal north to south Peru on Pacific coast and to at least Rio de Janeiro area on Atlantic coast, with only occasional records south to Magellan Straits. Mainly a freshwater species, preferring larger well-vegetated marshy areas, but also (especially in the non-breeding season) along coasts, lagoons and river mouths. Habitat destruction, as well as vulnerability of remaining suitable wetlands, are current threats to population, and could become a serious problem in foreseeable future.

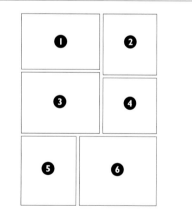

1 **Forster's Tern** (adult breeding pair, Cape May, USA)
2 **Forster's Tern** (adult non-breeding, Florida, USA)
3 **Forster's Tern** (first winter, Cape May, USA)
4 **Forster's Tern** (juvenile, New York, USA)
5 **Forster's Tern** (adult breeding, USA)
6 **Trudeau's Tern** (adult, Argentina)

TERNS

LITTLE TERN

Sterna albifrons L 23 cm (9 in), WS 52 cm (20 in)
Small, widely distributed, black-capped tern, with a triangular white forehead patch.

IDENTIFICATION Flight is fast with rapid wader-like wingbeats; forages usually in shallow inshore waters, where birds hover with downward-pointing bill and plunge-dive vertically from up to 10 m. **Juvenile** Forehead yellowish-brown with white streaking (soon turns white), becoming browner with less streaking on crown, and merging into darker brown eye streak from just in front of eye, through ear-coverts to nape; chin, throat, sides of neck, hindneck and underparts white. Saddle grey with blackish-brown 'V' markings; rump and uppertail-coverts pale grey; tail pale grey with whiter outer feathers (may show brownish tip). Outer three to six primaries and their coverts blackish-grey; inner primaries and secondaries paler whitish-grey; marginal and lesser coverts brownish-grey, forming indistinct carpal bar. Underwing white. Bill blackish with yellow base; legs and feet greyish-yellow. **First-year** Forecrown becomes whiter, saddle and wing-coverts become clearer grey, and bill and legs become dusky by summer. **Adult non-breeding** Much as breeding adult, but crown becomes mottled with white, and prominent black spot in front of eye; lesser coverts darker, and tail becomes greyer. Dark bill and dull legs. **Adult breeding** Forehead white, extending and narrowing over eye; crown and nape black, black extending narrowly through eye to base of bill; chin, throat, sides of face and underparts white. Saddle pale grey; rump and uppertail-coverts whitish-grey; tail white, short and forked (streamers). Upperwing pale blue-grey, with outer two or three primaries and their coverts blackish, forming dark leading edge to wing. Underwing white, outermost primaries with darker tips. Bill yellow with black tip; iris blackish; legs and feet yellow to orange-yellow. Compared with other terns, the wings appear pointed and very narrow in flight, with slender body and shorter tail. Perched birds look short-legged and compact, with head drawn into the body, while the bill looks long (about the same length as the head). The legs and tail-streamers are comparatively longer than on Saunders's Tern, which also has dark outer primaries, slightly paler grey upperparts, brown (not yellow legs), and no whitish supercilium behind the eye.

DISTRIBUTION AND STATUS Breeds colonially on beaches, islands and salt marshes in Europe, Africa, central and south-east Asia and Australia. Recent range expansion to Saipan (Northern Mariana Islands) and Hawaii. Total population c 70,000-100,000 pairs with c 50,000 pairs in Russia. Northern populations disperse southwards. Suffering from habitat loss habitat and disturbance.

SAUNDERS'S TERN

Sterna saundersi L 23 cm (9 in), WS 51 cm (20 in)

Small, black-capped tern of north-west Indian Ocean, very similar to Little Tern and previously regarded as a subspecies.

IDENTIFICATION Juvenile As Little Tern. Identification criteria still evolving, but probably identical. Some birds from Bahrain show a darker bar on the secondaries. **Adult non-breeding** Much as Little Tern. As adult breeding, but upperparts darker (and can be darker than Little Tern); uniform grey rump and back may not be entirely reliable for separating from Little Tern. Forehead, crown and lores may be whiter than on Little, and black mask is generally broader, imparting more of a Lesser Crested Tern pattern. Bill and legs blackish. **Adult breeding** Much as Little Tern, and probably reliably separated only by a combination of the following: white forehead patch extending only to eye, where it is rounded off or square-cut, thus lacking suggestion of a white supercilium; upperparts uniformly pale pearly-grey, generally paler than Little Tern and lacking the latter's contrast of paler rump and darker back; the tail-streamers are generally shorter; the black leading edge of the outer wing formed by the black outer three primaries is broader and blacker on most Little Terns and thus contrasts more with the paler grey of the rest of the wing. Legs mid brown to reddish-brown, generally shorter than on Little Tern. In areas where the two species breed together, Saunders's Tern tends to prefer a more marine environment.

DISTRIBUTION AND STATUS Breeds in loose colonies on mudflats and sand in the Red Sea, southern Somalia, Saudi Arabia and Oman, the Persian Gulf, north-west India, and Sri Lanka. May breed northern Indian Ocean islands (eg Maldives). Total population and dispersal unknown at present because of identification difficulties.

LEAST TERN

Sterna antillarum L 23 cm (9 in), WS 51 cm (20 in)
The North and Central American equivalent of Little Tern, from which it has been split as a full species.

IDENTIFICATION Flight and manner of foraging are identical to those of Little Tern. **Juvenile** Much as juvenile Little Tern. Pale spotting on nape. Upperparts have whitish to pale yellowish-brown edges in fresh plumage, dark 'V' markings and spots more rounded in shape, broader and browner than on Little; rump pale grey with paler narrow yellow-brown edges; tail with greyish-brown tip. Underparts white with yellowish-brown tinge. Lesser coverts have more distinct dark bar. Bill blackish; legs and feet yellowish-orange. **First-year** Much as Little Tern, although yellowish-brown edges retained longer. By summer much as adult non-breeding, but with forehead and crown mottled paler. Dark lesser coverts retained, tail darker. **Adult non-breeding** Much as Little Tern, but tail and rump darker. Bill blackish-brown with yellow base; legs greyish-brown with yellowish tinge.

Adult breeding White of forehead extends to eye only, generally shorter than on Little Tern; crown and nape black, this extending through eye as loral stripe to bill base (black on lores may be more extensive than on Little); chin, throat and sides of face white. Upperparts more bluish-grey than on Little Tern, extending onto rump and central tail. Underparts perhaps greyer than Little's. Upperwing bluish-grey; outer two to three primaries and their coverts blackish, forming dark leading edge to wing. Bill yellow with black tip (may be absent); iris blackish; legs reddish-orange, perhaps slightly greyer than Little Tern's. Differences from Little Tern are slight, subjective and still evolving. Structurally, Least Tern is slightly smaller, with shorter legs, a slimmer bill and longer tail-streamers; the most constant plumage difference is the rump and central part of the tail, which are the same shade as the rest of the upperparts (Little has a more contrasting white rump), and there may also be slight differences in head pattern and in colour of upperparts and underparts.

DISTRIBUTION AND STATUS Breeds usually colonially on beaches, sand bars and mudflats from California to Mexico (c 800 pairs), the northern Great Plains to Texas along rivers (c 1,000 pairs), Maine coastally to Florida Keys, and Texas to Honduras. Also Bermuda, Caribbean and northern Venezuela. Total population c 30,000+ pairs with most in eastern USA (c 21,500 pairs) and the Mississippi coast (c 7,000 pairs). Dispersal southwards as far as northern South America. Suffering habitat loss.

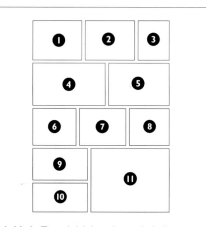

1 **Little Tern** (adult breeding with chick, Norfolk, England)
2 **Little Tern** (adult non-breeding, Sri Lanka, December)
3 **Little Tern** (adult breeding, Israel, May)
4 **Little Tern** (juvenile, Netherlands)
5 **Saunders's Tern** (adults, North Yemen)
6 **Saunders's Tern** (adult non-breeding, Azaiba, Oman)
7 **Least Tern** (adult breeding, Cape May, USA)
8 **Least Tern** (juvenile, New York, USA)
9 **Least Tern** (first winter, USA)
10 **Least Tern** (adult breeding, USA)
11 **Least Tern** (adult breeding, Cape May, USA)

TERNS

PERUVIAN TERN

Sterna lorata L 23 cm (9 in), WS 50 cm (20 in)
Small, uncrested South American tern, with black cap and white forehead suggesting Little Tern, black-tipped yellow bill, brownish-yellow legs, pale grey upperparts including rump and tail, outer primaries edged darker, and dusky grey underparts.

IDENTIFICATION Smallest tern of Humboldt region. Flight is hurried and fast, typical of small terns, with hovering before plunge-diving for food; usually forages over the sea and brackish water. **Juvenile** Variable, but generally much as juvenile Little Tern. Dark brown or blackish-brown face mask extends from the lores to the ear-coverts (a similar mask on Little is less pronounced or absent on the lores, but extends and broadens across the nape, giving the head a very different appearance). Upperparts as Little Tern. Underparts strongly buffish and lightly marked (whereas Little's underparts are white or very slightly washed buffish). **Adult non-breeding** Much as breeding adult, but crown whiter and extending back to upper nape, and underparts paler (almost white), with greyish wash across upper breast. Bill more extensively black with yellow base. **Adult breeding** Much as Little Tern. Forehead white, extending narrowly over eye; crown and nape black, black extending forward narrowly through eye as black eye mask to gape, isolating white forehead from greyish-white chin, throat and sides of face. Saddle slate-grey, rump and uppertail-coverts a shade paler; tail short and forked, greyish, with outer feathers whiter. Underparts pale greyish. Upperwing pale grey; outer webs of primaries one to three blackish, this decreasing inwards; secondaries have narrow white tips. Underwing greyish. Bill yellow with black tip; iris brown; legs and feet brownish-yellow. Although Peruvian recalls Little or Least Tern in size, jizz and general plumage, the darker grey of the rump, tail and underparts prevents confusion with those species.

DISTRIBUTION AND STATUS Humboldt Current. Breeds loosely colonially and solitarily on sandy beaches and dunes, also inland stony deserts of Peru and probably Chile. Total population unknown but about 5,000 pairs in Peru. Dispersal unknown, but recorded north to Guayaquil (Ecuador) and south to c 23°S in Chile.

FAIRY TERN

Sterna nereis L 25 cm (10 in), WS 50 cm (20 in)
Small, black-capped Australasian marine tern, with white forehead and lores, orange-yellow bill and legs, greyish upperparts and wings with slightly darker outer primaries, and white underparts. Classified as Vulnerable.

IDENTIFICATION Unlike Little Tern, Fairy Tern is very gregarious, often foraging in flocks, where hurried flight recalls that of Little, with similar hovering and plunge-diving. **Juvenile** Forehead dusky white; crown and nape brownish-black, extending narrowly over ear-coverts to enclose eye but not reaching bill. Saddle grey with blackish-brown edges; rump and uppertail-coverts white; tail white with brownish tip. Underparts white. Outer web of first primary black, remaining primaries grey, secondaries paler grey; coverts and tertials grey with brown tips. Underwing white. Bill and legs blackish-brown. **First-year** Much as breeding adult, but crown mottled white and blackish-brown; brownish tips to wing-coverts form faint carpal bar. Bill and legs blackish. **Adult non-breeding** Much as breeding adult, but crown white, imparting head pattern similar to Black-naped Tern. Bill yellow with dark tip; legs dull yellow. From similar-sized Little Tern by whiter crown and paler upperparts. **Adult breeding** Triangular spot in front of eye black, this extending through eye to blackish ear-coverts, nape and crown; lores, forehead, chin, throat, sides of face and underparts white. Saddle pale pearl-grey; rump, uppertail-coverts and forked tail white. Outer web of first primary black, visible at rest and in flight; otherwise upperwing pale pearl-grey as mantle, secondaries a shade paler. Underwing white (whiter than Little Tern). Bill and legs variable orange-yellow; iris brown. Superficially resembles Little Tern in plumage, jizz and flight, but distinguished by bill and leg colour, white (not dark) lores, more uniform upperwing, whiter underwing and paler underparts.

DISTRIBUTION AND STATUS Pacific Ocean. Breeds colonially or solitarily on sandy or coral islands and coastal dunes in western Australia (where population greatly reduced), South Australia, Victoria, Tasmania, the extreme north of North Island, New Zealand, and New Caledonia. Total population unknown, but c 2,000 pairs in Australia, c 10 pairs New Zealand, no data New Caledonia. Threats include flooding, human disturbance, predation, and possibly competition from Little Tern which is extending its range in South Australia. Some disperse to north-west Australia.

DAMARA TERN

Sterna balaenarum L 23 cm (9 in), WS 51 cm (20 in)
Small, black-capped, marine tern of southern Africa, with blackish bill, dark legs, and greyish upperparts and wings with black outer primaries forming dark leading edge. Classified as Near-threatened.

IDENTIFICATION Frequents inshore coasts, bays and lagoons, but does not form large flocks. **Juvenile** Head mainly white, with dark brownish-black cap extending backwards from eye across ear-coverts onto nape and lower crown; crown may show brownish and white flecking. Saddle grey, barred brownish and buff; rump, uppertail-coverts and tail white. Underparts white. Outer primaries and their coverts blackish-grey; inner primaries and secondaries grey; remaining coverts grey, barred darker, forming carpal bar. Bill and legs black. **Adult non-breeding** As breeding adult, but with lores, forehead and most of crown white. **Adult breeding** Full black cap from base of bill to nape; hindneck greyish; chin, throat and sides of face white. Saddle, rump and tail uniformly pale grey; tail short and forked, with slightly whiter outer feathers. Underparts white; sides of breast may be slightly greyer-white. Outer webs of outer primaries blackish (inner webs white); rest of upperwing pale grey as mantle. Underwing white with darker outer primaries. Bill black (some may show yellowish base); iris brown; legs and feet blackish-brown. Superficially resembles Little Tern, but has a heavier jizz, stronger and more even flight, and, in breeding plumage, a full black cap from bill base to nape; also a longer, slightly decurved, black bill and paler grey upperparts, including rump and uppertail, which tend to look white at a distance (as on Sandwich Tern).

DISTRIBUTION AND STATUS Southern Africa. Breeds loosely colonially on gravel and stony plains and dunes, up to 3 km inland (to minimize predation by Black-backed Jackal) in Namibia and the west and south coast of South Africa. Total population unknown accurately with varying estimates: probably several thousand pairs. Nesting birds disturbed by humans both on foot and in 4x4 vehicles while the exclusion of the general public from diamond-mining areas may actually aid protection. Disperses north in winter to Gulf of Guinea reaching Nigeria and Ghana – possible threats there unknown.

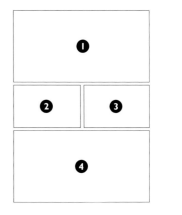

1 **Peruvian Tern** (adult, Chile, February)
2 **Fairy Tern** (adult breeding, New Zealand, December)
3 **Damara Tern** (adult breeding, Namibia, October)
4 **Damara Tern** (adult incubating)

TERNS

WHITE-CHEEKED TERN

Sterna repressa L 33 cm (13 in), WS 79 cm (31 in) Medium-sized, dark tern of north-west Indian Ocean.

IDENTIFICATION Normal flight is powerful, with deeper and faster wingbeats than Common Tern; plunges less frequently than other *Sterna* terns, with generally short dips to the surface, may hover near the surface. **Juvenile** Plumage as first-winter, except saddle feathers tipped brown with whitish fringes, and darker brown tip to tail. Bill blackish; legs yellow-brown. Similar to Common, but upperparts darker; generally more black on head than Common, which, with comparatively longer bill, gives Roseate-like appearance. **First-year** Forehead and forecrown white; blackish eye streak (broader than on Common) from eye through ear-coverts to crown and nape. Saddle medium grey; rump and tail greyish-white. Underparts white. Outer two primaries blackish (with white inner webs); remaining primaries and secondaries darkish grey with brownish tips and white fringes (indistinct dark secondary bar visible at close range); coverts grey, but blackish-grey marginal, lesser and outer primary coverts form dark carpal bar (more extensive than on Common). Underwing whitish (whiter than adults), with darker grey flight feathers. **Adult non-breeding** Much as non-breeding Common, but has darker grey upperparts, upperwings, rump and tail. Underparts white. Upperwing has outer web of outermost primary and remaining primary tips dark greyish, forming dark trailing edge to outer wing; secondaries have narrow whitish tips (can be difficult to see); outer primaries paler and more silvery than rest of upperwing. Underwing-coverts whitish-grey, contrasting with darker grey secondaries and primary tips which form dark trailing edge. Bill and legs dark, reddish-black. **Adult breeding** Full black cap from bill base enclosing eye to nape; whitish facial streak from base of bill below eye separates cap from dark greyish underparts. Plumage otherwise as non-breeding adult, but tail-streamers longer. Bill red with blackish tip; iris blackish-brown; legs and feet red. The darkest medium-sized *Sterna* tern. Recalls Common in size and jizz, but is slightly smaller, with shorter, more slender wings, and a longer bill which can droop at the tip.

DISTRIBUTION AND STATUS Breeds colonially with other terns on rocky, sandy and gravel substrates in the Red Sea, Somalia to Kenya, the Persian Gulf, Oman east to India. Total population unknown with variable estimates (eg 20,000-70,000 birds). Suffers from egg-collecting and avian predators. Dispersal to northern Indian Ocean, vagrants Eilat, South Africa.

ALEUTIAN TERN

Sterna aleutica L 36 cm (14 in), WS 78 cm (31 in) Distinctive, dark, medium-sized north Pacific marine tern.

IDENTIFICATION Flight strong and graceful, often high over the sea, with slower and deeper wingbeats than Common or Arctic Tern; the body rises and falls with the wingbeats, which are especially full on the downstroke. **Juvenile** Forehead, lores and crown fawn-brown, merging into darker brown nape forming black cap; chin, throat and sides of face whitish with variable light fawn wash. Saddle sepia-brown with lighter buffish or cinnamon-brown tips, heaviest on scapulars; rump and tail pale grey, tail fringed white. Underparts white, with yellowish-brown wash on sides of breast variably extending to flanks. Primaries slate-grey with brown subterminal tips and whitish fringes; inner primaries paler; secondaries grey with whitish tips; marginal coverts white, remainder as saddle. Underwing greyish-white with darker trailing edge. Bill and legs dull reddish-brown. **First-year/adult non-breeding** Much as breeding adult, but crown whiter, underparts whiter. **Adult breeding** Forehead white, extending narrowly over eye; crown and nape black, extending narrowly through eye to reach base of bill, thus isolating white forehead; chin and sides of face white, forming facial streak, shading to grey on throat. Saddle dark grey, contrasting with white rump, uppertail-coverts and tail, latter deeply forked. Underparts grey, a shade paler than upperparts, becoming white on vent and undertail. Outer webs of outer four or five primaries dark blackish-grey, forming dark wedge contrasting with paler whitish inner primaries; rest of wing dark grey, but with narrow white along inner leading and trailing edges. Underwing greyish-white with thin dark trailing edge, especially on secondaries. Bill and legs black. Similar in proportions and size to Common and Arctic, although the black bill is longer and narrower, and the wings longer and broader than on either.

DISTRIBUTION AND STATUS Breeds usually colonially on beaches, meadows and bogs from Sakhalin (2,100 pairs) and Sea of Okhotsk (c 1,000 pairs) to Kamchatka (500 pairs), Alaska and Aleutians. Total population probably under 15,000 pairs with most in Alaska. Dispersal south possibly to Philippines. Low breeding productivity, suffers both avian and mammalian predation. Vagrant Britain.

SPECTACLED or GREY-BACKED TERN

Sterna lunata L 36 cm (14 in), WS 74 cm (29 in) Medium-sized, black-capped, tropical Pacific tern.

IDENTIFICATION Juvenile Lower lores, forehead and narrow supercilium white, gradually merging on forecrown into darker blackish-brown of crown and nape which extends narrowly through eye as a loral streak to gape; chin, throat and sides of face white. Upperparts grey with buffish-brown and white fringes and edges, heaviest on scapulars; tail grey, outermost feather whiter. Underparts white, with variable greyish wash to sides of breast which may reach flanks. Primaries greyish-black, secondaries greyer; coverts grey, tipped buffish-brown, as mantle. Underwing mainly white, with browner flight feathers. **First-year** Similar to breeding adult, but crown and nape browner

with white streaking. Upperparts lose buff-brown and white fringes of juvenile. **Adult non-breeding** As breeding adult, but forecrown streaked white. **Adult breeding** White of forehead extends over eye as narrow supercilium; blackish of crown and nape extends narrowly through eye as loral streak to base of bill; chin, throat, sides of face and underparts white. Upperparts pale brownish-grey; tail brownish-grey, with outermost feather white. Primaries and secondaries blackish-grey, becoming paler and greyer towards saddle; marginal coverts white. Underwing white, with flight feathers browner. Bill, legs and feet black; iris brown. Spectacled Tern most closely resembles Bridled in both flight and appearance, but has a greyer saddle and inner upperwing, a slightly finer bill, whiter underparts and less white on the outer tail feathers. In paleness of the saddle and inner wings can resemble Aleutian Tern (ranges may overlap in the Pacific Ocean), but the dark (not white) rump and tail and whiter underparts of Spectacled prevent confusion. Sooty Tern is larger, darker, and has a different facial pattern.

DISTRIBUTION AND STATUS Breeds colonially on beaches, islands and low sea cliffs on the northern Mariana Islands east to Wake, northern Marshall and Hawaiian islands (estimates 18,000-51,000 pairs; heavy rat predation), Phoenix, Line (tens of thousands of pairs at each), Fiji, Australs and Tuamotu. Status on other islands unclear. Total population unknown. Dispersal to pelagic habitat, occasionally Moluccas and Caroline Islands.

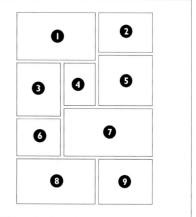

1 **White-cheeked Tern** (adult breeding, Saudi Arabia, June)
2 **White-cheeked Tern** (first winter, Egypt, October)
3 **White-cheeked Tern** (adult breeding, Saudi Arabia, June)
4 **Aleutian Tern** (adult breeding, Alaska)
5 **Aleutian Tern** (adult breeding at nest, Alaska)
6 **Aleutian Tern** (adult breeding, Alaska)
7 **Spectacled (Grey-backed) Tern** (adult breeding, Laysan Island, Hawaii)
8 **Spectacled (Grey-backed) Tern** (breeding adult on nest)
9 **Spectacled (Grey-backed)Tern** (adult breeding)

TERNS

BRIDLED TERN

Sterna anaethetus L 36 cm (14 in), WS 76 cm (30 in)

Medium-sized, long-winged, tropical marine tern found in all three oceans, with brownish to brownish-grey upperparts and wings, a white forehead (similar to Little Tern) contrasting with a blackish cap, and whitish underparts. **IDENTIFICATION** Normal flight is strong and purposeful, with the body moving up and down; forages normally by dipping and snatching food from the surface, with only the occasional plunge-dive. **Juvenile** Lower lores, forehead and narrow supercilium white, becoming buffish-brown on forecrown and merging evenly into blackish nape and hindcrown, this extending over ear-coverts to reach eye as a loral streak; chin, throat and sides of face white. Upperparts brownish-grey with buffish and white tips, heaviest on scapulars; tail brownish-grey. Underparts whitish, becoming greyer on sides of breast. Upperwing dark brownish-grey, with buffish tips to tertials and coverts. Underwing white, with brownish flight feathers. Bill and legs black. **First-year** Much as adult non-breeding, but juvenile wing and tail retained. **Adult non-breeding** Paler than breeding plumage. Mantle feathers and scapulars have pale edges. **Adult breeding** Forehead narrowly white, extending to just behind eye as a narrow supercilium; crown and nape black, this extending through eye as a loral streak to gape; white of chin, throat and sides of face extends to hindneck as a greyish-white collar separating cap from upperparts. Upperparts and tail brownish-black, outermost tail feathers white. Underparts white with variable light greyish tone. Upperwing blackish-brown, darker on primaries and secondaries; marginal coverts white. Underwing white, with brownish flight feathers. Bill (shorter than head length) and legs black; iris dark brown. Sooty Tern is similar in colour pattern, but is larger and a more black and white bird, with a darker underwing, and with white of forehead different in shape and not extending over the eye (also has less white on outer tail feathers); Bridled Tern, although a marine species, is less pelagic than Sooty and occurs more inshore, usually roosting ashore at night. Grey-backed Tern, which replaces Bridled in the tropical Pacific, is similar in size and pattern but has greyer upperparts and whiter underparts. **DISTRIBUTION AND STATUS** Pantropic. Breeds colonially, and usually annually on coral beaches, also rocky and sandy slopes on tropical and subtropical islands in all three oceans, although absent from central and eastern Pacific. Total population unknown, but probably exceeds 200,000 pairs with most (perhaps 130,000 pairs) in the Persian Gulf. Dispersive movements unclear, but widespread at sea eg very heavy southward passage observed off Sri Lanka. Prone to displacement by cyclones and hurricanes; has occurred Europe.

SOOTY TERN

Sterna fuscata L 43 cm (17 in), WS 90 cm (35 in)

Medium-sized, pelagic and tropical tern found in all three oceans, with blackish upperparts and cap, white forehead and white underparts; in flight appears long-billed, heavy-bodied and long-tailed. **IDENTIFICATION** Normal flight is strong, with deep wingbeats, often high over the ocean; forages in flocks, dipping and snatching food from the surface; does not plunge-dive, and rarely settles on the sea (plumage is not waterproof). **Juvenile** Head blackish-brown. Upperparts blackish-brown with buffish and sandy-white tips, heaviest on scapulars; tail shorter than adult's, lacking streamers, blackish with greyer outermost feather and tips. Underparts brownish-grey, with whitish tips to belly, becoming whitish-grey on vent, undertail-coverts and undertail. Upperwing blackish-brown, with whitish tips to tertials and coverts. Underwing mainly white, with brownish alula and flight feathers. **First-year** As juvenile, but forehead, nape and underparts paler. By summer, plumage more resembles adult, but underparts variable: generally, chin to upper breast blackish-brown, with rest of underparts white, or mainly white with duskier chin to upper breast. **Adult non-breeding** Much as breeding adult, but nape paler, and upperparts have variable white fringes. **Adult breeding** Forehead white, extending to above eye; crown, nape and hindneck black, this extending through eye as narrow loral stripe to base of bill, thus isolating white forehead from white underparts. Upperparts blackish-brown; tail blackish-brown, long outer streamers white. Upperwing mainly blackish-brown; marginal coverts white. Underwing white, with alula and flight feathers brownish. Bill, legs and feet black; iris brown. From smaller Bridled Tern by blacker upperparts, with cap and mantle appearing the same colour, white of forehead not extending over the eye and being more rounded in shape, lack of pale hindcollar, and broader dark trailing edge to the underwing; generally more pelagic than Bridled, usually returning to land only to breed. Has the longest-deferred maturity of any tern (six to eight years), and is prone to displacement by cyclones and hurricanes. **DISTRIBUTION AND STATUS** Pantropic. Breeds seasonally and aseasonally in large to huge colonies on sand, coral and rock, with or without vegetation, at many tropical and subtropical islands in all three oceans, although tends to avoid cool upwelling areas. Total population probably exceeds 25 million pairs – one of the most numerous seabirds with most in the South Pacific (eg 10,000,000 pairs Line Islands, c 1,500,000 pairs Hawaii, and over 1,000,000 pairs each at Phoenix and Marquesas). Some colonies suffer heavy predation (eg Ascension population reduced from 500,000 pairs to 200,000 pairs by cats), others have their eggs systematically collected,

with all first layings harvested. Dispersal to pelagic habitat in all three oceans; prone to displacement by cyclones and hurricanes. Vagrants Europe, South Africa, South Australia, New Zealand, western South America.

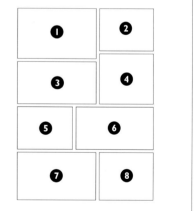

1 **Bridled Tern** (adult breeding, Australia)
2 **Bridled Tern** (adult breeding, Australia, October)
3 **Bridled Tern** (juvenile)
4 **Sooty Tern** (adult breeding)
5 **Sooty Tern** (first winter, Queensland, Australia, October)
6 **Sooty Tern** (first winter, Queensland, Australia, December)
7 **Sooty Tern** (juvenile, Queensland, Australia)
8 **Sooty Tern** (adult breeding, Queensland, Australia, October)

TERNS & NODDIES

BLACK TERN

Chlidonias niger L 23 cm (9 in), WS 66 cm (26 in)

Distinctive in summer plumage. Breeds inland, but, unlike other *Chlidonias* terns, winters mainly at sea.

IDENTIFICATION Juvenile Head as adult non-breeding, but cap browner. Mantle, scapulars, tertials and back brownish-grey (darker than adult) with blackish and buffish fringes; rump grey, paler than back; tail brownish-grey (may show dark terminal band). Underparts whitish, with brownish sides of breast (darker and more extensive than on adult). Upperwing brownish-grey, with darker leading edge (alula, marginal and lesser coverts). Bill blackish; legs orange-grey. From White-winged Tern by dark breast patches, darker and more extensive cap, and dark brownish-grey upperparts lacking saddle/rump contrast. **First-year** By winter, saddle becomes clearer grey: plumage much as adult non-breeding. By summer, underparts white or mixed black and white on throat, breast and belly; upperwings become faded and worn. May retain juvenile flight feathers, and tail very worn by summer. **Adult non-breeding** Dark cap extends to nape and ear-coverts; dark patch in front of eye, white eye-ring; forehead, chin, throat and hindneck band white. Upperparts pale brownish-grey; rump and tail may be greyer and less brown. Underparts white, with variable dark grey breast sides (absent on White-winged and Whiskered Terns). Upperwings silvery-grey; outer primaries may be darker. Bill and legs blackish-brown. **Adult breeding** Head blackish-grey. Mantle, scapulars and back slate-grey to blackish-grey; rump sides, uppertail-coverts and tail paler grey. Underparts blackish-grey from throat to lower belly; vent and undertail-coverts white. Upperwing slate-grey to blackish-grey with silvery tone when fresh, becoming darker with wear. Underwing greyish. Bill blackish; legs dark brown. *C. n. surinamensis* (North America) is generally darker: juvenile darker and more uniform above, especially on rump, with broader breastband merging into grey flanks; adult breeding more extensively and deeper black on head and underparts than nominate race. From White-winged Tern by slimmer jizz, proportionately longer wings, longer, more forked tail, longer bill, shorter and darker legs, and maritime winter habitat.

DISTRIBUTION AND STATUS Northern Hemisphere. Breeds colonially on well-vegetated inland lakes, marshes and peat bogs in Canada and North America, and in Europe from southern Scandinavia to Spain, eastwards across Europe and Asia to the Chinese border. Total population probably 500,000 pairs, with the majority in Russia and possibly 100,000 pairs in North America. Most populations now declining with land reclamation for agriculture. Dispersal south to winter at sea on both coasts of South America and west Africa. Vagrants Hawaii, Japan, Australia.

BROWN or COMMON NODDY

Anous stolidus L 42 cm (17 in), WS 82 cm (32 in)

Medium-sized, brownish, tropical pelagic tern found in all three oceans..

IDENTIFICATION Palest of the three *Anous* noddies. Forages by dipping, and snatching food from the sea surface; rarely plunge-dives, and infrequently settles on the sea. **Juvenile** As adult, but dark forehead and crown occasionally greyish. Whitish tips to mantle, upperwing-coverts, primaries and secondaries; blackish tail may show some paler tips; belly and vent area may be greyish-brown. Dark bill shorter and finer than adult's. **Immature** Generally as adult, with variable poorly developed white forehead. **Adult** White forehead and crown; sharp loral demarcation, but merging evenly into greyish-brown nape; small white crescents above and below eye. Upperparts dull brownish; tail blackish-brown. Underparts brownish, but belly and undertail-coverts greyer. Upperwing blackish-brown, primaries darker; lighter brownish median coverts across inner upperwing. Underwing dusky grey in centre, merging into darker margins (paler than either Lesser or Black Noddy). Bill short and powerful with curved upper mandible, black; iris dark brown; legs and feet dark brown. Wings are shorter and broader than on other terns of comparable size, and this, combined with the long tail, dark plumage and slow but powerful wingbeats, gives a distinctive heavier-looking jizz, with wings appearing well forward on the body. Identification of perched noddies is easier than with distant birds at sea, but Brown Noddy is larger and heavier than both Black and Lesser Noddies, with a more powerful flight, shows more contrast between the darker primaries and browner inner wing with paler coverts, and has a paler underwing than Lesser or Black.

DISTRIBUTION AND STATUS Pantropic. Breeds generally aseasonally and colonially on cliffs, flat beaches, bare ground, and in bushes and trees on tropical and subtropical islands in all three oceans. Total population 300,000-500,000 pairs, with most in Australia and on Phoenix and Society Islands. Tropical populations generally sedentary, subtropical populations more dispersive. Some displacement by cyclones and hurricanes.

BLACK or WHITE-CAPPED NODDY

Anous minutus L 34 cm (13 in), WS 76 cm (30 in)

Small to medium-sized, blackish, tropical pelagic tern of the Pacific and Atlantic Oceans.

IDENTIFICATION Juvenile Much as adult, but with less white on crown, which is sharply demarcated from blackish nape and similarly demarcated on lores. Buffish-white tips to upperwing-coverts and secondaries. **Immature** Much as juvenile, but lacks buffish-white tips to upperwing-coverts and secondaries. **Adult** White of forehead sharply demarcated from black lores, extending through white crown to merge evenly into greyer nape and hindneck (white cap generally more extensive than on either Brown or Lesser Noddy); small white crescents above and below eye. Upperparts, including tail, and underparts blackish-brown. Upperwing dark sooty-brown, primaries blacker. Underwing dark sooty-brown (unlike Brown Noddy). At all stages of plumage, appears darker and blacker than either Brown or Lesser Noddy. Bill long and thin, black; iris dark brown; legs and feet brown. Although the white forehead is more extensive and more conspicuous than on Brown Noddy, it merges into the greyish nape, and the border between the dark lores and the whitish forehead is straight and sharply demarcated (curved on Brown Noddy, though still sharply demarcated), while the bill is proportionately longer and thinner than on Brown Noddy, exceeding the head length (equal to head length on Brown); Black Noddy is also smaller and slimmer than Brown Noddy, with a faster and more fluttering flight. For differences from Lesser Noddy, see that species.

DISTRIBUTION AND STATUS Atlantic and Pacific Oceans. Breeds annually, often in dense colonies, preferably in bushes and trees on tropical and subtropical islands in the Atlantic and Pacific Oceans. Total population over 200,000 pairs with large numbers in Australia, Line and Phoenix Islands. Dispersal not well known; generally more sedentary than other noddy species. Vagrants Mauritania, Gambia and Nigeria.

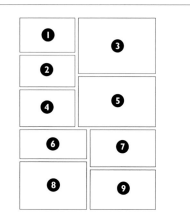

1 **Black Tern** (adult breeding, Merseyside, England)
2 **Black Tern** (juvenile moulting to first winter)
3 **Black Tern** (adult breeding, Greece, May)
4 **Brown (Common) Noddy** (juvenile, Lady Elliot Island, Coral Sea, March)
5 **Brown (Common) Noddy** (adult breeding)
6 **Brown (Common) Noddy** (adult breeding, Lady Elliot Island, Coral Sea, March)
7 **Black (White-capped) Noddy** (adult breeding)
8 **Black (White-capped) Noddy** (adult breeding, Norfolk Island, Australia)
9 **Black (White-capped) Noddy** (sub-adult)

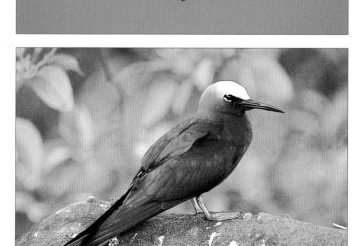

LESSER NODDY

Anous tenuirostris L 32 cm (13 in), WS 60 cm (24 in)

Small, dark brownish-grey, tropical pelagic tern of the Indian Ocean, with ashy-grey forehead and crown which usually merge evenly into the brown of the lores and the nape.

IDENTIFICATION Juvenile Resembles adult; some Australian birds may show whitish cap. Some appear drabber than juvenile Black Noddy. **Adult** Forehead and crown greyish-white, usually with no sharp loral demarcation and gradually merging into grey of nape and hindcrown (some Australian birds show atypically sharp demarcation between greyish-white forehead and blacker lores, more suggestive of typical Black Noddy); small white crescents above and below eye. Upperparts dark brown, shading to greyer on mantle; tail blackish-brown. Underparts brownish-grey. Upperwing and underwing dark brown, with slightly blacker primaries. Bill, legs and feet black; iris dark brown. From Brown Noddy by smaller size, narrower wings, lighter jizz with faster wingbeats, and longer and thinner bill; appears more uniformly dark-coloured than Brown Noddy, a shade greyer below, with more uniform upperwing and underwing patterns. From Black Noddy by slightly smaller size, browner-grey and less black plumage tone, and generally lacks sharp loral demarcation.

DISTRIBUTION AND STATUS Indian Ocean. Breeds colonially in trees and occasionally bushes in the Seychelles, Mascarene Islands, Cargados Carajos Shoals (St Brandon), Maldives, and Houtman Abrolhos Islands (Western Australia). Total population unknown at present – formerly abundant Western Australia, now reduced to *c* 30,000 pairs Pelsart Group (Houtman Abrolhos). Few known colonies but not endangered. Dispersal not well known; Western Australian birds are sedentary; fairly regular off eastern Africa.

BLUE-GREY or GREY NODDY

Procelsterna cerulea L 27 cm (11 in), WS 60 cm (24 in)

Small, dimorphic, distinct bluish-grey tern with black bill and black legs, until recently found only in the tropical and subtropical Pacific Ocean.

IDENTIFICATION Flight is buoyant and graceful; foraging birds pick food from the surface, and occasionally paddles on the sea surface. **Juvenile/immature** Generally bluish-grey, much as adult, but with some darker grey streaking on head, chin and throat. Light brownish cast to upperparts, underparts and wing-coverts. Primaries and secondaries blackish, forming conspicuous trailing edge to wing. **Adult pale form** (now usually, and probably correctly, treated as separate species, *P. albivitta*) Head and underparts pale greyish-white. Mantle bluish-grey; rump and uppertail-coverts white; tail slightly forked, light grey. Upperwing bluish-grey, with darker grey

primaries and secondaries; tertials, most coverts and secondaries show whitish tips. Underwing grey, with whiter coverts. **Adult dark form** (now normally treated as distinct species from *albivitta*) As pale morph but a shade darker, especially on head and underparts. Grey underwing-coverts give more uniform underwing. Bill black; iris black, with black ring around eye; legs and feet black with yellow webs. The combination of small size and greyish plumage should prevent confusion with other species, although in distant views pale-morph birds (can look white-headed) must be distinguished from superficially similar White Tern.

DISTRIBUTION AND STATUS Tropical and subtropical Pacific Ocean. Breeds loosely colonially on cliffs, rocky areas and bare substrate, and islands in lagoons. Both forms generally considered sedentary. Dark form (*cerulea*) breeds tropical Pacific on Marcus Island, Marshalls to Hawaiian archipelago, Christmas Island (Line Islands), Phoenix, Tuvalu (Ellice), Fiji, Western Samoa, Marquesas, Tuamotu, Society, Cook, Austral and Gambier Islands. Total population unknown, perhaps 100,000 pairs. Pale form (*albivitta*) breeds subtropical and temperate Pacific on Lord Howe, Norfolk, Kermadec, Tonga, Henderson, Easter Island, Sala y Gómez, Desaventurados (San Ambrosio and San Felix). Total population probably under 25,000 pairs with most in south-west Pacific. Recently recorded Andaman Sea, a significant range extension into Indian Ocean.

WHITE TERN

Gygis alba L 30 cm (12 in), WS 78 cm (31 in)

Small, delicate-looking, all-white, tropical marine tern found in all three oceans, with large black eyes and slightly upturned black bill with blue base.

IDENTIFICATION Compact jizz enhanced by short tail, broad and rounded white wings and a comparatively large head, yet flight is buoyant and graceful. **Juvenile** Much as adult, but with black ear spot, brownish mottling on nape, greyish-white upperwing, with brownish mottling and tips on saddle and wing-coverts. Black shafts to outer three to five primaries. Rump, underparts and underwing white. Tail short, pale grey, outer webs brownish. **Adult** White with faint ivory cast: the only completely white tern. Flight feathers and tail appear translucent from below, with darker underparts and underwing-coverts. Bill black, often with blue base; narrow black ring around eye; legs bluish. **Little White Tern (*G. (a.) microrhyncha*)** of the Pacific Ocean is treated as a full species by Sibley and Monroe, but included here as a subspecies (following Holyoak and Thibault): very similar to White Tern but noticeably smaller, and variously described as lacking blackish shafts on primaries, smaller-billed, with more black around eye and more shallowly notched paler tail. Apparently occurs on Paracel Islands

(South China Sea), as well as Phoenix, Line and Marquesas; those on the Marquesas interbreed with larger birds resembling *G. a. candida* (Holyoak and Thibault).

DISTRIBUTION AND STATUS Pantropic. Breeds solitarily or loosely colonially in trees and bushes, rocky slopes and cliffs on tropical and subtropical islands in all three oceans. Total population unknown but over 100,000 pairs with most in Western Samoa, Tokelau, Line and Phoenix Islands (over 10,000 pairs each): well distributed across the Pacific. Generally aseasonal breeding; unusual strategy laying single egg on tree branches, with no nest at all; most islands used are free from ground predators. Some populations sedentary, others disperse, but movements unknown.

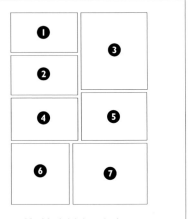

1 **Lesser Noddy** (adult breeding)
2 **Lesser Noddy** (adult breeding)
3 **Lesser Noddy** (adult breeding, Aride Island, Seychelles)
4 **Blue-grey (Grey) Noddy** (adult, Jarvis Island, central Pacific Ocean)
5 **Blue-grey (Grey) Noddy** (adult, Jarvis Island, central Pacific Ocean)
6 **White Tern** (adult breeding pair, Aride Island, Seychelles)
7 **White Tern** (adult breeding pair)

211

INCA TERN

Larosterna inca L 41 cm (16 in), WS ?
Large, uniformly dark bluish-grey, marine South American tern, with long rounded wings, shallow-forked tail, large bright red bill and red legs, indistinct blackish cap, conspicuous white moustache-like facial plumes, and a white trailing edge to the wing.
IDENTIFICATION Virtually unmistakable. Flight very buoyant and graceful; when foraging, hovers before dipping to the surface, showing rapid manoeuvrability for such a large bird. A very gregarious species found in harbours, roosting on beaches with gulls and foraging with marine cormorants and cetaceans.
Juvenile Wholly purplish-brown, with upperparts fringed greyish-buff, heaviest on scapulars and tertials, underparts greyer; no paler moustachial plumes. Blackish primaries and whitish trailing edge to wing. Bill and legs blackish. **Immature** More resembles adult, but generally darker, more brown-grey. Chin and throat paler grey; short pale grey moustache-like plumes appear from gape. Upperparts dark brownish-grey; tail blackish. Underparts brownish-grey. Upperwing dark brownish-grey, primaries and secondaries darker; inner primaries and secondaries tipped pale grey, forming whitish trailing edge. Bill and legs acquire dull reddish-horn tone. **Adult** Bluish-black cap from forehead to nape, merging into bluish-grey upperparts; yellow wattle at base of bill; conspicuous white moustache-like plumes from gape, curling downwards. Tail blackish. Underparts from chin and throat bluish-grey. Upperwing bluish-grey, primaries and secondaries darker; white trailing edge of wing from inner primaries inwards. Underwing bluish-grey, with coverts paler. Bill, legs and feet red; iris brown.
DISTRIBUTION AND STATUS Humboldt Current. Breeds loosely colonially and aseasonally on rocky sea cliffs, guano islands, often using abandoned petrel burrows, and on artificial structures from northern Peru to central Chile. Total population unknown, but estimated at about 50,000 pairs – variable with *El Niño* – found mainly on inshore guano islands of central Peru (eg Chinchas, Pescadores, Asia Island). Range extension south to Chile in 1930s, now common south to Valparaiso. Essentially sedentary, some dispersal north to Ecuador and south to Chiloé Island, Chile.

BLACK SKIMMER

Rynchops niger L 45 cm (18 in), WS 112 cm (44 in)
Largest and most marine of the three skimmers and the only one found in the Americas, where adults are unmistakable, with black upperparts, white underparts, white forehead, and black-tipped red bill with elongated lower mandible.
IDENTIFICATION Flight is graceful and buoyant, with measured beats of the long and pointed wings; forages low over the water surface, 'ploughing' with lower mandible in the water

until making contact with prey, when bill is snapped shut. Generally rests on beaches in the daytime, foraging more frequently early in the morning and towards dusk. Sociable. **Juvenile** Forehead white; crown, nape and hindneck dark brownish with black and white tips; lores, chin and throat white. Saddle dark greyish-brown with blackish centres and whitish fringes; rump and uppertail-coverts whiter, but soon turn browner; tail white with darker central feathers. Primaries and secondaries blackish, with white trailing edge from inner primaries; coverts as saddle. Underwing as adult. Bill reddish-horn with blacker tip, lower mandible longer than upper but shorter than adult's; legs horn-orange. **Adult non-breeding** Much as breeding adult, but upperparts browner, lower hindneck white, forming collar, and bill duller. **Adult breeding** Forehead white; crown, nape and hindneck black, continuous with black upperparts; rump, uppertail-coverts and tail white, tail with blackish central feathers. Underparts white. Upperwing black; inner primaries and all secondaries tipped white, forming white trailing edge. Underwing varies geographically; generally whitish with black primaries. Bill with elongated lower mandible, bright red with black tip; iris dark brown; legs short, bright red.
DISTRIBUTION AND STATUS Coasts, rivers and waterways of North and South America. Breeds colonially (occasionally solitarily) on sandbars and beaches of large rivers when water level is low, also increasingly on dredged islands, from Massachusetts and southern California southwards through Central America to Paraguay, Uruguay and Argentina. Total population unknown at present, but not endangered (USA population estimated at 68,000 birds in late 1970s with most in Louisiana and Texas). Northern populations disperse southwards to winter coastally. Numbers probably decreasing with human disturbance and loss of suitable habitat.

LITTLE AUK or DOVEKIE

Alle alle L 22 cm (9 in), WS 32 cm (13 in)
Small, short-necked auk, with black head and upperparts and white underparts, found in the higher latitudes of the Northern Hemisphere.
IDENTIFICATION Rapid wingbeats, small size and short bill impart characteristic 'plump' jizz. Gregarious, and may form large flocks at sea; can sit very low in the water. **Immature** Much as breeding adult, but bill smaller (75% of adult weight and adaptive to reduce gull predation). Head, neck and throat browner than adult, with paler chin. Mantle and back browner than adult. First-winter similar to non-breeding adult, but browner. **Adult non-breeding** Similar to breeding adult, but white on chin, throat, upper breast and ear-coverts: line of demarcation from lower mandible below eye to ear-coverts. **Adult breeding** Head and upperparts black, this extending on to upper breast. Underparts white from upper breast to tail. Upperwing black, with whitish tips to

secondaries and whitish streaking on scapulars. Underwing blackish, with variable whitish underwing-coverts. Tail black above, white below. Bill black; iris black; legs and feet dark grey. Distinctly different from any other high-arctic species, but beware of juvenile auks which have just taken to the sea.
DISTRIBUTION AND STATUS High Arctic, probably circumpolar in summer. Breeds in huge colonies on scree slopes of coastal cliffs from Baffin Island through Greenland and Iceland to Jan Mayen, Spitsbergen, Bear Island, Franz Josef Land, Novaya Zemlya, Severnaya Zemlya (Northland) to the Bering Sea (St Lawrence and Little Diomede Islands). May breed Ellesmere Island in the Canadian Arctic. Total population estimated at *c* 12,000,000 pairs with most (10,000,000 pairs) in north-west Greenland. The most abundant and the most northerly Atlantic alcid. Some birds winter within breeding range, some disperse southwards with the majority off the Grand Banks and Nova Scotia. Vagrants Cuba, Bermuda, Madeira, Mediterranean.

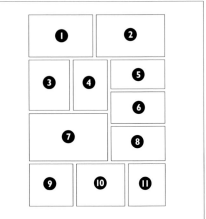

1 **Inca Tern** (juvenile)
2 **Inca Tern** (breeding adults and juvenile, Chile, February)
3 **Inca Tern** (breeding adult)
4 **Black Skimmer** (juvenile feeding by skimming, New York, USA, September)
5 **Black Skimmer** (juvenile, New York, USA)
6 **Black Skimmer** (first winter, Florida, USA)
7 **Black Skimmer** (adult breeding)
8 **Little Auk** (adult breeding, Spitsbergen)
9 **Little Auk** (adult breeding, Spitsbergen)
10 **Little Auk** (adult non-breeding, Kent, England, November)
11 **Little Auk** (adult non-breeding, England, January)

AUKS

GUILLEMOT or COMMON MURRE

Uria aalge L 42 cm (17 in), WS 71 cm (28 in)
Large, long-necked auk of the north Atlantic Ocean and north Pacific Ocean, with dark brown head and upperparts, white underparts and long black bill, more pointed than that of most other auks. 'Bridled' form found only in north Atlantic.

IDENTIFICATION Very similar to Brünnich's Guillemot. **Immature** At sea three to four weeks after hatching: unable to fly, length *c* 20 cm, dark brown above and white below (care with other smaller auks). Forehead, crown and hindneck dark brown to just below eye; ear-coverts whitish; chin white; throat brownish. Upperparts dark brown; underparts white. Partially developed wings lack white trailing edge to secondaries. By first winter similar to adult winter, but ear-coverts dark brown with line of demarcation below eye (thus with no dark post-ocular stripe of non-breeding adult). Bill shorter and deeper than adult's. **Adult non-breeding** Similar to adult breeding, except chin, throat, cheeks and ear-coverts white, with blackish post-ocular stripe from eye to ear-coverts. Forehead, lores (including eye) and crown blackish, narrowing on hindneck and then extending to partial collar at sides of neck.
Adult breeding Head and foreneck to upper breast dark brown; 'Bridled' Guillemots have narrow white eye-ring and white post-ocular stripe. Mantle, back and tail brownish-black (southern race *albionis* paler brown). Underparts from lower breast white, with thighs and flanks streaked brown (demarcation on upper breast more horizontal than on Brünnich's Guillemot). Upperwings dark brownish, with narrow whitish trailing edge to secondaries. Underwing dark grey, with whiter coverts and tips of secondaries. Bill black; iris black; legs and feet dark greyish. From Brünnich's Guillemot by slimmer body, more rounded crown, different pattern of demarcation on upper breast, browner upperparts (especially head and back), streaked flanks, longer and finer bill (usually) without white tomium stripe, and earlier timing of head moult.

DISTRIBUTION AND STATUS North Atlantic and north Pacific. Breeds highly colonially on ledges of steep sea cliffs and low flat islands, in the Atlantic from eastern North America and Greenland, east across northern Europe to Novaya Zemlya, and south discontinuously and sparsely to the Iberian Peninsula; in the Pacific from Korea and Japan coastally to the Bering Sea and the Aleutians continuing coastally to Washington and California. Total population estimate *c* 9,000,000 pairs with 4,000,000 pairs in the Atlantic and 5,000,000 pairs in the Pacific. Dispersal southwards from the Georges Bank (41°N) to the western Mediterranean and from southern Japan to southern California.

BRÜNNICH'S GUILLEMOT or THICK-BILLED MURRE

Uria lomvia L 45 cm (18 in), WS 76 cm (30 in)

Large, stocky, long-necked auk of the north Atlantic Ocean and north Pacific Ocean, very similar to Guillemot, but bill has a different shape with (usually) a white tomium stripe.
IDENTIFICATION Juvenile Length *c* 20 cm, with smaller bill than adult. Leaves colonies before it is able to fly. Blackish-brown upperparts and head resembling non-breeding adult, but with chin and throat grey. Upper breast grey, shading to white on lower breast. **Immature** Similar to non-breeding adult, but with chin and throat mottled dusky brownish. Bill smaller than adult's. **Adult non-breeding** Much as breeding adult, but blackish-brown head shades gradually to whitish chin and throat below eye level. Blackish-brown hindneck extends to form partial collar on lower sides of neck, much as Guillemot. Rest of upperparts and tail blackish-brown; underparts white. Upperwing blackish-brown, with narrow white secondary tips. Underwing blackish, coverts whiter. Bill may lack white tomium stripe. **Adult breeding** Much as Guillemot, with head and neck blackish-brown, but sharp demarcation from white underparts extends more vertically to a point on lower foreneck. See Guillemot for other differences. Post-nuptial head moult November (Guillemot July/August).

DISTRIBUTION AND STATUS North Atlantic and north Pacific. Breeds highly colonially on ledges of sea cliffs and islands from north-east Canada and Greenland eastwards around the Arctic Ocean at many localities, to Cape Parry in the Amundsen Gulf. In the north Pacific breeds Alaska, Aleutians and Pribilofs southwards to northern Japan. Generally more northerly than Guillemot. Total population estimated at 11,000,000 pairs, with *c* 6,500,000 pairs in the north Atlantic and 4,500,000 pairs in the north Pacific and Chukchi Sea. As with Guillemot most populations declining – attributed to direct or indirect human interference. Disperses to winter offshore mainly in low-arctic waters. Vagrants south to Washington and California, South Carolina, Britain, Holland and France.

RAZORBILL

Alca torda L 43 cm (17 in), WS 64 cm (25 in)
Large alcid confined to north Atlantic Ocean, with black head, upperparts and wings and white underparts; appears big-headed and thick-necked, with deep black bill with diagnostic white vertical band near tip and horizontal white stripe from upper mandible to eye.
IDENTIFICATION Juvenile (first-winter) Similar to non-breeding adult, but with breast sides darker. Bill is smaller, without whitish bands of adult. **Immature** (first-summer) Similar to non-breeding adult, but upperparts browner in tone, sides of breast and ear-coverts greyer. Bill develops faint white vertical bar near tip. **Adult non-breeding** Similar to adult breeding, but chin, throat and ear-coverts white; line of demarcation from bill below (thus enclosing) eye and then upwards (behind eye) towards crown. Bill has white vertical bar, but no white stripe from upper mandible to eye. **Adult breeding** Head, chin and throat black. Upperwings, mantle, back and tail black, with white sides to lower back and narrow white trailing edge to secondaries both visible in flight. Underparts white from throat (sharply demarcated) to vent. Underwing-coverts white, with primaries and secondaries blackish. Bill with both diagnostic stripes; iris brown; legs and feet blackish. From Guillemot by thickset jizz, with large head and deeper bill, pointed tail and blacker upperparts. From Brünnich's Guillemot by jizz, bill shape and whiter sides of face and ear-coverts.

DISTRIBUTION AND STATUS North Atlantic Ocean. Breeds loosely colonially on steep mainland cliffs and rocky offshore islands in eastern North America (Canada to Maine), western Greenland and Iceland, Jan Mayen, Faeroes, British Isles, Channel Islands, north-west France, Denmark, Baltic Sea, Norway, Bear Island, Murmansk and Kola Peninsula to the White Sea. Total population estimated at *c* 700,000 pairs, 70% of which are in Iceland and 20% in Britain and Ireland. Some populations have declined. Dispersal southwards further than either guillemot to New York, Azores, Iberian Peninsula, north-west Morocco, western Mediterranean. Has occurred Florida and Canary Islands.

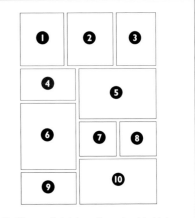

1 **Guillemot** (adult breeding pair with chick, Farne Islands, England, July)
2 **Guillemot** (adult non-breeding, Kent, England, November)
3 **Guillemot** (adult breeding (bridled), Shetland Islands, July)
4 **Guillemot** (adult breeding, Farne Islands, England, June)
5 **Brünnich's Guillemot (left) and Guillemot (right)** (adults breeding, Arctic Siberia, June)
6 **Brünnich's Guillemot** (adult breeding)
7 **Brünnich's Guillemot** (adult non-breeding)
8 **Razorbill** (adult breeding, Farne Islands, England, July)
9 **Razorbill** (adult non-breeding, Scotland, November)
10 **Razorbill** (adult breeding, Fowlesheugh, Scotland, June)

AUKS

BLACK GUILLEMOT

Cepphus grylle L 33 cm (13 in), WS 58 cm (23 in)

Medium-sized, blackish auk with contrasting white upperwing patches, slender black bill with red mouth, and red legs; winter and juvenile plumages much paler. Circumpolar in Northern Hemisphere, overlapping in range with Pigeon Guillemot.

IDENTIFICATION Most coastal and sedentary of Atlantic Alcidae, seldom seen far from shore. **Juvenile** Forehead, crown, lores, eye-stripe, nape and hindneck alternately barred blackish and grey, darker than non-breeding adult; chin, throat and sides of neck whiter with greyish tips. Upperparts blackish-grey, uniform on mantle, but scapulars, back and rump show small whitish tips. Underparts whitish with brownish-grey tips, especially along flanks. Upperwings blackish, with brown-mottled white coverts. Underwing has white coverts. Legs orange. **Immature** First-winter is similar to non-breeding adult, but crown and nape darker; whitish tips on mantle and back less conspicuous. By first summer similar to breeding adult, but with whitish tips to both upperparts and underparts; whitish wing patches reduced, with brownish edges. **Adult non-breeding** Head whitish, but barred duskier grey-brown on crown, nape and hindneck; small blackish eye-stripe and dusky ear-coverts. Mantle and back greyish-brown with white barring. Underparts white, with greyish-brown barring on flanks. Wings as adult breeding, but often with brownish edges. Tail blackish. **Adult breeding** Blackish, with conspicuous white upperwing patches. In flight, underwing shows white axillaries and white coverts. Adult Pigeon Guillemot has blackish bar in white upperwing-coverts and brownish-grey underwing-coverts; juvenile and adult winter Pigeon Guillemots more similar to Black Guillemot, but have darker brownish-grey underwing-coverts.

DISTRIBUTION AND STATUS Circumpolar in Northern Hemisphere. Breeds loosely colonially or solitarily in cliffs, scree slopes and boulder fields from arctic Canada and North America to Greenland and Iceland, Faeroes, British Isles, Scandinavia and the Baltic eastwards along northern Russia and arctic islands to the Chukchi Sea, Alaska and the Beaufort Sea. Total population unknown, but estimated at *c* 270,000 pairs, with *c* 50,000 pairs in arctic Canada, *c* 40,000 pairs in Greenland and *c* 50,000 pairs in Iceland. Uncommon in Bering Sea. Generally sedentary although northern populations move to find ice-free waters. Vagrants Long Island, New Jersey and northern France.

PIGEON GUILLEMOT

Cepphus columba L 32 cm (13 in), WS 58 cm (23 in)

Medium-sized north Pacific auk very similar in all plumage stages to Black Guillemot; some breeding adults show dark upperwings and thus resemble Spectacled Guillemot, but lack latter's white 'spectacles'.

IDENTIFICATION Juvenile Similar to adult winter, and resembles juvenile Black Guillemot. Forehead, crown, lores, eye-stripe and hindneck blackish-grey; rest of head dusky white with variable blackish-grey speckling. Upperparts and tail blackish with narrow whitish tips. Underparts whitish, with greyish tips on breast sides and flanks. Upperwing as adult winter, but with clear white wing patch. Underwing as adult, with greyish-brown coverts (whiter on Black Guillemot). Legs orange. **Adult non-breeding** Resembles Black Guillemot, but head whiter, with dusky grey crown, nape, eye-stripe and hindneck. Upperparts dark greyish with narrow white barring. Underparts white, with darker grey barring on flanks. Upperwing greyish; white wing patches have dark greyish-black marks (unlike Black Guillemot). Underwing as juvenile. **Adult transitional** Underparts become scaled light and dark: can resemble smaller non-breeding Marbled Murrelet, but has coverts (instead of scapulars) white. **Adult breeding** Plumage sooty-black with whitish wing patches (wing-coverts); unlike Black Guillemot, has blackish bars across coverts. Underwing-coverts brownish-white (whiter on Black Guillemot). Bill blackish, mouth red; legs and feet red. *C. c. snowi* has darker, mainly black (not white) wing-coverts and thus more resembles Spectacled Guillemot, but lacks white 'spectacles' and eye-stripe; also lacks whitish bill base and has smaller, slimmer bill.

DISTRIBUTION AND STATUS North Pacific. Breeds colonially or solitarily in cliffs and slopes, occasionally excavating a burrow, in north-east Siberia from the Chukotski Peninsula south to Kamchatka and the Kuril Islands, east through the Commander Islands and the Aleutians to the Bering Sea and Bering Strait, Alaska and British Columbia to California. Total population estimated at 235,000 birds, most of these in Farallon Islands (California) and Chukotski Peninsula; some populations are decreasing. Disperses from Bering Sea south to Japan and southern California.

SPECTACLED GUILLEMOT

Cepphus carbo L 38 cm (15 in), WS 67 cm (26 in)

Large, mainly dark guillemot of the north-west Pacific, in summer having white 'spectacles' and white post-ocular stripe, black bill and red legs.

IDENTIFICATION Juvenile Similar to adult non-breeding, with dark upperparts and white underparts. Chin and throat whiter, extending into whitish underparts with browner flanks. **Adult non-breeding** Similar to breeding adult, but with underparts white. Whitish 'spectacles' and white post-ocular stripe, with whitish at base of bill; remainder of head sooty-blackish, with paler barring on crown and nape. Upperparts sooty-black. Chin, throat, neck sides and underparts white, with pale greyish-brown tips on throat, foreneck and flanks. From Pigeon Guillemot by larger size, larger bill, darker head, nape and hindneck, and uniformly dark upperparts lacking whitish wing patches. **Adult transitional** Dark underparts scaled white and sooty-brown. **Adult breeding** Uniformly sooty brownish-black, with whitish at base of bill, whitish circular patch around eye ('spectacles'), and whitish stripe extending from eye backwards onto ear-coverts. Underwing-coverts and axillaries browner. Bill black with red mouth; iris black; legs red.

DISTRIBUTION AND STATUS North-west Pacific. Breeds colonially or solitarily on rocky mainland coasts in cliffs, slopes and boulder fields from Kamchatka and Sea of Okhotsk south to Ussuriland, north-east Korea, Sakhalin, Kuril Islands, and northern Japan on Hokkaido and north Honshu. Total population estimated at 71,000–74,000 pairs with 89% in the Sea of Okhotsk. Populations are decreasing for numerous reasons. Generally winters within breeding range; some dispersal southwards.

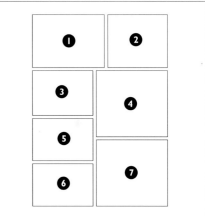

1 **Black Guillemot** (adult breeding, Shetland Islands, Scotland, June)
2 **Black Guillemot** (adult non-breeding, Norfolk, England)
3 **Pigeon Guillemot** (adult non-breeding)
4 **Pigeon Guillemot** (adult breeding, Alaska)
5 **Spectacled Guillemot** (adult non-breeding, Japan)
6 **Spectacled Guillemot** (adult breeding, Teuri Island, Japan)
7 **Spectacled Guillemot** (adult breeding, Teuri Island, Japan)

MARBLED MURRELET

Brachyramphus marmoratus L 25 cm (10 in), WS ? Medium-sized, dark, nocturnal, north Pacific alcid.

IDENTIFICATION Small 'neckless' alcid, with flight swift and direct; inshore feeder. **Juvenile** Much as non-breeding adult, but with clearer blackish-brown upperparts and dusky brown barring on underparts. **Adult non-breeding** Dark blackish-grey head and upperparts and white underparts. Blackish cap from base of bill, below eye through ear-coverts to back of nape; chin, throat, sides of face and sides of neck white. Upperparts blackish-grey with indistinct grey scaling; scapulars white (visible when swimming and in flight). Underparts white, with blackish collar on sides of breast; flanks greyish. Upperwing blackish-grey, and underwing dusky. From similar Kittlitz's Murrelet by longer, more slender bill, black cap extending below eye, darker hindneck, less extensive partial black collar at breast sides, and dark outer tail feathers. **Adult breeding** Forehead, crown, ear-coverts and hindneck dark brown, giving capped appearance; chin and throat whitish, mottled with dark brown. Upperparts dark brown as cap, with some barring; scapulars tipped greyer. Underparts olive-brown, darkest on breast, with pale buff-grey feather edges. Upperwing dark brown as upperparts; underwing dark brown. Tail brown. From Kittlitz's Murrelet by darker cap and upperparts, darker breastband and belly. **Long-billed Murrelet B. (m.) perdix** Recent molecular studies (Friesen and Baker 1994) indicate that this Asiatic form of Marbled Murrelet is the most genetically divergent of the brachyramphine murrelets and should be given specific status. It is heavier (296 g) than either *marmoratus* (241 g) or Kittlitz's Murrelet (225 g), with a much larger culmen (20.3 mm) than *marmoratus* (15.5 mm) and Kittlitz's (10.7 mm), as well as having larger wings, tarsus and tail. Plumage is essentially similar to that of *marmoratus*, but adults have a more conspicuous, well-developed white eye-ring in winter (less developed in *marmoratus*), whereas in summer the upperparts are dull tawny and buffish, lacking the cinnamon (or rufous-cinnamon) feather edges of *marmoratus*. Outermost tail feather has narrow white marginal stripe – not present in *marmoratus*. **DISTRIBUTION AND STATUS** Breeds non-colonially, usually within 60 km of the coast in coniferous forests (occasionally on the ground) in Alaska on Kenai Peninsula and Barren Islands, the Aleutians, west Washington and locally in north coastal California, south to Santa Cruz County; probably also in other places from Alaska to California, but nests difficult to find; North American population c 300,000 birds with 85% on the coast of the Gulf of Alaska and Prince William Sound. *B. (m.) perdix* is known only from forested coasts of Japan, Sea of Okhotsk, Kurils and Kamchatka (four nests have been found in Russia); population estimated at probably 50,000-100,000 birds, and distribution does not overlap with that of *marmoratus*. More dispersive than *marmoratus*, reaching Sakhalin and Japan. Both populations are declining. Threats include increasingly rapid logging of old-growth forests in Russia, as well as offshore oil developments. Vagrants have reached the west coast of America, as well as Florida.

KITTLITZ'S MURRELET

Brachyramphus brevirostris L 23 cm (9 in), WS ? Resembles Marbled Murrelet, with similar breeding and non-breeding plumages.

IDENTIFICATION Juvenile First-winter plumage similar to non-breeding adult, but with fine barring on face, nape, underparts and tail. **Adult non-breeding** Head white, with narrow blackish forehead, crown and nape (above eye), and dusky eye crescent. Upperparts blackish-grey with whitish spots; scapulars fringed white (visible when swimming and in flight). Underparts whitish, with narrow blackish partial breastband from sides of breast, flanks with dusky barring. Upperwing blackish-grey; underwing dusky. Tail brownish, with broad white fringe. From Marbled Murrelet by smaller bill, smaller cap not reaching eye, whiter hindcollar, more extensive partial breastband, and white outer tail feathers. From Least Auklet, which is smaller, by lighter head and no white auricular plume. **Adult breeding** Head sandy-brown with buff and fawn mottling. Upperparts and upper breast sandy-brown, marbled with buff and fawn, merging gradually into whitish belly. Upper primaries and secondaries blackish; wing-coverts sandy-brown, mottled buff and fawn. Underwing dark brown. Tail brown, narrowly fringed white. Lacks darker cap, darker breast and darker brown upperparts of Marbled Murrelet, and also has a shorter bill. **DISTRIBUTION AND STATUS** North Pacific. Breeds non-colonially on non-vegetated mountain scree slopes up to 75 km inland in Siberia at the northern extreme of the sea of Okhotsk (Shelikhova Bay) and the Chukotski Peninsula, in Alaska from Point Hope (Chukchi Sea) coastally to Glacier Bay (Gulf of Alaska) and the Aleutians. Total population unknown with estimates from 30,000 to 130,000 birds of which 70% are believed to be in Alaska. Dispersal mainly offshore near the breeding areas; recorded Washington, California. Threats include oil pollution, gill nets, diminished fish stocks.

XANTUS'S MURRELET

Synthliboramphus hypoleucus L 25 cm (10 in), WS 40 cm (16 in)
Small alcid with blackish upperparts and white underparts, thin black bill and bluish legs, very similar to Craveri's Murrelet.

IDENTIFICATION Flight low and very fast; gregarious. Both Craveri's and Xantus's Murrelets hold head high when swimming, giving grebe-like jizz (unlike other murrelets); swim very low in water, when white underparts not visible. **Juvenile** Similar to adult (no seasonal variation). Juveniles join adults at sea when two to four days old, before they are able to fly. **Adult** Head with blackish cap extending from gape, just below eye to hindneck and onto sides of breast. Upperparts and tail blackish with greyish suffusion. Chin, throat, lower sides of face and underparts white, with blackish flanks. Upperwing blackish; underwing mainly white, with dusky grey flight feathers. *S. h. hypoleucus* has prominent broad white crescents above and below eye, and white lower sides of face (eye crescents indistinct in *S. h. scrippsi* and also in Craveri's Murrelet, which have a partial white eye-ring; both also have dark ear-coverts). Both forms differ from Craveri's Murrelet in shorter, stouter bill, slightly larger size, demarcation of black on face from gape to only just below eye, less extensive partial collar at breast sides, greyer cast to upperparts, and whiter underwing.

DISTRIBUTION AND STATUS North-east Pacific. Breeds aseasonally in small colonies on offshore islands in steep cliffs, canyons, and rock crevices or on the ground under vegetation; nocturnal at colonies, and chicks go to sea with adults one to two days after hatching. Total population estimated at 5,600 birds concentrated at four main colonies: Santa Barbara (1,500 birds), Los Coronados (750 birds), San Benito (c 1,000 birds) and Guadelupe (2,400-3,500 birds) with smaller numbers on other islands. Both *hypoleucus* and *scrippsi* breed on Santa Barbara and San Benito, apparently with limited hybridization. Both populations have declined; should be classified as Vulnerable with many diverse threats. Some dispersal northwards, recorded Washington and Oregon.

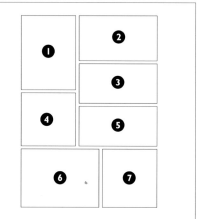

1 **Marbled Murrelet** subspecies *B. m. perdix*
2 **Marbled Murrelet** (adult breeding on nest platform in tree)
3 **Marbled Murrelet** (adult non-breeding)
4 **Kittlitz's Murrelet** (adult breeding, Glacier Bay, Alaska)
5 **Kittlitz's Murrelet** (adult non-breeding)
6 **Xantus's Murrelet** (adult breeding close to nest hole)
7 **Xantus's Murrelet** (adult non-breeding, off California, USA, September)

AUKS

CRAVERI'S MURRELET

Synthliboramphus craveri L 23 cm (9 in), WS ?
Small alcid with blackish upperparts and white underparts, black bill and bluish legs, very similar to Xantus's Murrelet and with a similar limited range in the north-eastern Pacific.
IDENTIFICATION Juvenile As adult, but with smaller bill, blacker upperparts, and blackish barring on sides of breast. **Adult** No seasonal variation. Black cap extends from bottom edge of lower mandible, below eye to hindneck, with partial breastband at sides of breast. Upperparts and tail blackish-brown. Chin, throat, lowermost sides of face and underparts white; blackish on flanks. Upperwing blackish. Underwing with whitish axillaries, dark greyish coverts, and blackish-grey flight feathers. Bill black; legs bluish. Very similar to Xantus's Murrelet but is slightly smaller, with finer and longer bill, black cap extending lower on face, darker upperparts, more extensive partial breastband, and darker underwing.
DISTRIBUTION AND STATUS North-east Pacific. Breeds loosely colonially on cliffs, slopes, rock crevices and burrows under vegetation on offshore islands in the Gulf of California north to Consag Rock, and also probably on islands on the Pacific coast of Baja California north to San Benito. Has the most restricted range of any alcid, occupying warmer water to the south of other alcids. Nocturnal at colonies; chicks go to sea with adults one to two days after hatching. Total population estimated at only 6,000-10,000 birds, with 90% at three islands in the Gulf of California (Partida, Raza and Tiburón). Population has recently declined with several local extinctions. Should be classified as Vulnerable, with many threats to both breeding birds and birds at sea. Dispersal to adjacent waters after breeding with some moving south along west coast of Mexico, and others north, especially in warm-water years. Vagrant Oregon.

ANCIENT MURRELET

Synthliboramphus antiquus L 26 cm (10 in), WS ?
Small to medium-sized north Pacific alcid, with black of head extending onto throat, whitish stripe behind eye, pale bill, bluish-grey upperparts and white underparts.
IDENTIFICATION Flight low and direct, with head held higher than in other murrelets. Sits low in water when swimming; springs clear of surface when diving. **Immature** Much as adult non-breeding, but bill darker and smaller, and chin and lower sides of face white (not black). From juvenile Marbled Murrelet by pale (not dark) bill, and contrast between black head and bluish-grey upperparts. **Adult non-breeding** Blackish on head and hindneck extends below eye and bill to chin and onto breast sides, to form hint of partial breastband. Upperparts bluish-grey, contrasting with black head. Underparts white, this extending onto lower throat and sides of

neck towards nape and forming partial white collar; flanks mottled blackish. Upperwing with bluish-grey coverts as upperparts, but flight feathers blackish-grey (thus darker trailing edge to wing). Underwing-coverts whitish, flight feathers darker. Tail blackish. **Adult breeding** As non-breeding adult, but black on chin extends over throat to top of breast, and has whitish stripe starting above eye and extending to nape, and white filoplumes on sides of neck. From superficially similar Japanese Murrelet by lack of crest and absence of white on hindneck.
DISTRIBUTION AND STATUS North Pacific. Breeds loosely colonially often with other alcids on islands with dense vegetation, normally on soft slopes using burrows, and occasionally in rock crevices and cavities, from the Yellow Sea and Sea of Japan north through Sakhalin and the Kurils to Kamchatka and the northern Sea of Okhotsk (Talan Island); also eastwards through the Commander and Aleutian Islands to southern Alaska, and south to Queen Charlotte Islands (British Columbia) and Carroll Islands (north-west Washington). Nocturnal at colonies, chicks go to sea with adults one to two days after hatching. Total population estimated at 1,500,000 birds with most in British Columbia. Populations declining probably most importantly from predation by foxes, rats and raccoons (eg Helgersen and Langara Islands). Dispersal generally within breeding range but also southward towards Korea and California, occasionally recorded inland North America. Vagrant England.

JAPANESE or CRESTED MURRELET

Synthliboramphus wumizusume L 26 cm (10 in), WS ?
Small to medium-sized north-western Pacific alcid, greyish-black above and white below, with pale bill, and with blackish head which in summer has a blackish crest and whitish crown sides meeting on the lower hindneck. Classified as Vulnerable.
IDENTIFICATION Juvenile Much as non-breeding adult, but browner on head and upperparts. **Adult non-breeding** As breeding adult, but lacks blackish crest and white on head. **Adult breeding** Head mainly black from chin below eye to lower ear-coverts; blackish crest from sides of head; whitish stripes on sides of crown from crest base meet on lower hindneck. Upperparts greyish-black, contrasting with black head. Underparts whitish, with greyish flanks. Upperwing greyish-black; underwing whitish, with darker flight feathers. Generally resembles Ancient Murrelet, but has blackish crest, white on head, and less black on chin and throat.
DISTRIBUTION AND STATUS North-west Pacific. Breeds loosely colonially in rock crevices and cavities, under boulders, also burrows where possible, chiefly on islands (but also on sea coasts). Most concentrated on five

main areas off south-east Japan: off Kyushu, 3,000 birds at Biro Island, 60 birds at Eboshi Island and 30 birds at Okinoshima; Izu Islands with 1,670 birds at eight sites; off Honshu, with 200+ birds at Mimiana Island, and small numbers at Kutsujima and Nanatsujima in the Sea of Japan; Shikoku, with small numbers on Koshima island; and Danjo Island with a few at two sites. Additionally under 10 pairs breed in South Korea with possibly a small population (under 100 birds) in Peter the Great Bay (south-east Russia). Nocturnal at colonies, chicks go to sea with adults one to two days after hatching. Total population estimated at 5,000-6,000 birds (1995) – the rarest and most threatened alcid. Populations are declining with some local extinctions, primarily as a result of predation by feral cats and rats. Dispersal offshore close to breeding localities; has reached Sakhalin, Kuril Islands, and Taiwan.

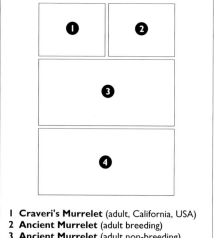

1 **Craveri's Murrelet** (adult, California, USA)
2 **Ancient Murrelet** (adult breeding)
3 **Ancient Murrelet** (adult non-breeding)
4 **Japanese Murrelet** (adult non-breeding)

AUKS

CASSIN'S AUKLET

Ptychoramphus aleuticus L 23 cm (9 in), WS ?
Small, plump, rather featureless grey auklet
with whitish belly, found in the north Pacific.
IDENTIFICATION Low, direct flight. Gregarious;
feeds well offshore in large flocks. At sea,
appears generally greyish-brown, with slightly
darker head and upperparts. **Juvenile** Much as
adult, but generally paler, with whitish chin and
throat, dark eye, and browner tone to wings
and tail. **Adult** Head dark greyish-brown, often
with paler grey stripe from eye towards nape;
white crescent above the eye; chin and throat
paler brown than head. Upperparts and tail
variable from dark slate to brownish. Upper
breast, flanks and undertail-coverts greyish-
brown (paler than upperparts), merging into
whitish on belly and vent. Upperwing-coverts
as upperparts, with flight feathers blackish-
brown. Underwing-coverts greyish-brown,
flight feathers darker. At very close range,
shows pale eyes and pale yellowish base to
lower mandible. From immature Crested
Auklet by white belly and dark bill. From
immature Whiskered Auklet by lack of whitish
facial streaks, by dark (not yellowish) bill which
is long and thinner, and by paler belly. Larger
Rhinoceros Auklet has yellow bill. Summer
Marbled Murrelet is browner, with a longer bill
and darker belly.
DISTRIBUTION AND STATUS North Pacific.
Breeds highly colonially on coastal islands with
or without trees in crevices, cavities, caves, and
also in burrows, from Buldir Island in the
Aleutians to south-west and south-east Alaska,
through British Columbia to southern Baja
California. Nocturnal at colonies, the only alcid
to produce two broods in one breeding season.
Total population estimated at 3,600,000 birds
(although Alaskan and Mexican populations not
thoroughly surveyed) with 2,700,000 birds in
British Columbia (including 1,095,000 birds on
Triangle Island). Despite being one of the most
widespread alcids, populations have declined,
with some local extinctions, mainly the result
of mammalian predators (foxes, cats, rats and
goats) combined with human predation,
pollution and fisheries. Southern populations
are generally sedentary while those of Alaska
and British Columbia disperse southwards as
far as California.

PARAKEET AUKLET

Cyclorrhynchus psittacula L 25 cm (10 in), WS ?
Small, dark north Pacific auklet with stubby red
bill, sooty-black head (with yellowish auricular
streak in summer), wings and upperparts, and
white underparts.
IDENTIFICATION Flight strong and direct,
generally at higher altitude than other auks;
swims buoyantly. Less gregarious at sea than
most other auks. **Immature/adult non-
breeding** Plumage much as breeding adult, but
with chin, throat and foreneck whitish,
auricular streak whitish and reduced. Bill is dull
brownish-red. From non-breeding larger

Rhinoceros Auklet by whitish breast and flanks,
and one (not two) whitish facial streaks. **Adult
breeding** Head sooty-blackish, with single
yellow auricular plume starting from behind
eye. Upperparts and upperwings sooty-blackish;
tail black. Underparts white from foreneck to
undertail, with dark mottling on upper breast
and flanks. Underwing greyish. Bill large, stubby,
with upward-curving lower mandible, red with
yellowish at base; iris yellow; legs and feet
yellowish-grey.
DISTRIBUTION AND STATUS North Pacific.
Breeds colonially, mainly on offshore islands, in
crevices and cavities of steep sea cliffs, boulder
fields and talus slopes with vegetation, from
Chukotski Peninsula south to Sea of Okhotsk,
Kamchatka and Commander Islands, and west
Alaska from Diomede Islands, Fairway Rock,
Sledge Island and Norton Sound south to
Pribilofs and Aleutians, east to islands in Prince
William Sound. Total population not well
known, but estimated at 1,200,000 birds with
800,000 birds in west Alaska and 400,000 birds
in east Siberia; populations probably reduced
historically. Current threats include human
disturbance, introduced predators, commercial
fisheries and marine pollution. Dispersal south
to pelagic habitat in winter, reaching Japan and
California.

CRESTED AUKLET

Aethia cristatella L 27 cm (11 in), WS 45 cm
(18 in)
Medium-sized, generally uniformly sooty-grey
north Pacific auklet, with dark recurved crest
on forehead, stubby red bill with yellow tip,
yellowish-white iris, and a single white auricular
stripe extending backwards from eye.
IDENTIFICATION Juvenile Much as non-
breeding adult, except bill yellowish-brown and
smaller, and no crest or auricular stripe: thus
uniform sooty-grey head, upperparts and wings,
shading to brownish-grey underparts. From
similar Cassin's Auklet by lack of whitish eye
crescent, pale (not dark) bill, darker
underparts. From juvenile Whiskered Auklet by
larger size and darker head, without whitish
streaks on sides of face. **Adult non-breeding**
Much as breeding adult, but with smaller yellow
bill (as bill sheath shed), dark recurved crest on
forehead reduced, whitish auricular stripe
reduced. **Adult breeding** Head sooty-grey;
dark recurved crest on forehead; thin white
auricular stripe from eye across ear-coverts.
Upperparts, wings and tail sooty-grey.
Underparts entirely brownish-grey. Bill orange-
red with yellow tip. Whiskered Auklet is
similarly coloured, with a recurved crest, but is
smaller, with three (not one) thin white facial
stripes.
DISTRIBUTION AND STATUS North Pacific.
Breeds highly colonially on remote islands and
cliffs, preferring scree slopes, but also sea cliffs,
boulder fields and lava flows, generally with
other alcids, from Chukotski Peninsula south to
Kamchatka, Sakhalin and central Kuril Islands in
Bering Sea on Diomede, Fairway Rock and

Sledge Island, and west Alaska in Norton
Sound, south to Pribilofs and Aleutians east to
Shumagin and Semidi Island (but not Near
Island). Total breeding population unknown,
but estimated at 6,000,000 birds (or 4,100,000
pairs) with an estimated North American
population of 3,000,000 birds (c 2,100,000
pairs) and an estimated Russian population of
2,900,000 birds (c 2,000,000 pairs). The
Alaskan population may be as large as
6,000,000 birds. Some colonies are huge eg
Talan Island with c 1,000,000 birds. Populations
slowly declining from human predation and
disturbance, mammalian predators, commercial
fisheries and oil pollution (particularly
susceptible to the latter since species forms
large flocks at sea all the year round).
Disperses in open water around Bering Sea in
winter reaching the Gulf of Alaska and Japan.
Has occurred California.

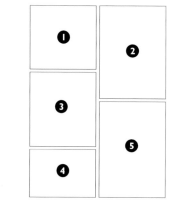

1 Cassin's Auklet (adult breeding at nest site,
Farallon Island, off California, USA)
2 Parakeet Auklet (adult breeding)
3 Parakeet Auklet (adult breeding, St Paul
Island, Alaska, June)
4 Crested Auklet (adult breeding)
5 Crested Auklet (adult breeding)

WHISKERED AUKLET

Aethia pygmaea L 20 cm (8 in), WS ?
Tiny sooty-grey auklet, only slightly larger than Least Auklet, with, in summer, a short red bill, dark recurved crest from forehead, and three thin white facial streaks (crest and streaks retained but reduced in winter).

IDENTIFICATION Flies low and fast; forages close to shore, springing clear of water when diving. Nocturnal at colonies. **Juvenile** Generally uniform sooty-grey on head, upperparts and wings, with paler chin and lower underparts. No crest. Sides of face show traces of three white facial streaks, which help distinguish it from Cassin's and Crested Auklets. **Adult non-breeding** Much as adult breeding, but with reduced crest and less obvious white facial streaks; upperwing-coverts greyer. **Adult breeding** Head slate-grey; long, recurved dark crest from forehead, drooping forward over bill; white facial plume from behind eye over ear-coverts, and two more facial plumes both starting at lores, one going above eye and the other below eye. Upperparts, wings and tail slate-grey; wing-coverts may be paler. Underwing dark brownish. Underparts from chin sooty-grey, lighter than upperparts, gradually becoming greyish-white by vent. Bill red with white tip; iris white.

DISTRIBUTION AND STATUS North Pacific. Breeds highly colonially preferring unvegetated talus slopes, also boulder fields, rock crevices, and lava flows on islands and cliffs, usually with other alcids, from the north-east Sea of Okhotsk and Commander Islands south to the Kurils and east to the Aleutians. Total population unknown, but not large and estimated at 100,000+ birds with *c* 75,000 in North America (mostly in the Aleutians: 30,000 pairs at Buldir Island) and *c* 25,000 in Russia. Population trends unknown, but current threats primarily from mammalian predation, oil pollution, and human disturbance. Often found in large flocks. Dispersal in winter to adjacent seas; has reached Japan.

LEAST AUKLET

Aethia pusilla L 15 cm (6 in), WS 35 cm (14 in)
Tiny, the smallest north Pacific auklet, with blackish head, upperparts and wings; whitish below, in summer mottled with grey across breast, isolating white throat from pale lower underparts.

IDENTIFICATION Possibly the most abundant seabird of the north Pacific: colonial and gregarious, forming large rafts at sea. Springs clear of water when diving. **Juvenile** Much as non-breeding adult, but upperparts darker, and lacks white auricular streak. **Adult non-breeding** Head blackish-grey, with indistinct whitish streaking on forehead and lores, and more conspicuous central white auricular stripe extending back over ear-coverts from behind eye; chin, throat and sides of neck whitish. Upperparts and wings blackish-grey, with white scapulars visible on closed wing. Underwing-coverts whitish, flight feathers blackish. Underparts white from chin to tail. Tail black. Bill black. From non-breeding Marbled and Kittlitz's Murrelets (which have whitish scapulars) by smaller size, more extensive dark on head extending well below eye level, and white auricular streak. **Adult breeding** Head blackish with indistinct whitish streaking on forehead, a whitish stripe from gape to below eye, and more conspicuous white auricular stripe from behind eye over ear-coverts; chin and upper throat white. Upperparts blackish. Wings blackish-grey; white on scapulars less apparent than in non-breeding plumage. Below white chin, variable greyish mottling usually forms a continuous breastband, less dense on lower breast and flanks, merging into white on belly and vent. Bill with small knob at base of upper mandible, red with whitish tip; iris white.

DISTRIBUTION AND STATUS North Pacific. Breeds highly colonially on islands and cliffs in crevices and preferably in bare talus slopes, but also in boulder and lava fields, generally with other alcids, from Chukotski Peninsula south to the Sea of Okhotsk and the central Kuril Islands, and west Alaska from Diomede Island and Cape Lisburne south to the Aleutians and east to Sumigan and Semidi Islands in the Gulf of Alaska. Total population unknown, but roughly estimated to be *c* 12,000,000 pairs or *c* 17,000,000 birds with approximately equal numbers in Russia and North America. The most abundant auklet, concentrated at a few huge colonies, *eg* Matykyl Island (Sea of Okhotsk) holds at least 6,000,000 birds and possibly 10,000,000 birds. Population trends unknown but some local declines probably as a result of human predation and disturbance, mammalian predation, oil pollution and commercial fisheries. Dispersal to winter in ice-free seas within breeding range, occasionally Japan and British Columbia. Vagrant California.

RHINOCEROS AUKLET

Cerorhinca monocerata L 37 cm (15 in), WS ?
Large, sooty-brown, north Pacific auklet, more closely related to the puffins, with whitish underparts, two thin white facial streaks and, in summer, a pale yellow 'horn' at the base of the yellowish-orange bill.

IDENTIFICATION Flight is strong and direct. Feeds far out at sea; sits low in water, appearing 'neckless'. Nocturnal at colonies. **Juvenile** Much as adult non-breeding, but generally darker, no whitish facial streaks, and a smaller, finer, more pointed bill. **Adult non-breeding** Plumage as adult breeding, but whitish facial streaks reduced; 'horn' is absent, and bill colour generally duller. From superficially similar juvenile Tufted Puffin by size and shape of bill, whiter underparts, more pointed wings. Parakeet Auklet is smaller, with whiter underparts and a reddish bill of different shape. **Adult breeding** Head brownish, with two long and thin white facial streaks, uppermost from behind eye to nape, lower from gape across upper throat. Bill yellowish-orange, with short whitish 'horn' from base of upper mandible. Upperparts and tail brownish, as head, but with paler buffish edges imparting scaled effect. Underparts as upperparts but paler, becoming mottled on lower breast and whitish on belly. Upperwing brownish, with paler edges to wing-coverts; underwing brownish-grey. Iris yellow; legs and feet greyish-yellow.

DISTRIBUTION AND STATUS North Pacific. Breeds highly colonially in burrows in maritime and inland grassy slopes, occasionally on flat ground on forest floors, usually with other alcids, from the western Sea of Okhotsk, Sakhalin, and the southern Kuril Islands south to Japan and north-east Korea. Also from the Aleutians east to south and south-east Alaska, south through British Columbia and Washington to California. Total population estimated at 1,250,000 birds with *c* 347,000 birds in Asia and *c* 903,000 birds in North America with the majority in British Columbia. Some historical population decline with local extinctions, also some recolonization (*eg* Farallon Islands in 1970s) and recently recorded Channel Islands. Threats today are predation, oil pollution affecting large flocks, and commercial fisheries. Dispersal to adjacent seas in winter.

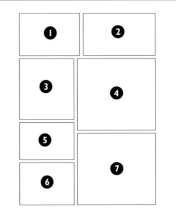

1 **Whiskered Auklet** (adult breeding, north Pacific Ocean, June)
2 **Whiskered Auklet** (adult breeding, Kuril Islands, Pacific Ocean, June)
3 **Least Auklet** (adult breeding)
4 **Least Auklet** (adult breeding, St Lawrence Island, Alaska, June)
5 **Least Auklet** (adult non-breeding, St Paul Island, Alaska, June)
6 **Rhinoceros Auklet** (adult non-breeding, California, USA)
7 **Rhinoceros Auklet** (adult breeding, Farallon Islands, off California, USA)

PUFFINS

ATLANTIC PUFFIN

Fratercula arctica L 32 cm (13 in), WS 55 cm (22 in)
Medium-sized, dumpy auk, confined to north Atlantic, with blackish upperparts and white underparts, large black head with greyish-white sides of face and ear-coverts enclosing eye, and distinctive three-coloured bill and red legs.

IDENTIFICATION Generally spends more time in the sea than other auks, and more pelagic than Razorbill and Guillemot in winter. **Juvenile** Similar to non-breeding adult, but with smaller, greyish bill lacking triangular shape of adult's; legs yellowish. Upperparts generally browner. Grey on sides of head from bill to eye, with sides of face and ear-coverts whitish (head appears dark from a distance). **Immature** Similar to non-breeding adult, but bill smaller and darker, with dull reddish tip with only one to two grooves. **Adult non-breeding** Sheds bill sheath, and bill grooves less noticeable; bill yellowish at tip, dusky grey at base. Legs yellowish. Dusky grey on sides of head. **Adult breeding** Forehead, crown, nape and hindneck black, this extending to throat and foreneck as a narrow black collar isolating greyish-white sides of face; chin darker grey. Upperparts to tail black. Underparts white, with darker flanks. Upperwing black, without whitish trailing edge to secondaries shown by Razorbill, Little Auk and Guillemot. Underwing grey, with paler coverts. Bill larger and triangular, greyish at base, red at tip, with transverse yellow bands and cere; legs and feet red. In flight, appears smaller than Razorbill and Guillemot, with shorter, rounder wings and short tail; lacks whitish sides to lower back of those species, and also lacks their whitish trailing edge to secondaries.

DISTRIBUTION AND STATUS North Atlantic. Breeds highly colonially, mostly in burrows on grassy maritime slopes and sea cliffs, also in boulder fields and scree slopes, in Canada and Greenland, south to Maine, Iceland, Jan Mayen, Faeroes, Spitsbergen, Bear Island and Novaya Zemlya and north-west Russia (White Sea), coastally through Norway, Sweden, British Isles and Ireland to the Channel Island, and north-west France. Total population estimated at 6,000,000 pairs with most in Iceland (3,000,000 pairs) and Norway (1,200,000 pairs). Populations have been reduced historically mainly through predation; current threats are many, varied and complex, but include continued predation, marine pollution and overfishing. Dispersal to sea in winter south to New Jersey, Azores, Canaries, Morocco and western Mediterranean.

HORNED PUFFIN

Fratercula corniculata L 38 cm (15 in), WS 57 cm (22 in)
North Pacific puffin, very like Atlantic Puffin in all plumages, breeding adults having large triangular-shaped bill, yellow at base and red at the tip, with an orange wattle at gape and a small horn of tissue over the eye.

IDENTIFICATION Flight strong, high over water, with fast wingbeats. Swims buoyantly; springs clear of surface before diving. **Juvenile** Much as non-breeding adult, but sides of face duskier, and bill smaller, darker and more pointed. **Adult non-breeding** As breeding adult, but bill sheath shed to give smaller, dusky bill with reddish tip; no horn of tissue over the eye; sides of face dusky grey, upperparts browner. From both guillemot species by larger head, deeper chest, more rounded crown, and heavier bill. From Tufted Puffin by white underparts. **Adult breeding** Forehead, crown and nape black, this extending to chin and neck and enclosing whitish sides to face and cheeks. Upperparts and tail black. Underparts white, with mottled black flanks. Upperwing blackish; underwing mainly dark. Bill yellow with red tip, orange wattle at gape; horn of tissue over eye; legs and feet orange to reddish.

DISTRIBUTION AND STATUS North Pacific. Breeds colonially mainly on rocky cliffs, boulder areas and talus slopes, less frequently in burrows in grassy maritime slopes, from Wrangel and Heard Islands, Chukotski Peninsula south through Kamchatka and Commander Islands to the Sea of Okhotsk, Sakhalin and the northern Kurils. Also west Alaska from Diomede Island and Cape Lisburne south to the Aleutians and east through the Gulf of Alaska to Queen Charlotte Islands (British Columbia). Total population estimated at *c* 1,220,000 birds with *c* 292,000 birds in Asia and *c* 928,000 birds in North America. Most are found in the Alaskan Peninsula with *c* 762,000 birds including *c* 250,000 birds on Suklik (Semidi Islands). Populations have probably declined historically mainly from predation by foxes; current threats include continued mammalian predation, oil spills and commercial fisheries. Dispersal generally within breeding range, but occasionally to Japan, Hawaii, Oregon and California.

TUFTED PUFFIN

Fratercula cirrhata L 38 cm (15 in), WS ?
Medium-sized to large, mainly black, north Pacific puffin with, in summer, a striking white face mask, yellow head plumes from crown, and large orange-red bill which is greenish at base.

IDENTIFICATION Flight strong and direct, requiring long run to become airborne. Colonial breeder, but solitary at sea; forages widely from colonies. **Juvenile** Much as non-breeding adult, but with smaller, more pointed, yellowish-grey bill; face sides and underparts whiter. From young Rhinoceros Auklet by larger and less pointed bill, more rounded head shape, less pointed wings. **Adult non-breeding** Bill loses sheath to become less triangular-shaped, with grey base and red tip. White sides of face and yellow head plumes also lost. Head blackish, with pale superciliary stripe. Upperparts, wings and tail dull blackish-grey. Underparts brownish-grey; breast and belly may have some white feather tips. **Adult breeding** Plumage entirely blackish, except for conspicuous white face mask, with yellowish head plumes from crown sides over nape. Bill orange-red with greenish base; legs and feet orange-red.

DISTRIBUTION AND STATUS North Pacific. Breeds colonially, mainly in burrows, on maritime slopes and tops of islands, also cliffs and crevices in boulder beaches, from Chukotski Peninsula south to Commander Islands and Sea of Okhotsk, Sakhalin, Kuril Islands to northern Japan. Also west Alaska (Diomede Island and Cape Thompson) south to the Aleutians, east through the Gulf of Alaska, to British Colombia and California. Total population estimated at *c* 3,502,000 birds with *c* 764,000 birds in Asia and *c* 2,738,000 birds in North America, with most in the Aleutians and Alaska. Populations have declined historically through predation, and there have been local extinctions. May have recently recolonized Channel Islands off California. Disperses pelagically in winter more than other alcids, including central north Pacific and south to Japan and California.

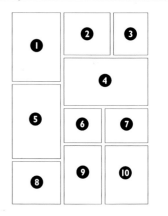

1 **Atlantic Puffin** (adult breeding, Shetland Islands, Scotland, June)
2 **Atlantic Puffin** (adult non-breeding, Netherlands, January)
3 **Atlantic Puffin** (adult breeding, Fidra Island, Scotland)
4 **Horned Puffin** (adult breeding, St Paul Island, Alaska, June)
5 **Horned Puffin** (adult breeding)
6 **Horned Puffin** (adult non-breeding)
7 **Horned Puffin** (adult breeding, Valen Island, Siberia)
8 **Tufted Puffin** (adult breeding, Valen Island, Siberia)
9 **Tufted Puffin** (adult non-breeding, Cordell Banks, California, USA)
10 **Tufted Puffin** (adult breeding)

APPENDICES

NON-MARINE SPECIES OMITTED

Pelecaniformes:
Great White Pelican *Pelecanus onocrotalus*
Pink-backed Pelican *P. rufescens*
Dalmatian Pelican *P. crispus*
Spot-billed Pelican *P. philippensis*
Australian Pelican *P. conspicillatus*
American White Pelican *P. erythrorhynchos*
Reed (Long-tailed) Cormorant *Phalacrocorax africanus*

Pygmy Cormorant *P. pygmeus*
Little (Javanese) Cormorant *P. niger*
Little Pied Cormorant *P. melanoleucos*
Little Black Cormorant *P. sulcirostris*

Lariformes:
River Tern *Sterna aurantia*
Yellow-billed Tern *S. superciliaris*
Black-bellied Tern *S. acuticauda*

Black-fronted Tern *S. albostriata*
Whiskered Tern *Chlidonias hybridus*
White-winged Tern *C. leucopterus*
Large-billed Tern *Phaetusa simplex*
African Skimmer *Rynchops flavirostris*
Indian Skimmer *R. albicollis*

APPENDIX II:

IUCN CRITERIA

Critical (Critically endangered):
Facing an extremely high risk of extinction in the wild in the immediate future.
CRITERIA: rapid decline (80% over ten years); small population (under 250 mature birds) or very small population (under 50 mature birds); probability of extinction 50% within five years.

Endangered:
Not Critical, but facing a very high risk of extinction in the wild in the near future.

CRITERIA: rapid decline (50% over ten years); small population (2,500 mature birds) or very small population (250 mature birds); probability of extinction 20% within 20 years.

Vulnerable:
Not Critical or Endangered, but facing a high risk of extinction in the wild in the medium-term future.
CRITERIA: rapid decline (50% over 20 years); small population (10,000 mature birds) or very

small population (1,000 mature birds); probability of extinction 10% within 100 years.

Near-threatened:
Species close to qualifying for any of the above threatened categories.

SELECTED BIBLIOGRAPHY

BAILEY, S.F., PYLE, P., and SPEAR, L.B. 1989. Dark *Pterodroma* petrels in the North Pacific: identification, status and North American occurrence. *Am. Birds* 43: 400-415.

BOURNE, W.R.P. 1967. Long-distance vagrancy in the Petrels. *Ibis* 109: 141-167.

COLLAR, N.J., CROSBY, M.J., and STATTERSFIELD, A.J. 1994. *Birds to Watch 2. The World List of Threatened Birds.* Birdlife International. Cambridge.

CRAMP, S., and SIMMONS, K.E.L. (eds) 1977. *The Birds of the Western Palearctic.* Vol. 1. Oxford University Press. Oxford.

CROXALL, J.P., EVANS, P.G.H., and SCHREIBER, R.W. 1984. *Status and Conservation of the World's Seabirds.* ICBP Tech. Pub. No. 2. Cambridge.

CROXALL, J.P., *et al.* 1991. *Seabird Status and Conservation: a Supplement.* ICBP. Cambridge.

DEL HOYO, J., ELLIOTT, A., and SARGATAL, J. (eds) 1996. *Handbook of the Birds of the World.* Vols 1 and 3 Lynx Edicions, Barcelona.

DEVILLERS, P., and TERSCHUREN, J.A. 1976. Observations de la Sterne Péruvienne (*Sterna lorata*) au Chili et illustration de son plumage juvénile. *Gerfaut* 66: 261-265.

GRANT, P.J. 1982. *Gulls: A Guide to Identification.* Poyser. Berkhamsted.

HARPER, P.C., and KINSKY, F.C. 1978. *Southern Albatrosses and Petrels.* Victoria University Press. Wellington.

HARRISON, P. 1983. *Seabirds: an Identification Guide.* Croom Helm. Beckenham.

HARRISON, P. 1987. *Seabirds of the World: A Photographic Guide.* Christopher Helm. Bromley.

HOLYOAK, D.T., and THIBAULT, J.C. 1976. La variation géographique de *Gygis alba. Alauda* 44: 457-473.

HOWELL, S.N.G., SPEAR, L.B., and PYLE, P. 1994. Identification of Manx-type shearwaters in the eastern Pacific. *Western Birds* 25: 169-177.

HOWELL, S.N.G., WEBB, S., and SPEAR, L.B. 1996. Identification at sea of Cook's, De Filippi's and Pycroft's Petrels. *Western Birds* 27: 57-64.

IUCN. 1996. Final Draft Resolution: Seabird By-catch in Longline Fisheries. (13 June 1996)

JOHNSGARD, P.A. 1993. *Cormorants, Darters and Pelicans of the World.* Smithsonian Institution Press. Washington.

MALLING OLSEN, K. 1989. Field identification of the smaller skuas. *Brit. Birds* 82: 143-176.

MALLING OLSEN, K., and LARSSON, H. 1995. *Terns of Europe and North America.* Christopher Helm. London.

MARCHANT, S., and HIGGINS, P.J. 1990. *Handbook of Australian, New Zealand and Antarctic Birds.* Vol. 1, Pt A. Oxford University Press. Oxford.

MURPHY, R.C. 1936. *Oceanic Birds of South America.* Vols 1 and 2. Macmillan. American Museum of Natural History, New York.

NELSON, J.B. 1978. *The Sulidae: Gannets and Boobies.* Oxford University Press. Oxford.

RASMUSSEN, P.C. 1986. Molts of the Rock Shag and new interpretations of the plumage sequence. *Condor* 89: 760-766.

READERS' DIGEST. 1985. *Complete Book of New Zealand Birds.* Readers' Digest. Sydney.

ROBERTSON, D., and BAILEY, S.F. 1992. *Cookilaria* petrels in the eastern Pacific Ocean. *Am. Birds* 45: 1067-1081.

SCAR Bird Biology Subcommittee. 1996. Distribution and numbers of the Antarctic Petrel *Thalassoica antarctica.* Unpubl. report.

SERVENTY, D.L., SERVENTY, V., and WARHAM, J. 1971. *The Handbook of Australian Seabirds.* A.H. & A.W. Reed. Sydney.

SHIRIHAI, H., SINCLAIR, I., and COLSTON, P.R. 1995. A new species of *Puffinus* shearwater from the western Indian Ocean. *Bull. B.O.C.* 115 (2): 75-85.

SIBLEY, C.G., and MONROE, B.L. 1990. *Distribution and Taxonomy of Birds of the World.* Yale University Press. New Haven.

SPEAR, L.B., HOWELL, S.N.G., and AINLEY, D.G. 1992. Notes on the at-sea identification of some Pacific Gadfly Petrels (genus: *Pterodroma*). *Colonial Waterbirds* 15: 202-218.

TENNYSON, A. 1990. Seabirds in strife. *Forest and Bird* 21: 23-30.

YÉSOU, P., PATERSON, A.M., MACKRILL, E.J., and BOURNE, W.R.P. 1990. Plumage variation and identification of the 'Yelkouan Shearwater'. *Brit. Birds* 88: 299-319.

YORIO, P.M., and HARRIS, G. 1991. Actualización de la distribución reproductiva, estado poblacional y de conservación de la Gaviota de Olrog (*Larus atlanticus*). *El Hornero* 13: 200-202.

ZINO, P.A., and ZINO, F. 1986. Contribution to the study of the petrels of the genus *Pterodroma* in the archipelago of Madeira. *Bol. Mus. Mun. Funchal* 38: 141-165.

229

PHOTOGRAPHIC ACKNOWLEDGEMENTS

Numbers in bold type in these acknowledgements refer to the page number and those in parentheses refer to the actual picture number. An asterisk indicates that the picture also appears on the dust cover.

The following abbreviations have been used:

FLPA: Frank Lane Picture Agency
NP: Nature Photographers
NZ Dept of Cons: New Zealand Department of Conservation
OSF: Oxford Scientific Films
WR: Windrush Photos

Noriyuki Aoki/Nature Production 217(5)
John Archer 151(2)
Yuri Artukhin/FLPA
Stephen Bainbridge/David Wingate 65(7)
Peter Basterfield/WR 163(9), 167(7), 171(3), 171(11), 189(8), 207(2), 207(5), 207(8), 215(4), 227(3)
N. J. Bean/Aquila 89(1)
Nigel Bean 107(7), 207(3), 211(7)
Giff Beaton 67(1), 75(10), 133(4), 219(7), 223(3), 224(4), 225(5), 227(4)
B. D. Bell/NZ Dept of Cons 131(3)
Richard Bevan 127(1), 127(2), 127(3)
Louise Blight 93(1)
Mark Bolton/NP 75(9), 101(1), 101(2)
R. and N. Bowers/Vireo 159(11), 159(12)
Alan Brady 55(5)
Mark Brazil 29(1), 77(1), 77(2), 77(3), 123(9), 123(10), 217(6), 217(7)
Roy Broad 109(3), 211(3)
Michael Brooke/OSF 55(1), 59(5)
J. J. Brooks/Aquila 203(4)
Richard Brooks/WR 165(6), 167(2), 183(11), 183(12)
S. C. Brown/FLPA 211(1)
Robin Bush/NP 113(4)
Mike Carter 33(6), 39(8), 41(5), 41(7), 49(1), 49(2), 49(5), 51(6), 71(1), 71(3), 79(2), 87(1), 87(8), 95(2), 95(5), 107(9), 117(2), 119(4), 131(8), 141(2), 147(7) 209(8)
C. Carvalho/FLPA 209(7)
Richard Chandler/WR 163(12)
Robin Chittenden 151(12), 153(2), 153(8), 153(9), 161(9), 215(9)
Brian Chudleigh 23(1), 23(3), 51(8), 61(4), 67(3), 67(7), 79(1), 89(6), 93(4), 95(6), 107(6), 113(2), 113(3), 123(1), 123(2), 137(1), 137(4), 137(5), 139(9), 139(10), 139(11), 139(12), 171(6), 171(8), 171(9), 171(11), 193(1), 195(6), 203(2), 209(4), 209(6)
Paul Cook 35(6), 77(6), 77(8), 131(2),
Simon Cook 19(3), 19(4), 19(5), 19(6), 21(3), 21(4), 21(5), 21(8), 27(3), 33(5), 35(5), 71(6), 97(5), 127(8), 127(9), 129(4), 131(1), 133(1), 185(1)
Bill Coster 41(6), 81(5), 115(2), 127(6), 183(8), 199(6), 227(7), 227(8)
David Cottridge/WR 99(3), 141(4), 145(10), 163(4)
G. Cubitt 129(3), 131(4), 131(6)
Mark Cubitt 101(6), 101(7), 101(8)
John Davies/WR 15(6), 17(6), 19(1), 19(2),

21(6), 21(7), 23(2), 39(5), 127(4), 137(2), 137(3), 147(5), 147(8), 171(10), 189(5), 193(2)
P. Devillers 83(5), 149(4), 151(1), 175(11), 191(3), 203(1)
Wendy Dickson/WR 181(7), 213(8), 213(9), 215(5)
Paul Doherty/WR 123(4), 123(8), 161(3), 175(5), 195(4), 201(3)
Goran Ekstrom/WR 61(3), 135(5), 145(5), 149(6), 149(7), 149(8), 167(6) 169(1), 185(5), 213(4)
Tom Ennis/WR 135(3), 135(4), 155(2), 155(10), 159(1), 161(5), 161(13), 163(13), 165(5), 165(7), 165(9), 171(4), 195(1), 207(6)
Jim Enticott 15(4) 15(5), 17(5), 17(9), 17(10), 25(5)*, 31(5), 31(8), 31(9), 33(2), 33(4), 33(7), 33(8), 35(1), 35(3), 35(4), 37(1), 37(2), 39(1)*, 39(6), 39(7), 43(2), 43(3), 43(9), 45(2), 45(3), 45(4), 61(5), 63(6), 65(1), 65(2), 65(3), 65(4), 67(5), 71(7), 75(4), 75(5), 75(6), 75(8), 73(6), 79(7), 81(4), 89(5), 97(4), 97(6), 117(6), 117(7), 119(3), 125(4), 125(5), 139(2), 141(8), 143(1), 143(2), 143(6), 177(9), 177(10), 197(2), 197(4), 197(5)
Hanne and Jens Eriksen/Aquila 201(6)
Ian Fisher/WR 83(2), 147(9), 177(5)
I. Flux/NZ Dept of Cons 87(5)
T. and P. Gardner/FLPA 49(3), 115(3)
Roy Glen 115(6)*
Chris Gomershall/RSPB 191(7)
G. K. Gordon 25(7), 25(8), 33(1), 79(3)
Michael Gore/NP 211(6)
Michael Graybill/Earthviews 217(3)
D. Hadden/Vireo 75(3), 91(1)
T. Hamer 219(2)
J. C. Haney 67(2)
Phil Hansboro 61(8)
Michael Harris/NP 17(7), 21(2), 25(6), 27(6), 33(9), 37(5), 43(1), 71(2), 81(3), 129(5)
Richard Heermann/OSF 117(4)
Mike Hill/OSF 125(2)
J. Hoffman/Vireo 99(5)
Brenda Holcombe/WR 15(1), 15(3), 17(1), 17(4), 23(6), 25(1), 25(2), 25(5), 27(7), 27(8), 27(11), 29(5), 77(5), 79(4), 79(5), 99(7), 113(5), 119(2), 137(7), 149(1), 149(2), 175(10) 187(7), 189(3), 213(10)
Brayton Holt 39(2), 193(5)
E. and D. Hosking/FLPA 187(8),
David Hosking 205(4), 211(2)
M. Imber/NZ Dept of Cons 61(7)
Karou Ishie/Nature Production 103(6), 221(4)
E. A. Janes/WR 173(5)
R. Jones/FLPA 111(8)
Kevin Karlson 115(4), 115(9), 161(6), 161(10), 161(12), 175(4), 185(7), 207(4), 209(5), 209(9), 215(7)
A. J. Knystautas/Vireo 177(6)
P. La Tourette/Vireo 49(4)
Gordon Langsbury/WR 137(6), 153(5), 183(10), 193(9)
Ed Lemon/NP 43(5), 43(7), 43(11), 69(3), 93(7)
Tony Leukering/Vireo 219(1)
Tim Loseby 121(11), 121(12), 155(1), 155(4)
R. J. Lowe 57(8), 57(10), 53(1), 53(2), 53(3)
Mark Lucas/WR 187(2)

Horst Ludeke/FLPA 125(6)
Tony Marr 43(6), 63(5), 67(4), 143(7)
David Mason/WR 133(5), 191(1), 201(1)
D. and N. Massie 203(3)
Mike McDonnell 83(6)
P. Meeth 103(4), 103(5)
D. Merton/NZ Dept of Cons 47(4), 47(5), 49(6), 57(6), 57(7)
G. Moon/FLPA 51(9)
Arthur Morris/WR 107(8), 109(5), 109(6), 109(7), 109(8), 115(7), 115(8), 117(8), 117(9), 117(10), 117(11), 117(12), 121(3), 121(4), 121(5), 121(6), 121(7), 135(2), 137(9), 145(8), 151(4), 151(5), 151(6), 151(7), 151(8), 153(4), 155(5), 155(6), 155(7), 155(8), 155(9), 157(1), 157(2), 157(3), 157(4), 157(5), 157(6), 157(10), 159(2), 159(3), 159(4), 159(5), 159(6), 159(7), 159(8), 159(9), 159(10), 159(13), 161(4), 163(3), 163(5), 163(7), 175(2), 175(3), 179(6), 179(7), 179(8), 179(9), 179(10), 179(12), 179(13)*, 179(14), 181(11), 185(8), 185(9), 185(10), 187(1), 187(3), 187(4), 187(5), 187(6), 191(2), 191(4), 191(5), 191(8), 191(9), 191(10), 195(2), 195(8), 195(12), 199(1), 199(2), 199(3), 199(4), 199(5), 201(7), 201(8), 201(9), 201(10), 201(11), 213(5), 213(6), 213(7)
Pete Morris 73(8), 75(1), 87(3), 111(10), 121(13), 193(3), 193(4), 197(3)
R. B. Morris/NZ Dept of Cons 71(4), 75(2), 131(5), 131(7)
K. Mullarney 161(7), 191(9)
J. P. Myers/Vireo 213(1)
Maura Naughton 29(2)
Mark Newman/FLPA 125(7)
Howard Nicholls/WR 27(10), 31(7), 77(4), 89(3), 119(1), 127(5), 133(2), 139(4), 139(7), 139(5), 141(5), 143(3), 147(6), 157(13), 179(4), 183(6), 183(7), 183(9), 207(1)
NZ Dept. of Cons 57(9), 87(4), 93(3)
David Osborn/NP 139(1)
Tony Palliser 55(4), 61(1), 61(2), 63(1), 63(2), 69(2), 73(7), 87(2), 87(6), 93(5), 93(6), 95(4), 97(1), 97(2), 97(3), 109(1), 111(1), 111(2), 111(3), 117(3), 141(1), 141(3)
D. & E. Parer-Cook/Ardea 69(1)
T. Parker/Vireo 135(7)
Chris Patrick 37(4), 65(5), 109(10), 129(1), 129(2), 193(6), 197(1)
Alan Petty 41(2)
R. L. Pitman 97(7), 97(8), 97(9)
R. L. Pitman/Vireo 49(7), 57(1), 57(2), 57(3), 57(4), 57(5), 59(3), 81(7), 85(1), 103(3), 105(1), 105(2), 121(1), 121(10), 151(3), 153(1), 219(6), 221(2), 221(3)
A. R. Plant 53(4)
René Pop/WR 15(2), 17(8), 21(1), 31(1), 31(6), 39(3), 39(4), 69(6), 73(3), 79((6), 81(1), 81(2), 83(3), 95(3), 99(1), 117(1), 117(5), 133(3), 141(7), 141(9), 145(2), 145(9), 147(3), 151(9) 155(3), 157(14), 173(2), 195(9), 195(11), 201(4), 227(2)
S. Pujol 27(1)
R. F. Porter 63(3), 63(4), 71(8), 73(1), 75(7), 75(11), 79(9), 89(4), 93(9), 107(3), 163(6), 173(12), 201(5)
P. Pyle 47(1), 47(2), 47(3)

P. Pyle/Vireo 59(4)

Mark Rauzon 29(6), 51(1), 51(2), 51(3), 51(5), 55(2), 55(3), 59(2), 81(6), 81(8), 85(2), 85(3), 99(6), 103(1), 103(2), 107(1), 107(2), 113(7), 113(8), 189(6), 205(6), 205(7), 205(8), 205(9), 211(4), 211(5), 213(3), 223(1), 225(6), 225(7), 227(6), 227(9)

Mark Rauzon/Vireo 53(5)

Martin Reed 59(1)

Richard Revels/WR 183(2)

G. Roberts/NZ Dept of Cons 77(9)

John Roberts/WR 173(10), 185(4), 209(3)

D. Robertson/Vireo 91(2), 221(1)

J. P. Roux 27(2)

B. W. Rowlands 45(1)

Chris Schenk/WR 123(5)*, 181(12), 215(6)

Hadoram Shirihai 75(12), 87(9), 87(10), 87(11)

Rich Stallcup 29(3), 85(4), 85(5), 105(3)

Paul Sterry/NP 25(3), 89(2), 107(4), 107(5), 217(4), 223(2), 223(5), 225(3), 227(5), 227(10)

Alan Tate 25(9), 27(4), 27(5), 29(4), 31(2), 31(3), 31(4), 33(10), 37(3), 41(3), 43(10), 51(7), 69(4), 69(5), 73(5), 77(7), 91(3), 93(2), 109(9), 113(6), 127(7), 133(6), 135(1),

137(8), 139(3)*, 143(4), 149(3), 149(5), 151(11), 151(13), 151(14), 153(3) 157(11), 163(8), 165(1), 165(2), 165(3), 165(4), 169(7), 175(7), 175(8), 177(7), 177(8), 179(3), 179(5), 185(2), 185(3), 205(2), 213(2), 213(11), 223(4), 225(1), 225(2)

G. Taylor/NZ Dept of Cons 61(6)

G. & V. Thomson/WR 111(12)

Roger Tidman 23(4), 33(3), 35(2), 41(4), 43(4), 79(8), 93(8), 93(10), 143(5), 145(1), 145(3), 161(1), 161(2), 169(5), 173(9), 191(6), 217(2)

David Tipling/WR 41(1), 83(1), 83(4), 111(4), 111(5), 111(6), 111(7), 111(9), 123(3), 123(7), 135(6), 147(1), 147(2), 163(1), 163(11), 167(1), 167(4), 167(5), 171(1), 171(2), 173(4), 173(8), 177(1), 177(2), 181(10), 189(7), 215(1)*, 215(2), 215(3), 215(10), 217(1), 227(1)

Ray Tipper 109(2), 109(4)*, 123(6), 163(10), 169(3), 169(4), 169(6), 175(6), 175(9), 185(6), 201(2)

Ralph Todd/WR 17(2), 17(3), 27(9), 95(1), 115(1) 115(6)*, 139(6), 157(12), 179(1)

David Tomlinson/WR 15(7), 23(5), 23(7), 23(8)*, 23(9), 111(11), 113(1), 169(8), 169(9),

171(5), 171(7), 173(1), 173(3), 175(1), 183(5), 193(8)

C. R. Tyler/WR 189(4), 207(7)

Arnoud B. van den Berg/WR 73(2), 115(5), 125(1), 125(3), 151(10), 153(7), 161(8), 169(2), 177(3), 177(4), 179(2), 181(8), 189(1), 189(2), 205(1), 205(3)

Gus van Vliet 219(4)

U. Wand 43(8)

B. P. Watkins 73(4)

Alan Williams 25(4), 147(4), 167(8), 183(1), 183(3), 215(8)

M. Williams/NZ Dept of Cons 71(5)

David Wingate 65(6)

E. Woods/WR 121(2), 165(8)

Steve Young 99(2), 101(3), 101(5), 141(6), 145(4), 145(6), 145(7), 153(6), 157(7), 157(8), 157(9), 161(11), 163(2), 167(3), 173(6), 173(7), 181(1), 181(2), 181(3), 181(4), 181(5), 181(6), 181(9), 181(13), 183(4), 183(13), 195(3), 195(5), 195(7), 209(1)

D. & M. Zimmerman/Vireo 99(4)

Francis Zino 63(7), 63(8)

T. Zurowski/Vireo 219(3), 219(5)

INDEX